PUBLIC RELATIONS WRITING

Fourth Edition

PUBLIC RELATIONS WRITING

The Essentials of Style and Format

THOMAS H. BIVINS
UNIVERSITY OF OREGON

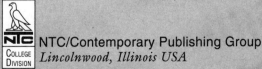

NTC/Contemporary Publishing Group
Lincolnwood, Illinois USA

Sponsoring Editor: Marisa L. L'Heureux
Product Manager: Judy Rudnick
Art Director: Ophelia Chambliss
Production Coordinator: Denise M. Duffy-Fieldman

ISBN: 0-8442-0351-3 (student text)
ISBN: 0-8442-0352-1 (student workbook)

Published by NTC/Contemporary Publishing Group, Inc.,
4255 West Touhy Avenue, Lincolnwood (Chicago), Illinois 60646-1975 U.S.A.

Library of Congress Cataloging-in-Publication Data
Bivins, Thomas H. (Thomas Harvey).
    Public relations writing: the essentials of style and format /
Thomas H. Bivins.--4th ed.
        p. cm.
    Rev. ed. of: Handbook for public relations writing.
    Includes index.
    ISBN 0-8442-0351-3 (softbound: student text).--ISBN
0-8442-0352-1 (student workbook)
    1. Public relations--United States. 2. Public relations--United
States--Authorship. I. Bivins, Thomas H. (Thomas Harvey).
Handbook for public relations writing. II. Title.
HM263.B538 1999
659.2--dc21   98-45630
890 QB 0987654321   CIP

CONTENTS

CHAPTER 11   SPEECHES AND PRESENTATIONS   235

CHAPTER 12   DESIGN, PRINTING, AND DESKTOP PUBLISHING   250

CHAPTER 15   THE BASICS OF STYLE   340

This is a handbook for those who, by intention or by accident, find themselves in the position of writing for public relations. In my years of experience I have been asked as many questions concerning public relations writing from those not in public relations as from those in public relations. Countless inquiries have come from the teacher who has suddenly been "appointed" publicity chair for his committee; from the office manager who has been assigned, ad hoc, the job of putting out a newsletter; or from the small-company president who wants to create her own brochures on the new desktop publishing software she just acquired but doesn't know how to proceed. That's why you'll find this book begins with the basics and pretty much sticks with them.

Public Relations Writing: The Essentials of Style and Format is designed to aid both the beginner and the advanced public relations writer. In it you will find most of the forms of public relations writing, including news releases, backgrounders, newsletter and magazine articles, brochures, print advertising copy, and broadcast scripts.

Formerly titled *Handbook for Public Relations Writing*, we renamed this book in conjunction with a thorough revision. This latest edition now includes

1. a more in-depth look at the "why" of public relations writing (Chapters 1–3),
2. a greatly expanded discussion of the legal and ethical issues of public relations writing (Chapter 4),
3. a whole new section on feature writing (Chapter 8),
4. and a newly combined chapter on the basics of design, printing, and the interface with desktop publishing (Chapter 12).

Finally, another entirely new chapter is devoted to writing on and for the computer, including information on composing alone or with others and the uses and techniques of Internet writing (Chapter 13). While others may champion the computer age as the answer to modern communications problems, I persist in believing that the computer, in the words of Paul Brainerd (the "father" of desktop publishing), is simply another tool. In the right hands, it can communicate effectively; in the hands of the incompetent or mediocre, what is produced is simply more clutter. At its best, the computer can enhance our understanding, bring us closer together in a nearly instantaneous manner, and allow us to interact in ways never before imagined. Whether the best of this new technology is realized is up to us—the writers and users. Some of what is included in this chapter and elsewhere throughout the book may help point the way.

In addition to the myriad content changes, improvements have also been made to the book's design and user-friendliness. For one, the trim size has been expanded to 7¼-by-9⅛ inches in order to better accommodate the many sample documents scattered throughout the book. Also, new pedagogical elements have been added. There is a lot of information packed into this book; I encourage you to use the learning objectives and key terms for help in understanding the most important points and the exercises for practicing your skills in these areas.

Many of the recommendations contained in this handbook are based on years of experience as a writer, both in public relations and in general business practice. It is my belief that any public relations writer worthy of the name should become familiar with all forms of writing. After all, good writing is good writing, no matter what the form. The truly good writer, like the good artist, is able to work in any medium. This book is an attempt to put most of the reference material that you, as a public relations writer, would need to successfully complete the work that is such a vital part of your chosen profession: writing.

Acknowledgments

A number of people have helped make this new edition possible. First, I would like to acknowledge the reviewers who took the time to critique the third edition of *Handbook for Public Relations Writing*. Their many suggestions are evident throughout this new edition: Anne Marie Arzt, Oakton Community College; David L. Dollar, Southwest Missouri State University; Charles T. Glazer, University of Pittsburgh at Greensburg; Shelly A. Green Wright, State University of New York at New Paltz; Leo J. McKenzie, Marist College; Jane W. Peterson, Iowa State University; Michael B. Shelly, Illinois State University; and John N. Weis, Winona State University.

In addition, Marilyn Milne, John Mitchell, and Dan Steinberg, colleagues and professionals all, took time out from their busy lives to provide many of the new examples included in this edition. My brother, Chris, provided me with a number of examples from his vast design repertoire. Andi Stein, former public relations pro turned doctoral student, shared her expertise in employee communications and new technology. Much of the chapter on digital media was gleaned from her experiences and her writings, especially her Masters thesis and subsequent article, which dealt with the changes in employee communications and new technology. Andi's research help, writings, and advice have been invaluable. My colleague and co-author, Bill Ryan, was gracious enough to allow me to "borrow" his introduction to design from our book *How to Produce Creative*

Publications (also from NTC). I couldn't imagine writing a better one myself.

Finally, I would like to thank the folks at NTC/Contemporary Publishing, namely Marisa L'Heureux, who kept pestering me to get going on this new edition (and who hasn't left me alone yet), and Liz MacDonell, my editor, who so expertly corrected my mistakes, asked the many needed questions, and politely kept the pressure up until it was all done.

My thanks go to them all. They share in whatever usefulness this book provides to you, the reader.

About the Author

Thomas H. Bivins is a Professor in the School of Journalism and Communication at the University of Oregon, where he teaches public relations and mass media ethics. He received his Ph.D. in telecommunication in 1982 from the University of Oregon and taught for three years at the University of Delaware before returning to the University of Oregon. Bivins received a B.A. in English and an M.F.A. in creative writing from the University of Alaska, Anchorage, and has nearly twenty years of professional media experience, including work in radio, television, advertising, public relations, and editorial cartooning.

## CHAPTER 1

WRITING FOR PUBLIC RELATIONS

FOR IMMEDIATE RELEASE

In this chapter you will learn:

- Why good writing is important to a public relations professional.

- The difference between uncontrolled and controlled information.

- The most often-used tools of public relations writing, and how they differ.

- The process of public relations writing.

All public relations practitioners write at some time. Public relations is, after all, communication, and the basic form of communication is still the written word.

Regardless of the prevalence of television, radio, cable, DTV, and increasingly the Internet, the written word is still powerful. Even the events we witness on television and hear on the radio were written down originally in the form of scripts. News anchors on television are not recounting the day's events from memory; they are reading from a teleprompter. Nearly every entertainment program is precisely scripted—from your favorite sitcom to the MTV Video Music Awards. And while it may not seem so, most of what you see on the Internet has been carefully thought out and prewritten prior to its placement on that Web site.

It is no wonder today's employer values an employee who can communicate through the written word. Employers want people who can write and communicate ideas—who can pull complex or fragmented ideas together into coherent messages. This requires not only technical skill but also intelligence. It also requires a love of writing. Be forewarned: The subjects of public relations writing can seem to many to be crashingly dull; however, for writers who love their craft, the duller the subject, the greater the challenge. Even the most mundane subject can shine with the right amount of polish.

So, the place of writers in public relations is assured. From the president or vice president of public relations to the lowliest office worker, writing is a daily part of life. From enormously complex projects involving dozens of people and whole teams of writers to the one-person office cranking out daily news releases, editing weekly newsletters, or updating Web pages, writing will continue to be the number-one concern of public relations. Through it, your publics will come to know you and, for better or worse, develop a permanent image of who you are. It is in your best interest and that of the people you work for to ensure that this image is the one you want to portray.

What is needed before you begin to write, however, is knowledge. Being able to spell and string words together effectively does not make a good writer. First and foremost, a good writer must be able to think. A good writer must be aware of the world around him or her and understand how his or her writing is going to affect that world.

It is absolutely essential that you think before you write, otherwise your writing will be only empty words, disconnected from reality or, worse, unintentionally misleading or false.

What Is Public Relations Writing? ──────

All **public relations writing** attempts to establish positive relations between an organization and its various publics, usually through image-building techniques. Most writing in the realm of public relations falls into two rather broad categories, uncontrolled information and controlled information.

Uncontrolled Information

Information that, once it leaves your hands, is at the mercy of the media is **uncontrolled information.** In other words, the outlet in which you want the information placed has total editorial control over the content, style, placement, and timing. Such items as news releases are totally uncontrolled. For example, you may write what you think is the most effective, well-thought-out news release ever presented to your local paper, but you never see it in print. Or maybe they do use it, but they leave out all of your skillfully crafted sentences about your employer. In these cases, the newspaper editors have exercised their prerogative to control your information. Once you put it in their hands, they get to decide what to do with it.

Then why, you're probably asking yourself about now, even use uncontrolled information? For at least two reasons. First, it's generally cheaper because you don't have to pay for production or placement costs. Second, your message gains credibility if you can pass it through the media on its way to your target public. I've sometimes referred to this technique as "information laundering" (humorously, of course). The fact is, our messages often are viewed by our target publics as having a vested interest—which of course they do. However, when those same target publics see the same message served up by the media, it seems to gain credibility in their eyes. Obviously, this is also true for passing the information through any credible second party, such as magazines, opinion leaders, or role models. Thus, the loss in control is usually more than balanced by the overall gain in credibility.

Controlled Information

Information over which you have total control as to editorial content, style, placement, and timing is **controlled information.** Examples of controlled information are institutional (image) and advocacy advertising, house publications, brochures, and broadcast material (if it is paid placement). Public service announcements (PSAs) are controlled as far as message content is concerned but uncontrolled as to placement and timing.

In order to get the most out of any message, you should send out both controlled and uncontrolled information. That way, you can reach the broadest possible target audience, some of which will react more favorably to one type of approach.

The Tools of the Public Relations Writer ———

As with any trade, public relations writing makes use of certain tools through which messages are communicated. The most common are listed here:

- **News releases**—both print and broadcast. The most widely used of all public relations formats, news releases are used most often to disseminate information for publicity purposes and are sent to every possible medium, from newspapers to radio stations.
- **Backgrounders**—basic information pieces providing background as an aid to reporters, editors, executives, employees, and spokespersons. This is the information used by other writers and reporters to "flesh out" their stories.
- **Public service announcements (PSAs)**—the broadcast outlet most available to not-for-profit public relations. Although the PSA's parameters are limited, additional leeway can be gained by paying for placement, which places it in the category of advertising.
- **Advertising**—the controlled use of media, ensuring that your message reaches your public in exactly the form you intend and at the time you want. Advertising can be print or broadcast.
- **Articles and editorials**—usually for newsletters, house publications, trade publications, or consumer publications. In the case of nonhouse publications, public relations articles are submitted in the same way as any other journalistic material. Editorials can be either paid for, as are Mobil's editorials and *Fables*, or submitted uncontrolled and vie for placement with comments from other parties.
- **Collateral publications**—such as brochures, pamphlets, flyers, and other direct marketing pieces. These are usually autonomous publications, which should be able to stand on their own merits but which can be used as supporting information for other components in a package. They might, for instance, be part of a press packet.
- **Annual reports**—one of the most-produced organizational publications. Annual reports not only provide information on the organization's financial situation, they also act as a vehicle for enhancing corporate image among its various internal publics.
- **Speeches and presentations**—the interpersonal method of imparting a position or an image. Good speeches can inform or persuade and good presentations can win support where other, written, methods may fail.

Although these are not the only means for message dissemination at the disposal of the public relations writer, they are the most often used. Knowing which to use requires a combination of experience, research, and intuition. The following chapters were not designed to teach you these qualities. Instead, they attempt to provide you with a framework, or template, that will enable you to perform basic tasks as a public relations writer. The rest is a matter of experience, and no book can give you that.

The Process of Public Relations Writing ━━━━━

All forms of writing for public relations have one thing in common: they should be written well. Beyond that, they are different in many ways. These differences are related primarily to purpose, strategy, medium, and style/format. As you will see, these elements are extremely interrelated, and you really can't think about any single element without conceptualizing the others. For example, purpose and strategy are intimately related, and choice of medium is inextricably bound to style/format.

As to purpose, there are basically only two reasons for a public relations piece to be produced: to inform or to persuade. Strategy depends almost completely on the purpose to which the piece is to be put. For instance, if your purpose is to persuade a target audience to vote for a particular mayoral candidate, you might choose a persuasive strategy such as argument to accomplish your purpose.

The medium you choose to deliver your message will also dictate its style and format. For example, corporate magazines and newsletters employ standard magazine writing style (which is to say, a standard magazine style of journalism). Newsletter writing, on the other hand, is leaner, shorter, and frequently uses a straight news reporting style. Folders (commonly referred to as brochures) are, by nature, short and to the point. Copy for posters and flyers is shorter still, while pamphlets and booklets vary in style and length according to purpose. Writing for the Internet may incorporate any or all of these styles in slightly to greatly abbreviated formats. All of this is packaged within organizational patterns that generally vary according to a relational logic (based on the ability to jump from one point to another led by the relationship of one piece to the other).

Throughout this book, we will be dealing with these elements of public relations writing: purpose, strategy, medium, and style/format. Before we begin looking at each element, however, we need to address the broader issue of planning. That is the subject of the next two chapters.

KEY TERMS ━━━━

public relations writing

uncontrolled information

controlled information

news release

backgrounder

public service announcement (PSA)

advertising

articles and editorials

collateral publication

annual report

speeches and presentations

## CHAPTER 2

PLANNING YOUR MESSAGE

FOR IMMEDIATE RELEASE

In this chapter you will learn:

1. • The four steps in the planning stage of writing.

2. • What an issue statement is, and why and how it is developed.

3. • Why it is important to know your target audience before you develop a PR piece.

4. • The two types of formal research, and their advantages and disadvantages.

5. • The three types of objectives used in public relations writing.

Almost all writing goes through (or should go through) several stages, the first—and some say the most important—of which is planning. Planning incorporates practically everything you need to know, both about your subject and your audience, in order to produce a successful written piece—a piece that accomplishes what you need it to do. The planning process includes developing an issue statement (the *purpose*), selecting the proper *strategies* for accomplishing that purpose, choosing the most effective *media* to deliver the message, and adhering to the correct *style* and *format* as dictated by the media choices. Inherent in all of these steps is research— research into whom to communicate with and how to best communicate with them, and research into how well you communicated. We'll talk about the planning stage of writing in this chapter and the next. This discussion will include all of the elements just mentioned, with the exception of style/format. That is the focus of the remainder of the book.

Developing an Issue Statement ————

All communication in public relations has some purpose. It may be to encourage people to vote, or to join your organization, or not to litter, or it may be simply to raise their level of knowledge about your issue. Thus, the first step in any plan whose goal is to reach a specified audience with a specified purpose in mind is to define the issue or problem[1] addressed by the communication. Working without a precise definition of the issue is analogous to writing a college term paper without a thesis statement: you have no clear direction to show where you are going and, thus, no way to determine whether you got there.

The first step in defining the issue is to develop an issue statement. An **issue statement** is a precise definition of the situation, including answers to the following four questions:

1. What is the problem or opportunity to be addressed?
2. Who are the affected parties? At this point, it is only necessary to list the concerned parties. A precise definition of publics comes later in the planning process.
3. What is the timing of this issue? Is it an issue of immediate concern (one needing to be addressed right now), impending concern (one that will have to be addressed very soon), or potential concern (one that you are tracking as needing to be addressed in the near future)?

---

[1] The terms *issue* and *problem* are relatively interchangeable depending on how you view the situation. *Issue* is a more generic term and covers both problems and opportunities; however, many people in public relations persist in viewing most responses in terms of problems. For our purposes, we will use the term *issue* as being more inclusive.

4. What are your (or your organization's) strengths and weaknesses as regards this issue?

In answering these questions, you should take care to be as precise as you can. Succinctness is important to clarity, and clarity is of primary importance in the planning process. It is often wise to answer these questions in outline form and then, working from the outline, develop an issue statement. Consider the following example. It is necessarily simplistic for demonstration purposes. Most issue analysis at this stage is far more complex; however, the approach is the same and the need for precision and succinctness is no less important:

1. **Issue:** Your company has recently developed a new line of educational software targeted to school-aged children from first grade through high school. Development was time consuming and expensive, and was based on previous research showing a marked trend in education toward computers in the classroom. Marketing and advertising of the new software will be taken care of by your company's marketing department and its outside advertising agency. From a public relations perspective, however, you see an opportunity to capitalize on the growth in educational computers by raising the awareness of key publics to the importance of this trend and by tying your company's name to that growth.

2. **Affected publics:** Your publics have already been determined in part by the markets that will be using your new line of software. They are educators, administrators, parents, and students.

3. **Timing:** Because this is an opportunity and not a problem, timing is essential. Most opportunities require that you act quickly in order to capitalize on them. Your software is already developed, as is a marketing program. You need to move in advance of, or, at the very least, simultaneously with, the marketing effort.

4. **Strengths and weaknesses:** Your strengths include the availability of existing marketing research that has already determined your target publics, advance knowledge of how the new software will enhance the educational process so that you can focus on those elements, and a wide-open opportunity to set the scene for your product through some advance public relations work.

   Weaknesses might include competition, potential perception of vested interest in any philanthropic effort you might suggest, and the necessity to move almost immediately because of the availability of the product.

An issue statement based on this information might look like the following:

The recent development of our new line of educational software and the coincidence of current trends in educational computing present an opportunity for our company to align itself as a leader in modern education. To do so, we will need to raise the level of attention of key publics concerning the importance of computers in the classroom in such a way that we become closely associated with the trend. We are in a unique position to alert educators, administrators, and parents to the multiple uses of classroom computers and the availability of educational software as an answer to many current classroom problems. A well-placed publicity effort outside of and separate from our marketing plan could help pave the way for eventual increased sales of our software. This publicity effort should not seem to be connected to our product; however, we should not appear to hide our interests in increased sales either. A joint effort with an educational nonprofit organization might be the best approach.

This issue statement covers all of the questions posed earlier. The only qualitative difference between the original answers provided to the questions and this statement is the narrative format of the statement. Stating the issue in this form helps others to conceptualize what you already understand and sets the groundwork for further analysis of the issue.

A useful device in helping you lay the groundwork for an issue statement is a *direction sheet*. This is a series of questions you should answer when you begin an assignment. Exhibit 2.1 describes how to use a direction sheet to plan your written piece. No public relations writer should begin an assignment without one.

EXHIBIT 2.1

Preparing a Direction Sheet

A basic direction sheet might include the following information:

- **Subject of the piece.** Is it going to be a new product publicity piece, an announcement of employee promotions, or news about a special event such as a fund-raiser or a grand opening?

- **Format.** What form will the information take? Will it be a news release, a magazine article, a television PSA, or a brochure?

- **Objective.** What do we hope to accomplish by producing this piece? Do we want to educate the general public concerning our

(Continued)

(Continued)

hiring policies? Do we want to make engineers aware that we have developed a new product for their use? Do we want to promote the Olympics by associating ourselves with the event?

- **Intended audience.** Exactly who is our target public? Is it home-makers, businesspeople, children, staff members? Who we decide to communicate with will determine the form of the message and probably the medium.

- **Angle.** The angle "hooks" the audience and establishes the context of the message. It is all-important and one of the toughest compo-nents to establish. The angle must be new and interesting. In a print ad, it could be a bold headline. In a television PSA, it might be a peaceful, scenic shot juxtaposed with abrasive audio. In a radio PSA, it might be a humorous context.

- **Key ideas.** These are the salient points you wish to make through your communication. Establishing key ideas is important because they serve as an outline for writing a successful message.

- **Length.** This depends to a great extent on format. The length should be agreed upon in advance by the party requesting the piece and the writer. News releases, for instance, can be from one to five pages long. Article length is usually determined by the publication for which it is intended. Brochure length varies according to layout.

- **Deadline.** This element is usually the most inflexible. Unfortunately, in public relations writing as in most writing, the finished product is usually needed "yesterday."

When you receive an assignment, try to get as much information as you can in one "client" meeting. This means, be prepared ahead of time with a complete list of questions. Once you have left your "client," it is usually difficult to get back in touch.

Researching the Topic ———

As is the case in all forms of writing, you must know your topic before you can write about it. Research techniques for this purpose can run the gamut from formal research, such as surveys and questionnaires, to simply check-ing the library or on-line services for useful information. Increasingly, for instance, information on thousands of subjects can be found free of charge on the Internet.

Regardless of whether it is on line or in a file cabinet, organizational research material is generally readily available to most public relations writers. You can check with various departments within your organization for information on your topic and obtain previously published material from in-house and other sources. After you have been at this type of work for a while, you will undoubtedly have a well-stocked *swipe file* in which you have collected everything ever written about your subject area—by you or anyone else. In essence, you become a standard journalist gathering background information for a story. You should never start writing until you have sufficient background on your subject.

For many articles, human interest is important. This is where interviews come in. Firsthand information is always best when you can get it. Interview those who are intimately involved with your topic and use their information when you write. Interviewing is a special skill and it takes a lot of practice. The people you interview will determine how informative or interesting the interview will be. Although you can't always control who you interview, you can prepare so that you can make the most of your meeting. Exhibit 2.2 gives some tips for a successful interview.

EXHIBIT 2.2

Tips for a Successful Interview

- **Do your homework.** Collect background information on the people you're going to interview, as well as on the topics. Don't be embarrassed by your own ignorance of the topics; the better you know the topics, however, the more time you can save by asking for specific details rather than for in-depth explanations.

- **Prepare your interviewees in advance of the interviews.** Contact your interviewees well in advance, set a time for the interview that is convenient for them, and make sure they know exactly what you are going to cover and why. That way, they can also prepare for the interview by gathering pertinent information as well as their thoughts. Ask if you can "talk with them" rather than "interview them." A talk puts people at ease; an interview can make them tense and formal.

- **Write down a list of questions you want answered, working from the general to the specific.** But be prepared to let the interview range according to the interviewee's responses. Often, an answer will open new areas of inquiry or suggest an angle you hadn't thought of before. Be ready to explore these new avenues as they come up. Ken Metzler, journalist, educator, and author of *Creative Interviewing*, claims that the best interviewers should not

(Continued)

(Continued)

only expect surprises, but should ask for surprises in their willingness to explore rather than follow a strict set of questions.

- **If you are going to use a tape recorder, check to make sure that your interviewee is comfortable with being taped, and that you have fresh batteries or that an electrical outlet is available.** And, even though you are taping, always take notes. This physical activity usually puts the interviewee at ease by showing that you are listening, and it serves as a good backup if your recorder stops functioning or your tape runs out. Your recorder should not occupy the space between you and your subject. Move it a little to the side, but make sure the microphone isn't obstructed. The space between you and your subject should be free of any object that may be a source of distraction. (You should also keep your notepad in your lap, if possible, or simply hold it.)

- **Break the ice.** Open your interview with small talk. Try a comfortable topic, such as the weather, or, if you know something about your interviewee, a familiar, nonthreatening topic. For example, if you know your interviewee is an avid golfer, ask if he or she has had a chance to play much lately. Almost any topic will do—in fact, most of the time, something will suggest itself naturally.

- **As your interview progresses, don't be afraid to range freely, but return occasionally to your prepared questions.** Although the information you gather exploring other avenues may add greatly to your collection of relevant facts, remember to cover all the ground necessary for your article.

- **If you are ever unsure of a quote or think you might have misunderstood it, ask your subject to repeat it.** Even if you are taping the interview, accuracy on paper and in your own mind is worth the slight pause.

- **Finally, be prepared to remember some key conversation after your interview is officially over.** Most of us are aware of the phenomenon that Ken Metzler calls the "afterglow effect"—when dinner guests, for example, stand at the door with their coats on ready to go and talk for another 30 minutes. The same thing usually happens in an interview. You have turned your recorder off and put your pad away, and on your way out the door you have another 10 minutes of conversation with the interviewee. In this relaxed atmosphere, important comments often are made. Remember them. As soon as you leave, take out your pad and write the comments down or turn on your recorder and repeat the information into it. However, always make sure that your interviewee realizes that you are going to use this information as well. Don't violate any assumed "off the record" confidences.

Remember: Get as much as you can the first time out. Most interviews range from thirty minutes to two hours. A follow-up interview, providing you can get one, will never be as fruitful or relaxed as the first one.

Analyzing the Target Audience ──────

Imagine holding a complex conversation with someone you don't know at all. If you are trying to persuade that person to your point of view, you will have a better chance if you know his or her predispositions in advance. The same holds true for written communication. In order to write for an audience, you have to know that audience intimately.

A **target audience** is typically defined as the end users of your information—the people you most want to be affected by your writing. What you need to know about your target audience depends to a great extent on your objectives. As discussed previously, public relations writing is typically used either to perform or to persuade. The type of information you gather on your target audience depends a lot on which of these two uses your particular piece will be put to. If you are writing a persuasive piece, for example, you need to know not only who your prospective readers are, but also how much they know about your topic, how interested they are, and whether they feel they can—or want to—do anything about it. With this information in hand you can inform them, address their concerns and, hopefully, move them to action. On the other hand, think of all those publications you have seen at government agencies or received through the mail as a result of having requested information. Writers of these types of pieces need to know only that you desire their information.

Knowing for whom you're writing is probably the most important factor in planning your message. The success of your writing will be determined, to a great extent, on how well you have "aimed" your message. The best way to aim your message is to write for an imagined reader, someone to whom you are speaking directly. In order to understand this individual, you need to know him or her personally. To do this, you will have to develop a profile of this "typical" reader, citing both demographic characteristics (age, sex, income, etc.) and psychographic information (behavior patterns, likes and dislikes, attitudes, etc.).

Another important factor to consider at this point is how your target audience feels about your subject. In most persuasive endeavors, there are three types of audiences: those already on your side, those opposed to your point of view, and those who are undecided. As most experienced persuaders know, convincing the hard-core opposition is not a reasonable objective. Persuading those already on your side is like preaching to the converted: Unless you want to stir them to some action, it is a waste of time. Thus, most persuasion is aimed at the undecided. Remember, however, that even the undecided have opinions. However, those opinions may not be fully crystallized, which leaves this group particularly open to persuasion.

Conducting Target Audience Research

Methods for collecting information on your target audiences range from informal methods such as simply asking the person who gave you the assignment who the audience is, through secondary research gathered from such sources as the library, the Internet, or your own organization, to fairly expensive formal research. Many writers are put off by the notion of having to gather hard-core information about their readers. Unfortunately, many a message has totally missed its audience because it was not built around this information.

While an in-depth discussion of formal research techniques is beyond the scope of this book, it is important that you understand the significance of such techniques and a bit about how they work. At the very least, you should know enough to ask the right questions of the people you hire to do the survey for you and then to translate what they find out into plain English. Briefly, then, here are some of the things to look for.

There are essentially two types of formal research: primary research and secondary research. **Primary research** is data collected for the first time and specifically for the project at hand. This type of research is generally more expensive because you have to do everything from scratch, including developing the questions, printing up the survey, collecting the data, and analyzing it. Whether you hire a research firm or do it yourself, primary research will be costly and take more time. The upside is that primary research will be completely relevant to your current issue (ideally, at least).

Secondary research includes data previously collected, often by third parties, for other purposes and adapted to the current needs. This can include demographic information already gathered by another department in your organization, or information gained from research done by other parties entirely outside your company. Secondary research is generally less expensive to obtain and quicker to get hold of. However, it does have to be adapted to your uses and will not always answer all your questions. A combination of primary and secondary research is usually the best approach.

Regardless of the type of research you use, it must fit your needs. The best way to ensure that it does is to set an objective for your research and then compare the results of your efforts with your original objective. This is most important if you decide to do primary research.

Secondary Research. A visit to the library or Internet can yield volumes of secondary data. For example, government documents such as the *American Statistics Index (ASI)* can be invaluable sources. *ASI* is a compendium of statistical material including the U.S. census and hundreds of periodicals that can be obtained directly from the sponsoring agencies, from the library itself, or on the Internet. *ASI* also publishes an alphabetical index arranged by subject, name, category, and title.

Other sources of market information include the Simmons Market Research Bureau's annual *Study of Media and Markets.* This publication includes information on audiences for over one hundred magazines, with readership delineated by demographic, psychographic, and behavioral characteristics. When using secondary research such as this, be aware that you will find much information that is not directly applicable to your target audience. You not only have to know where to look, but you also have to know how to interpret what you read and apply it to your needs.

Primary Research. Once you have decided to use primary research, you will need to decide how to collect it. The two most common methods of primary research are focus groups and surveys.

Focus Groups. Focus groups have become a fairly commonplace practice for those in advertising, marketing, and public relations. The technique requires that you assemble a small group (usually not more than 10 people or so) from your target audience, present them with questions or ideas, and ask for their reactions. Your approach can be relatively formal (a written questionnaire to be filled out following the presentation) or informal (open-ended questions asked in an open discussion among the participants).

The key to a successful focus group is to design your questions in advance and cover all the areas you need to analyze. Be sure to explore whether your message's language is appropriate to your audience. Some of the questions to be considered are: Is the message difficult to follow, or does it have too much jargon or too many technical terms? Does your audience understand the message? Does the message speak to them, or do they feel it is meant for someone else? Is the medium appropriate? Would your readers take time to read the message if it came to them in the mail? As an insert in their paychecks? In the corporate magazine? Answers to these questions should give you a fair idea of how your larger audience will react to your message.

The best way to set up a focus group is to hire a moderator who is experienced in asking these questions and interpreting the responses properly. Don't assume that because you are the writer and the closest to the project that you can interpret audience feedback clearly. Indeed, in most cases you are *not* the one best suited to act as the focus group's moderator. Moderators are generally trained in marketing and/or sociology and are used to eliciting responses from people without biasing the answers. This is not a skill that is beyond most PR people, but it does take a bit of training. Exhibit 2.3 describes in detail how to conduct a focus group.

EXHIBIT 2.3

How to Conduct a Focus Group

- **Specify what you are trying to find out before you conduct the focus group.** Don't go into a focus group without a clear idea of your objective. Instead, develop a list of objectives for your focus group study. List exactly what you hope to discover from this meeting. Are you trying to find out whether your target audience will read stories about other employees? Do the people in the target audience react differently to different colors? Which color or combination of colors do they react most favorably to? You are trying to get your group to react to various stimuli you present to them.

- **Decide on a moderator.** It is best to hire someone who has done this before. Focus group moderators are experienced people with special skills. Without revealing what they are looking for, they can lead others into answering questions and reacting to stimuli. Moderators moderate—that is, they lead the discussion, call on different respondents, and keep the discussion going without allowing a free-for-all to occur. If cost is a factor (and good moderators can cost a bit), you might consider conducting the focus group yourself. However, if you have never conducted a focus group or seen one conducted, you should attend a session or two before you attempt it yourself.

- **Schedule according to your participants' needs, not yours.** If members of your target audience are busiest during certain hours of the day or days of the week, don't hold your focus group during those times. Make the meeting convenient for them. This courtesy will help put them in a cooperative frame of mind. Know your audience and their special needs when you schedule. For example, if day care is an issue, perhaps you can arrange for it. If lunch is the only time you can hold your meeting, provide lunch.

- **Select your participants properly.** Develop a valid method for picking members of your target audience. In most cases, you only need a representative cross-section of your audience. For example,

if 60 percent of your readers are women aged 25 to 35, make sure
that 60 percent of your focus group are women with those demo-
graphics. Holding a focus group with nonrepresentative participants is self-defeating. If you are in doubt about whom to select,
develop a screening questionnaire that will tell you whether the
respondents are really part of your target audience.

- **Provide for payment.** Nearly all focus group participants are paid.
  Most people won't participate for the fun of it (although some like
  having their opinions counted). Base what you pay on whom you
  are interviewing. Professionals, such as physicians and attorneys,
  should receive around $100, while others may be happy with
  $20–$50 for the session. Make sure your participants know they
  will be paid. The screening questionnaire is a good place to mention it.

- **Like the airlines, always overbook.** If you need ten people, book
  fifteen or twenty. Some will invariably not show up. If everyone
  does, just take them as they arrive, and turn away the rest when
  you have reached the number you need. But pay everyone, including those you don't use.

- **Meet with your moderator and set up guidelines for the study.**
  It is best to use your objectives as a starting point and develop a set
  of procedures from them for the focus group interview. Lay out
  these procedures step by step so that if you conduct more than one
  focus group, you will be able to follow exactly the same procedures
  in each session.

- **Sit in on the focus group as an observer if possible,** and if your
  moderator doesn't think it will be obtrusive. Always allow yourself
  to be introduced and don't interrupt or talk during the session.

- **Provide refreshments, even if it's just coffee or juice.** Most people expect some amenities in addition to the payment they
  receive—and it helps to put them in a better frame of mind.

- **The day of the focus group, check to make sure everything you
  will need for the meeting is ready and on hand.** You will be surprised how often you show up to find that someone else is using
  your reserved room. Or you count on someone else to bring the
  overhead projector, and they forget. Or you find you need to have
  pencils on hand, or paper, or wastebaskets, or any number of small
  items that can make or break a focus group meeting. As with everything else, it is best to make up a list of everything you will need to
  do or bring prior to the meeting. Then arrive an hour early and
  check off your items.

(Continued)

(Continued)

- **Hold the focus group.** Whether you are the moderator or someone else is, the following guidelines apply equally:

  - **It is a good idea to audiotape or videotape a focus group.** Many nuances of expression and voice aren't captured by simply taking notes or relying on written responses. If you use audiotape, make sure you have enough tape for the entire session. Also make sure that it is good quality tape, and that your recorder will actually pick up everyone in the room. Don't rely on that tiny recorder you use to tape reminders to yourself. If you videotape, you will need to hire a camera operator. Just positioning a stationary camera and turning it on won't do because you will never be able to cover everyone in the room at once. And, if you do decide to tape, let your participants know in advance and remind them again when they are seated and ready to start. Don't rely completely on the tape, however. Use it as a backup and always take complete notes. If the tape fails, for whatever reason, notes may be the only ally you have. Also, note taking makes the participants feel that you are doing your part as well.

  - **Always put your group at ease by telling them something about yourself, why you are conducting this study, and the fact that it is entirely informal and open.** Have the participants introduce themselves. Make sure they understand that you expect each one of them to play a part and that everyone's opinion counts equally. Stress that there are no right or wrong answers.

  - **A warm-up question that is easy to handle is a good way to get started**—something fun, yet thought-provoking. For example, if part of your study is to gauge reactions to the new look of your newsletter, you might begin by asking each participant what his or her favorite color is.

  - **Remember, a moderator moderates.** Don't lose control of the group discussion. To ensure that everyone gets an opportunity to speak, try going around the table allowing each member of the group to answer each question, and don't ask a new question until everyone has answered the question on the floor. On the other hand, don't be afraid to veer from the point if an interesting side issue is raised. Just make sure everyone has a chance to respond to each issue in turn. If you find that one or two people tend to dominate the answers, focus on the quiet ones for a while, draw them out, and encourage their participation. Remind the group that everyone's opinion counts.

- **Keep an eye on the clock.** An hour to an hour and a half should be enough time to get what you need without tiring your participants. If you do go 90 minutes or longer, take a break midway through.

- **When the meeting is over, thank the participants personally for their help and make sure they are paid before they leave.** You want to leave the participants with a good impression, so treat them well until they depart.

- **Immediately after the focus group study is over, sit down with your notes and begin answering the questions you developed as objectives when you began this whole process.** This is only the beginning, however. Don't draw hasty conclusions until you have had a chance to look at everything in context (including any tape you might have made of the meeting). Once you have a handle on the big picture, assemble all the evidence in the form of answers to your questions. Be sure to note if anything is incomplete. Perhaps you should have asked something else about reader interest in a particular area. Maybe you didn't probe deeply enough as to color preferences. Make a note of these shortcomings so that if you conduct another focus group study, you can include expanded questions.

- **Draft a final report, even if it's to yourself, covering everything you found out through the focus group study.** Send copies to appropriate parties and file a couple for future information. (Or for future editors of your newsletter. They'll thank you for it.)

Surveys. Another, equally important primary research option is the survey. The three most common methods of survey data collection are the face-to-face interview, the telephone interview, and the mailed questionnaire. Each has advantages and disadvantages.

The *face-to-face interview* allows you to interpret body language, facial expressions, and other nonverbal clues that help "flesh out" the responses you're getting verbally. A good interviewer will know how to gauge these nonverbal clues and evaluate them within the context of the verbal answers. The disadvantages of face-to-face interviewing include potential inconsistency in the abilities of interviewers and the general reluctance of most people to agree to any but the most perfunctory personal interview.

The *telephone interview,* by far the most common type of interview, also has its advantages and disadvantages. It must be brief (usually five minutes or so) or people won't agree to it. You can interview far more people this way, but you don't get much depth. Random dialing is most often used for telephone interviews; however, not everyone has a phone and thus the sample is not truly random. Lastly, not everyone likes to be interviewed over the phone. If the information you need can be gathered in only a few questions, though, the telephone may be your best bet.

The *mailed questionnaire* is usually the most effective way of gathering in-depth information from a great many people at the same time. While this method may not clarify ambiguous questions the way face-to-face interviews can, it does provide for more questions and longer responses than telephone interviewing. And it has a built-in consistency the other methods don't have. Answers aren't biased by interviewer miscues (facial expressions, body language), and each question is asked in a uniform way.

There are generally two types of data collected by survey. *Descriptive data* is basically information that "paints a picture" of the public being studied by its distinctive demographic characteristics—such as age, income, sex, education, nationality, and so on. This is information you need for your reader profile.

Inferential data is information that allows for generalizing about a larger group or population. Of course, the people you choose for your survey must be entirely representative of the larger population you want to reach. This allows you to "sample" a small segment of your target public and, from their reactions, "infer" the reactions of the larger audience. Inferential research can only work, however, if the sample is chosen completely at random from your larger population. This means that everyone in your target public has an equal chance of being chosen. How do we assure an equal chance? Easy. Computers have made this type of selection process much easier than it was in the past. All you need is a list of your target population (usually gathered by voter lists, DMV records, and such). Numbers are assigned to each person, and a computer selects, at random, those to be surveyed. There are, however, some variations in the selection process you should be aware of. These processes, or sampling methods, are listed in Exhibit 2.4.

The final question on any survey is one you must ask *yourself:* What does it all mean? If you have asked the right questions, and if you have selected your samples according to your needs and totally at random, then you should be able to analyze the answers in a way that is meaningful to you and your employer. This implies that you have carefully planned out the survey in advance, including the questions to be asked and the method of gathering the data. It also assumes that everyone involved knows what they're doing.

Typical problems in survey design include: not enough people were sampled, the sample wasn't truly representative of your overall population, important questions were left out or questions were too open to interpre-

EXHIBIT 2.4

Sampling Methods

Several types of sampling methods are used in survey sampling. Each fits a specific need of those asking the questions:

- *Simple random sampling* is the easiest method. You simply select the number you need from a master list, at random. This will usually be sufficient if you have a relatively homogeneous group with few or no differentiating characteristics.

- *Systematic sampling* adds a bit more process to this method by assigning (again by computer) an interval number. This means that the computer will select, at random, a starting number followed by another number that will decide who is chosen next. For example, the computer chooses person number 2,067 as the first person to be mailed a survey. It then picks an interval number, say 43. This number is added to 2,067, giving us 2,100—the next person to be sent a survey—and so on. The same interval number is used each time.

- *Cluster sampling* is useful if you need to interview only the head of each household, for instance, or 20 out of 56 houses in a subdivision, or people in four of the ten counties of a state. Clusters are chosen using the same methods as described above, only the "population" list is shorter because we're using larger initial units than individuals.

- *Stratified random sampling* implies that you will randomly select your sample based on further defining characteristics. For example, if your population is divided by income level (say, 20 percent over $50,000, 30 percent over $30,000, and 50 percent under $20,000) you would select the same percentages in your sample.

- *Quota sampling,* by contrast, uses a set number from each mutually exclusive grouping within your population. This way, every voice is given attention. So, for example, within your population you may have a group (say, rape victims) that comprises a very small percentage of the overall target public. Using a stratified sample, you might not get the input you need from this group. Why? Because in the sample you may end up with only one or two people who fall into that category, yet their opinions may be very important to you. If you draw an equal number of people from each of the subgroups whose opinions you need, you will have a better idea of the variance of opinion. Or, you may not get a valid reading of opinions

———— *(Continued)* ⌐

(Continued)

> within that group if you limit yourself to a truly representative sampling size relevant to the population. In fact, many researchers will simply oversample a smaller subgroup in order to get a valid response from within that group, then weight the response in the overall final analysis.

---

tation (see Exhibit 2.5 for types of survey questions), and your findings aren't related to your objective. It's important that you think about the possible shortcomings of any survey prior to spending your valuable time and money on something that might not prove to be worth it.

Anticipating Audience Expectations

Once you know who your audience is and how they feel about your subject, one final question must be answered if you expect to be successful: Why are they going to be paying attention to what you have written? If you don't know why your audience is reading your message in the first place, you certainly can't know what they expect to get from it. Ask yourself these questions:

- **What does my audience already know about my topic?** Never assume they know anything about your subject, but don't talk down to them either. How do you reach a compromise? Find out what they do know. Remember, people like to learn something from communication. It is best, however, to limit the amount of new information so as not to overwhelm your readers.

- **What is my audience's attitude toward me or my organization?** Remember the three basic audiences for any persuasive piece? You will need to determine whether your audience is on your side, against you, or unconvinced. To the extent possible, it is also a good idea to try to determine what your audience's image of you or your organization is. Determining audience attitude is often an expensive proposition because it usually requires formal research. If time or money constraints only permit you to make an educated guess based on a small focus group or even on intuition, that's better than nothing at all. It is much easier to convince others when you know that you already have credibility with them.

- **Is my publication to be used in a larger context?** In other words, is your publication part of a press kit, for instance, or a direct-mail package, or one of many handouts at a trade show? This knowledge will

EXHIBIT 2.5

Types of Survey Questions

1. An open-ended question:

   Who would you like to see elected president?

2. A closed-ended question with unordered answer categories:

   Who would you like to see elected president?

   1. Larry
   2. Mo
   3. Curly
   4. Mickey Mouse
   5. Donald Duck

   [handwritten: • NO PARTICULAR ORDER]
   [handwritten: ADVANTAGE • 5 ANSWERS • EASY TO ANALYZE]

3. A closed-ended question with ordered answer categories:

   For each of these candidates, please indicate how much you would like that individual to be elected president.

	Strongly favor his election	Somewhat favor his election	Somewhat oppose his election	Strongly oppose his election
a. Larry	1	2	3	4
b. Mo	1	2	3	4
c. Curly	1	2	3	4
d. Mickey	1	2	3	4
e. Donald	1	2	3	4

   [handwritten: ADVANTAGE • GIVES MORE CHOICES]

4. A partially closed-ended question: *[handwritten: COMBINES OPEN & CLOSED.]*

   Who would you like to see elected president?

   1. Larry
   2. Mo
   3. Curly
   4. Mickey
   5. Donald
   6. Other (specify)

5. Ladder Scale question:

   On a scale from 0 to 10, where 0 means you rate the job the president is doing as extremely poor and 10 means you rate the

   (Continued)

(Continued)

> job the president is doing as extremely good, how would you rate the job President Fillmore is doing now?
>
> **Extremely Poor**   **Extremely Good**
>
> 0   1   2   3   4   5   6   7   8   9   10

6. Lickert Scale question:

    How likely do you think you will be to vote for President Fillmore in the upcoming election?

    1. Very likely
    2. Somewhat likely
    3. Neither likely nor unlikely
    4. Somewhat unlikely
    5. Very unlikely

7. Semantic Differential question:

    Question: How would you characterize Millard Fillmore as president?

    Good -- Bad
    Weak -- Strong
    Decisive --- Indecisive
    Immoral -- Moral
    Intelligent --- Stupid

determine your readers' level of attention and their receptiveness. Always consider the surroundings in which your piece will be used if you want it to have the maximum impact.

Setting Objectives ━━━━

While the overall goals of a public relations campaign are generally broad (such as "To improve employee moral"), **objectives** set the concrete steps you need to take to reach your goal. A project's objectives must relate to the purpose of your message and should be realistic and measurable. For public relations writing, there are three types of objectives: informational, attitudinal, and behavioral.

Informational objectives are used most often to present balanced information on a topic of interest to your target audience. For instance, if you are simply attempting to let your employees know that your organization has developed a new health care package, your objective might read something like this:

> To inform all employees of the newest options available in their health care benefits package by the beginning of the October open enrollment period.

Notice that the objective begins with an infinitive phrase ("to inform"). Objectives should always be written this way. Notice, too, that the number of employees is addressed ("all"), and a specific time period for the completion of the objective is also included. In a complete communications plan, this objective would be followed by the proposed tactic for its realization and a method by which its success could be measured. For example:

> To inform all employees of the newest options available in their health care benefits package by the beginning of the October open enrollment period by placing informational folders in each employee's paycheck over the next two months. Personnel will keep a record of all employees requesting information on the new health care plan during the open enrollment period.

If your objective is *attitudinal* or *behavioral* rather than informational, your message is probably going to be persuasive. There are three ways you can attempt to influence attitude and behavior:

- You can create an attitude or behavior where none exists. This is the easiest method because there is usually no predisposition on the part of your target audience.
- You can reinforce an existing attitude or behavior. This is also relatively easy to do because your target audience already believes or behaves in the way you desire.
- You can attempt to change an attitude. This is the most difficult to accomplish and, realistically, shouldn't be attempted unless you are willing to expend a lot of time and energy on, at best, a dubious outcome.

An example of an attitudinal objective is:

> To create a favorable attitude among employees concerning the changeover from a monthly pay disbursement to a twice-monthly pay disbursement.

Methods for measuring this type of objective range from informal employee feedback to formal surveys of attitudes some time after the changeover has gone into effect.

An example of a behavioral objective is:

> To increase the number of employees in attendance at the annual company picnic by 25 percent by mailing out weekly reminders to the homes of employees four weeks prior to the picnic.

Obviously, measuring the effectiveness of this objective is easier; however, if you don't see an increase in attendance, you will have to do some serious research into the reasons why. Be aware, however, that these reasons might not involve your message or its presentation at all. You might simply have picked the Sunday of the big state fair to hold your picnic. Don't automatically conclude that your message is the problem without exploring all variables affecting its desired results.

KEY TERMS

issue statement   objectives

target audience   secondary research

primary research

EXERCISES

1. Imagine you are developing an article for a new type of golf club for a trade publication. Profile your target audience by developing a rough, off-the-top-of-your-head description of the typical reader. Next, check several directories (*Simmon's,* for example) to determine media usage, create a demographic profile, and extrapolate some basic psychographic information about your target audience.

2. Now, based on its stated ability to reach the target audience profiled in Exercise One, pick an appropriate publication, cite its circulation and publication policy, and state why this is the most appropriate publication for your message.

3. Write down your goal for learning to write for public relations. In general terms, what do you hope to accomplish or where do you hope to be after you learn how to write for PR? Now, based on your goal, list several objectives that you will need to accomplish in order to reach your goal.

## CHAPTER 3

CHOOSING THE RIGHT MESSAGE AND MEDIUM

In this chapter you will learn:

- What a message strategy is, and why it is important to develop one before you develop a public relations piece.

- The purpose of informative and persuasive public relations pieces.

- What message strategies work best for conveying information and for persuading, and how each of these strategies works.

- How to choose the appropriate medium (or media) for conveying the message.

Once you have developed an issue statement, researched your topic and audience, and set objectives, you are ready to complete the planning process by choosing a message strategy and a medium for conveying that message. These final stages are the topic of this chapter.

Setting Message Strategy ──────

Message strategy has to do with developing a message, or messages, that will reach and have the desired effect on your target audiences. Your message strategies should logically follow your objectives and contribute either directly or indirectly to them. You will need to develop individual message strategies for each of your target publics, based on what you have learned about them through your research. Remember: The strategy or strategies you employ will be determined to a great extent by your audience's make-up, predispositions, and perceived needs.

Most public relations writing is either informative or persuasive by intent, and there are a number of strategies for accomplishing both of these outcomes. Information, for example, may be imparted in a straightforward, expository manner, indicating by style that the message is unbiased. Information may also be imparted using entertainment, as anyone who has ever watched "Sesame Street" knows. In fact, if you are trying to reach an ambivalent audience with information, getting their attention through entertainment may help ensure your success. Persuaders may use entertainment as well, or reason, or emotion to convey their message.

While persuasion may seem to be separate from "pure" information, it is most certainly not. Most public relations people know, for example, that whether or to what extent a target public changes its mind is due to three variables: (1) whether they are even aware of the issue you are talking about, (2) whether or not they believe it is important to them personally, and (3) whether or not they believe they can do anything about it. The extent to which each of these variables is in play with any given target public will dictate what strategy you use in your writing. For example, if the target public is largely unaware of the issue you are dealing with, you will need to inform them before anything else can be attempted. If they are aware of the issue but don't see its relevance to their personal agendas, then you will have to do some persuading. If they are aware of both the issue and its importance to them but they feel constrained (for whatever reason) from acting, then your job becomes a combination of information and persuasion.

What you have found out about your publics from your prior research will then dictate which strategies to take in your information and persuasion approaches. For example, while entertainment may work well with children, something approaching logic (argument) might have a better effect on business people. Both strategies could be said to be persuasive, their styles simply dictated by the target public.

An *informative piece* should be balanced and complete. Its purpose is to let readers in on something they may not know or may have an incomplete picture of. The intent may be to publicize a new product or service, to set the record straight on a vital issue affecting your organization, or simply to let your readers know what's happening in your organization. Whatever the intent, the informational publication has to stick to just that—information. If your point of view is so strong as to evoke opposition, you probably should be writing a piece to persuade.

A *persuasive piece,* on the other hand, usually is heavy on the positive attributes of your service, product, or point of view. Persuasive pieces need to be written in terms the audience can relate to, and they frequently benefit from the use of words with emotional impact. Information pieces can get away with far fewer emotionally packed words and are frequently longer. After all, their aim is to inform an audience that is assumed to be already convinced of, or at least interested in, the subject.

Informative Strategies ━━━━━━

Writing informative messages is one of the most straightforward tasks in public relations writing. Informative messages should be balanced and unbiased in presentation. Naturally, you can put your own "spin" on anything you write, but in the information piece you should keep to the facts—most audiences will see through a persuasive piece thinly disguised as information. Indeed, this is one of the major objections journalists voice concerning news releases. They often say that much of what they receive is really advertising (persuasion) in disguise.

Information can be presented in a number of ways, from dissemination of pure information (called **exposition**) to entertainment. Two of the most-used forms of *exposition* are narration and description.

- **Narration (storytelling).** Telling stories is a natural human inclination. Fortunately for us, it also seems to be a natural need as well. The popular appeal of documentaries is evidence of our love of storytelling, and the enormous success of such cable television innovations as the Discovery Channel speaks to the widespread appeal of this form of information dissemination. Keep in mind that narration as well as the other approaches that follow can also be used as persuasive strategies.

- **Description.** Description is a method of sharing with our audiences those aspects of our surroundings that have had an impact on us. When used together with narration, we get a very expressive form of narration: fiction. The two most common forms of description are technical description and suggestive description.

- *Technical description* is relatively free from impression. We see it most often in technical journals and manuals. Its purpose is generally instructional.

- *Suggestive description* is more impressionistic and can also be used for persuasion. This is the form taken most often in feature or non-fiction writing.

Entertainment ("sugar-coated" information) is the second major information strategy. While entertainment is often thought of as not imparting information, like all forms of communication it informs to some extent. While referring to entertainment strategies as "sugar-coated" may seem a bit harsh, remember that the purpose of encapsulating information within entertainment is to make it "easier to swallow." We are much more easily informed if we are entertained simultaneously. Again, think of how hugely popular and effective "Sesame Street" has been, or how successful the show "Biography" has been for the cable network A&E. Entertainment strategies will be addressed further in the discussion of persuasion that follows. For a short prewriting checklist for information pieces, see Exhibit 3.1.

EXHIBIT 3.1

A Prewriting Checklist for Information Pieces

When writing an informative piece, ask yourself the following questions:

- Why would my target audience want to know about this topic?

- What would they want to know about it?

- Is the topic tied to a particular strategy? If so, what strategy? If it is part of an overall persuasive campaign, why am I using an informative approach?

- How much material should I leave for "further information"?

- Am I expecting any results from this approach? Make your objectives clear enough to be measurable so that you can later evaluate the results of information dissemination effectively.

Remember: The most valid objective of information is to raise the level of knowledge or understanding of your target audience. The reason behind PR writing may be ultimately to persuade, but in informative pieces bias should be kept to a minimum.

The Process of Persuasion ———————

In order to write persuasively you must understand the process of persuasion, what it is and how it either works or doesn't work. Let me begin by stating that **persuasion**—moving someone to believe or act a certain way—is difficult in most cases. That's why so many public relations campaigns strive for understanding, not persuasion. The problem, as it turns out, is that human beings have an interesting and frustrating ability to not listen to what is being said to them. This is particularly annoying for public relations people, who are constantly trying to communicate with publics who are simply not paying attention. Once we understand why they aren't listening, we have a much better chance of getting them to pay attention. Ready for a little theory?

Theory of Cognitive Dissonance:
Why They Are Not Listening

Dissonance theory, formulated in the 1950s, says that people tend to seek only messages that are "consonant" with their attitudes; they do not seek out "dissonant" messages. In other words, people don't go looking for messages they don't already agree with (who needs more conflict in their lives, right?). This theory also says that about the only way you are going to get anybody to listen to something they don't agree with is to juxtapose their attitude with a "dissonant" attitude—an attitude that is logically inconsistent with the first. What this means (theoretically) is that if you confront people with a concept that radically shakes up their belief structure, you might get them to pay attention. For example, this is the technique employed by some anti-abortion activists when they force us to look at graphic images of aborted fetuses. While the experience may be truly uncomfortable, it does remind even the most ardent pro-choice among us of the costs of the procedure. The idea is to shock unbelievers into questioning their loyalties.

Later research revealed that people use a fairly sophisticated psychological defense mechanism to filter out unwanted information. This mechanism consists of four "rings of defense":

- **Selective Exposure.** People tend to seek out only that information which agrees with their existing attitudes or beliefs. This accounts for our not subscribing to *The New Republic* if we are staunchly liberal Democrats.

- **Selective Attention.** People tune out communication that goes against their attitudes or beliefs, or they pay attention only to parts that reinforce their positions, forgetting the dissonant parts. This is why two people with differing points of view can come to different conclusions about the same message. Each of them is tuning out the parts with which they disagree.

- **Selective Perception.** People seek to interpret information so that it agrees with their attitudes and beliefs. This accounts for a lot of misinterpretation of messages. Some people don't block out dissonant information; they simply reinterpret it so that it matches their preconceptions. For example, while one person may view rising interest rates as an obstacle to her personal economic situation, another may view the same rise as an asset. The first person may be trying to buy a new home; the second may be a financial investor. Both are interpreting the same issue based on their differing viewpoints.

- **Selective Retention.** People tend to let psychological factors influence their recall of information. In other words, we forget the unpleasant or block out the unwanted. This also means that people tend to be more receptive to messages presented in pleasant environments—a lesson anyone who has ever put on a news conference understands.

What does all this mean? For those of us in the business of persuasion, it means we have a tough job ahead of us! The outlook isn't all that bleak, however. Since the time of the ancient Greeks (and probably before), we have known that people can be persuaded. Once you know how resistant they can be, half the job is done. The rest is in knowing how to break down those defenses (or, at least, how to get around them).

Persuasive Strategies

Writing a message that persuades is not easy. First, you must have a crystal-clear understanding of what it is you want your readers to do in response to your persuasive effort. This means that you have to be able not only to convey your message in the clearest possible terms, but also be responsive to opposing points of view.

It is important to note here that the persuasive message is normally audience-centered—that is, persuasive strategy is based on who your audience is and how they feel about your topic. The approach you use probably will be based on audience analysis. For example, your knowledge of your target audience should indicate how receptive they are to either an emotional or a rational appeal. Historically, audiences react best to a combination of both. There are times, however, when a purely emotional or purely rational appeal will be most effective.

In general, audience-centered persuasion will be more successful if you adhere to the following simple principles:

- **Identification.** People will relate to an idea, opinion, or point of view only if they can see some direct effect on their own hopes, fears, desires, or aspirations. This is why local news is more interesting to most people and why global issues remain so distant from most of our daily lives.

- **Suggestion of Action.** People will endorse ideas only if they are accompanied by a proposed action from the sponsor of the idea or if the recipients themselves propose it—especially if it is a convenient action. Every time you see a tear-off coupon at a grocery store, the manufacturer is using a suggestion of action.

- **Familiarity and Trust.** People are unwilling to accept ideas from sources they don't trust. Why does Bill Cosby sell Jell-O? Because we trust him, and the folks at Jell-O know this well.

- **Clarity.** The meaning of an idea has to be clear, whether it is an event, situation, or message. One of the most important jobs of public relations is to explain complex issues in simple terms. In today's "sound-bite" environment, this has become increasingly difficult. No one is more aware of this than political campaign advisors. When was the last time you saw a political ad that said anything substantive in thirty seconds? Despite this, research shows that some of the best of these ads actually work.

Remember: A hostile audience usually won't be convinced; a sympathetic audience doesn't need to be convinced; and an undecided audience is as likely to be convinced by your opposition as by you. Different strategies must be employed for each of these audiences. For instance, if you are writing for a friendly audience, an emotional appeal may work very well. For an undecided audience, a rational appeal supported by solid evidence may work best. If your audience is neutral or disinterested, you will have to stress attention-getting devices. If they are uninformed, you will have to inform them. And if they are simply undecided, you will have to convince them.

As already mentioned, certain strategies are more appropriate to persuasion than to information dissemination. For example, emotional appeals are most often associated with persuasion, not information. That's why, for instance, straight news stories are generally free of such appeal. They are supposed to be as objective (informative) as possible. The most common strategies for persuasion are compliance strategies, argument strategies, and emotional strategies.

Compliance Strategies

Compliance strategies are persuasive strategies designed to gain agreement through coercion. **Coercion** refers to techniques of persuasion not based on reasoned argument (although they may appear to be), but rather on some other method of enticement. For example, offering a reward for the return of stolen merchandise doesn't exactly appeal to altruism, yet it's not considered an unacceptable method for regaining what is yours. So, while coercion may appear at first blush to be unethical, a quick review of the following three compliance strategies will reassure you that it need not be.

Sanction strategies use rewards and punishments controlled either by the audience themselves or as a result of the situation. For example, if I'm trying to persuade you that supporting the state lottery is a good thing because the proceeds go to fund education, I can offer you the potential reward of big winnings. Of course, you control whether you are eligible or not. If you buy a ticket, you are; if you don't, you're not. However, I made you aware and offered you the choice.

Appeal strategies call upon the audience to help or come to the aid of the communicator or some third party represented by the communicator. For instance, I might urge you to "save the whales." I am counting on your sense of altruism to act, mostly because it is so difficult to tie the fate of whales to any personal interest beyond altruism. Of course, this strategy only works on publics who are prone to act sympathetically.

Command strategies come in three forms:

- They may employ direct requests with no rationale or motivation for the requests. The famous "I Want You" poster for the U.S. Army is still a great example of this strategy. A more current example is "Got Milk?"—the campaign of the American Dairy Council.

- They may provide explanation accompanied with reasons for complying. The Army's "Be All You Can Be" campaign is a good example of this one. One of the newer versions of that message plays heavily on the college tuition benefit, for example.

- They may provide hints and suggest circumstances from which the audience draws the desired conclusions and acts in the desired way. This technique implies that your audience shares certain implied suggestions. For example, the famous (or infamous) Virginia Slims ads suggest that smoking promotes thinness. Another example is the now-famous Mafia explanation, "I made him an offer he couldn't refuse." The implicit suggestion is understood between communicator and audience. Nothing explicit need be said.

Argument Strategies

Democratic debate is at the heart of our system of government. It is no surprise then that argument strategies are among the oldest types of persuasion at your disposal. **Argument strategies,** which are persuasive strategies designed to oppose another point of view and to persuade, come in two types: reasoned argument and emotional appeal. Both attempt to persuade by arguing one point of view against another.

Reasoned argument (also known as *logical argument*) uses the techniques of rhetoric as handed down from the ancient Greeks. For persuasive messages it is important to understand the psychological state of your audience and build your message around this. This audience-centered approach includes three basic techniques of reasoned argument: the motivated sequence, the imagined Q & A, and messages aimed at attitude change. We will discuss each of these briefly.

A common tactic used by persuaders is the *motivated sequence,* which involves the following five steps:

1. **Attention.** You must first get the attention of your audience. This means that you have to open with a bang.

2. **Need.** Establish why the topic is of importance to the audience. Set up the problem statement—a brief description of the issue you are dealing with.

3. **Satisfaction.** Present the solution. It has to be a legitimate solution to the problem.

4. **Support.** Support fully your solution and point out the pitfalls of any alternatives. Otherwise, your audience may not be able to comprehend completely the advantages of your solution over others.

5. **Action.** Finally, call for action. Ask your audience to respond to your message, and make it as easy as possible to take action.

In the *imagined Q & A,* the message is structured into a series of questions that the audience might have, followed by your answer to each. Ask yourself the questions your audience might be asking you, such as:

- **Why even talk about this subject?** Tell them the importance of your topic to them. Tie your topic to their concerns.

- **For example?** Don't just leave them with your point of view. Give them examples. Support your proposal.

- **So what?** Let them know what all of this means to them, and tell them what you want them to do.

If you really are going to try to change attitude, you had best be aware of the most common techniques: messages aimed at attitude change. Following are some guidelines for constructing persuasive messages designed to change attitudes or opinions. The strategy employed here is argument.

1. If your audience opposes your position, present arguments on both sides of the issue. Remember: They already know you have a vested interest in giving your side of the story. By presenting both sides, you portray an image of fairness and willingness to compare arguments. The process appears to be more democratic that way. In most cases, it is advisable to address counterarguments only after you have presented your own side. Here's how it works:

- State the opposing view fairly. Make your audience believe that you are fair-minded enough to recognize that there is another side and that you're intelligent enough to understand it.

- State your position on the opposing view. Now that you have shown you understand the other side, state why you don't think it's right—or better yet, not totally right. This indicates that you find at least some merit in what others have to say, even the opposition.

- Support your position. Give the details of your side of the argument. Use logic, not emotion. Show that you are above such tricks; however, don't avoid emotion altogether. Try to strike a balance while leaning toward logic and emotional control.

- Compare the two positions and show why yours is the most viable. If you have done your work well up to this point, then your audience will already see the clear differences between the two sides. Strengthen their understanding by reiterating the differences and finishing with a strong statement in support of your arguments.

2. If an audience already agrees with your position, present arguments that are consistent with their favorable viewpoint. This will tend to reinforce their opinions. Not much can be gained by presenting opposing arguments to this audience since they already agree with you. In fact, it might work against you.

3. If your audience is well educated, include both sides of the argument. Intelligent people will judge your argument by how well you are able to refute counterarguments (as in Strategy One).

4. If you do use messages containing both sides of the argument, don't leave out relevant opposition arguments. Audiences who notice the omission (especially well-educated ones) will probably suspect that you can't refute these arguments.

5. If your audience is likely to be exposed later to persuasive messages countering your position, present both sides of the argument (as in Strategy One) to build audience resistance to the later messages. This is known as the "inoculation effect," which basically states that once you have heard me present both my side and the opposing side of an argument, and heard me soundly refute the other side, you are far less likely to listen to the other side at a later time. You have, after all, already heard their side—from me.

Emotional Strategies

Emotional strategies are persuasive strategies designed to gain support through the use of emotional appeal. Because emotion is common to all human beings, it should come as no surprise that its use as a persuasive strategy is widespread. Most advertising uses emotional appeal to sell products. Parity products, especially, benefit from this technique. A *parity product* is one that is virtually indistinguishable from other similar products. Bath soaps, soft drinks, and perfumes are examples of parity products. Think about the type of ads you have seen that deal with these products: They are almost always based on an image created by emotional appeal. And not to let public relations off the hook, think of all those politicians who seem to be pretty much alike. How are they differentiated in our minds?

Emotional appeal can be fostered in several ways, the most important of which are the use of symbols, emotive language, and entertainment strategies. We will discuss the use of symbols and emotive language in the section on ethics in Chapter 4. Here, we will concentrate on entertainment as a way of creating emotional appeal.

Like the techniques of argument, the techniques of *entertainment* have been handed down to us from the ancient Greeks. The masks of comedy and tragedy are part of our cultural symbolism in the West. Entertainment, by nature, appeals to the senses. As a culture we constantly refer to a person's "sense of humor" or someone's "sense of the dramatic." As anyone who has kept track of the evolution in beer commercials knows, humor has become the primary focus of many beer manufacturers' ad campaigns. Think of the recent Budweiser campaign using frogs (and then lizards) to imprint name recognition, or the "Bud Bowl," now a staple of Super Bowl mythology. Like many other products, beer is a parity item, and parity products are best differentiated by image—which is often the result of entertainment strategies.

While it's easy to spot the uses of drama and humor in advertising, public relations campaigns frequently use the same approaches in order to persuade. Humor, for example, is especially useful if what you have to "sell" is either opposed by your audience or appears to be distant from their experience. Politicians needing image revamps often turn to humor. Vice President Al Gore could be seen a few years ago cracking jokes about his own stiffness on "Late Night with David Letterman." This was not an accident, but rather a carefully planned public relations move to soften his image.

Emotional appeal, like compliance strategies, may seem to be unethical; however, using emotion to draw attention is not inherently so. While it may be manipulative (in the sense that it's sole intent is to "hook" the audience), it is unethical only if it hides the true objective of the message: to persuade.

Choosing the Appropriate Medium or Media

The final step in the planning process is choosing the appropriate medium or media for your message. Any assumptions you make at this juncture could be disastrous. Selecting the right medium or media is a decision that should be based on sound knowledge of a number of factors. Public relations educators Doug Newsom, Alan Scot, and Judy VanSlyke Turk, in their book *This Is PR: The Realities of Public Relations,* have suggested a series of important considerations to be used in choosing the right medium for your message:

1. **What audience are you trying to reach and what do you know about its media usage patterns and the credibility ratings for each medium?** Many target audiences simply do not watch television or listen to the radio. Others don't read newspapers regularly or subscribe to magazines. You need to know, first, whether your intended audience will even see your message if it is presented in a medium they don't regularly use. Research tells us, for example, that businesspeople read the newspaper more than some other groups do, and rely on it for basic news and information. Other groups may rely on television almost exclusively for their news and information. For each of these groups, the credibility of the medium in question is vital. For example, businesspeople cite newspapers as a more credible source for news and information than television; however, for many people, television is far more credible.

2. **When do you need to reach this audience in order for your message to be effective?** If time is of the essence, you would best not leave your message for the next issue of the corporate magazine.

3. **How much do you need to spend to reach your intended audience, and how much can you actually afford?** It may be that the only way to achieve the result you're looking for is to go to some extra expense, such as a folder with more glitz or a full-color newsletter. Although every job has budget constraints, it's best to know from the start exactly what it will take to accomplish your objectives.

After these tough questions have been answered, you will still need to ask four others:

1. **Which medium (of those you have listed in response to the first three questions) reaches the broadest segment of your target audience at the lowest cost?** The answer to this question will give you a "bottom-line" choice of sorts because cost is the controlling factor in answering it. It might be that you can reach all of an employee audience with an expensive corporate magazine, but two-thirds of it with a less expensive newsletter.

2. **Which medium has the highest credibility and what does it cost?** Here, the correct answer will give you the additional factor of credibility that is key if your audience is at all discriminating. There are

always those for whom the least credible of sources is still credible (otherwise gossip tabloids would go out of business). But, for the honest communicator, credibility is important to the success of any future messages.

3. **Which medium will deliver your message within the time constraints necessary for it to be effective?** Again, a critical letter distributed via the company Intranet may be a lot more timely than a well-written article in next month's corporate magazine.

4. **Should a single medium be used or a combination of complementary media (media mix)?** Remember, each element in an overall communications program may require a specialized medium in order for that portion of the message to be most effective.

The more you know about your audience, the better you will be at selecting just the right medium for your message. However, you must also understand that media criteria often dictate message and message format. For instance, brochures "demand" brevity, as do flyers and posters; corporate magazines allow for fuller development of messages; newsletters offer more space than folders but less than magazines; pamphlets offer space for message expansion and place fewer demands on style; annual reports require strict adherence to SEC (Security and Exchange Commission) guidelines; and Web pages allow for detailed information on numerous topics. You must also consider cost, lead time for writing, editing, layout, typesetting, paste-up, printing, and distribution.

In short, selecting the most appropriate medium for your message is a complex endeavor. Be forewarned that no assumptions should be made about the acceptability of any particular medium. Until you have at least considered the questions posed earlier, you will probably only be guessing on your choice of an ideal medium.

Learning to Adapt ━━━━━

One of the hallmarks of a good writer is the ability to adapt to the needs of the audience, the message, and the medium. Public relations writing, unlike many other forms of writing, requires this flexibility. In the following chapters, you will find a variety of writing styles used in different formats. The key to writing for public relations is to learn these formats and adapt your style to each as needed. The road to becoming a good public relations writer has many sidetracks, and it is quite easy to let yourself become specialized. But the trick to becoming the best kind of writer is not to let that happen. The greater the variety of writing styles you can learn to use well, the better your chances of becoming an excellent writer.

KEY TERMS

message strategy	compliance strategies
exposition	coercion
persuasion	argument strategies
dissonance theory	emotional strategies

EXERCISES

1. Find a persuasive public service advertisement in a magazine. (Many of the major "consumer" magazines carry them.) Assess whether the ad is using a compliance, appeal, command, or argument persuasive strategy, and explain your reasoning. Rewrite the copy using each of the approaches not used originally.

2. Write down three reasons why you believe this ad was placed in this particular magazine. Based on your reasoning, list three other magazines in which you would place this ad.

3. If you were to use this advertisement in media other than magazines, what would those media be, and why would you pick them?

4. Look through your local newspaper for examples of persuasive writing, excluding advertising. Bring in copies of what you find along with an analysis of which persuasive techniques are being used.

## CHAPTER 4

ETHICAL AND LEGAL ISSUES IN PUBLIC RELATIONS WRITING

FOR IMMEDIATE RELEASE

In this chapter you will learn:

- Some of the ethical considerations of public relations writing, including unethical persuasive techniques and unethical language use.

- The guidelines for how to ghostwrite ethically.

- The legal aspects of public relations writing, including defamation, invasion of privacy, and copyright and trademark considerations.

Public relations is fraught with ethical and legal dilemmas—no one working in public relations would deny this. But for the writer, these dilemmas take a slightly different form than the types of problems faced by others in the field. Many of the ethical quandaries facing public relations people have to do with decisions on large issues—whether to handle a particular political candidate or ethically suspect client; how to deal with the media on a day-to-day basis without lying; what to keep confidential and what to disclose; and whether to do what the client says, no matter what. It's not that such decisions are beyond the scope of the public relations writer. It's that a writer spends much more time dealing with the technical aspects of his or her job than with the bigger picture. This tight focus, however, comes with its own set of ethical and legal considerations, among which are such quandaries as how to persuade without violating the basic tenets of ethics and good taste, how to write words that will later be claimed by someone else as their own, and how not to invade privacy or infringe on another's copyright.

Ethical Considerations of Public Relations Writing

Some people consider persuasion unethical by nature. They believe in a very strict version of the "marketplace of ideas" theory that if you provide enough unbiased information, people will be able to make up their own minds about any issue. Of course, we all know that isn't true. While our political system is based on this theory, to some extent it is also based on the notion of reasoned argument—that is, persuasion. People who believe fervently enough in a particular point of view aren't going to rely on any marketplace to decide their case. They're going to get out there and argue, persuasively, for their side. Since the time of Aristotle we've had access to a number of persuasive techniques, some already mentioned.

We also are aware, however, of how easily many of these techniques can be turned to unethical purposes. In fact, the most frequent complaint against any form of communication is that it is trying to persuade unethically. While this may seem to be leveled most often at advertising, public relations isn't off the hook entirely. Following are a number of techniques which, in varying degrees, can be used unethically. All of these have been used in propaganda campaigns, but you will recognize many of them as still being used in both PR and advertising.

Unethical Persuasive Techniques

By far the most unethical of the persuasive techniques are those codified by the Roman orators over a thousand years ago. These are commonly referred to as **logical fallacies** because they are both illogical and deceptive by nature. Let's look first at these:

- **Cause and Effect** (*post hoc ergo propter hoc*). Don't be put off by the Latin. We see cause and effect in operation all the time. It means that because one thing follows another in time, it was necessarily caused by it. This is most often used to infer that one thing is the result of the other. Politicians are particularly adept at using this argument. For example, an incumbent may suggest that the national drop in crime rate is the result of his policies when, in fact, it is the continuation of a drop that began before his administration. A recent television ad for plastic implies that we are a healthier society because meat is no longer sold in open-air markets, exposed to the elements. While this may be partially true, the overall longevity of any society is the result of multiple factors, not just one.

- **Personal Attack** (*ad hominem*). This means "against the man," and is a technique used to discredit the source of the message regardless of the message itself. Again, we see this one time and again in politics, where policies are left unconsidered while personality assassination runs rampant. Any time you see an argument turn from issues to personality, this unethical strategy is being used.

- **Bandwagon** (*ad populum*). This is an appeal to popularity. In other words, if everyone else is doing it, why aren't you? McDonald's has been using this approach for years in its "xxx billion sold" byline. Since human beings are, by nature, group oriented, they already tend to want to go with what's popular. However, as Thoreau pointed out, the group isn't always right.

- **Inference by Association.** This is an argument based entirely on false logic, most often thought of as "guilt by association," or, in some cases, credit by association. The argument usually takes the following form:

   Chemical weapons are evil.
   X company makes chemical weapons.
   X company is evil.

Of course, the argument is logically inconsistent. While chemical weapons may, in themselves, be evil, this does not automatically make the entire company evil. The same sort of argument can be made by associating a product or idea with another, already accepted idea. For example, the statement, "from the people who brought you . . ." assumes that because one product is successful or satisfying, all products from the same company will be. And, of course, this argument is used in all those celebrity endorsements: "Wheaties, the breakfast of champions!"

There are several other tactics closely related to inference by association that are not necessarily unethical by nature, but that can be used unethically. Some of the most common are the following:

- **Plain Folks.** This is an appeal to our need to deal with people who are like us. "Plain folks" proposes that the speaker is just like the listener and thus "wouldn't lie to you." Politicians are adept at this approach, and so are corporate executives who sell their own products. For example, almost everyone who watches TV knows that Dave Thomas owns Wendy's and that he seems to be a regular guy, just like you and me. But Dave Thomas isn't just like the average "you and me." He is a very wealthy corporate executive who happens to star in his own commercials. Do you know anyone like that in your circle of friends?

- **Testimonials.** This tactic is directly related to inference by association; however, testimonials are actually implying that the celebrity spokesperson uses the product or supports the cause. And, of course, this may or may not be true.

- **Transfer.** This is the deliberate use of positive symbols to transfer meaning to another message not necessarily related. The use of religious or patriotic symbols such as a "heavenly choir" or an American flag during a commercial not directly related to such symbols is an example of transfer. Most recently, the ubiquitous use of Beethoven's "Ode to Joy" in everything from the Olympic Games to cable channel promos is a blatant attempt to bring a sense of high, nearly religious, meaning to the message being imparted.

Unethical Language Use

Another area of ethical consideration as it relates to persuasion has to do with the actual use of language. Often called **language fallacies,** these techniques are nearly always used intentionally. The most common are the following:

- **Equivocation.** Words can be, and often are, ambiguous. Many words have more than one meaning. *Equivocation* refers to using one or both meanings of a word and then deliberately confusing the two in the audience's mind. For example, the word "free" is tossed about quite a bit by advertisers, but does it literally mean "without cost"? When you purchase that big bottle of shampoo that claims you are getting "12 more ounces free!" are you really getting it free? When a press release states that a senior executive has "resigned," does it mean he has quit or that he was fired? In fact, the word "resign" has become something of a euphemism in business and government for being asked to leave.

- **Amphibole.** This is the use of ambiguous sentence structure or grammar to mislead. For example, "new and improved" products imply that there is a logical comparison to be made. But what are these products' "newness" and state of improvement being compared to? How about, "X cereal: part of a nutritional breakfast"? Which part? Is it nutritional without the other parts? If not, what are the other parts? And if something only "helps" you obtain whiter teeth, what else plays a part?

- **Emotive Language.** This is the use of emotionally charged words to shift response from the argument itself to the images invoked by these words. It is a bit like transfer except that it uses words instead of images. Think of the ads that use words such as "freedom," "miracle," "powerful," "younger looking." Or the news release that refers to a product as "revolutionary," or a person as "dynamic." When we use these words, we've strayed from fact to opinion.

Ultimately, whether what you have written is ethical or not will depend on being as objective as possible about your own motives. If you wish to deceive, you will. A technically good writer has access to all the tools needed to write unethically. The decision is yours. Remember: *Persuasion is ethical, manipulation is not.*

Ethics and Ghostwriting

Ghostwriting refers to writing something for someone else that will be represented as that person's actual point of view. Public relations writers ghostwrite speeches, letters to the editor, annual report letters from the president, and even quotes. Ghostwriting is ubiquitous, to say the least. Rhetoricians point out that no president since Abraham Lincoln has written his own speeches in entirety. You will recall that Lincoln wrote the Gettysburg Address on a train ride between Washington and Gettysburg—and, by most accounts, did a fairly nice job.

The days when the busy corporate executive or politician had the time (or the skill) to write his or her own speeches have long since vanished. In fact, we can no longer take it as a given that most of what passes for their words—either in print or spoken forms—are really *their* words. When President Reagan's speechwriter, Larry Speakes, indicated in his book that he had not only written all of the president's speeches but had made up quotes (even "borrowed" quotes from others and attributed them to Reagan), many seemingly incredulous journalists cried foul. Surely they, like most of us, realized that a president simply doesn't have the luxury to write his own speeches any more. Even John Kennedy, famous for his speeches, didn't write his own.

However—and this is a big however—something still bothers all of us about a writer we don't even know putting words into the mouth of someone we do know, or thought we knew. So, the question is, if ghostwriting is to be taken as having been produced by, or at least prompted by, the person under whose name it will appear, is it unethical? Well, yes and no. Some of the best guidelines I know of have been set down by Richard Johannesn in his book *Ethics in Human Communication,* in which he analyzes the ethics of ghostwriting by posing the following series of important questions:

- **What is the communicator's intent, and what is the audience's degree of awareness?** In other words, does the communicator pretend to be the author of the words he speaks or over which his signature appears? And how aware is the audience that ghostwriting is commonplace under certain circumstances? If we assume, as most of us do, that presidential speeches are ghostwritten, then the only unethical act would be for the president to claim to author his or her own speeches.

- **Does the communicator use ghostwriters to make himself or herself appear to possess personal qualities that he or she really does not have?** In other words, does the writer impart such qualities as eloquence, wit, coherence, and incisive ideas to a communicator who might not possess these qualities otherwise? The degree to which the writing distorts a communicator's character has a great deal to do with ethicality.

- **What are the surrounding circumstances of the communicator's job that make ghostwriting a necessity?** The pressures of a job often dictate that a ghostwriter be used. Busy executives, like busy politicians, may not have the time to write all the messages they must deliver on a daily basis. However, we don't expect the average office manager or university professor to hire a ghostwriter. Part of the answer to this question lies in the pressures of the job itself, and the other part has to do with the need and frequency of communication.

- **To what extent do the communicators actively participate in the writing of their own messages?** Obviously, the more input a communicator has in his or her own writing, the more ethical will be the resultant image. We really don't expect the president to write his or her own speeches, but we do expect that the sentiments expressed in them will be his or her own.

- **Does the communicator accept responsibility for the message he or she presents?** Part of the problem with Larry Speakes's revelation was that President Reagan denied the accusations. Most communicators simply assume that whatever they say or whatever they sign their names to is theirs, whether written by someone else or not. This is obviously the most ethical position to take.

Remember: If you ghostwrite, you are as responsible for the ethicality of your work as the person for whom it is written. Be sure that you have asked yourself these questions before you give authorship of your work over to someone else.

The Legal Aspects of Public Relations Writing ———

All those who deal in public communication are bound by certain laws. For the most part, these laws protect others. We are all familiar with the First Amendment rights allowed the press in the United States. To a certain degree, some of those rights transfer to public relations. For example, corporations now receive a limited First Amendment protection under what is known as commercial speech. **Commercial speech,** as defined by the Supreme Court, allows a corporation to state publicly its position on controversial issues. The Court's interpretation of this concept also allows for political activity through lobbying and political action committees.

But, as with most rights, there are concomitant obligations—chief among them is the obligation not to harm others through your communication. The most important "don'ts" for public relations writers concern slander or libel (defamation), invasion of privacy, and infringement of copyrights or trademarks.

Defamation

Defamation is the area of infringement with which writers are most familiar. Although it is variously defined (each case seems to bring a new definition), **defamation** can be said to be any communication that holds a person up to contempt, hatred, ridicule, or scorn. One problem in defending against accusations of defamation is that there are different rules for different people. More specifically, it is generally easier for private individuals to prove defamation than it is for those in the public eye. Celebrities and politicians, for example, open themselves to a certain amount of publicity, and, therefore, criticism. While a private individual suing for libel must only prove negligence, a public figure must prove malice.

In order for defamation to be actionable, five elements must be present:

- There must be communication of a statement that harms a person's reputation in some way—even if it only lowers that person's esteem in another's eyes.
- The communication must have been published or communicated to a third party. The difference here is that between slander and libel. *Slander* is oral defamation, and might arise, for example, in a public speech. *Libel* is written defamation, although it also includes broadcast communication.

- The person defamed must have been identified in the communication, either by name or by direct inference. This is the toughest to prove if the person's name hasn't been used directly.

- The person defamed must be able to prove that the communication caused damage to his or her reputation.

- Negligence must also be shown. That is to say, the source of the communication must be proved to have been negligent during research or writing. Negligence can be the fault of poor information gathering. Public figures also must prove *malice*—that is, that the communication was made with knowing falsehood or reckless disregard for the truth.

There are defenses against defamation. The most obvious is that the communication is the truth, regardless of whether the information harmed someone's reputation or not.

The second defense is privilege. Privilege applies to statements made during public, official, or judicial proceedings. For example, if something normally libelous is reported accurately on the basis of a public meeting, the reporter cannot be held responsible. Privilege is a tricky concept, however, and care must be taken that privileged information be given only to those who have a right to it. Public meetings are public information; however, only concerned individuals have a right to privileged information released at private meetings.

The third most common defense is fair comment. This concept applies primarily to the right to criticize, as in theater or book critiques, and must be restricted to the public interest aspects of the work under discussion. However, it also can be construed to apply to such communications as comparative advertising.

Privacy

Most of us are familiar with the term *invasion of privacy*. For public relations writers, infringing on privacy is a serious concern. It can happen very easily. For example, your position as editor of the house magazine doesn't automatically give you the right to use any employee picture you might have on file, or to divulge personal information about an employee without their prior written permission.

Invasion of privacy falls roughly into the following categories:

- *Appropriation* is the commercial use of a person's name or picture without permission. For instance, you can't say that one of your employees supports the company's position on nuclear energy if that employee hasn't given you permission to do so—even if they do support that position and have said so to you.

Private facts about individuals are also protected. Information about a person's lifestyle, family situation, personal health, etc., is considered to be strictly private and may not be disclosed without permission.

- *Intrusion* involves literally spying on another. Obtaining information about another's private affairs by bugging, filming, or recording in any way is cause for a lawsuit.

Copyright

Most of us understand that we can't quote freely from a book without giving credit, or photocopy entire publications to avoid buying copies, or reprint a cartoon strip in our corporate magazine without permission. This is because most forms of published communication are protected by copyright laws.

The reasons for copyright protection are fairly clear: Those who create original work, such as novels, songs, articles, and advertisements, lose the very means to their livelihood each time that novel, song, or advertisement is used without payment.

All writers need to be aware that copyrighted information is not theirs to use free of charge, without permission. Always check for copyright ownership on anything you plan to use in any way. You may want to rewrite information, or paraphrase it, and think that as long as you don't use the original wording you are exempt from copyright violation. Not so. There are prescribed guidelines for use of copyrighted information without permission. You may use a portion of copyrighted information if:

- It is not taken out of context.
- Credit is given to the source.
- Your usage doesn't affect the market for the material.
- You are using the information for scholastic or research purposes.
- The material used doesn't exceed a certain percentage of the total work.

Just remember: Never use another's work without permission.

Trademarks

Trademarks are typically issued for the protection of product names or, in certain instances, images, phrases, or slogans. For example, several years ago Anheuser-Busch sued a florist for calling a flower shop "This Bud's For You." The reason, of course, is that the slogan is commonly recognized as referring to Budweiser beer. Similarly, the Disney studios have guarded their trademarked cartoon characters jealously for over fifty years, and their trademark appears on thousands of items. Charles Schultz's "Peanuts" characters also are used for hundreds of purposes, all with permission. Even advertisements that mention other product names are careful to footnote trademark information.

One of the main reasons for trademark protection is to prevent someone not associated with the trademarked product, image, or slogan from using it for monetary gain without a portion of that gain (or at least recognition) going to the originator. Another important concern is that the trademarked product, image, or slogan be used correctly and under the direction of the originator. Certain trademarked names, such as Xerox, Kleenex, and Band-Aid, have for years been in danger of passing into common usage as synonyms for the generic product lines of which they are part. The companies that manufacture these brand names are zealous in their efforts to ensure that others don't refer to photocopying as "Xeroxing," for example, or to facial tissue as "Kleenex." In fact, one of the legal tests for determining whether a brand name has become a synonym for a generic product line is to determine whether it is now included in dictionaries as a synonym for that product.

As harmless as it may seem, using the term "Xeroxing" in a written piece to refer to photocopying, or the simple use of a cartoon character on a poster announcing a holiday party may be a trademark violation. The easiest thing to do is to check with the originator before using any trademarked element. Often the only requirement will be to either use the true generic word (in the case of a brand name) or mention that the image, slogan, or name is a trademarked element and give the source's name. Exhibit 4.1 defines symbols indicating protected material.

KEY TERMS

logical fallacy	commercial speech
language fallacy	defamation
ghostwriting	

EXERCISES

1. Look for a print advertisement in a magazine or newspaper that you think uses unethical or questionable persuasive techniques. Indicate which techniques are used in the ad and answer the following questions:

   • What do you find unethical about the ad and the approach taken?

   • Why do you think this approach was used?

   • What would you do differently to sell this product or service in order to make the persuasive appeal ethical?

EXHIBIT 4.1

Symbols for Protected Material

© **Copyright.** Used to protect copy of any length. Can be "noticed"—or marked—either without actual federal registration (which limits protection under the law) or with registration (which expands the degree of legal protection).

® **Registered Trademark.** Used to protect any word, name, symbol, or device used by a manufacturer or merchant to identify and distinguish his or her goods from those of others. This mark indicates that the user has registered the item with the federal government, allowing maximum legal protection.

™ **Trademark.** Similarly used, but as a "common law" notice. In other words, material marked this way is not necessarily registered with the government and thus has limited and not full legal protection.

## CHAPTER 5

MEDIA RELATIONS AND PLACEMENT

FOR IMMEDIATE RELEASE

In this chapter you will learn:

- How journalists judge news value.

- The difference between hard news and soft news.

- How to work with the media, including getting to know journalists and their jobs.

- How to successfully get your public relations message placed in the media.

Public relations practitioners are professionals. So are journalists. Professionals, in the ideal sense, work together for the public welfare. Why, then, do public relations people see members of the media as adversaries who go out of their way to dig up the dirt? And why do reporters— whether print or broadcast—often see public relations people as "flaks" paid to run interference for their clients?

Actually, there is a little truth in both points of view and there are a number of legitimate complaints on both sides. Public relations people often are charged with covering up or stonewalling, while reporters often do seek only the negative in any issue. Obviously, this is a far from perfect relationship between professionals.

Part of the problem stems from a lack of real understanding in both camps of how the other operates. There is little you can do to make journalists find out more about PR, but you can do much to improve your own knowledge of how the media operate, what media people want from you, what they are capable and not capable of providing, and how to get your public relations piece placed in the media.

What Is News?

The most common stumbling block to a good working relationship between public relations and media professionals is a mutually agreeable definition of the concept of *news*. Research has shown that most journalists judge news value based on at least some of the following characteristics:

- **Consequence.** Does the information have any importance to the prospective reading, listening, or viewing public? Is it something that the audience would pay to know? News value is frequently judged by what the audience is willing to pay for.

- **Interest.** Is the information unusual or entertaining? Does it have any human interest? People like to transcend the everyday world. Excitement—even vicarious excitement—often makes good news.

- **Timeliness.** Is the material current? If it isn't, is it a whole new angle on an old story? Remember: The word *news* means "new." This is one rule frequently broken by public relations practitioners. Nothing is more boring than yesterday's news.

- **Proximity.** For most public relations people seeking to connect with the media, a local angle is often the only way to do it. If it hits close to home, it stands a better chance of being reported.

- **Prominence.** Events and people of prominence frequently make the news. The problem, of course, is that your company president may not be as prominent to the media as he or she is to you.

If your story contains at least some of the above elements, it stands a chance of being viewed as news by media professionals.

Journalists often make a distinction between hard news and soft news. While there are no fixed definitions of hard and soft news, there are some pretty self-evident differences between the two. **Hard news** is information that has an immediate impact on the people receiving it. By journalists' definition, it is very often news people need rather than news they want. **Soft news** is just the opposite: It is news people want rather than news they necessarily need. A story about a local teachers' strike is hard news; one about a new swimming program at the YMCA is soft news. A story about a corporate takeover is hard news; one about the hiring of a new celebrity spokesperson is not.

The problem is that many public relations people believe journalists view everything that the public relations people send them as soft news. Of course this isn't so, and many public relations writers have discovered that both hard and soft news often will be used by media outlets looking to fill time and/or space. In addition, much of what passes for soft news often is viewed as public-interest information by the various media.

The other notion to understand about hard and soft news is that hard news frequently is perishable while soft news is not. In other words, a story on an important stockholders' meeting in which a buyout is announced is not only perishable, it is very timely. On the other hand, a new development in a product line or a promotion within your organization probably is not perishable—it will still be news a week from now.

Working with the Media

The media are a powerful force, and they can do a lot for you—or a lot against you. The determining factor may well be how much you know about media professionals and appreciate their jobs, and how well you get to know them as people. Following are some suggestions for doing just that, along with some guidelines for dealing with the media, interviewing, and correcting errors.

Getting to Know Journalists' Jobs

Getting to know journalists' jobs starts with learning all you can about the media outlets and the individuals with whom you will be dealing on a regular basis. Journalists have a tough life. (I know, so do you.) Having some journalism experience goes a long way toward understanding the frustrations of the job. Many public relations practitioners have had prior journalistic experience or education. Most journalists, however, haven't experienced public relations work firsthand. Thus, it is often up to you to make the relationship work.

Talk to journalists. Ask them for their guidelines on gathering news. Get to know how they write and what they choose to write about. Most news outlets will gladly provide you with guidelines for submitting everything from feature stories to publicity. Follow them. Know their deadlines and keep them as if they were your own—in a way, they are. At the same time, try to let media people know what you do. Show them your style. Ask them for hints on how to make it more acceptable to their needs. Everybody likes to be asked his or her professional opinion.

Getting to Know Journalists as People

In order to begin working with media people, you have to meet them first. If you're new to your job, the first step is to get out and introduce yourself. Of course, no self-respecting reporter is going to be in his or her office when you drop in. They're busy people and they're probably out covering a story. If they have an 11:00 P.M. deadline, they may not be back in the office to write their stories until after 6:00 P.M. And with the advent of laptop computers and online transmission capabilities, many reporters now file directly from the field. So how do you meet them?

Call first. Tell them who you are and how what you're doing relates to their work. Keep it brief, just a quick "Hello, I'm new in town, you will be hearing from me soon, anything I should know?" If you can't get them by phone, try e-mail (although many reporters give out e-mail addresses only to their closest contacts to keep the traffic volume down). If you get a chance to meet in person, do so. Again, be brief, keep it professional, and don't get away without asking them what you can do to make *their* jobs easier.

Remember: This relationship is two-way. Journalists need your information as much as you need their medium for your messages. Be available at all times and make sure they know how to get in touch with you at a moment's notice. Always give them your home phone. News happens after five o'clock too. If you cooperate, they'll cooperate.

Establishing a rapport with the media is your first concern; however, a word needs to be said here about courting the press. Most journalists who deal in hard news don't react well to being courted. That is, they aren't likely to change anything they think or write because you invited them out to lunch. Although we've all heard stories about unethical journalists, I prefer to assume that every reporter has professional scruples. You should too. They may well go out to lunch with you, especially if you have a story that may interest them, but they are very likely to pick up their own checks. The sole exception might be the trade press. Trade journalists are used to receiving samples of products that they are writing about. Everything from small parts to expensive equipment is loaned out to the various trade publications for these purposes. For most media, though, the golden rule of media relations is, *Let them know you by your work, not by your checkbook.*

Guidelines for Dealing with the Media

So now you're ready to meet the media in a working situation. What do you do? Although there are no guidelines that can cover every possible situation, the following are a few that will help you to keep your encounters professional and as pleasant as possible:

- **Always be honest.** It takes a lot of hard work to build credibility, and nothing builds credibility like honesty. It takes only one mistake to ruin months of credibility building. If you are honest with the media, they will be fair to you. But remember, "fair" to them means balanced and objective. They will tell all sides of a story, even the negative. You should be willing to do the same.

- **Establish ground rules early in your relationship.** Among the most important of these rules is that everything is "on the record." If you don't want to see it or hear it the next day in the newspaper or on TV, you would best not say it to a journalist today. While I usually advise public relations practitioners (and others) to always stay on the record, there are two accepted circumstances under which journalists are *supposed* (and that's a big *supposed*) to honor your off-the-record comments:

  - *Not-for-attribution*—This is the home of the "sources close to the White House" quote. Honest PR practitioners generally stay away from this one. It smacks of leaks and fear of attribution. This is one of the key ways the media often are manipulated into running with information on which they would normally require confirmation. Let's face it, without attribution, how does anyone know the opinion is even valid?

  - *Background*—In my estimation, this is the only useful justification for going off-the-record. Going off-the-record in order to fill in background without which a reporter might misconstrue your statements or misunderstand your position is a legitimate procedure. Keep in mind, however, that it is open to the same potential abuse as any other off-the-record comment.

- **Always answer a reporter's phone calls.** Never avoid returning a call, either because you're afraid of what they will ask (in which case, you're in the wrong business), or because you haven't done your homework. If they don't get it from you, the ideal source, they'll have to get it from less reliable sources, and you don't want that to happen.

- **Give media people what *they* want, not what *you* want.** Ideally, they can be the same thing. The key, of course, is to make your information newsworthy, following the criteria listed earlier.

- **Along the same lines, don't bombard journalists with a daily barrage of press releases.** Nothing that happens every day is newsworthy. The reporters and editors who receive your releases know this and are very likely to stop reading your information.

- **Don't assume reporters are out to get you.** If you have established a good working relationship with them, they are probably going to seek out your help, not try to assassinate you.

- **Don't try to intimidate reporters.** They'll resent it. Don't let your boss talk you into this one. You are the liaison, the media relations person. It's your job to get along, and nobody wants a friend who tries to intimidate them into doing something.

- **Don't plead your case or follow up on stories.** The nature of publicity is to let the media handle it once you have released it. If you want more control than that, take out an ad.

Guidelines for Media Interviews

While being interviewed by reporters and/or setting up interviews for reporters with your clients aren't exactly public relations writing, they do help you visualize further the proper relationship between reporter and public relations person. With that in mind, some guidelines for interview situations follow. Some are similar to the guidelines already covered; others are specific to the interview situation:

- **Everything in an interview is on the record.** Like everything else in which a reporter is involved, keep any comments strictly on-the-record. If you don't want your words printed on the front page of tomorrow's paper, don't say them out loud to a reporter.

- **Provide background.** Give interviewers all the background they need to bring them up to speed on the topic at hand before you begin the "official" interview. They may not have read your media backgrounder or done any homework on your client prior to the interview (although they have if they're good reporters). As with everything else you say, keep the background information free of anything you don't want printed or run on the air.

- **Know the topic.** If you don't know the topic, why are you being interviewed? The same applies to any spokesperson you may have chosen for the interview. Always choose the person who knows the most about the issue being discussed; that person is not necessarily the company president or yourself. Nothing is more embarrassing than to have to constantly plead ignorance.

- **Anticipate touchy questions.** If something hot is happening with your client, the interviewer is there to ask about it. Assume this always to be true. If they don't ask the tough question, just consider yourself lucky; however, be prepared to answer it in your way and with your spin if they do ask.

- **Always answer questions that are already a matter of public record.** For example, if you have just filed a quarterly return with the

SEC and it contains information about your organization's economic status that is less than flattering, guess what? It's public information by law and you might as well be prepared to address it if it comes up.

- **Be completely honest.** Truth is the major responsibility of all communicators. If you ever lie to a journalist, he or she will never trust you again. Remember: Credibility is very difficult to obtain, but it only takes one lie to lose it forever. The following three guidelines are related to this one:

  - *Answer questions directly.* Don't rush, guess, dodge, or stonewall when answering questions. Reporters quickly become frustrated when you try to avoid answering a question. Ultimately, it's best just to get to the point if you want to maintain your credibility.

  - *If you don't know the answer, say so.* Offer to get back to them with the answer as soon as you can. You can also offer to put them in touch with someone who does know the answer, but then you lose control of the spin factor.

  - *Keep it cordial, no matter what happens.* Never lose your cool. That would put you at a disadvantage because you automatically become defensive in such situations. If that happens, you lose control of the interview and hurt your own image as a public relations professional.

- **Look professional.** This may seem self-evident, but you're a professional. If you look like one, you will enhance your credibility, and this will enhance your message's importance.

- **Offer help later if needed, and give it.** If you have promised to follow up, do it. Make yourself available for any follow-up questions that they may have and assure them that it is no trouble. However, don't call them just to check on the progress of the story.

Guidelines for Correcting Errors

What do you do if you discover an error in the subsequent story a reporter produces? If the error is minor, ignore it—no sense badgering a reporter or editor over minor details. If the error is important, however (regardless of whether the error was caused by you or by the reporter), it needs to be corrected. Here are some guidelines for doing so:

- Always be as diplomatic as possible.
- Contact the reporter immediately. If it's your fault, say so and ask if it's too late to get the error corrected before publication. And don't take a great deal of time pointing out the error. Just mention it and ask if it can be fixed.
- Remain calm and courteous. If you seem agitated, the reporter will get suspicious. If it's the reporter's fault, the individual may even get angry.

- If the story has already been run, ask for a correction.
- If the reporter is unwilling or unable to redress the error, don't automatically go over his or her head—unless correcting the error is worth more than your relationship with the reporter.
- If all else fails, write a letter to the editor correcting the error. Keep it short and to the point. And, above all, keep it rational. Don't pout and don't point fingers.
- Finally, ask the reporter if there is anything you can do in the future to try and prevent this sort of thing from happening again.

Placing Your Public Relations Piece in the Media ———

Knowing journalists will enhance your chances of placing valuable information with them. But you can't rely on personal contact for everything. Placing public relations materials with the media requires up-to-date information on all of the possible outlets for your materials, as well as the ability to physically get your message to the media.

Deciding Where to Place Your Message

Naturally, the number and type of media outlets will depend on your business. If you are in the automotive industry, trade journals will be a vital link between you and your publics. If you work for an organization that is strictly local, then your media contacts will be limited to the local media. Local interest news will be important, too, within the communities in which your plants or offices are located. If you work for a regional or even a national operation, then your contacts will expand accordingly. Whatever media you deal with, it is important to keep updated directories and lists that meet your particular needs with the least amount of waste information.

Media Directories. A good directory is an indispensable tool for the media relations specialist. **Media directories** come in all sizes and address almost every industry. Publishers of directories offer formats ranging from global checkers that include a variety of sources in every medium, to specialized directories dealing with a single medium.

There are a number of excellent directories for media placement. Here are some of the major ones:

- *Bacon's Public Relations and Media Information Systems*—a series including *Bacon's Publicity Checker* (two volumes covering editorial contacts in the United States and Canada, magazines organized by industry, daily and weekly newspapers, and all multiple publisher groups); *Bacon's Media Alerts* (a directory of editorial profiles cover-ing editorial features and special issues, often planned months in advance, for both magazines and newspapers); *Bacon's Radio/TV Directory* (a listing of every TV and radio station in the United States, listed geographically); and *Bacon's International Publicity Checker* (editorial contact information on magazines and newspapers in fifteen Western European countries). Bacon is also available on line at www.baconsinfo.com. Like many of the other services listed below, Bacon online offers sales of its directories, links to online sites for media outlets, and a host of other Internet services.

- *Burrelle's Media Directory*—organized similarly to *Bacon's* and pub-lished on a similar schedule. Both *Bacon's* and *Burrelle's* also provide clipping services separate from their directories. Burrelle is online at www.burrelles.inter.net.

- A series published by Larrison Communications that includes *Medical and Science News Media; Travel, Leisure and Entertainment News Media;* and *Business and Financial News Media.*

- *Editor & Publisher*—a series of several media guides including the well-used *Editor & Publisher International Yearbook* (a collection of newspapers divided into dailies and weeklies and covering everything from local and national publications to house organs and college papers). *Editor & Publisher* hosts a comprehensive online service with links to hundreds of media outlets worldwide from its address at www.mediainfo.com.

- *Standard Rate and Data Service (SRDS)*—used primarily by advertis-ers, this multivolume set is one of the most exhaustive around for sheer inclusion. If you are looking for every magazine published in the United States, in every category imaginable, this is your directory. *SRDS* also provides information on electronic media and newspapers. *SRDS* can be found online at www.srds.com, and it provides an exten-sive electronic service as well as links to many other useful sites.

- Two other Internet sites, useful because of their multiple links to other media outlets online, are www.prplace.com and www.publicity.org.

Most of the online sites listed here don't substitute for printed direc-tories. In fact, most of them offer these directories for sale as part of their online services. For the time being, printed directories (in some cases available on CD-ROM) are still the industry standard. Because the prices of these directories range into the hundreds of dollars, you will need to be fairly selective. When choosing a directory, keep the following key points in mind:

- The directory should be current. If it is not updated at least once a year, its uses are limited.

- The directory should cover the geographic area in which you operate and in which you want your organization's message to go out. You may not need a national directory if your operation is strictly local or statewide. Many states publish directories of all kinds of information, such as almanacs, that include media addresses.

- If your primary target is trade publications, then you need to choose a directory that lists them. *Standard Rate and Data Service,* for instance, publishes a constant stream of listings, including business and industry directories.

- If you are a heavy user of broadcast media, your directory should include broadcast listings.

- The directory should list names of editors, news directors, and so on, and their addresses. Make sure these are current. Nothing is more embarrassing to you and more infuriating to them than to receive a press release addressed to the previous editor.

- Make sure circulation is listed for print publications and listening/ viewing audience for broadcast outlets. You don't want to waste an excellent story on a tiny circulation trade magazine when you might have reached a much larger audience.

The most important point to remember about media selection is never to place anything in a publication you haven't read personally. What may sound like an excellent publication in a directory may turn out to be second-rate for your purposes. After some time in your particular field, you will become familiar with its leading publications. Until then, read them all. Remember: Your image is tied to their image.

Media Lists. Directories are essential, but they are not the only tools you will need to keep up to date with media relations. **Media lists** are just as vital to your job. They are a more personal tool than directories because they contain details about local contacts and all the information you need to conduct business in your community. Media lists may include regional and even nationwide contacts, depending on the scope of your operation. A media list, once compiled, should be updated by hand at least once a month. This job can usually be handled efficiently by clerical staff once the list is compiled. It only takes a 30-second phone call to each of the media outlets on your list to verify names and addresses. In the long run, the routine of updating will pay off. A computer is a great tool for compiling and maintaining a media list. Computer software designed specifically for media lists is available from a number of distributors.

In compiling a media list, try to include most of the following:

1. Name of the publication, radio/TV station, particular show (for talk shows), and so on.

2. Names of editors, reporters, news directors, etc.

3. Addresses, including mailing and street addresses if they are different. You may need to hand-deliver a press release on occasion, and this can be difficult if all you have is a P.O. Box number.

4. Telephone and fax numbers for the media outlets as well as for each of the people you have on your list. Many media outlets can now accept computer-generated press releases through normal telephone lines or satellite-transmitted video or audio actualities. Include such details in your media list.

5. Any important editorial information such as style guidelines, deadlines, times of editions (morning/evening), dates of publication for magazines, times of broadcasts, use of actualities, photo requirements, and use of fax or electronic transmission (and applicable phone numbers).

Getting Your Message to the Media

Once you have decided where to place your information, you have to get it there. Again, you have a number of choices, dependent on what you are sending and to whom. The first option is to deliver the message yourself, using one of the following methods:

- You can mail it. This takes more time, but if your information is not perishable, this may work just fine. Thousands of news releases and information pieces are still mailed every day.

- You can hand-deliver it. Reserve this one for really important or really timely information. Hand delivery used to be the norm; now it's a lot of trouble. However, it can pay off in that it still receives a bit more attention than other forms of delivery.

- You can fax it. Nearly everyone has a fax these days. The biggest problem with this delivery method is quality. If all you're sending is text, OK. But if pictures are an important consideration, a fax may not be your first choice.

- You can transmit it electronically via computer. This can be accomplished in several ways. You can use standard e-mail, e-mail attachments, Web site message dumps, or direct dumps to the medium itself. Many media have direct lines for such purposes. One of the benefits of using a computer is that images can also be transmitted, often with excellent results.

In lieu of delivering the message yourself, you may choose to use a placement agency. **Placement agencies** are outfits that will take your information, such as a press release, and send it out to a great many media outlets using their regularly updated media lists and computerized mailing services. Many of these firms mail out hundreds of releases for you—at a tidy cost.

Placement agencies will provide you with many more mailings than you might have garnered from your personal mailing list, but much of what is mailed out is not correctly targeted and ends up as waste coverage. As any business editor will tell you, the majority of press releases received are not relevant to the publication, and many originated from placement agencies in other states. You are often better off targeting those media with which you are most familiar and who are at least interested in your information.

The sole exception might be the computerized agencies such as *PR Newswire*. Organizations such as this send out your release electronically, over a newswire, just like the Associated Press. Media outlets can subscribe (free of charge) to the service and will receive your release—along with hundreds of others—sorted by subject and other descriptors. They can scan by subject, look at the lead only, or pull up the whole release. This method substantially reduces the amount of paper they have to plow through and guarantees at least subjects of interest to them. Your advantage is that you can target locally, regionally, or nationally. Of course, the price of placing the release increases with its coverage.

Fitting Your Information to Your Outlet

It is essential to know as much as possible about the media outlet to which you are sending your information. Never submit information blindly to publications or stations you have never read, watched, or listened to. Picking a trade publication out of *Standard Rate and Data Service* just because it has a large circulation doesn't ensure that it is the type of publication in which you want to see your story.

The key, of course, is to read the publication, watch the TV station, listen to the radio station, or browse the Web site first. By doing so, you also will learn about the outlet's style and will be able to tailor your release accordingly.

If you are writing for a trade journal, don't automatically assume that the one you have chosen is similar in style to others in the industry. Remember that publications often are differentiated by their styles when they deal with similar subject matter.

Understanding Radio and Television Placement.
Before placing information on the radio, you will need to understand the concept of **format**. Whereas placement of your message on television requires a familiarity with the various program offerings of the stations you are dealing with, placement on radio is usually determined by the format of the station—usually designed around the type of music it plays or information it provides. For example, some stations play only Top-40 hits. These stations

usually cater to a teenage audience. Other stations play only Classic Rock or jazz, or provide news. Their listeners vary according to their format.

Deciding what radio station you place your message on depends on what your target audience listens to, and that is determined through audience research. Any radio sales manager will be able (and quite willing) to provide you with detailed analyses of the station's listening audience. All you have to do is to match your target audience profile with its listener profile. If, for instance, your target audience regularly listens to jazz, then you would be best served to place your message on a station using a jazz format. Exhibit 5.1 lists the most common radio formats.

Examine the formats and styles of all publications or broadcast shows you would like to accept your information, then prepare your material in a style as close to theirs as you can. For example, if you are prerecording PSAs (public service announcements) for use on various stations, you might want to put a different music track on each spot depending on the format of the station with which it will be placed. Nothing is quite so jar-

EXHIBIT 5.1

Standard Radio Formats

Adult Contemporary (AC)	New Adult Contemporary/Smooth Jazz
Adult Standards	New Country
Album-Oriented Rock	New Rock
All News	News/Talk/Information
All Sports	Nostalgia
Alternative	Oldies
Children's Radio	Religious
Classical	Rhythm & Blues
Classic Country	Seventies Oldies/Classic Hits
Classic Rock	Seventies Rock
Contemporary Hit Radio	Soft AC
Country	Southern Gospel
Easy Listening	Spanish Contemporary
Educational	Spanish Language
Ethnic	Talk/Personality
Gospel	Urban AC
Jazz	Urban Contemporary
Modern AC	Urban Oldies
	Variety

ring to listeners of a classical music station as to have their entertainment interrupted with a message surrounded by a rock music background. Although a rock music station might carry a spot with a classical music background, the opposite is probably not true.

Television is much easier to figure out. It is the medium that reaches the broadest segment of the population. Rather than depending on formatting to attract a single audience, television depends on different programs and times of day to attract different audiences. Program types include drama/adventure, news, talk, daytime serials, and sports, among others. Each program type draws a particular target audience. Time of day is also a factor in determining when to air a TV commercial. Standard television time blocks (known as *dayparts*) are listed in Exhibit 5.2.

Just as in radio, a TV sales manager will be able to give you detailed statistics on viewing audiences by program and time of day.

You will need to consider the following questions before you place your message with either a radio or television station:

- If radio, what format does the station use? If television, what programs are appropriate to my message?

- Will the station take taped actualities (for interviews or reactions)? If so, what kind of tape? Reel-to-reel? Cassette? If it is video for television, will the station want one-inch tape, or three-quarter or half-inch cassette? Can they use slides? How about slidetape?

- Will the station use 10-, 20-, 30-, or 60-second spots?

EXHIBIT 5.2

Standard Television Dayparts

Early morning	Monday–Friday, 7:00 A.M.–9:00 A.M.
Daytime	Monday–Friday, 9:00 A.M.–4:30 P.M.
Early fringe	Monday–Friday, 4:30 P.M.–7:30 P.M.
Prime access	Monday–Friday, 7:30 P.M.–8:00 P.M.
Prime time	Monday–Saturday, 8:00 P.M.–11:00 P.M.
	Sunday, 7:00 P.M.–11:00 P.M.
Late news	Monday–Sunday, 11:00 P.M.–11:30 P.M.
Late night	Monday–Sunday, 11:30 P.M.–1:00 A.M.
Saturday morning	Saturday, 8:00 A.M.–1:00 P.M.
Weekend afternoon	Saturday–Sunday, 1:00 P.M.–7:00 P.M.

- Who will write the copy? Will you write and submit it or will you simply give the station the information? Will the station use scripts you have written for its announcers to read?

- Will the station provide production services, or will you have to have your message prerecorded?

- How much lead time does the station need? For production? For placement?

All of these considerations—and probably a few more—will have to be taken into account before you can work successfully with the broadcast media. Note that all this information should be included in your media list.

Broadcast Cover Letter. Before you send any information to a radio or television station in the form of a **spot** (a written script or prerecorded message designed specifically for broadcast), make sure it is accompanied by a cover letter explaining the content and a mail-back card of some kind so that the station can let you know when and if your spot was aired. Exhibit 5.3 is a generic example of such information.

Using Press Kits

One of the most common methods of distributing information to the media is via the **press kit.** Press kits are produced and used for a wide variety of public relations purposes. They are handed out at product promotion presentations and press conferences; they are used as promotional packages by regional or local distributors or agencies; and they are part of the never-ending stream of information provided by organizations to get their messages out. When a press kit (also known as a *press packet*), is used properly, it can effectively aid message dissemination by adding the right amount of unduplicated information to the media mix.

A press kit is usually composed of a number of information pieces designed specifically for use by the media (see Exhibit 5.4). Enclosed within a folder with a cover indicating who is providing the kit and its purpose, a press kit usually includes something like the following:

- A table of contents.
- A news release.
- A backgrounder or fact sheet.
- One or two other information pieces such as:
  - Already-printed brochures.
  - Company magazines or newsletters.

EXHIBIT 5.3   Cover Letter and Mail-Back Card

The American Tuberculosis Foundation
1212 Folger Street
New York, New York 00912

Dear Program Director:

Smoking and lung disease are issues that affect all of us in some way. The recent concern over secondhand smoke has resulted in considerable debate. In an effort to help "clear the air," the American Tuberculosis Foundation hopes you will run the enclosed radio/TV spots for the education of your listening/viewing audience.

Since our campaign started in January, over 300 radio/TV stations around the country have responded by airing the "Your Good Health" spots. We hope that you will join them in serving your listening/viewing audience.

For your convenience, we have provided you with a mail-back card. By filling out this important evaluation, you will help us to better serve our common interests in the future.

Thank you,

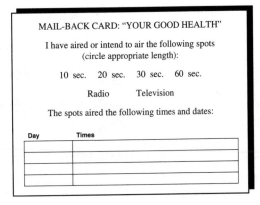

MAIL-BACK CARD: "YOUR GOOD HEALTH"

I have aired or intend to air the following spots
(circle appropriate length):

10 sec.   20 sec.   30 sec.   60 sec.

Radio   Television

The spots aired the following times and dates:

Day	Times	

- An annual report.
- A feature story or sidebar, if appropriate to the subject matter.
- A biography (or biographies) and accompanying photos.

A press kit with fewer items is generally a waste of folder space. If you have only a few items to disseminate and wish to avoid the cost of producing folders, use plain, manuscript-sized envelopes. These are cheaper

EXHIBIT 5.4   Press Kit Designed for a Press Conference

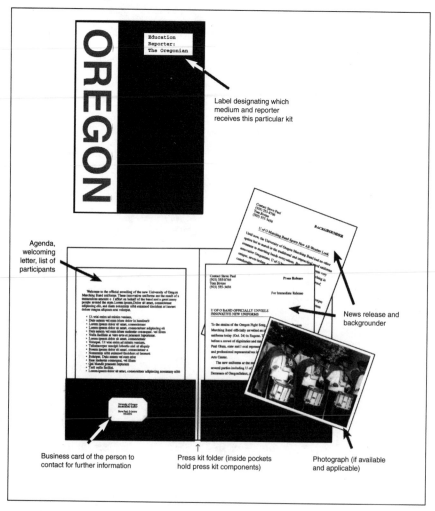

than folders, you might already have them in stock with your address printed on them, and they are ready for mailing.

The contents of a press kit can vary greatly, depending on the intent of the kit. For example, a press kit for a corporate product introduction briefing might include these items:

- News release on the new product.
- Color photo and cutline (caption).
- News release on the product content (the material used to manufacture the product).

- Black-and-white photos and cutlines of other products made from the manufactured material.
- News release describing another application of the material.
- Black-and-white and color photos of that application.
- Backgrounder on the material.
- In-house magazine article tear sheet on the material.
- Color brochure on the material and its uses.
- News release on new materials being developed.
- Hard copy of the product presentation speeches.

Press kits can serve many purposes and should include enough information to meet the needs of their audiences. The key to assembling a useful kit is to keep in mind the needs of those receiving the information.

If you are providing a press kit to the media for a press conference, it should include some, but not necessarily all, of the following items:

- A cover letter explaining the kit and a table of contents listing each item in the kit, with each item listed as appearing on the right or left side of the folder.
- A basic facts sheet outlining the participants at the press conference, the relevant dates, and any facts or figures that might be unclear.
- A backgrounder explaining the relevance of the current topic in a historical context.
- News releases of about one and one-half pages for both print and broadcast media. Give both releases to each reporter.
- Any feature stories or sidebar-type information that might be of interest to reporters. Be sure it is relevant.
- Any photos or other visual materials that might add to the stories. Include cutlines.
- Biographies on any individuals playing an important part in the event the press conference covers. Include photos, if available.
- Any already-produced information pieces that might be of interest to the media, such as brochures, in-house publications, etc.

Once you have assembled a press kit, make sure that all of the media get a copy, even those reporters who do not attend the event your press kit is designed to cover. Press kits are most effective when used with a good, up-to-date media list. By labeling your press kits with the name of the various media outlets prior to your event, you will know immediately after the event who showed up and who didn't. You can then mail the remaining kits to the prodigal media.

Other Information Pieces. You should be aware that there are several other types of "kits" designed either for use by the media or for in-house use. The most common of these are the publicity kit and the information kit. The **publicity kit** is designed to be something of a "how-to" aid for those in your organization who are unfamiliar with publicity techniques. It provides basic training and support in garnering publicity. For example, if your organization is a large not-for-profit agency with a national headquarters and chapters in every state, it probably doesn't have PR people in every chapter. As the national media relations director, you may help alleviate this problem by designing a publicity kit for the employee with little or no experience in dealing with the media. The American Lung Association distributed just such a publicity kit to its regional offices. For a detailed list of its contents, see Exhibit 5.5.

Information kits are developed to provide generic background that reporters can then place on file. For example, let's say you work in PR for the State Association of Ophthalmologists. Since ophthalmology is a complex science and frequently is confused with such related practices as optometry, it is in your client's best interest to provide clarification in advance of any stories that might be forthcoming from you. A piece containing facts, figures, and definitions pertaining specifically to ophthalmology could be developed and distributed to, for instance, local science reporters. These information pieces often are produced in kit or booklet form and are meant to be kept on file for future reference (see Exhibit 5.6). The State Association of Ophthalmologists' information kit might include the following pieces of information:

- Definition of ophthalmology.
- Definitions of key terms used in ophthalmology.
- Differences between ophthalmology and optometry.
- Medical information on the human eye and typical eye ailments.
- Easy-to-follow illustrations of typical eye ailments.
- How to obtain further information concerning ophthalmology and the association.

Depending on the size and scope of your organization, an information kit might also include a list of corporate media contacts, organization charts, or trademarks. Increasingly, such information also can be provided electronically by setting up a Web site containing the same information, then providing that Web address to the media.

Pitch Letters or Media Advisories. It is sometimes useful to submit a **pitch letter** (also known as a *media advisory*) in advance of your self-produced news package. This letter alerts the reporter or editor of a

EXHIBIT 5.5

American Lung Association's Publicity Kit

A publicity kit the American Lung Association sent to its state offices included the following:

- Cover letter.
- Table of contents.
- Clipsheet (photos and logos for newspaper placement).
- Magazine ad folder with sample return order card.
- Magazine drop-in ad instructions.
- Suggested cover letter for magazine ad folder.
- Newspaper clipsheet instructions.
- Captioned photo.
- Direction sheets titled "How to Get the Best Use of TV PSAs" and "How to Get Local ID on TV Spots."
- Radio scripts (tapes sent with kit).
- Radio usage report and cover letter.
- Report of use card.
- Radio station phone call (scripted inquiry used to contact radio station program directors).
- Radio PSA distribution report card.
- Television scripts (tapes sent with kit).
- Storyboard for TV spot.
- Cover letter for TV stations.
- TV PSA delivery report card.
- Report of use card for TV PSAs.
- Supply service memo and order form for more of any of these items.

story opportunity. The best of all worlds is to have the media cover your story without your having to write it for them. The pitch letter is generally sent to reporters and editors you are most familiar with and with whom you have already established a working relationship—they are much more likely to respond to your tips than are journalists who don't know you.

EXHIBIT 5.6 Information Kit

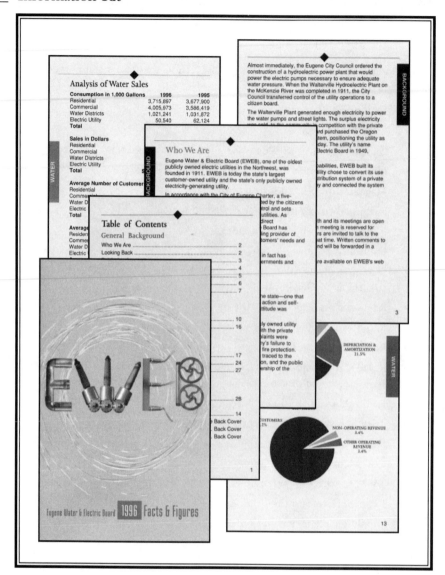

This information booklet produced by the Eugene (Oregon) Water & Electric Board contains everything from a company profile to the location of bill payment stations and is intended for both consumers and media.

The standard pitch letter should avoid hard sell and simply rely on the news value of the story to entice the media. Present the basic facts of the story without embellishment. Include a solid rationale for news coverage by pointing out how important this information might be to the medium's constituency. Finally, let them know how to get further information—make it easy for them. Exhibit 5.7 is an example of such a letter.

EXHIBIT 5.7   Media Pitch Letter

```
Crime Team
The Oregonian
1321 SW Broadway
Portland, OR 97201

Re: Criminals and Addictions

Serenity Lane's Straight Facts, in Salem, works with prison-
ers and parolees who have drug and/or alcohol addictions but
would not succeed in traditional treatment centers. Straight
Facts is unique in its work as an outpatient program that suc-
cessfully addresses criminality and addictions.

"We do just as much work on lifestyle as on alcohol and drug
abuse," says Jeri Moeller, the director. Jeri, who was in the
criminal justice system, founded the program in 1986 with
Marion County Corrections. The county funds it, along with
grants and the Oregon Health Plan.

Statistics from Straight Fact's 1993-94 programs show that
success rates ranged from 68 percent to 79 percent. Since
then, Straight Facts has tripled the number of clients it
serves.

In 1991, Straight Facts became part of Serenity Lane. Serenity
Lane is a licensed specialty hospital and is included in the
book "The 100 Best Treatment Centers for Alcoholism and Drug
Abuse." It is headquartered in Eugene, with facilities and
outpatient programs throughout Oregon.

You are welcome to attend groups and talk to counselors and
clients. If you would like to explore Straight Facts, please
call me toll free at 1-888-644-7989 or use my e-mail:
mm@prpr.com.

Thanks for your time.

Sincerely,


Marilyn Milne
Public Relations Services for Serenity Lane/Straight Facts
```

Cooperation Is the Key

Whether your message is delivered to your target audience or not depends a great deal on the cooperation of the mass media. It is in your best interest to foster a professional relationship with those media representatives with whom you deal regularly. If they respect your professionalism in meeting their (and by inference, their audiences') needs, you will be rewarded with cooperation—and that is a major step in the right direction.

KEY TERMS

consequence	soft news	press kit
interest	media directory	publicity kit
timeliness	media list	information kit
proximity	placement agency	pitch letter
prominence	format	
hard news	spot	

EXERCISES

1. Assume you work for a local not-for-profit agency that works with homeless youth. Put together a media list composed of those outlets most likely to publish information on your organization. Explain why you have chosen these media and not others.

2. Call local media outlets and ask for copies of their publicity guidelines. Write up a comparison of how they differ and how they are alike, and what you make of the differences.

3. Tour a local newspaper, a local radio or TV news operation, or any other appropriate location where news is a primary part of the operation. Write a brief report explaining what you learned and how you think it would affect your ability to do your job as a publicist.

4. Visit a local not-for-profit agency and see what kind of printed information they have available. Do you think it is enough? Do you think it is effective? If possible, meet with the agency's public relations person and see if you can obtain copies of any materials produced specifically for media use.

5. Look through your local paper for any articles you suspect were the result of publicity placement. Explain why you think so.

6. Put together an informational press kit on an organization of your choice. This could be the place where you work or are an intern. It could be your school or department, the student union, or an organization where you volunteer. Find as many informational pieces as you can for inclusion in the kit. Write up a basic explanation of the purpose of the kit and a table of contents. Pick an appropriate folder design and color, and assemble the final product. Be prepared to explain why you chose the pieces you included and why you left others out.

## CHAPTER 6

NEWS RELEASES AND BACKGROUNDERS

FOR IMMEDIATE RELEASE

In this chapter you will learn:

- What a news release is and why it is important to public relations professionals.

- How to write various forms of news releases, including publicity releases, product news releases, and news releases for broadcast.

- What a backgrounder is, and how to write one.

- What a fact sheet is, and how to write one.

The news release has been called the workhorse of public relations. Every day, thousands of news releases are sent out all over the country to newspapers, magazines, and radio and television stations. Some newspaper editors receive as many as a thousand a month. Of these, only a minuscule number are ever used, and most of these are severely edited. Why, then, do public relations professionals and the people who employ them continue to use news releases? Because they are still effective. They are used by newspapers and trade journals to pass along information about events and occurrences that reporters might not otherwise have the time or the inclination to cover.

The key to effective news releases is not so much in the writing, although we will certainly concentrate on that, but in the placement. As we saw in the previous chapter, knowing when something is newsworthy and when it is not, and knowing your contacts in the media and their schedules and guidelines, are the most important elements of news release writing.

As a writer of news releases, you will become a reporter. It is essential that you understand journalistic style in order to present your releases in the proper format. Remember that reporters and editors are used to seeing one style of writing on a daily basis. That style fits their papers and they are unlikely to print anything that doesn't conform. Remember, too, that although the reporter is responsible only to his or her editor, you are responsible to both the editor and the people you work for. This means that you must accommodate both the style of the newspaper and the needs of your employer. It is not an easy fence to walk, but as a public relations practitioner you have to try to keep your balance.

What Is a News Release? ━━━━━

A **news release** is information that you wish released to the press, usually the print media. Although all news releases have format in common, there are different emphases.

- Basic **publicity releases** cover any information occurring within an organization that might have some news value to local, regional, or even national media.

- **Product releases** deal with specific products or product lines. These are usually targeted to trade publications within individual industries. They can deal with the product itself, consumer use of the product, or a particular business or marketing angle.

- **Financial releases** are used primarily in shareholder relations; however, they are also of interest to financial media. Many local, regional, and national general media have financial highlights sections, as well.

One of the most important points to remember is that all news releases should contain at least three elements: *publicity, angle,* and *story.* These elements may overlap or be quite distinct from each other, but they are all there. The publicity value of a news release is sometimes hidden, while the story is the perceived reason for writing the release—at least from the media's point of view. The angle, on the other hand, may be simply the hook that attracts media attention. Often it is the same as the story, but it is not as often the same as the publicity value. The reason, of course, is that most media aren't interested in your organization receiving publicity; they are interested in a story their audience wants to know about.

Writing a News Release ━━━━━━

The style of the news release is that of the straight news story: It begins with a lead, expands on the lead, and proceeds to present information in decreasing order of importance. This style, known as the **inverted pyramid style,** allows an editor to perform his or her job—that is, to edit—from the bottom up. A good news release also utilizes accurate quotes.

The Lead

The **lead,** or opening sentence of the news release, is all-important. As every journalist knows, the lead is the hook that entices the reader into your story. For the public relations practitioner, too, the lead is a hook to entice the editor into running your release. Don't ever get the notion that any news release you send out will automatically be printed or that it will even be printed the way you wrote it. The fact is, even if you have written the most appealing news release ever seen at the *Daily Planet,* most editors feel an obligation to edit. Indeed, you will be lucky to have the information in your release placed at all. This should not deter you, however, from writing a good release. You have to sell the editor first before your release will ever be seen by anyone else, and that's where a well-written lead comes in.

Editors often take fewer than 30 seconds to peruse a news release. Their decision to print the message or not depends a lot on how you present yourself in the headline (title) and the lead. Most editors use several measures to determine whether your release will be used. Who you are, as regards your past record of providing only legitimate news, is the first important consideration. Once past that, your headline or title should tell them whether your release is important to them or not (more on this later). Finally, your lead should summarize the relevancy of your story.

The *summary lead* is by far the most common type of news release lead. A good summary lead will answer the key questions—who, what, when, where, why, and how. The *delayed lead* is used to add drama to a news story; however, this type of lead is usually reserved for feature stories and is not appropriate for straight news. Thus, we concentrate here on summary leads.

Before you write the lead, you must first decide on a theme. Try to determine what is unique about the event covered by your release. Although news releases should generally be considered as straight news stories and must be informative, they don't have to be boring. To illustrate, look first at the summary lead from a release distributed by the Electronic Products Producers Association:

> "The present condition of the software market is such that companies involved in software development should be able to capitalize on current economic trends. This means that new product development should allow the earliest investors a significant niche in the market." This statement was made by Mr. James L. Sutton, president of Associated Products Corporation, during a speech at the fall convention of the Electronic Products Producers Association held in Syracuse, New York.

Now consider this revised version of the same lead:

> A leading electronics industry executive declared today (October 21) that the computer software market is wide open to new investors.
>
> "The present condition of the software market is such that companies involved in software development should be able to capitalize on current economic trends," said James L. Sutton, president of Associated Products Corporation. "This means that new product development should allow the earliest investors a significant niche in the market."
>
> Sutton's prediction of a dynamic market was made in a speech given at the fall convention of the Electronic Products Producers Association in Syracuse, New York.

Notice how the second lead has broken up the quote and used the proper journalistic form for *attribution* ("said James L. Sutton"). The opening paragraph has been rewritten to include most of the pertinent information:

Who?   A leading electronics industry executive.

What?   Declared a wide-open computer software market.

When?   Today (October 21). Notice the inclusion of the actual date in parentheses. This is to let the editor know that the "today" you are speaking of is October 21. If the paper receives the release on October 20 but doesn't publish the information until October 22, they will need to correct the copy to read "yesterday."

Where?   Left until the final paragraph. (It isn't always necessary to squeeze all of the information into the first paragraph.)

Why?   Included in the explanatory paragraph following the lead. Of all the information, "why" is the most likely to be left out of the lead because it usually takes the most explanation and invites the interested reader to look further.

How?   In a speech. Also left for the final paragraph.

Remember that you are responsible for the ordering of points in your lead and in your news release. The more interesting you can make the information by order of presentation, the better it will read. Notice also how much shorter the sentences seem in the revised version. In fact, there is only one more sentence than in the original, but because the quote is broken up and the attribution is placed in the middle, the sentences seem much shorter. Although it is wise to present most of the key information early in the release, only the most important elements need appear in the lead. The rest can follow in logical order.

Note also that a publicist's lead is likely to differ from one written by a newspaper reporter. The following examples, written for a local newspaper, serve to illustrate the difference:

Publicist's Lead

Francis Langly, former Director of Research and Development at Rogers Experimental Plastics Company, will be awarded the prestigious Goodyear Medal on June 6 in Indianapolis at a banquet held in his honor. Awarded by the American Chemical Society, the Goodyear Medal is the premier award for work in the field of specialty elastomers.

Reporter's Lead

Francis Langly, 24 Cedar Crest Drive, will receive the Goodyear Medal at the annual meeting of the American Chemical Society. The conference is being held in Indianapolis on June 6.

Although neither of these examples is particularly original—public relations releases rarely are—there are still reasons for the differences in content and style. Consider these questions:

- Why is the address left out in the publicist's lead?
- Why is Langly's title included in the publicist's lead?
- What is the difference between the phrases "will receive" and "will be awarded"?
- What is the significance for the publicist in pointing out that the Goodyear Medal is the premier award in the field?

Answers to these questions illustrate the differences between hard news and publicity, and between the publicist's and the journalist's objectives.

Quotations and Attributions

Quotations add interest to your news release. It is always good to obtain usable quotations and place them at appropriate spots throughout the release. Note that it is never a good idea to begin a news release with a quote—because news releases are considered straight news stories, a quote fails to come to the point soon enough. As was illustrated above, quotes need not be written as complete sentences followed by the attribution; they can be broken up by the attribution. Also, you don't need to follow every quotation by an attribution, especially if it is understood that the same person quoted earlier is still being quoted. A good rule is to repeat an attribution if more than one paragraph has elapsed since it was last given. Of course, if you change the source of the quotation, you will need to designate the change by a new attribution. Don't be afraid to work with the form of attribution, and don't use the same form each time. Consider the following:

> Johnson, a longtime trucker, doesn't like the strike. "This layoff has really affected my family," he said. The strike has been in effect for three months. "We're down to eating beans out of a can," he said. Johnson has three small children and a $500-a-month house payment. "I don't know what I'm going to do about my bills," he said.

Although the form of attribution ("he said") is correct, its repetition is monotonous. There are a number of ways of attributing a quotation that can add variety to releases. For example, you can paraphrase points of the quote, combine quotes, or simply use one attribution between two quotes. Look at this revised version:

> Johnson, a longtime trucker, doesn't like the three-month-long strike. "This layoff has really affected my family," he says. "We're down to eating beans out of a can."
>
> Johnson, who has three small children and a $500-a-month house payment, says he doesn't know what he's going to do about his bills.

Notice that the tense of the attribution has also been changed to the present. News releases need to sound as timely as possible, which includes using the present tense in attributions if possible. If you are dealing with a story that is obviously past, then the attribution must reflect this.

Most newswriting classes and most journalists adhere to the rule of using only the last name in an attribution. News releases, on the other hand, must follow the conventions set up by the originating organization. In most cases, even if you do insist on attributing a quotation to "Mr. Jones" or "President Smith," the news editor will delete the honorific. You will have done your job by using the conventions of your employer, however, and in the long run, that is all you are expected to do.

The accuracy of quotations is obviously important, but while reporters must be absolutely accurate, public relations writers have some leeway. An illustration will help explain. Suppose you work for Rogers Experimental Plastics Company (REPC). You are writing a release on a new product line and are quoting the company president. You have interviewed the president and he knows you are writing the release. He is also aware of what he said; however, because he will probably be reviewing the release before it is sent out, he will correct anything he doesn't like. As a writer and an employee, you have the creative ability and leeway to "invent" a quotation as long as he approves it. No employer will fault you for putting well-written words in his mouth. Suppose in your interview the president had said:

> I don't think anything like this new plastic has ever been seen—at least not around this area of the world. It may be the greatest thing since sliced bread and who knows how much money we'll make from it.

You may actually write in your release:

> Paul Johnson, president of REPC, is excited about the new product. "We've come up with a totally new concept in plastic," he says. "I expect that the market for 'Plagets' in the West will be tremendous."

All you have done is tidy up the quotation and make it more interesting. Remember that you may only "doctor" quotations that will be checked for accuracy and approved by the party to whom they are attributed. It is a good rule to make sure that anyone you interview receives a copy of the finished release before it is distributed. There is nothing like a libel suit to sober up a writer! Another legitimate way of presenting unclear or clumsy quotations is to paraphrase or use indirect attribution. This is fine for news stories written by reporters, but news releases can benefit a great deal from well-written quotations.

Finally, if you want to help prevent serious editing—or even elimination—of your quotations (and your sources' names) you must learn to "protect" your quote. In other words, learn to use information that is vital to the understanding of the story as quotes rather than the "fluff" quotes often provided by the those giving you the assignment. For example, consider the following:

> "This is an exciting day for all of us," says Delphi CEO Robert Altus.

As you can probably guess, any self-respecting editor would cut out this nearly meaningless quote. It's painfully clear that it was included in order to get the CEO's name in the release. Now consider this quote as an alternative:

> "The merger of Delphi and TransAmerican airlines will more than double the workforce available to both companies currently," says Delphi CEO Robert Altus.

While it may still be clear that this quote provides for mention of the CEO's name, there is a greater chance that it will stay because it provides important information. Used in this way, quotes can be placed strategically, based on the level of importance of the information. "Fluff" quotes, of course, belong at the end of the release—if used at all.

Local Interest

Local media outlets like local stories. For most public relations writers, news releases can almost always be oriented to a local audience. The real problem is finding just the right local angle—the one that will entice the newspaper into running the story. Some basic guidelines will help you in your placement:

- If you are releasing a story with national as well as local interest, try to construct your release so that any local information is interspersed throughout the release. By doing so, it will be difficult to cut out the national information, which might not be of interest to a local editor, without harming the local angle.
- Avoid commercial plugs. Editors recognize advertising instantly and will simply round-file (trash) your release. Keep your local angle newsworthy.
- If you are sending only to local media and you reference a local city in your release, omit the name of the state.
- Above all, don't strain to find a local angle where there is none.

Suppose you are assigned to write a release that has national importance and you want to target it for a local paper, say, the *Seattle Times*. You know from your interview with William J. Hoffman, chief systems engineer of Associated Products Corporation of Syracuse, NY, that he went to high school and college in Seattle. Based only on this little bit of knowledge, the piece can be localized. In addition, you could try to place a version of the release in the *Lincoln High Review* and another version in the University of Washington *Husky* (the alumni paper). Your leads might look like these:

For the Seattle Times

William J. Hoffman, Seattle native and Chief Systems Engineer for Associated Products Corporation (APC) of Syracuse, N.Y., has been credited with developing a revolutionary educational software line.

For the **Lincoln High Review**
   William J. Hoffman, a Lincoln High School graduate and former president of the LHS Electronics Club, has been credited with developing a revolutionary educational software line.

For the *University of Washington* **Husky**
   William J. Hoffman, a University of Washington graduate with honors in Engineering, has been credited with developing a revolutionary educational software line.

If you think the Lincoln High School angle is too much of a stretch, don't use it. Every angle, however, is worth at least some consideration. You will be surprised how your placements can multiply if you ask the right questions in your interviews and construct the right angles from the answers.

Remember, though, that the focus of your release isn't always the local angle; that is only the hook. Don't slight your real story in favor of the local angle, no matter how interesting it is. In the samples above, for instance, Hoffman is the angle, but the software is the story. The trick is to lead with the angle, move to the story, and keep the two so intertwined that any editor will have difficulty separating them.

Formatting a News Release ─────

Although public relations practitioners often incorporate the conventions of their organization into their news releases, there is a standard news release format, as described below. Exhibit 6.1 provides a sample news release with the format elements in place.

1. News releases typically are written on plain, white bond paper with no decorative border.
2. Margins are one to one and a half inches on all sides.
3. The address of the sender is placed in the upper left-hand corner of the first page. This identifying block should include the complete address, name of the contact person (usually the person who wrote the release), and telephone numbers. It is especially important to include a night telephone number as well as a daytime number— newspapers don't shut down at night, and if an editor wants to use your release but needs further or clarifying information and can't reach you, the release may get dumped.
4. The release date appears on the right margin, slightly lower than the bottom of the address block. This portion provides the editor with exact information concerning the appropriate timing for the release. More about release dates later.

5. The body of the release begins about one-third of the way down the page, allowing some white space for comments or notes from the editor. If there is to be a title—and titles are entirely optional—it should come between the address block and the body of the release, flush left. Typically, the title does not extend beyond the address block by more than a few characters, which usually means that it will be stacked (set in two lines on top of each other). The title should be all caps, single-spaced, with the last line underlined.

6. The body of the news release is double-spaced. Never single-space a news release. Paragraphs usually are indented with normal spacing between paragraphs. Some companies prefer no indention and triple-spacing between paragraphs, but the standard is indented.

7. If the release runs more than a page, the word "more" is placed in brackets or within dashes at the bottom of the page.

8. Following pages are identified by a "slug line" followed by several dashes and the page number at the top of the page, usually either flush left or flush right.

9. The end of the release is designated in one of several ways. Use the word "end" or the number "30" either in quotation marks or within dashes, or the symbol #####.

Release Dates and Times

When do you want your release to be published or broadcast? If you have just written a release about an important meeting that will be held tomorrow (January 23) but you don't want the information that will be presented at that meeting to reach the public prior to the meeting, you will have to say so on your release. Although it is wise not to send out releases too far in advance of an event, it is also wise to be as timely as possible—which means getting your release to the media outlet beforehand.

There are a number of ways to designate release dates and times. Regardless of which method you choose, the time and date belong just slightly below the address block, flush right. The two most common designations are:

• Release with no specific time frame. By far the mostly widely used type of release, and usually designated by *For Immediate Release.* Other phrases include *For Release on Receipt* or *For Release at Will.* It is unnecessary to add a date to this type of release statement.

• Release with specific date. An example would be *For Release January 23 or Thereafter,* or if you need to be even more specific, *For Release January 23, 10:00 P.M. or Thereafter.* Other options are *Hold for Release, Friday, January 23, 10:00 A.M.,* or *For Release after 10:00 A.M., Friday, January 23.* This type of release statement could be used, for

EXHIBIT 6.1   News Release Format

```
            Company or Client Name
            and Address Here
            Contact: (Your Name)
            Day Phone:
            Night Phone:

                                        Release Date and Time

            THE TITLE GOES HERE, ALL UPPER CASE
            AND UNDERLINED LIKE THIS
                The Point of Origin Dateline Goes Here—The body of the
            release should begin one-third of the way down the page to
            leave enough room for the editor or copy person to write
            remarks. The release proper should be double-spaced for ease
            of readability and editing.
                Be sure to use normal indents and consistent spacing
            between paragraphs. It is not necessary to triple-space
            between paragraphs. All information should be presented in
            descending order of importance, ending with the least impor-
            tant items in case last-minute editing results in the bottom
            of your release being lopped off.
                Remember to leave at least one-inch margins all around, but
            resist the urge to leave huge right-hand margins in order to
            stretch your information.
                When you arrive at the bottom of the first page, leave at
            least a one-inch margin and indicate either the end of your
            release (-30-) or that more information follows (-more-). If
            more information follows, try not to break paragraphs or sen-
            tences in the middle. Never break a word and complete it on
            the next page.

                                    -30-
```

instance, if you want all the media to carry it at one time, or if the
event is actually occurring at a future date but you want to release the
information early.

Datelines

Datelines are used to indicate the point of origin of your news release if,
for some reason, that is important. Datelines are important to foreign cor-
respondents to enable readers to appreciate that a story originated at the

location where it happened. For public relations practitioners, a dateline may serve the same purpose. It alerts the editor to the fact that your release concerns an event either reported from or happening at a certain geographical location. Datelines should be placed immediately preceding the opening of your release proper, on the same line, as in the following:

> SPRINGFIELD, Ohio—Rogers Experimental Plastics Company (REPC) has announced the development of a versatile new plastic widget that has the potential for use in a number of industries from automotives to electronics.

If the city is well known (New York, Los Angeles, etc.), there is no need to include the name of the state. In the case of a city whose name may be popular in a number of states, you would want to designate the state (as in the example above to differentiate Springfield, Ohio, from Springfield, Oregon, or Springfield, Kentucky, or any number of Springfields). If the release is intended for a statewide press only, you can get by with just the name of the city. Finally, if there is any possibility that confusion might arise from use of the city name only, include the state (Moscow, Idaho, or Moscow, Russia).

Exclusives and Specials

If your release is an **exclusive** (intended for only one paper), make sure the editor knows it. Remember that an exclusive can be sent to only one publication. A **special,** on the other hand, is a release written in a certain style, intended for a specific publication but being released elsewhere as well (see Exhibit 6.2.). Both designations should be noted immediately below the release information as follows:

> For Immediate Release Exclusive to the *Daily Planet*
> For Release February 24 or Thereafter Special to the *Daily Planet*

Product News Releases ————

Product publicity often has little or nothing to do with advertising. In its strictest sense, advertising refers only to the purchasing of time or space in which to run a message. Product publicity is not paid for; it is a far more subtle art. You must be able to construct informative passages concerning a given product without actually "pitching" the product. This is not an easy task. The minute an editor detects a sales pitch, the release gets pitched.

Most product publicity goes through several stages: product introduction (usually via news releases to trade media), articles in which the prod-

EXHIBIT 6.2   Exclusives and Specials

```
Deer Point Development, Inc.
Box 1387
Deer Point, Michigan 72493
Contact: Warren Bailey
Day Phone: (714) 555-6635
Night Phone: (714) 555-1765
```

For Immediate Release
Special to the *Deer Point Sentinel*

NEW PLANT TO OPEN IN DEER POINT

    A new plant designed to manufacture high-tech components for automobiles is scheduled to be opened in late July according to Eleanor Maston, president of Deer Point Development, Inc. (DPD). The two-building facility will encompass over 55,000 square feet and be housed on a five-acre plot near the Doe River. Maston's company was instrumental in the planning, acquisition of land, and contracting of firms for the construction of the new plant. The plant will be owned and operated by Auto-Tech, Inc. of Albatross, Maine—a longtime member of the automotive peripherals industry.

    Maston predicts that over 800 new jobs will be created by the plant's construction. "Auto-Tech has assured us that they intend to hire the majority of their plant workers from the local community," she says. "They plan to bring in only a bare-bones management crew from the outside to begin with, and train local people from the ground up."

    According to Maston, DPD first learned of the scheme last December when Auto-Tech president Wilson Klatchki contacted her. The New England-based company was seeking to expand into the high-tech industry and needed a plant close to the major automobile manufacturers in Detroit. Deer Point seemed like the perfect solution.

    "Auto-Tech felt that our proximity to Detroit was ideal," Maston says. "They wanted to be close without having to build in the city itself."

    The site was chosen for its availability and scenic location, according to Maston. "Because high tech is basically a 'clean' industry, building the plant near Doe River poses no environmental problems," she says.

    Construction of the plant began in February and is expected to continue through the summer.

-30-

---

uct is reviewed after testing (written by the trade publications themselves), and "user articles" (submitted by the public relations writer focusing on actual users of the new product). This section covers only product introduction releases.

EXHIBIT 6.3   Product News Release

 Tall Drink of Water, Inc.
435 Lasado Circle
Watertown, NY 10056
Contact: Myrna Hofman
Phone: (121) 555-1222   For Immediate Release

NEW FOUNTAIN DISPENSES
COLD, HOT, AND ICE WATER

   Watertown, NY—A new water fountain that dispenses cold
water, hot water, and ice water has been marketed by Tall Drink
of Water, Inc. (TDW), of Watertown, N.Y. The new fountain,
which already is appearing in offices across the country,
operates on an entirely new system for compartmentalizing
water supplies.

   According to TDW president and co-founder Willis Reed, the
new fountain represents four years of hard work. "We spent a
lot of time on this new fountain," he says. "It's a whole new
concept in water fountains. We did some initial research on
office water consumers and found that they wanted not only
cold water, but also hot and ice water as well."

   The new fountain uses a system of valves that pass the water
from the building plumbing system through the fountain in a
series of stages. The incoming water is captured first in a central reservoir. From this central pool, the liquid is siphoned
off to the cold-water tank. This tank feeds the main drinking
spout for normal water needs. Ice is produced in a refrigerat-
ed tank located next to the cold-water reservoir and dispensed
through a separate opening in the side of the fountain. On the
opposite side of the fountain is the hot-water dispenser, which
feeds off a heater tank located above the main reservoir.

   "It's the addition of the icemaker that makes our fountain
unique," says Reed. "We use a Handy-Ice III manufactured by
FREON, Inc., in Asbury Park, N.J.," he says. "The Handy-Ice
III produces ice at a rate that far exceeds anything else on
the market today. A number of other manufacturers already make
dual-purpose fountains, but ours covers the entire range of
drinking needs."

-more-

Product introduction releases serve a multitude of purposes, from
pure information about a single product to publicity for other companies
and other products. It is quite common to mention contributing manufacturers in a product release. For example, if you develop a basic plastic that
is then used by a leading headphone manufacturer in its product design, it
is usually acceptable to mention that company's use of your product. There
is always the chance that the headphone manufacturer will reciprocate. In

```
New Fountain--2

    Reed indicates that the new fountain will probably be mar-
keted in areas with noticeable seasonal shifts. "We expect
that areas that have pronounced seasonal temperature fluctu-
ations will have the greatest need for our fountain," he says.
But almost any office where people have different tastes in
beverages is a potential market." Reed explains that in any
given office environment, 75 percent of the staff will be sat-
isfied with just plain water; however, the other 25 percent
will use a fountain for making hot drinks such as tea and soup
in the winter and iced drinks in the hot months. He also
expects that the very availability of such a fountain will
increase its usage.


                          #####
```

fact, many such joint arrangements are formalized when products are pub-
licized. Consider the release in Exhibit 6.3 about a new water cooler.

Can you tell whom the publicity is for? From the address block you
learn that the company that manufactures the fountain is sending out the
release; however, a second company is also mentioned. The manufacturer
of the icemaker is given some free publicity. In many cases, this is a good
thing to do. Of course, you don't want to give your competition a helping
hand, but it never hurts to help your friends. Often, it's difficult to tell
what the real publicity point is in a product release. If the above release

had been written and distributed by an agency or by FREON, Inc., then the "bottom line" publicity would actually be for the icemaker, through publicity for the fountain. This is not an uncommon approach in product publicity and is not normally considered unethical.

Product news releases are arranged slightly differently from other releases. Although they certainly follow the normal inverted pyramid style of decreasing order of importance, they are quite obvious in their inductive approach to the product definition. In other words, product releases normally proceed from a general statement concerning the product (often an announcement that the product is on the market) to specific information about the product's attributes, characteristics, and applications. The end of the release is usually reserved for company background—full name, relationship to parent or subsidiary companies, and branch locations or the location at which the specific product is made. The release in Exhibit 6.4 reflects this pattern of organization.

Writing News Releases for Broadcast ━━━━━

Radio is meant to be heard and television is made to be seen and heard. That means you have to write for the ear or for the ear and eye. Simplification is the key to broadcast writing. Because it is harder to absorb the spoken word than the written word, concepts need to be pared down to the bare bones. Sentences must be shorter, speech more colloquial, and complex issues distilled to their essence. One of the major advantages of using broadcast media is repeatability—listeners may hear or see a message many times in the course of a single day or a single week. Even so, you must learn to write as though your audience will hear or see your message only one time.

Consider the differences between the following leads written for two different releases—one meant for print, the other for radio.

Print
INDIANAPOLIS, June 6—Francis Langly, former Director of Research and Development for Associated Products Corporation (APC), today received the American Chemical Society's (ACS) Goodyear Medal—ACS's most prestigious award—for his work in the field of specialty elastomers.

Radio
At an awards luncheon in Indianapolis today, a Wilmington native received the highest honor of the American Chemical Society. The prestigious Goodyear Medal—awarded for work in the field of specialty elastomers—went to Francis Langly, former Director of Research and Development for Associated Products Corporation.

EXHIBIT 6.4   Product News Release with Company Information at the End

NEWS RELEASE

Associated Products Corporation
1800 Avenue of the Americas
Syracuse, NY 10025-1234

Contact: Mark Spanger
Day telephone: (315) 555-9836
Night telephone: (315) 555-5467

                                    For Immediate Release

VERSATILE NEW ELASTOMER
<u>HAS INDUSTRY-WIDE APPLICATIONS</u>
    Associated Products Corporation (APC) has announced the
development of a versatile new elastomer with the potential
for use in a number of industries. The new compound, dubbed
PLIENT, is a vacuum-molded elastomer product displaying characteristics of both plastic and rubber.
    "We've worked for almost five years on this product," says
Raoul Simpson, materials engineer for APC. "We think PLIENT
will revolutionize the way designers think about certain
applications from now on." Simpson led the team that developed PLIENT and has begun experiments designed to test its
broad range of applications. "We already know it can be used
in the automotive industry replacing the heavy two-piece metal
widgets now being used," he says. "We suspect that it will be
useful in a number of related and unrelated industries as a
more cost-effective replacement for fiberoptics."
    The key element to the success of PLIENT is its ability to
withstand temperature extremes and its resistance to oil and
abrasive chemicals. And because of its characteristic conduc-
tive nature, it has the potential for a number of applications in the electronics industry.
    Paul Johnson, vice president of the Elastomers Division of
APC, is excited about the new product. "We've come up with a
totally new concept in versatility," he says. "I expect that
the market for PLIENT in the West will be tremendous."
    Associated Products Corporation has been developing plas-
tics products for uses in industry since its founding in 1979.
Its Elastomers Division is located in Springfield, N.Y., with
a subsidiary in Cleveland, Ohio.

                            #####

Although both releases are approximately the same length, there are some noticeable differences that raise some interesting questions:

- Why doesn't the broadcast release start with a dateline?
- Why not use the abbreviations ACS and APC in the broadcast release?
- What is the reason for beginning the broadcast release with the location rather than the name, as in the print release?

The answers are simple: Datelines are not needed in broadcast releases because they won't be read. The point of origin usually becomes clear through the narrative. Abbreviations are too confusing when heard on the air. It is always advisable to use the entire name, unless the abbreviation has become commonplace usage. Finally, beginning with location in broadcast helps set the scene. This is peculiar to broadcasting and is a carryover from drama, in which a scene is set prior to any dialogue.

Use the medium to your advantage. If you are using radio, set the scene first, then populate it with real people and easy-to-understand facts. Remember: A news release for radio or television is just that—news. It is intended for the same purpose as a print news release—to be used as news. The closer to acceptable news style it is, the better your chances of getting it broadcast. Prepare your releases for broadcast media using the same format you would use for a print release. Exhibit 6.5 illustrates this.

After reading Exhibit 6.5, consider these questions:

- Why is a paraphrase used instead of a direct quotation in this release?
- Does the lead establish a sense of place prior to coming to the point?
- Can you locate all the elements of a lead within the release? Are they where they should be in order of importance?
- If you were a news announcer, what additional information would you want to have before you ran this story?

Remember, no matter what the type of news release, it is still information you will lose control over once it is sent out to the media. They are your primary audience. You must learn to write for them first. To the extent that you do this, your releases will have a greater chance of reaching any other audience.

Backgrounders

Backgrounders are in-depth information pieces. As the name implies, they provide background information for anyone wishing it—reporters, ad copywriters, speechwriters, and editors. Backgrounders are almost

EXHIBIT 6.5   Broadcast Release

```
Society for Needy Children
4240 Welxton Avenue
Newhope, MN 78940

Contact: Lucille Bevard
Day Phone: 555-8743
Night Phone: 555-9745

                                    For Immediate Release

    A little girl stood for the first time today to receive a
new teddy bear and a check for $75,000 from the Society for
Needy Children. Eight-year-old Mary Patterson accepted the
check on behalf of the children at the St. Mary Martha's
Children's Hospital. The money represents the culmination of
a year-long fund-raising drive by the Society.
    The money is earmarked for a new ward to be devoted exclu-
sively to the treatment of crippling diseases in children.
One of the first beneficiaries will undoubtedly be little
Mary, who has been disabled by congenital arthritis since
birth. Along with her new teddy bear, Mary and the other
children at the hospital will be using a new physical ther-
apy center donated through a matching grant from the Friends
of St. Mary Martha's.
    Hospital Administrator Lois Shelcroft says that the check
and the new therapy center are just the first step, and that
the Society for Needy Children has promised to continue their
fund-raising efforts on the hospital's behalf in the coming
year. Society spokesperson Jane Alexander says that the next
fund-raising drive, scheduled to begin in September, will pro-
vide funding for a new lab.

                            #####
```

always prepared by the public relations staff. Good backgrounders are comprehensive yet concise. They should never be used to espouse company policy or philosophy—that is reserved for controlled media, such as ads and editorials.

Backgrounders frequently accompany news releases in press kits. They usually supply enough information to fill in any gaps left by the release. Often, they are just insurance against getting called in the middle of the night by a reporter who is editing your news release and in need of some "background." Other times they are important "sales pieces," setting up an historical need for a new product.

In order to make a backgrounder comprehensive, the public relations writer must research as many sources as possible, including old articles, brochures, reports, news releases, and materials published outside the organization. Backgrounders can also benefit from personal interviews. As with news releases, backgrounders are more readable if they contain first-hand information.

A backgrounder should begin with a statement of the issue being addressed. Because it is not a news story or news release, it need not be presented as a lead nor need it follow the inverted pyramid style. Most backgrounders, however, do follow a basic pattern:

1. Open with a concise statement of the issue or subject on which the accompanying news release is based. Try to make it as interesting as possible. This opening statement should lead logically into the next section.

2. Follow the opening with an historical overview of the issue. You should trace its evolution—how it came to be—and the major events leading up to it. It is permissible here to use outside information. For instance, if you were writing a backgrounder on a new surgical technique, you would want to trace briefly the history of the technique's development and tie this in with information on techniques that had been used in the past. It is advisable to name your sources in the body of the text when appropriate. Readers of backgrounders want to know where you got your information.

3. Work your way to the present. This is the meat of your backgrounder. You want to explain the issue you opened with and its significance. Be factual. Remember: A backgrounder is an information piece, not an advertisement or the place to sell your company's philosophy.

4. Present the implications of the issue being discussed and point the direction for future applications. Even though a backgrounder is a public relations piece, it needs to be carefully couched in fact-based information.

5. Use subheads where appropriate. Subheads negate the need for elaborate transitions and allow you to order your information logically. Subheads need to be carefully chosen and should contribute to understanding.

6. Most backgrounders are four or five pages in length. Let your information dictate your length; however, don't become long winded or pad your document. Editors will recognize fluff immediately. The object of a backgrounder is to provide information and answer anticipated questions, nothing more.

EXHIBIT 6.6   Backgrounder

Contents, Not Structure, Pose the Most Fire Hazards

Losses to fires are costing billions of dollars and claiming thousands of lives each year in the United States. The National Fire Protection Association handbook states: "Fire-resistive construction is an important life-safety measure. However, severe fires may occur in the contents of fire-resistive buildings, and highly combustible decorations and interior finish materials may more than offset the value of noncombustible structurals." In fact, of all the contents common to residential, commercial, and institutional occupancies, the most often underestimated is the hazard from burning upholstered chairs and mattresses.

Although the many desirable features of a fire resistive building cannot be overlooked, there is no such thing as a "fireproof" building. Regardless of the construction type, there are always combustibles within the building. Generally, contents fires present a greater life-safety hazard to building occupants than the eventual ignition of the structure. In fact, the cause and early stages of fires are related to the building contents and interior finish materials and not the structure.

No matter what the construction type, the contents fire must be controlled in order to achieve life safety. A parallel may be drawn between a contents fire in a fire-resistive building and a fire in a furnace. The contents are the fuel and the building is the furnace.

Statistics Show Furniture Fires on the Rise

The Consumer Products Safety Commission recently stated that last year there were about 62,000 bedding fires, which caused 930 fatalities. Another 35,000 fires in upholstered furniture took 1,400 lives, prompting the Commission to declare that these materials are the "biggest killer of all the products under the jurisdiction of the agency."

The National Bureau of Standards had earlier reported that mattresses, bedding, and upholstered furniture were involved

-more-

The backgrounder in Exhibit 6.6 was used as an accompanying piece to a news release touting the advantages of a fire-resistant latex foam for use in upholstered furniture and mattresses. After you have read it, consider the following questions:

- How does it follow the recommendations for writing a backgrounder?
- How does it differ?

```
Fire Hazards--2

in 45 percent of the fatal fires they reviewed where the mate-
rials first ignited could be identified. They concluded that
"any inroads that can be made into the furniture problem
promises greater fire-death reduction than any other type of
strategy."

Building Design Not the Answer
    As for building design, recent well-publicized fires have
resulted in new provisions to building fire codes; however,
over 90 percent of the buildings that will be in use in the
year 2000 have already been built. Reliance on these new fire
codes for personal safety may, in fact, be unwarranted.
    Although building design and fire protection devices are
important, they do not guarantee the safety of the occupants.
Many fires develop too rapidly for fire systems, such as
sprinklers, to control. Fires can spread past a sprinkler head
to another area before the sprinkler head operates. Another
fire might smolder for hours, producing deadly smoke and gases
but not enough heat to cause operation for the sprinkler sys-
tem. In addition, property loss is most closely related to
fire-resistant building materials which would have to be
incorporated into future structures. Building contents most
strongly affect human safety.

Fire Reduction Not Yet a Reality
    A decade ago, the National Commission on Fire Prevention
and Control reported that fire was a major national problem,
ranking between crime and product safety in annual cost.
They were appalled to find "that the richest nation in the
world leads all the major industrialized countries in per
capita deaths and property loss from fire." The efforts of
this commission focused attention on fires and resulted in
the establishment of a goal to reduce the nation's fire loss-
es by 50 percent in the next decade. That goal has not been
realized.

                          -more-
```

- Does it trace the history of the issue adequately?
- Does it bring the reader up to the present and cover the current status of the issue?

Can you tell from reading this backgrounder that it was meant to sell a product? Probably not, unless you knew in advance that it was part of a product-related press kit. The object of a backgrounder is to provide background, not to "sell" anything. In the case of this particular backgrounder,

Fire Hazards--3

Recent fire loss data from the National Fire Prevention Association suggests that we have performed poorly in our efforts to reduce the nation's fire losses. Multiple-death fires, killing three or more people, have increased 70 percent in the past decade. In fact, fatalities in this group rose 37 percent between 1972 and 1980, and fires in this category are increasing at an average of 7.5 percent a year.

The estimated property loss from just building fires in the United States last year was about $6 billion, an increase of almost 7 percent from the year before. Further analysis of the estimate for fire-loss data this year shows that:

- Educational facilities lost $184 million, an increase of 82.2 percent over last year's figures.
- Institutional facilities lost $38 million, up 52 percent.
- Areas of public assembly lost $356 million, up 9.2 percent.
- And residential occupancies, such as hotels, motels, and apartments, lost $3.3 billion, up 7.1 percent from last year.

Judging from these data, it is apparent that the goal of reducing fire losses by 50 percent has not been met. In fact, fire losses are steadily increasing in most cases. Why? In answering this question, some important points must be taken into consideration:

- Contents may more than offset the value of noncombustible building materials, and
- The flammability properties of the contents are critical to life safety.

Although most new buildings are constructed in accordance with a national building code such as the National Fire Protection Agency (NFPA) 101 Life Safety Code or a similar

-more-

information is provided concerning fire safety and the need for purchasers of upholstered furniture to be aware of the dangers of fire.

The next step is to present the readers with a suggested action. This can, and often does, come in the accompanying product news release. Thus, the trick to writing backgrounders is to make them relate to your subject without actually "pushing" your product, philosophy, or service.

```
Fire Hazards--4

code, no national code regulates upholstered seating or mat-
tresses. And although a federal mattress flammability stan-
dard exists, its effectiveness has been questioned by both the
Consumer Products Safety Commission and the National Bureau
of Standards. As a result, a concrete fortress could be built
according to code and filled with furniture that burns like
gasoline. Larger buildings can contain tons of such furniture.

The Burden of Safety Is on the Buyer
    In the absence of codes specifically meant for furniture,
the burden of safety falls on the person selecting furniture
for a residence, commercial structure, or installation.
Greater care must be taken to select the most fire-resistant
furniture available for a particular need. In judging these
needs, the hazards to which the furniture might be exposed
should be considered, such as the likelihood of cigarette
burns, open flames, proximity of fuel or other combustibles,
and population density. For example, in areas with a high
level of vandalism, materials with a good open-flame resis-
tance might be needed, while furniture prone to accidental
ignition may only need to be cigarette resistant.
    The ultimate test of any furniture is, of course, how it
will perform in an actual fire. It is obvious that fire-resis-
tant structures are not enough to ensure life safety. If the
nation's fire losses are to be reduced, then the potential
hazards of furnishings must be considered.

                        #####
```

Fact Sheets ————

Fact sheets contain just that—facts—and nothing more. If you have a lot of figures, for example, or a few charts that help explain your topic more easily, or simply a few itemized points you want to make, then a fact sheet is the form to use. A fact sheet is usually only one page, sometimes printed on both sides. It should elaborate on already presented information, such as a news release, and not merely repeat what has already been said.

For example, if you have written a news release about the relocation of a facility to a new site, the news release undoubtedly discloses the news-

EXHIBIT 6.7   Museum Fact Sheet

University of Northern Washington

```
University of Northern Washington
2900 Provender Drive
Alderdale, Washington 99304
Contact: Richard Lawson, (206) 555-1234

          Museum of Natural History Fact Sheet

The University of Northern Washington Museum of Natural
History will move into a new building on the east side of
campus by March of 1996. The museum is being relocated as
part of the university's $45-million project to expand and
modernize its science facilities.

Future Location:
On the northwest end of a university-owned parking lot on East
23rd Avenue, between Renton and Box Streets. The parking lot
is being redesigned so that no parking spaces will be lost as
a result of the new building.

Construction timeline:
Five months, beginning in late summer.

Cost:
$635,000

Fund-raising goal:
$150,000 to complete and equip the building.

Balance left to be raised by mid-August:
$72,500

                          -more-
```

worthiness of the event with particulars on when the move is to take place, for what reasons, etc. A fact sheet, however, can elaborate in interesting ways. For example, you might want to itemize costs, or break out major donations made toward the move, or elaborate on the size of the facility with square foot comparisons.

Take a look at Exhibits 6.7 and 6.8. These fact sheets are slightly different, but each contributes to forming a more complete story. The first fills in the numbers on a museum move and the second supports a product press kit for a line of vitamins.

Museum--2

Pledges to date:
$77,000
- $32,500 from former UNW football coach Arlyss Thompson to
  build the storage area for the geology collection.
- $22,500 on a one-to-two challenge match pledged by
  Thompson for construction costs.
- $22,500 from Seattle philanthropist Frazier Crane to
  match half of the Thompson challenge, on the condition
  that the rest of the money be raised from other sources.

Other funding sources:
$485,000 allocated by the university from the $8.1-million
Department of Energy grant for the first phase of the capital construction program to build modern science facilities
on campus.

Square feet:
11,000 square feet with a 9,100-square-foot courtyard. Total
square footage of existing building is 10,689.

Special features:
Air-conditioned and climate-controlled to protect the highly
fragile collections.

Advantages:
Improved public access and increased public parking.

#####

EXHIBIT 6.8   Weight-Control Fact Sheet

VITAMIX VITALSTATS

Vitamix International
P.O. Box 9234
Westphalen, Ohio 76456

<u>Vitamix Vital Statistics</u>

- About two-thirds of U.S. households reported making dietary changes in the past survey year for reasons of health or nutrition. Of these, 43 percent cited weight control as the primary reason for the changes.
- 53 percent of the adult population surveyed have tried to control weight during the past year by "staying away from fattening foods and/or eating less"—up from 48 percent the year before.
- 18 percent of the adult population surveyed this year reported the use of "low-fat" food/beverage options as part of weight-control strategy.

<u>Population Overweight/Obese</u>

- According to the data collected in the most recent Health and Weight Loss Survey (HWLS), 32 percent of the men and 36 percent of the women aged 20-27 were 10 percent or more above their desired weight.
- 14 percent of the men and 24 percent of the women were 20 percent or more above their desired weight in the same HWLS survey.
- 7 million Americans are classified as extremely obese.
- 30 percent of all males and 49 percent of all females surveyed by the National Center for Vital Statistics said they considered themselves overweight.
- More than half of those surveyed in a recent Aerobic 4 National Fitness Survey said "it would be beneficial to lose weight."

-more-

```
Vitamix--2

                        Weight-Control Diets

• At any given time, at least 20 percent of the population
  are on some kind of weight-loss diet.
• 33 percent of those surveyed in the Aerobic 4 National
  Fitness Survey said they are dieting either to lose or
  maintain weight.
• In a recent Nielsen Survey, 56 percent of women aged
  25-34 said they were dieting.

                             #####
```

KEY TERMS

news release	dateline
publicity release	exclusive
product release	special
financial release	backgrounder
inverted pyramid style	fact sheet
lead	

EXERCISES

1. Tape a talk show on TV. As you view the tape, take notes of the answers of the person being interviewed. Write up your "quotes." Watch the tape again, comparing the actual answers to your cited quotes. Note the differences.

2. Pick a news story from your local paper. Rewrite the lead of the story stressing as many different facets of the story as possible. Turn in both the original story and your leads. Work up each lead and the following paragraph ideas using the form on the next page.

3. Pick a product that interests you. Write a product news release targeted to a trade publication in that industry outlining the virtues of your product in a *nonadvertising* approach. Use a media directory such as *Standard Rate and Data Service* to pick out a publication, or go to the library or local newsstand and pick out a target publication. Be prepared to explain why your release shouldn't be considered advertising.

4. Assume you are writing a news release on yourself highlighting a recent accomplishment—it can be on literally anything. Where would you place the release? Think of where you have been and what you have done and what potential media sources serve those locations. Make a media list complete with addresses. Devise a separate lead for each outlet.

5. Locate a product-oriented feature story from a mass consumer magazine or trade publication. Go over the story carefully and pull out items that relate only to pure information about the product and develop an outline for a product backgrounder based on this information. State what further information you think you would need to work up a complete backgrounder on the product.

News Release Outline Form

Objective of Release:

_____

_____

Lead:

_____

_____

_____

Paragraph 1 (Main Idea):

_____

_____

Paragraph 2 (Main Idea):

_____

_____

Paragraph 3 (Main Idea):

_____

_____

Paragraph 4 (Main Idea):

_____

_____

Paragraph 5 (Main Idea):

_____

_____

CHAPTER **7**

ANNUAL
REPORTS

In this chapter you will learn:

- What an annual report is, and who its audiences are.
- The contents of a typical annual report.
- How to write an annual report.

Annual reports are probably one of the least read of all house publications. Recent research indicates that about half the shareholders who receive them spend fewer than 10 minutes looking at them. And, believe it or not, 15 percent of all stock analysts don't read them at all. So why is corporate America spending $5 billion a year producing annual reports?

Part of the reason is that the federal government requires it. The Securities Exchange Act of 1936 requires publicly traded companies to provide their investors with a yearly financial statement. This law also requires that an annual report be delivered to stockholders no later than 15 days before the annual meeting. Quarterly reports also have to be filed.

Beginning in 1980, the Securities and Exchange Commission (SEC) mandated that additional information be added, including financial data covering the past five years and an expanded discussion and analysis of the company's financial condition. It's not surprising that annual reports began to increase in size and complexity—so much so, in fact, that a few years later General Motors asked the SEC to allow them and other companies to develop and file an abbreviated "summary" annual report.

In 1987, the SEC ruled that companies could indeed publish such a report as long as they included all of the elements required by law as either appendices to the abbreviated report or in another formal document, such as the already required Form 10-K. Critics continue to contend that this new flexibility allows companies to selectively cut bad news from their most visible communication vehicle. They argue that most stockholders will read only the annual report, believing it complete. Although some companies have experimented with the "summary" annual report, most companies still produce the lengthy report already familiar to stockholders.

These days, most large corporations, and many small ones, have their own Web sites on the Internet. And most of these sites include links to the companies' annual reports. However, many of these are abbreviated reports or reports that contain only what the company considers to be the important sections (generally the president's letter and some summary tables). For now, it appears that hard-copy annual reports are still the best way to get a complete financial picture of an organization—at least for the time being.

Annual Report Audiences

When you produce an annual report, you're writing for a primarily internal audience, one with a vested interest in the well-being of your organization. That's why many annual reports gloss over the bad news, even though research shows that most stockholders would feel a lot better about a company if it were open and honest with them.

Stockholders aren't the only audience for annual reports, however. These organizational summaries are excellent information sources for media people, especially financial reporters. They also provide valuable background for financial analysts, potential stockholders, nonshareholding employees and customers, and opinion leaders such as legislators and community leaders.

Before you write an annual report, you must first decide which of these audiences you are writing for. Don't ever assume that you are talking only to shareholders; rank the other potential audiences in order of their importance to you, and be sure to address them, too.

Annual Report Contents

No two annual reports are alike; however, the SEC does require that certain elements be present including:

- Certified financial statements for the previous two years.
- An explanation of any difference between these financial statements and statements filed in another form with the SEC.
- A summary management analysis of operations for the past five years.
- Identification of the company directors' principal occupations.
- Stock market and dividend information for the past two years.
- Notice of Form 10-K availability.
- A brief description of both business and line-of-business in the "audited footnote."
- Any material differences from established accounting principles reflected in the financial statements.
- Supplementary inflation accounting.

The form this information takes is what makes annual reports different from each other. To accommodate the SEC guidelines, annual reports have developed certain standard mechanisms for housing the required information:

- A description of the company including its name, address (headquarters, subsidiaries, and plant sites), its overall business, and a summary of its operations, usually in both narrative and numerical form.
- A letter to stockholders that includes an account of the past year's achievements, an overview of the industry environment and pertinent markets, and a discussion of future business and investment strategies.
- A financial review as set forth by the SEC regulations listed previously.
- An explanation and analysis of the financial review that outlines the factors influencing the financial picture over the past year.
- A narrative report covering anything from a discussion of subsidiaries to details on corporate philanthropy. Many companies use the annual

report as a forum in which to discuss social issues or beat their own public relations drum, as it is one of the best publicity tools available.

Exhibit 7.1 shows the cover, president's letter, and an inside spread from a public utility company's annual report.

Writing for Annual Reports ───────

There are generally two ways to produce an annual report: you can write it in-house, or you can farm it out to an agency. Frankly, agencies—including those that specialize in annual reports—produce the bulk of these publications. However, with the advent of desktop publishing, more organizations are considering in-house writing and production.

No matter who writes it, the bulk of an annual report is taken up with tables, charts, and flashy photographs. In fact, critics charge that annual reports often try too hard (and too blatantly) to sweeten a bitter financial pill with a lot of pretty sugar coating. Many annual reports do stand guilty of this, but countless others perform a valuable informational service to their stockholders. In fact, because they are good message vehicles, a great many nonprofit organizations are now producing annual reports even though they don't really have to. The modern annual report has become a major tool in any organization's public relations arsenal.

Writers produce only two small portions of the annual report, but they are the portions most read by shareholders: the president's letter and the narrative report.

The President's Letter

There are some really awful president's letters in annual reports. The reason most cited is the SEC guidelines telling them what they have to talk about. Fortunately, these guidelines don't tell writers how to talk about what they have to talk about. There is no reason these letters have to be crashingly dull, wordy, and confusing. What impresses the everyday shareholder is honesty, a straightforward writing style, and no fluff.

Both of the following examples opt for the "numbers up front" approach on the mistaken belief that readers want it that way:

> [Company name] expanded its financial base in 19__ and substantially increased the number of property interests in its investment portfolio. A $47-million common stock offering, completed in June, plus a $40-million public offering of mortgage notes and common stock purchase warrants in December 19__ were among the financial resources that permitted [company name] to increase the number of its property interests to 191 by adding 99 real estate investments during the year.

EXHIBIT 7.1   Elements of an Annual Report

The annual report for the Eugene, OR, Water and Electric Board (EWEB) is typical of many corporate annual reports, even though EWEB is a publicly owned utility. It utilizes large, colorful pictures in a standard magazine format.

(Continued)

(Continued)

Surging Power Plays

Like the city it serves, Eugene Water & Electric Board exists in a rapidly changing environment. What was once a sleepy university and logging town has transitioned to a diverse city. Similarly, the small publicly-owned utility that was born in 1911 has evolved to an innovative, responsive water and energy utility perfectly suited to serve this high-energy community.

Preparations continued at high speed in 1997 for a new business environment where a slippery combination of customer service and price will be prominent. The prospect of a restructured electric industry, already has played a role in utility business for several years, but in 1997 the potential of industry restructuring shifted to the foreground and resulted in Oregon House Bill 2821.

The bill would have opened Oregon's electric industry to competition. Although HB 2821 never made it to the House floor, the effort prompted comprehensive discussion by the EWEB Commissioners regarding the consumer and environmental protections considered vital in any proposed restructuring bill.

EWEB joined consumer groups, advocates for low-income interests and others in support of HB 2821, largely because the bill addressed issues the Board flagged as crucial, including recovery of stranded costs and continued support of renewable resources and low-income energy assistance.

consumer protections

Competition

HB 2821

The year 19__ was a successful one for [company name]. Net income was up substantially, over 27 percent greater than 19__'s results, to a record $305.6 million, as the economy moved into a strong recovery. On a per share basis, our earnings were $9.50, an increase of 13 percent, reflecting both the issuance of additional common stock during this past year, as well as the preferred stock issued during 19__.

The next example at least begins with an interesting image of a "corporate renaissance":

We are in the midst of a corporate renaissance, and 19__ was a strong reflection of the growth, diversification, and enthusiasm that typifies [company name].

We had a record performance in 19__ in many areas. For the first time, net income exceeded $1 billion, at $1.2 billion. Sales reached an all-time high of $13.4 billion—up more than $2 billion from the 19__ level. The list of records also included earnings per share at $6.47; and operating income, which at $2.3 billion was up 69 percent from the previous record.

And what about bad news? This letter buries it under a barrage of industry buzzwords such as "maximizing profitability":

[Company name] continued its strategy of maximizing profitability in basic markets and businesses in 19__. All these areas of the Corporation had a truly excellent year. Unfortunately, the property and casualty reinsurance lines of the Insurance Group, which are not a part of our basic long-term strategy, incurred continuing heavy losses, significantly lowering our overall profitability. Reflecting this impact, [company name]'s consolidated net income of $106.3 million was about flat with 19__, although earnings per share increased marginally to $4.02 from $3.96, reflecting a slightly reduced number of common shares outstanding.

Finally, here's a letter that approaches a mixed year with an interesting, number-free narrative approach:

External forces produce both opportunities and challenges—and 19__ had its share of both for [company name] and its businesses.

During the year, some of the external forces facing our four business segments served to expand revenues and growth. Others had a dampening effect, calling for effective countermeasures.

The mix of forces at work included . . . [bulleted list follows]

We worked to take advantage of those external forces that offered opportunities, and to overcome the challenges posed by others.

If you can write the letter yourself, and simply route it for the president's approval, you will get better results than you would if the president drafted it. When you do it yourself, keep in mind a few points: First, because most of the rest of the report is numbers, it's best to keep numbers in the letter to a minimum. Also, keep your letter short, and keep its language friendly and simple. This way, you will be able to cover the SEC bases without boring your readers.

The Narrative Report

The body of the annual report is your only chance to write anything without numbers—or, at least, with a minimum of numbers. Here is where you get to describe the company, its operations, its people (a favorite focus of many reports), and its future in detail. The only problem is one of space. Remember: You can't leave out anything required by the SEC. And you don't want to leave out anything that really makes your company look good.

One of the best ways to decide on content is to have the people in charge of the various divisions or subsidiaries submit brief lists of the year's highlights from their "down-in-the-trenches" perspective. Make your needs known in plenty of time to get responses from your contacts. And leave the final compiling and writing to one person so that the entire report has a single style.

A quick word about that style: Depending on a company's image, the style of an annual report can vary greatly. Some are formal to the point of being stiff. Others are too informal and leave shareholders with a feeling that the company is being loosely run. The best and most appropriate style is somewhere in the middle.

As with the president's letter, you don't have to begin your narrative report with numbers. In fact, it benefits greatly from a little introduction. There is no reason why annual reports have to be boring reading. The following introductions to the narrative report sections of two different annual reports are fairly good examples of what can be done to lend a modicum of interest to an otherwise often dull subject:

> To come up with a winner in global competition, you have to provide the highest quality . . . the greatest number of choices . . . and the most innovative solutions to a customer's needs, regardless of location.
>
> In meeting that challenge, [company name] uses a system of "global networking" to choreograph its worldwide response by product, function, and geographic area. Networking teams enable [company name] to draw upon its resources around the world and to respond quickly no matter where customers may be headquartered.
>
> There are many ways to define shareholder value . . . and many ways that companies strive to create it. But at [company name], the strategy has been three-pronged:

- Utilizing existing resources within the company to diversify into four separate businesses.
- Acting on opportunities to build and strengthen these existing businesses.
- Keeping abreast of trends that hold promise for the future.

Use numbers to augment your narrative—but don't let numbers be the entire focus. Although annual reports are intended to spell out a company's financial environment, they communicate more often with average people than with financial analysts. Financial analysts don't rely on an annual report as their sole information source; many shareholders will, however, so it has to be written in a style they can understand.

Striking just the right tone, in both writing and design, is the most important ingredient in producing an annual report. In fact, so much depends on design that many annual reports emphasize form at the expense of its function.

Design for design's sake is still common. Be careful not to let your "look" overpower your written information. Ideally, form and function should work together to achieve a real sense of the company that readers care enough to own part of.

Exhibit 7.2, a complete annual report, illustrates how all these elements come together in a polished final product.

EXERCISES

1. Bring in an annual report for either a for-profit or nonprofit organization. Be prepared to analyze its approach including writing style, layout and design, and "approachability."

2. Critique the narrative portion of the annual report you have chosen. Analyze its strengths and its weaknesses. Rewrite any portions that you think could benefit from your changes.

3. Imagine yourself as an organization seeking investors. Describe yourself in a president's letter for your personal annual report. Consider the following: What was your past year like? How would you state your shortcomings so that they don't sound quite so "short"? What do you see as the strengths that would make you a good investment? Why would anyone want to invest in you? Paint as good a picture as possible about your potential for success next year.

EXHIBIT 7.2   Complete Annual Report

The annual report of the Southern Willamette Private Council (SWIPIC), a not-for-profit social service agency, is fairly small and simple, signifying by its presentation its status as a publicly funded agency.

Welcome To SWPIC

As the only Oregon PIC to exceed state averages, the Southern Willamette Private Industry Council delivered more services to more people in 1995. We made a substantial contribution to helping business have a well-trained workforce.

And we will continue to add more value to the community through our innovative programs and services. As part of our broader vision, we're establishing the Willamette Career Center, a "one-stop delivery center" for everyone to access career placement, job search and job training programs.

Many risks and challenges still face us, however. Significant funding reductions for job training and youth services have already hit home. Programs for dislocated workers and low-income adults will see severe federal funding reductions. Proposed federal workforce legislation will dramatically change how job training is delivered in Lane County.

With the support of Oregon's officials and with renewed local commitment, our experience will guide us to extend our vision and continue to provide benefits for businesses, the community, and our clients. We'll meet this chal

Taking Care of Business

SWPIC's employment services help fuel motor coach expansion

Human Resource Director Dan Bedore knows that finding the right employees can dramatically impact a company's bottom-line. At Country Coach in Junction City, Dan is responsible for hiring the 500 employees that sand, paint, weld, detail, and otherwise, build each new luxury coach.

When the company expanded operations, Dan turned to SWPIC as a source for workers. First SWPIC organized a special industrial technology course with Lane Community College that taught students production line and safety skills. Then SWPIC screened a pool of employees and presented the applicants to Dan.

"SWPIC provided us with workers tailored to our needs," Dan says. "Things that we take for granted — job and safety skills, productivity, reliability — I couldn't find addressed in any other program." SWPIC also reduced costs by reimbursing Country Coach for half of each eligible worker's wage during the training period.

Tax exemptions are available to businesses using SWPIC as a "first source" for hiring.

But as Dan Bedore knows, the benefits extend beyond good business practices and tax breaks. "Preparing people and getting them into the workforce helps business and the community," Dan says. "SWPIC gives us an opportunity to develop a person who otherwise might not have a chance to succeed."

> "Things that we take for granted — job and safety skills, productivity, reliability — I couldn't find addressed in any other program."
>
> **Dan Bedore**
> (pictured right)

(Continued)

(Continued)

PUTTING THE PIECES TOGETHER

Gayle Heimbuck planned to take another waitress job. She was submitting applications when the Employment Department referred her to SWPIC. Within two weeks, SWPIC placed Gayle at Country Coach, learning to assemble drawers for installation into recreational vehicles. She's been there for nearly two years.

"I take the raw lumber, cut the pieces to size, rout, dovetail and shape them, put the drawer together and send it to the paint booth," Gayle says.

Conducting Community Business

All community members profit from SWPIC

Here's how Jim Griffith, vice president and general manager of Shorewood Packaging, discusses the benefits of SWPIC: "Without SWPIC, employers would miss good employees and the community would pay the price."

Board member Gary Pierpoint, senior vice president of South Umpqua Bank, agrees. "SWPIC serves as a catalyst for the community, bringing together the employment division, LCC, and assistance agencies all under one roof. It's a very positive step."

Small business operator Jill Davis also agrees. Jill owns Springfield's Classic Letterpress, one of more than 300 businesses that works with SWPIC. She used traditional employment avenues to search for a press operator. It was SWPIC, however, that screened applicants and recommended Lynn Stutts (see sidebar). Jill thanks SWPIC for its support of workers and businesses.

"In the long run, the worker, business, and community all benefit," Jill says. "Everyone wins."

U.S. Representative Peter DeFazio dedicates his congressional pay raise to scholarships for workers needing education and retraining. "SWPIC provides my scholarship recipients and thousands of other Lane County residents the training and job opportunities they need to meet the challenges of the future."

"In the long run, the worker, business, and community all benefit. Everyone wins."

Jill Davis
(pictured right)

REACHING GREATER HEIGHTS

"I have the energy of a fireball," proclaims Lynn Stutts, who at five feet tall must rank among the nation's shortest press operators. Springfield's Classic Letterpress runs Lane County's only specialty printing press. In a trade formerly dominated by men wearing aprons and leather visors, Lynn stands tall.

"When SWPIC sent me for an interview, everyone was worried about my size," Lynn says. "I told them I've been stuck with this size all my life and it's not the

Getting Down to Business

A caring, professional staff and board run SWPIC's award-winning programs

While much of SWPIC's success comes from the heart, a large part can also be attributed to the expertise of its staff and board of directors, representing a cross-section of the entire community.

SWPIC's staff is instrumental in facilitating new training to assist clients and meet specific business needs.

Lane County Commissioner Ellie Dumdi says the staff's work has extended SWPIC's reputation beyond the community. "Through-out the past 13 years SWPIC has enjoyed the benefits of outstanding leadership. It is recognized as one of the best service delivery organizations in Oregon and in the nation."

Board member Don Casler, Lumber and Sawmills Workers Union business manager, sees the board getting well-rounded ideas for solutions because the private business sector, local government, employment division, welfare department, labor, and private citizens are all represented.

"SWPIC's expertise is in meeting the specific needs of local workers to overcome their employment obstacles," says Paul Wostmann, board member and general manager of Gunderson Springfield, Inc. "Our services and training give our clients a better chance of succeeding over the long term."

> "Our services and training give our clients a better chance of succeeding over the long term."
>
> **Paul Wostmann**
> (pictured right)

(Continued)

(Continued)

Managing the Business

SWPIC's books demonstrate excellent fund management

The Southern Willamette Private Industry Council managed a budget of $8.9 million with most money coming from state and federal grants. Of the budgeted amounts, $7.8 million were expended. Funds remaining at the end of the year are carried into the next year.

Major funding categories include the Dislocated Worker Program (25.2 percent), the Job Training Partnership Act (40.8 percent), the Family Support Act (23.2 percent), and other funding provided for Corrections, the Regional Workforce Quality Council, and Veterans programs (10.7 percent). JTPA funds support both low-income adults and youths and the Family Support Act funds the JOBS (welfare-to-work) program.

While funding originates from these sources, money is tracked through 21 individual fund, and 75 sub-fund, accounts. Each fund account is tracked separately, and reports are submitted to state and federal agencies as required by law.

SWPIC is audited annually and adheres to state and federal laws and Generally Accepted Accounting Principles (GAAP).

"Lane County has received tremendous benefits through SWPIC's ability to attract federal and state funds."

John Lively
Executive Director
Eugene/Springfield
Metro Partnership

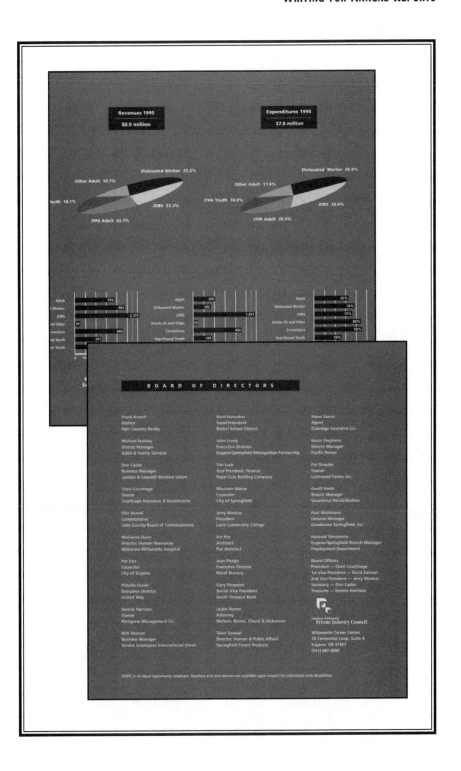

## CHAPTER 8

NEWSLETTERS, MAGAZINES AND FEATURE WRITING

FOR IMMEDIATE RELEASE

In this chapter you will learn:

- The various types of newsletters and why they are used.

- How to research, write, and design a newsletter.

- The purpose of house magazines and how to create them.

- How to write in the feature style.

In public relations writing, and in other forms of journalistic writing as well, we often talk about producing "newsletter articles" or "magazine articles." What we really mean is "feature articles," as differentiated from "news articles." The feature article or story is really what defines the nature of both newsletters and magazines. While both media may—and often do—contain straight news stories, as well as other forms of information such as calendars and fact sheets, their primary content is the feature. In this chapter we will discuss the art of feature writing as it pertains to newsletters and magazines.

The other element that links newsletters and magazines is the look. Increasingly, newsletters are adopting magazine-type layout techniques in place of the historically more common newspaper approach. Some of the design "quirks" of both publication types are mentioned here, while others are covered in Chapter 12, "Design, Printing, and Desktop Publishing." Thus, you will find in this chapter information that is relevant both to newsletters and magazines, with the differences, such as length and layout, pointed out along the way. You will also find that the commonalties far outweigh the differences.

Newsletters ━━━━━━━━

Every day in the United States thousands of newsletters are published and distributed to hundreds of thousands of readers. It is estimated that some 50,000 corporate newsletters alone are published each year in this country. Most newsletters are internal publications in the sense that they reach a highly unified public—employees, shareholders, members, volunteers, voting constituencies, and others with a common interest. In fact, if you ask any self-respecting communications professional for the most effective means of reaching a primarily internal audience, the response will most likely be the newsletter.

Types of Newsletters

Newsletters are as varied as the audiences who read them; however, they do break down into several different types:

- *Association newsletters* help a scattered membership with a common interest keep in touch. Profit and nonprofit associations and almost every trade association in the United States publish newsletters for their members, often at both national and regional levels.
- *Community group newsletters* are often used by civic organizations to keep in touch with members, announce meetings, and stimulate attendance at events. The local YWCA or Boys Club newsletter might announce their schedules, while a community church group newsletter

distributed throughout surrounding neighborhoods might be a tool for increasing membership.

- *Institutional newsletters,* perhaps the most common type of newsletter, are usually distributed among employees. Used by both profit and nonprofit organizations, they are designed to give employees a feeling of belonging. They frequently include a balanced mix of employee-related information and news about the company.

- *Publicity newsletters* often create their own readers. They can be developed for fan clubs, resorts (some resort hotels mail their own newsletters out to previous guests), and politicians. Congressional representatives often use newsletters to keep their constituencies up to date on their activities.

- *Special-interest newsletters* developed by special-interest groups tend to grow with their following. *Common Cause,* for instance, began as a newsletter and has grown into a magazine representing the largest lobbying interest group in the United States.

- *Self-interest* or *"digest" newsletters* are designed to make a profit. The individuals or groups who develop them typically offer advice or present solutions to problems held in common by their target readers. These often come in the form of a sort of "digest" of topics of interest to a certain profession. In the public relations profession, for instance, you'll find *PR Reporter, PR News, Communicate, O'Dwyer's Newsletter, Communication Briefings,* and many more.

Why a Newsletter?

Why, indeed? Most newsletters address an internal public (see Exhibit 8.1), with the exception of those that target single-interest groups—such as professionals and executives—outside a formal organizational structure. In the ideal organizational structure, communication flows both vertically (upward and downward) and horizontally. The newsletter is a good example of **downward communication:** It fulfills part of management's obligation to provide its employees with formal channels of communication. **Upward communication** provides employees a means of communicating their opinions to management. Ideally, even downward communication channels such as newsletters permit upward communication through letters to the editor, articles written by employees, surveys, and so forth. Newsletters can also provide horizontal communication—that is, from group to group—but this type of newsletter is rarely produced within an organization; rather, it originates from outside.

But why a newsletter instead of a magazine, booklets, bulletin boards, or (heaven forbid) more meetings? There are several questions you can ask yourself when deciding whether a newsletter is the publication that best suits your purpose:

EXHIBIT 8.1   Newsletter Examples

Once a newsletter is deemed a successful way to reach constituents, many companies use them for multiple purposes. Here and on the following two pages we see three different uses of the newsletter format from the same company. *Pipeline* is the regular quarterly newsletter of the Eugene (Oregon) Water and Electric Board. Its general focus is news about how to save energy and its associated costs.

(Continued)

(Continued)

EWEB AT 85
1911-1996
ENERGIZED BY CHALLENGE

Turn-of-the-Century Typhoid Epidemic Spurs Public Utility

Turn-of-the-Century Eugene, from the top of Skinner's Butte. Old water reservoir in foreground.

Photo Courtesy of Lane County Historical Museum

In 1908, the City of Eugene purchased a local, privately owned water system for $140,000.

In 1911, Eugene became the first city in the Pacific Northwest to use chlorine to purify water.

In 1961, EWEB's Hayden Bridge Filtration Plant changed to a PitCon process, the first major breakthrough in water filtration and purification since 1895.

In November, 1964, Eugene voters approved fluoridation of EWEB's water; in September, 1965, voters reversed the decision and fluoridation stopped. In the mid-seventies, the same thing happened again.

In 1990, EWEB water was recognized as the "Best Tasting Water in the Pacific Northwest" in a taste-test sponsored by a Washington state utility.

In 1992, EWEB installed a state-of-the-art, computerized Supervisory Control and Data Acquisition (SCADA) system to monitor the water system daily.

In 1906, typhoid fever hit Eugene. It soon became known as "the worst epidemic in the history of Oregon." When an Oregon State University scientist injected a guinea pig with water from a downtown well, it died immediately. "Experiments Made Prove Conclusively That Cause of Eugene's Terrible Malady is in the Water Supply" read the headline in the *Eugene Guard*. The public became enraged.

Rising to the challenge, Eugene's citizens approved a bond measure in 1908 to buy the privately-owned water company and establish a public water system. In 1911, the Eugene Water Board began operations.

With such a history, it's not surprising that Eugene Water & Electric Board (EWEB) has installed a water treatment system that's among the "best in the West," according to Water Division Director Dick Helgeson. "We keep ahead of the curve," says Helgeson. "Each time the federal government tightens up national water quality standards, we're ready to comply, usually without much upgrading of equipment and operations."

To begin with, says Helgeson, EWEB is fortunate to draw its water from one of the purest sources in the nation: the McKenzie River. EWEB then takes every precaution to provide customers with the highest quality drinking water:

■ The water goes through a full treatment and disinfection process at EWEB's Hayden Bridge Filtration Plant, one of the largest full-treatment filtration plants in the Pacific Northwest.

■ Treated water moves through a completely enclosed system of pipes and reservoirs, eliminating the possibility of outside contamination.

■ Pipes and hydrants are flushed and reservoir water is turned over regularly to keep it fresh.

■ Water is tested hourly, seven-days-a-week, in an environmental laboratory at the Hayden Bridge Filtration Plant; more than 85,000 tests are performed each year.

■ All Filtration Plant employees are fully cross-trained, so every operator at the Filtration Plant is also a Level IV Technician, certified to work in the lab.

■ EWEB has encouraged thousands of commercial/industrial businesses and residential customers to install 'backflow' devices to guard the water system from accidental contamination by customers.

Even with all these water quality measures, EWEB's water rates are among the lowest in the region. "Drink up," says Helgeson. "You can fill 100 glasses with pure, good-tasting EWEB water for only one cent."

"Over many years EWEB has tended to function in a light-cavalry mode. It has avoided the pitfall of becoming a sluggish bureaucracy. It has moved quickly and decisively when required to do so in the interests of its customers. And it seems to have understood the dynamics of change."

Beautiful McKenzie: The Story of Eugene Water & Electric Board, Norman F. Stone, 1981

EWEB at 85 was a specialty newsletter on the occasion of the utility's 85th anniversary and was designed as a sort of nostalgic image piece.

Changing Currents

Taking a Look at a Deregulated Electricity Market

February 1997

Buying Electricity Before Deregulation

Generating Facilities → Utilities → Consumers

WIRED FOR WHEELING

Generating Facilities → { Marketers / Utilities / Brokers } → Consumers

Buying Electricity After Deregulation

Future shock is rippling through the electric utility industry — the last big monopoly in the American economy is about to be deregulated. Ironically, most electric consumers — and that's just about everybody — are not clear on the significance of the revolutionary changes on the horizon.

The drive for increased competition is fueled on the premise that restructuring will lower electric bills. The catalysts for change in the electric industry are companies, which now include power marketers and independent power producers as well as traditional utilities,

eager to sell power outside their traditional markets. Electricity customers — particularly heavy users — are also joining the fray, noting that customers want more choices and should be free to select or purchase the services they want.

Today, the electric utility that provides your power has been determined solely by where you live. With competition, that would change. The idea of having customers pick their power provider, just as consumers select their long distance telephone service, is cutting edge stuff in the electric industry.

"In the past, electric customers have been able to buy their retail electricity with all the related services from a single provider," says Eugene Water & Electric Board General Manager Randy Berggren. "In the future, you might choose to deal with several different suppliers."

Electrifying Changes

For the past century, the electric utility business has been heavily regulated by government. The current move to restructure the industry started with the passage of the Energy Policy Act of 1992, which encourages unprecedented competition in the wholesale energy market.

As a result, Congress set the stage to allow each state the right to enact rules giving power customers more choices. Last year, the Federal Energy Regulatory Commission opened up access to transmission lines across the country, allowing

anyone with power to sell to have access to the regional electrical network. Power generators cannot be denied access to another utility's transmission lines, and users must be charged reasonable fees.

Some states are already experimenting with what's known as "retail wheeling" or "retail access." Earlier last year, New Hampshire began a two-year pilot program with approximately 17,000 residential and commercial customers (see related story this page). The pilot represents about three percent of the state's electric consumption and allows customers to choose from about 32 electricity suppliers.

With retail wheeling, a customer can contract with a power provider to deliver electricity to a distribution network. The distribution system owner, usually the customer's existing utility, may no longer be the original source of the power supply. However, the utility may continue to supply the use of the network and other services, such as metering and billing.

In the new world of retail competition, a customer might choose different suppliers of the many services necessary to deliver electricity. Likewise, consumers would have a wide array of choices in terms of buying electricity from a utility for whatever reason — whether because it is cheaper or because it's generated by renewable resources. Beyond the generated power source, the local distribution or "wires" utility (in this case, EWEB) will likely remain unchanged.

continued on page 2

New Hampshire Braves New World

"Live Free or Die"

— General John Stark,
in appealing to the
colonial New Hampshire
legislature to participate
in a war against
England in 1776.

Yankees from the Granite State had a rather black-and-white view of their world prior to the Revolutionary War. Now, more than 200 years later, the State of New Hampshire is participating in a new kind of revolution — the deregulation of the electric utility industry.

In June 1996, the New Hampshire legislature passed a bill requiring that the state's retail electricity market be open to competition by January 1998. The bill also directed the New Hampshire Public Utilities Commission to create a retail competition pilot project.

As a result, New Hampshire began the pilot project, with 17,000 business and residential customers — about 3 percent of the state's electric customers — choosing their electricity supplier. The pilot has several objectives:

★ determine level of interest among customers and suppliers for competitively provided retail electricity services.

★ develop rates that separate the costs of electricity or energy, transmission, distribution and energy services, such as metering and billing.

★ resolve technical questions.

The New Hampshire pilot was designed to give utilities, power marketers, customers and regulators some experience with competition. In the experiment, customers were able to choose a supplier for only the energy portion of their service, representing about 30 percent of the total electric bill for residential customers and 30-40 percent for commercial customers. The rest of the bill covered such expenses as transmission, distribution and capital costs, which continue to be paid to the distribution utility.

continued on page 2

Changing Currents is an update on the deregulation of the utility industry nationwide. It serves to alert customers of the impending change and to sell the company as a viable provider once this change occurs.

- **What is the purpose of the publication?** Is it to entertain? Inform? Solicit?

- **What is the nature and scope of the information you wish to present?** Longer information is probably better suited to a longer publication such as a magazine; shorter, to brochures or folders. If your information is strictly entertaining or human interest, it may also be better received within a magazine format.

- **Who, exactly, are you trying to reach?** All employees from the top down? A select few (the marketing department, the credit department, the vice president in charge of looking out windows)?

- **How often do you need to publish it to realize the objectives you set in answering the previous questions?** Newsletters are best suited to situations requiring a short editorial and design lead time.

Keep in mind also that newsletters are best for small publication runs and information that needs a quick turnover. They handle information that is considered necessary but disposable (much like a newspaper, which in a sense the newsletter mimics). However, this is generally, but not universally, true. Many fine newsletters are designed to be kept. Health and financial newsletters, for instance, are often hole-punched so that the reader can save them in ring binders. For the most part, though, they are considered disposable.

Newsletter Content

To determine a newsletter's content, you must first know your audience. Is it totally internal, totally external, or a combination of internal and external? Your audience and its interests will dictate, to a large extent, the topic and direction of your articles.

Depending on the type of newsletter you are publishing, the focus will be broad or narrow. For example, when you write for an internal, employee public, you must carefully balance information with entertainment. You must please management by providing information it wants to see in print, and you must please the employees by providing information they want to read. Otis Baskin & Craig Aronoff, in their book *Public Relations: The Profession and the Practice,* present a guideline for an appropriate mix in an internal publication (not necessarily a newsletter) aimed primarily at an employee audience:

- 50 percent information about the organization—local, national, and international.

- 20 percent employee information—benefits, quality of working life, etc.

- 20 percent relevant noncompany information—competitors, community, etc.
- 10 percent small talk and personals.

Given that most newsletters are fairly short, such a complete mix may be impractical; however, a close approximation will probably work. Remember, though, that this mix is only appropriate for publications such as institutional newsletters.

By comparison, most external (horizontal) publications tend to focus on items of interest to a more narrowly defined target public. For example, a newsletter for telecommunications executives may concentrate on news about that industry, omitting human interest items, small talk, or industry gossip. In fact, almost every newsletter targeted to executives contains only short, no-nonsense articles. The reason, of course, is that busy executives simply don't have the time to read the type of article that interests the average employee.

Newsletter Objectives

Newsletters, like any well-managed publication, will achieve best results if objectives are set and all actions follow logically from them. Objectives relate to your publication's editorial statement. Editorial statements shouldn't be pie-in-the-sky rhetoric; they should reflect the honest intent of your publication. If your intent is to "present management's story to employees," then say so up front. An editorial statement can be an objective, or it can serve as a touchstone for other objectives.

For example, from the editorial statement in the previous paragraph you could reasonably derive an objective such as "To raise the level of awareness of management policies among all employees by X percent over the next year." Or, "To provide an open line of upward and downward communication for both management and employees." Whatever your objectives, make sure they are measurable. Then you can point to your success in reaching them over the period of time you specified. You should also have some means by which to measure the success of your objectives. If your objective is simply "To present management's message to employees," how will you measure its success or failure? Don't you want to find out if just presenting the message was enough? How will you tell if anyone even read your message, or, if they did, whether they responded in any way?

Make your objectives realistic and measurable, and once you have set them, follow them. Use them as a yardstick by which to measure every story you run. If a story doesn't help realize one of your objectives, don't run it. If you just can't live without running it, maybe your objectives aren't complete enough.

Newsletter Articles

Most newsletters are journalistic in style. They usually include both straight news and feature stories and range from informal to formal depending on the organization and its audience. Usually, the smaller the organization, the less formal the newsletter. Large corporations, on the other hand, often have a very formal newsletter with a slick format combining employee-centered news with company news.

The responsibility for writing the newsletter is almost always handled in house, although some agencies do produce newsletters on contract for organizations. In-house personnel tend to be more in tune with company employees and activities. Sometimes the writing is done in house and the production, including design, layout, and printing, is done by an agency.

If you produce your own newsletter, you are limited only by expense and imagination. A standard newsletter is usually 8½-by-11 inches or 11-by-17 inches folded in half. It averages from two to four pages in length and is frequently folded and mailed. Many are designed with an address area on the back for mailing (see Exhibit 8.2).

The length of articles varies. Some newsletters contain only one article, while others include several. An average four-page newsletter uses about 2,000 words of copy. Depending on the focus of the newsletter, articles can range in length from "digest" articles of fewer than 100 words to longer articles of 600 words for newsletters that cover only one or two topics per issue. The trend today is toward shorter articles, especially for the newsletter aimed at the businessperson or corporate executive. Even for the average employee, newsletter articles usually need to be brief. Most newsletters make use of simple graphics or photographs. Most are typeset or, increasingly, desktop published.

Because newsletters inform and entertain, articles should be written in an entertaining way. Usually, news about the company or strictly informational pieces use the standard news story style (see Chapter 6), except that there is no need to use the inverted pyramid because newsletter stories are seldom edited for space from the bottom up. Employee interest pieces tend to use the feature-story style. Feature-type articles for newsletters should be complete, with a beginning and an ending.

Where Do Stories Come From?

There are many ways to come up with acceptable ideas for articles. Sometimes you might receive ideas from employees or management. Sometimes a news release or a short piece done for another publication will spark enough interest to warrant a full-blown newsletter article. Whatever the source of the idea, you must evaluate the topic based on reader interest and reader consequence.

If you're familiar with your audience's tastes, you can quickly determine their interests. To evaluate consequence, ask yourself what readers will

EXHIBIT 8.2   Newsletter Folds

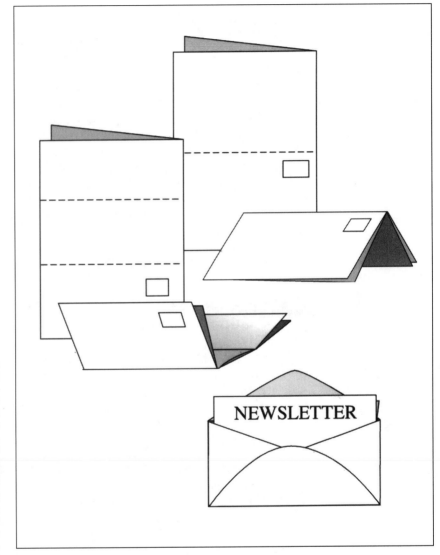

Clockwise from bottom: standard 11-by-17-inch, four-page folded in thirds and mailed in business envelope; standard 11-by-17-inch, single folded in thirds with Post Office indicia on bottom third (usually folded and stapled); standard 11-by-17-inch, folded in half with indicia on bottom half (usually folded and stapled).

learn from the article. Although light reading is fun for some, an organizational publication isn't usually the place to engage in it.

Every newsletter editor will tell you that getting story ideas isn't all that hard. Finding someone to write the stories is. There are several methods for enlisting writers. If you are putting out an in-house publication, try assigning "beats" like a newspaper does. If you're lucky enough to have a staff, assign them to different types of stories—perhaps by department or division, or by product or service. If you don't have a staff, rely on certain people in each department or division to submit stories to you. Sometimes the promise of seeing their name in print is inducement enough.

You can also send employees a request form, spelling out exactly what you are looking for. The information you get back will be sketchy, but you can flesh it out with a few phone calls (see Exhibit 8.3). This is an especially good method of gathering employee-related tidbits that don't deserve an entire story but should still be mentioned. One method for organizing your shorter stories is to group them according to topic. For example, group all stories relating to employee sports, or all stories about employee community involvement, or promotions, and so on.

Of course, if your publication is a narrowly focused horizontal publication, you may end up doing most of the research and writing yourself. Many such newsletters are truly one-person operations. Because desktop publishing allows a single person to act as reporter, editor, typesetter, and printer, this type of publication is enjoying a rebirth.

Whatever system you use to gather stories, as editor you will probably be doing most of the writing as well as the editing.

Researching Stories

If you write most of your own stories, you know that every topic must be researched thoroughly. The first step in a normal research process is to do a "literature search" to determine whether your article has already been written. If it has, but you still want to explore the topic for your specific audience, then try another angle.

Next, gather background information. Try to get specifics—you can't write about something you don't know a lot about personally. It also pays to get firsthand information. Interview people who know something about your topic. Not only will you get up-to-date information, you also may end up with some usable quotes and some new leads (see Chapter 5 for some tips on interviewing.)

And don't forget the library and Internet. Many a fine article has been written based on a library or Internet visit. These are both among the most valuable—and cheapest—forms of research around. In any event, most articles will be fairly complete and accurate if you do a little background research and conduct an interview or two. Because newsletter articles are usually short, this is about all the information you can use.

Design Considerations

Most people who engage in newsletter writing and editing today also lay out their own newsletters as well. And with the advent of desktop publishing, that job has become increasingly easy. Thus, no discussion of newsletters would be complete without some mention of design.

EXHIBIT 8.3   Employee Information Sheet

Employee Name: _____

Department: _____

Position: _____

Do you have any information pertaining to promotions, awards, service recognition, and so on, that might be of interest to fellow employees? If so, please give details below.

Do you have any story ideas for the employee newsletter? Please list your suggestions below.

If you are directly involved in any of the above information, would you be willing to be interviewed?

Would you be willing to write any or all of an article relating to any of the ideas mentioned above?

Please return this form to the Corporate Communications Department, #302.

We've already seen how most newsletters are simply 8½-by-11-inch or 11-by-17-inch pages folded in half, giving us four pages, or "panels," to work with. However, once we include the design elements that will make our newsletter attractive enough to be picked up by readers, there's not all that much room left for words. Exactly how much room will depend on your design capabilities.

What many designers love most about newsletters is the wide variety of available formats. Just picking one can be a challenge. A newsletter can take on any number of disguises, ranging from the standard 11-by-17-inch format folded down to a four-page 8½-by-11-inch size, to a lengthy, magazine-like format folded and stapled, to a tabloid newspaper, to a tabloid-sized magazine-type format known as a *magapaper.* Audience needs and cost are the most important deciding factors in picking a format for your newsletter.

The point to remember is that no matter what format you ultimately decide on, you will be stuck with it for quite some time. If you are going to have enough information to fill a 12-page magazine format four times a year, good—use a magazine format. If not, try something smaller. If you need to insert your newsletter in a monthly billing envelope, try something even smaller. If size is what attracts your audience, and you usually don't have to mail your newsletter, try a magapaper or a tabloid (even these can be mailed—they just cost a lot more).

Whatever you decide on, remember that your design elements must fit your format. Large formats call for larger artwork. Small formats call for shorter articles. White space is an extravagance in a bill stuffer, but not in a tabloid. Folding and mailing differs immensely among the various sizes. Suit your format to your needs.

The well-designed newsletter won't shout, "Look at my look." Instead, it will simply say, "Pick me up and read me." More than anything else, the design you choose and the skill you use in implementing that design will be nearly subliminal to the message you impart. The non-verbal message imparted through choices of paper, color, and format is as important as anything you have to say, because if you fail to entice your readers through these subtle nuances, you may not have any readers.

In order to get the most out of a newsletter, you must design it with your target audience always in mind. Are they a conservative, business-executive group? Shouldn't your newsletter reflect that conservatism? Are they an artistic, easygoing audience? Shouldn't your newsletter appeal to their sense of freedom of expression? In fact, your newsletter has to appeal to your readers' sense of what is correct for them—both in the information you provide, and in the packaging in which you provide that information.

Take a look at Exhibit 8.4 for some of the essential elements of a newsletter front page. While there isn't time or space to cover newsletter design in detail here, refer to Chapter 12 for more information on design and working with printers.

Style Sheets

In order to maintain consistency in your newsletter from issue to issue, you will need to develop a style sheet. A style sheet is a listing of all of the type specifications you use in your newsletter. It should be as complete as possible, and every member of your staff should have a copy. Style sheets are especially important if you are sick or on vacation and someone else has to produce an issue or two of your newsletter. It will tell them at a glance

EXHIBIT 8.4 A Newsletter Front Page

Some of the more important design elements of a typical newsletter front page are: (1) The banner, or name, of your newsletter. Make sure it neither overpowers your front page nor is overpowered by other elements on the page. (2) The headline. Typically, there should be only one major head on the front page. Make it large enough to draw attention but not so large as to overpower your banner. (3) Photos and illustrations. Don't scrimp on size. Draw attention to your stories with large photos and illustrations. Just make sure they are of a quality worthy of the attention. (4) Body copy. Flush left, ragged right if columns are wide (two or three columns), justified if narrow (four or more columns). (5) Table of contents. Don't assume it has to be boxed. Try an open format for a change. (6) Rules and boxes. Use them to delineate your columns or to set items apart.

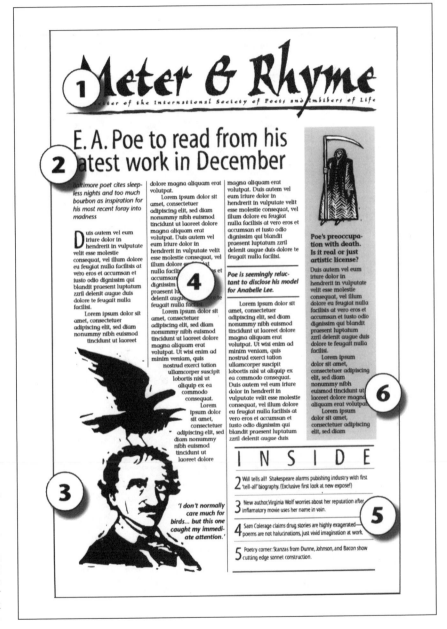

what it probably took you hours to determine when you first started. Exhibit 8.5 shows a typical style sheet. As you can see from this simple example, you'll have to make numerous design decisions as editor of your

EXHIBIT 8.5   Style Sheet

```
Style Sheet: On Line
Newsletter of the Public Relations Student Society of America,
University of Oregon Chapter

Page size—11 by 17 inches, one page, printed front and back,
vertical tabloid layout. Margins three-quarter inch on all
sides. Folded in thirds for mailing. Self-mailer on bottom
third of back page. 60 pound, white, semi-matte finish.

Grid—Five columns for normal text layout. Four or five columns
for boxed or feature items. One pica between columns with a
hairline rule.

Body text—10-point Times, auto leaded, flush left, first
indents one-quarter inch.

Captions—9-point Times italic, flush left, run width of photo,
1/2 pica beneath photo.

Lead article headline—24-point Optima bold, set solid,
reversed on 40 percent screen. Run full width of page (five
columns).

Two and three-column heads—18-point Optima bold, leaded 19,
flush left running width of article. Reversed on 40 percent
screen.

Pull quotes—14-point Optima italic, centered, one- to three-
column width as needed. Two-point line one pica above and one-
point line below as needed to fill space.

Masthead copy—9-point Optima, flush left, one-column width.

Ink color—Black ink run on preprinted blanks with banner in
PMS 4515.
```

own newsletter. The fun is in the experimenting. Don't give up until you have it the way you want it.

Magazines ━━━━

When we speak of magazines, most of us think of our favorite consumer publication (*Time, Newsweek, National Geographic,* the *Atlantic,* etc.). For our purposes, however, we are speaking primarily, but not exclusively, of the house publication. Recent research has shown that house publications are the least looked-to form of organizational communication. Guess what's first? Face-to-face communication. That's not surprising, but it doesn't mean that the house magazine is dead. What it does mean is that magazines should contribute to open communication rather than be relied upon as the sole source.

The house magazine plays another role as well: Unlike most print media an organization might have access to, the house publication is a totally controlled medium—that is, the organization producing it has sole editorial control. The company can go on record through its house organ, state its position on a controversial issue, or simply tell its story its way. In other words, the house organ is still a good public relations tool.

The typical house organ is meant for an internal public—usually employees, shareholders, and retirees. Sometimes, though, it is offered to the external public. A publication like *Weyerhaeuser Today* stresses a broader emphasis, with articles often dealing with the industry as a whole and subjects of interest to those outside the company. However, because the house organ is, at bottom, still a public relations piece, its thrust remains company oriented. Even a seemingly unrelated story will, in some way, eventually relate to the organization.

The house publication is usually in either magazine or newspaper format (or sometimes a magapaper). Both communicate with their various publics efficiently. Unless the company is large enough to produce a slick in-house publication, the house organ will be sent out to an agency for design and printing. Sometimes the agency will even provide writers to work up the stories; however, the best articles still come from writers inside the company who know and work with the people they write about.

Magazine Content and Format

Like its smaller cousin the newsletter, the house magazine usually presents the following editorial mix:

- 50 percent information about the organization—local, national, and international.
- 20 percent employee information—benefits, quality of working life, raises, etc.
- 20 percent relevant noncompany information—competitors, the community, etc.
- 10 percent small talk and personals.

How you organize these elements is important. You should lead your reader through your magazine in a logical order, and one that is pleasing and interesting.

There is no single organizational format for house magazines. What is important is that you find a place for all relevant information, a place inclusive enough to house similar information from issue to issue.

Before you even start (or if you're overhauling an existing publication), you need to set some objectives. To make sure your reasons for publishing a house magazine are realistic, ask yourself some questions:

- **Are my goals and objectives consistent with the goals and objectives of the organization itself?** What am I trying to get out of this? The temptation is very real, especially for creative people, to produce a magazine for simple ego gratification. Don't succumb to it. Have good, solid reasons for publishing.
- **Can I attain these objectives through another, more effective method?** Can I achieve good downward communication through an existing newsletter or more frequent meetings?
- **Can I attain these objectives in a more cost-effective way?** House magazines are expensive to produce. As usual, budget restrictions will have the final say.

Once you have answered these questions, and you have satisfied yourself that your prospective audience will benefit from your publication, you can decide on its proper organizational format.

Most house magazines contain very much the same type of editorial information as newsletters. The following items are listed in the approximate order in which they might appear (allowing for overlap in the case of articles):

- *Table of contents:* Usually run on the front page.
- *Masthead:* Gives publication information (editor, publisher, etc.) and is usually run on the table of contents or second page.
- *Editorial:* Can be in the form of a "President's Column," a signed editorial from management or the publication's editor.
- *Letters:* If the publication is designed for two-way communication, a letters column is a common addition.
- *News Notes:* A quick (and brief) look at what's happening around the organization. You can get a lot of these in two or three pages. This is a good place for employee information as well.
- *Articles:* News and feature articles make up the bulk of the magazine and should have a consistent order of their own. For instance, the cover story should always appear in the same approximate location each issue.
- *Announcements:* Usually boxed, but sometimes run as regular columns for job placement, promotions, etc. This is another good place for employee-interest pieces.
- *Calendar:* Upcoming events of interest to readers.

Remember: There are no hard-and-fast rules for formatting your magazine, but once you choose a method, stick to it. Your readers look for consistency. If the format changes every two issues, you'll lose them quickly.

Magazine Articles

House publication articles range from straight news to complete fiction, and include everything in between. Most, though, are either straight news or feature. A vast array of writing styles can justifiably be called "magazine writing." Articles or ideas for articles that don't seem to fit one particular magazine format, or even one section of a magazine, may well fit into another. For example, let's say you interview an employee on a job-related topic such as benefits. In the course of your conversation you discover that your interviewee builds model ships as a hobby and, in fact, has won several competitions. You actually gather enough information for a how-to article on building model ships as well as enough for a feature on the employee. Neither of these ideas may fit into the story you originally set out to do; however, they may fit into another section on employees or one on hobbies. The lesson, of course, is to never discard information just because it doesn't fit into your present assignment. Even if the tone or style of the article or information doesn't seem to fit one category, it may well fit another.

Articles for house publications tend to be shorter than those for consumer magazine articles or even trade journals (dealt with below). The average length of most house publications in magazine format is around 12 pages. Article length runs about 1,000 words or fewer for features (about four typed pages). Considering that magazine column width is about 14 picas for a three-column spread, and that articles are usually accompanied by photographs or artwork and headlines, subheads, and blurbs—a 750-word article may cover several pages.

Trade Journals

Trade journals are a valuable source of information for those who work within a specific industry. They provide news and stories dealing with the concerns and products of that industry. Trade journals accept product press releases readily and are an excellent target for placement. They usually have a section devoted specifically to new products and will normally place your release—edited of course—in this section.

For those desiring more attention, trade journals also accept articles written on products, concepts, and services of interest to their specific audiences (i.e., the industries they serve). These are normally submitted in the manner of any free-lance magazine article. First, you query the journal by letter explaining that you have an article idea, what it is, and why you think it might fit the journal's format and be of interest to its readership. If you receive a positive response, send the article, carefully following the journal's editorial style.

Trade journals, like consumer magazines, often have a sheet of "author's guidelines" explaining the journal's style, average article length, manuscript requirements, and so on. Follow these guidelines explicitly if you want to get published or get your client the publicity you were hired to provide.

The variety of trade journal articles is immense. They can range from feature-type articles using human interest, through straight news stories on products and services, to light fluff articles on travel and entertainment. In order to determine what style best fits your idea and their magazine, obtain a copy of the publication and read it thoroughly. Never submit an article to a magazine you haven't read.

Get a copy of one of the numerous "publicity checkers" that list all of the publications by industry. For my money, *Standard Rate and Data Service (SRDS)* provides the most comprehensive look at trade publications of any publicity checker on the market. Almost every industry has a trade journal, sometimes a number of them. For instance, there are trade journals for golf course groundskeepers, racetrack owners, thoroughbred breeders, paper manufacturers, supermarket owners, table waiters, bartenders, railroad workers, airline workers, and almost every other trade imaginable. One or more of these undoubtedly will fit your needs.

Feature Writing for Newsletters and Magazines

We saw in Chapter 5 that much of what public relations writers produce is in so-called "straight news" format, or inverted pyramid. This is always true of news releases and can be true of anything written that is deemed "straight news" as opposed to a "feature." So now you know what straight news is, but what is a feature?

A feature can be construed as almost anything that isn't straight news. In fact, *feature* has several meanings. As used in the term "feature story," it simply means the main story or cover story in the publication. In its broader sense, feature means an article that features something as its central point or theme. This "something" may not necessarily be the message of the story or its publicity angle. It is most often the story itself. For example, let's say you've been asked to do a story on a new product—a plastic underlining that can be used as a bed for soil or sod to keep it from eroding or slipping. Instead of doing a straight news story on the product itself, you opt to do a feature story on a user of the new product. Maybe you find a golf course that's using the new underliner to rebuild its greens and the focus of the story becomes the golf course. The publicity angle or the message about the new product becomes almost secondary. Featuring the golf course adds an extra dimension to your product story and sets it in context. In fact, the most useful element of the feature story approach is that it presents a context. Not every straight news story can do that.

EXHIBIT 8.6   Straight News Story

```
Newsletter
AMHCA story
Page 1 of 1

Counselors' Association "hires" PRSSA

    The American Mental Health Counselors Association (AMHCA),
a representative association for community counselors, has
hired the Public Relations Student Society of America (PRSSA)
to develop and implement a series of communication projects.
The projects began last spring when a committee of five PRSSA
members developed a public relations plan for AMHCA. The com-
prehensive plan is targeted at present and potential members.
The two main objectives of the plan are to strengthen AMHCA
as a membership organization and to create awareness of AMHCA
among its target audiences.
    After receiving approval for the plan from AMHCA board mem-
bers, PRSSA was asked to develop more specific projects. This
fall, a committee of eight PRSSA members worked on two pro-
jects. The first was to develop a logo and slogan for AMHCA
to be used on all informational materials. The logo, now fin-
ished, symbolically represents the safety and shelter of a
hearth, utilizing a stylized Hebrew symbol for home and well-
being. The second project involved redesigning an existing
AMHCA brochure. The committee developed a whole new layout and
cover design.
    The committee will also continue to develop projects for
winter and spring terms. The main project will be a series of
brochures for AMHCA. The brochures will range from informa-
tion on membership to information on mental health counsel-
ing. Other upcoming projects include writing a series of pub-
lic service announcements to be broadcast nationally for
Mental Health Week in March.
    "Overall, the project has been a great experience for all
of us involved," said committee chairperson, Wendy Wintrode.

                            -30-
```

Feature Style

Feature style usually is less objective and provides less hard information than straight news style. Features generally take a point of view or discuss issues, people, and places. The style is more relaxed, more descriptive, and often more creative than straight news style. Read over the straight news story in Exhibit 8.6. Next, look at the opening paragraphs of the feature story in Exhibit 8.7. This story is on the same topic as the straight news example, but the approach is extremely different.

EXHIBIT 8.7   Feature-style Article

```
AMHCA story
Page 1 of 1

Clearing Up the Confusion over Mental Health

    What's the difference between a therapist, psychologist,
psychotherapist, psychiatrist, and counselor? If you don't
know, you're among the millions of people who are confused
about the multi-tiered mental health counseling field.
    In an effort to clear up some of the confusion, the
American Mental Health Counselors Association (AMHCA) has
"hired" a university student group to produce a public infor-
mation campaign for them.
    The Public Relations Student Society of America (PRSSA) at
the University of Oregon has been retained by the association
to develop a program of information that will better define the
various roles contained under the umbrella term "mental health
counselor." Jane Weiskoff, regional director of AMHCA says that
the confusion seems to stem from a misconception over what con-
stitutes a "counselor." "In the mental health profession, there
is a perceived hierarchy," she says. "Psychiatrists are seen
as being at the apex of the field with psychologists, thera-
pists, and other counselors falling into place under them. We'd
like to clarify and possibly alter that perception."
    Part of the plan, which has already been produced and
approved, is to establish and maintain contact with current
AMHCA members through a series of brochures and an updated and
redesigned association newsletter. These informational pieces
will carry the message that mental health counselors come in
a variety of forms with a variety of educational and train-
ing backgrounds, and that each of these levels is suited to
certain types of counseling. . . .

    [For illustration purposes, part of the story has been
deleted here]

    If committee chairperson Wendy Wintrode has her way, the
term "mental health counseling" will soon have a completely
different, and definitely more expanded, definition. "We want
everyone to know that professionalism doesn't begin and end
with a small clique at the top—it is the guiding force behind
the entire field of mental health counseling."

                              -30-
```

Although the same facts are present in the feature story, the focus is on creative information presentation. The lead is a question (a typical delayed lead strategy). Answering that question becomes part of the story itself. Quotes are used liberally, and they not only validate and lend credibility to the subject discussed, they add human interest.

Human interest is a key characteristic of much feature writing. It can be simple inclusion of the human "voice" in a story, or it can be an entire profile, featuring a single person. Although the term *profile* usually refers to a feature story done on a person or on one aspect or issue relating to a person, individual companies or products may be profiled as well. (We'll talk more about profiles later in this chapter.)

The following is from a profile on a corporate legal department and its new head. Notice how the scene is set in the lead before the subject is introduced:

> Sitting behind a cluttered desk, boxes scattered around the office—some still unopened—is the new head of Associated Products Corporation's Law Department, Ed Bennett. Ed is a neat man, both in appearance and in speech. As he speaks about the "new" Law Department, he grins occasionally as though to say, "Why take the time to interview someone as unimportant as a lawyer?" That grin is deceiving because, to Ed and the other attorneys who work for Associated Products Corporation, law is serious business.

To add human interest is merely to add the human element to a story. Information without this element is only information. With it, information becomes more interesting, more personal, more attuned to readers' experiences. As a further example, consider the following lead:

> Somewhere north of Fairbanks, long after the highway disappears into the low growth and stubby trees, Seth Browner is stalking an elusive prey—his health. Seth is one of 20 hikers involved in the inaugural "hiking for health" program. Seth hopes the program will give him an opportunity to see the outdoors up close for the first time in his life and provide him with something he badly needs right now. Six months ago, Seth's doctor told him if he didn't exercise he would die.

And, if you're trying to reach people with your message—I mean really reach them—injecting human interest is often the best way to do it.

Writing the Feature Story

Feature stories, unlike straight news stories, must have a defiinite beginning (the *lead*), middle (the *body*), and end (the *ending*). Developing these elements takes patience, practice, and organization.

The Lead. Always start at the beginning. A good lead is the hook that entices the reader into reading the complete piece.

Your lead must tell the reader what the story is about. It is not necessary to cram everything into the lead; however, you must include enough information that the reader doesn't have to search for your topic. For straight news articles, the lead needs to come right to the point with the facts up front. For a feature, on the other hand, the delayed lead may be used. In this type of lead you create ambiance, then place your story within the environment you have created, but it must still come to the point before the end of the second paragraph. Consider the following delayed leads:

A Lead for a Horse Racing Trade

For some time now, the sound of heavy machinery has echoed through the rolling green countryside and heavily forested groves of Eastern Maryland. But that sound will soon be replaced by the sound of galloping horses as they take to the newly banked turns and straightaways at what is being billed as "the most innovative thoroughbred training and sports-medicine facility in North America."

A Lead for the Hospital Industry

The scene is a standard hospital room designed with fire safety in mind: a very low fuel load, floors of asbestos tile, walls of gypsum board on steel studs, and a ceiling of fiberglass panels. The hospital is built in accordance with the National Fire Protection Agency Life Safety Code and has received the Joint Commission on Accreditation of Healthcare Organization's maximum two-year approval.

Late in the evening, a patient accidentally ignites the contents of his trash can, which in turn ignite the bedclothes and, eventually, the mattress. The ensuing fire is a disaster, and despite the correct operation of all fire systems, multiple fatalities occur and the entire hospital wing is a total loss. Why? There are no fire standards on the upholstered furniture in this hospital, and the mattresses meet a federal code designed to retard fires from smoldering cigarettes, not from open flames.

A Lead for a New Product Aimed at Highway Engineers

You're traveling along at high speed, the familiar "clackety-clack" of the rails beneath your feet. But wait a minute. You're not on a train, you're in an automobile, and that familiar sound beneath your feet is the result of deteriorating pavement joints that have been repaired with the usual "hot pour" method.

A Lead for an Article for Golf Course Superintendents

Valleyview Country Club had a problem—the twelfth hole was sinking again. For almost 40 years, the facilities people at Valleyview had been rebuilding the green. In fact, it had been rebuilt three times over that period of time, but each time with the same results—in a matter of a few years the green would begin to sag again. This time, it was almost bowl-shaped and was acting as a funnel for rainwater draining from its outer edges into its concave center.

Although you may not have guessed it, all of these leads come from articles announcing new products or new applications for established products. Remember, even the most mundane subject can benefit from a creative treatment. Your readers will read your story only if they like your lead.

Other techniques for beginning your story include leading with a quote and placing it in context, or using metaphor, simile, analogy, anecdote, and other interest-getting devices. Although most of us forgot these literary tools the minute we left freshman composition, we shouldn't assume that good writing can get along without them. Look over the following literary uses of metaphor, simile, and analogy and then compare them with the feature article leads that follow them:

- A *metaphor* says that one thing is another:

  Cauliflower is nothing but a cabbage with a college education. (Mark Twain)

  Tree you are,
  Moss you are,
  You are violets with wind above them. (Ezra Pound)

- A *simile* says that one thing is *like* another:

  Though I must go, endure not yet
  A breach, but an expansion,
  Like gold to airy thinness beat. (John Donne)

  In time of peril like the needle to the lodestone, obedience, irrespective of rank, generally flies to him who is best fitted to command. (Herman Melville)

- An *analogy* makes hard-to-understand ideas easier to grasp by placing them in context, or, as in the following example, by making a point of view more understandable through humor:

  Soap and education are not as sudden as a massacre, but they are more deadly in the long run. (Mark Twain)

The following leads show that even the most mundane subject is of interest to someone and deserves the most interesting treatment possible. Pay particular attention to the number of scene-setting or descriptive words used in these leads.

Leading with a Quote

"Steelhead trout are an elitist fish; they're scarce, big, beautiful and they're good fighters," says Bob Hooton, Fish and Wildlife biologist responsible for steelhead on Vancouver Island. (*Salmonid*, newsletter of the Canadian Dept. of Fisheries and Oceans)

Leading with an Anecdote

If past experience is an indication, the telephones at our Client Services Center in Laurel, Maryland, will rarely stop ringing on December 16. That day the Center begins accepting calls for appointments to review diaries from the Fall radio survey. (*Beyond the Ratings*, national newsletter of Arbitron)

April 1 marks the beginning of a new era in banking—and a new dawn of satellite communications. On that day a clerk in Citicorp's Long Island, NY, office will make history by picking up the phone and dialing a Citicorp office in California. (*Telecommunications Week*, national newsletter published by Business Research Publications, Inc.)

Leading with an Analogy

You've heard the adage "two heads are better than one." What about 40? The Division's plants, more than 40 of them, are "putting their heads together" in the form of a division-wide information-sharing project recently released. (*Action Connection*, employee newsletter of Weyerhaeuser Packaging Division)

Setting the Scene

It's 5:30 on a Monday afternoon and you've just finished one of those days. Not only did the never-ending pile of work on your desk cease to go away, but you just received two additional "A" priority assignments. On top of that, the phones wouldn't stop ringing and the air conditioning wouldn't start working, even though the temperature hit 95. (*Spectra*, employee newsletter of the SAIF Corporation)

It's pretty quiet at Merwin Dam in southwest Washington. Two generators are running. The water level is down a little so folks along the reservoir can repair some docks while the weather stays nice.

For the 21 people working at the dam, it's business as usual. But, there is a subtle change. There's no longer a threat hanging over their heads that Pacific might not own or operate the dam. The court case that could have forced Pacific to give it up was finally resolved at the end of February. (*Pacific Power Bulletin*, employee newsletter of Pacific Power)

Leading with a Metaphor/Simile

Recession fears faded like presidential candidates this spring. Markets were jolted by the February employment release, which showed an increase in employment of over 500,000. . . . The mood has gone full circle as there is renewed focus on the strength of the economy with its

5.4 percent unemployment rate, and the whiff of higher inflation in the air. (*Northwest Business Barometer,* a quarterly economic review for customers from U.S. Bank)

The Body. Once the lead is conceived and written, the story must elaborate on it. If possible, make points one by one, explaining each as you go. Get the who, what, when, where, why, and how down in the most interesting way possible—but get to the point early.

The body of the article must support your main point, preferably already made in the lead, and elaborate on it. It should contain all the information your reader needs to understand what you are trying to say. Obviously, it's in your best interest to present your ideas clearly. Working from an outline is the best way to ensure that you have covered all of your key points in a logical order. (Several methods for organizing an outline are presented in Chapter 15.)

You should anticipate questions your reader might have, and answer them satisfactorily. Remember to utilize logical transitional devices when moving from one point to another. Subheads, although helpful to the reader, don't alleviate the need for thoughtful transitions. Back up your statements with facts and support all generalizations with specifics. Although magazine and newsletter feature stories seldom use footnotes, they are not completely inappropriate. Usually, however, citation can be taken care of in the body of the text. If, however, you are quoting someone, be sure to use attribution (see Chapter 5). Don't just give the person's name. A person's title or job may lend your quote authority if that person is considered knowledgeable or an expert on your subject.

In a feature, cover the news angle in a more people-oriented way. Paint word pictures to help readers hear, smell, and feel the story. If your story has a possible human-interest angle, use it. It helps your readers relate to the message through other human beings. Above all, don't be afraid to experiment with different approaches to the same topic. Try a straight news approach, then a human-interest angle or maybe a dramatic dialogue. The two articles in Exhibits 8.8 and 8.9 reflect two different approaches to the same story. Exhibit 8.9 is, in fact, a sustained analogy. In the longer article in Exhibit 8.10, notice the organizational concept and transitional devices that move the article from point to point, and the contributions of the lead and ending.

Whatever approach you use, try to make your story specific to your audience. Remember, they are major players in your scripts, in reality or vicariously.

The Ending. The most powerful and most remembered parts of your article will be the beginning and the end. Good endings are as difficult to write as good beginnings. However, there are only a few ways to wrap up an article and bring your readers to closure (a sense that they are sat-

EXHIBIT 8.8   Feature Story, Version A

<u>Three Reasons to Use Business Plans—Besides Raising Money</u>

Home-based businesses need business plans, and Tim Berry knows why. Berry, an internationally known business planning expert and principal author of Business Plan Pro™ business-planning software, says that business plans do more than raise money.

"People mistakenly think business plans are just for bankers or venture capitalists, but they are just as important for home-based entrepreneurs," Berry says. "If you are running a business or thinking about starting one, then you need a business plan."

Berry names three key benefits of creating a business plan:

- Knowledge of the market, potential sales, potential costs and expenses, and monthly cash flow.
- Commitment to actions that will lead to success.
- Communication with vendors, allies, and banks.

"The most important benefit is knowing what you're risking," Berry believes. A monthly cashflow statement helps you understand how much money you need and how much you might lose. For example, a hypothetical home-based mail-order business that is supposed to sell $2,500 per month could easily spend $7,500 on expenses and goods. That same business could also lose $15,000 or more by waiting two months for sales. The business plan for a home-based business should always include a month-by-month cash plan, which tracks where the money is going and how much is needed. "Unless you take the time to do the monthly analysis in a business plan," says Berry, "you won't realize what's at stake."

A business plan also provides better organization of the business and allows managers to focus on priorities. Properly developed, the plan provides an overview while organizing the details. A mail-order business whose objective is increasing sales must first focus on the product, then the mailer and the mailing list, and finally the system for answering calls.

                            -more-

---

isfactorily finished): summarize your main points (*summary ending*), refer back to the beginning in some *way* (*referral ending*), or call for action (*response ending*), although this last method is rarely used in feature article writing. Consider the following leads with their respective endings:

- Posing a question in the lead/summary ending:

```
    Berry points out that a well-developed plan can make a
home-based business look good to vendors, allies, and banks.
It can sway a vendor in deciding to grant distribution rights
to the business, enable companies to establish alliances with
related businesses, and help the graphic designer or Internet
consultant understand the company's needs. It can also assist
when a business seeks a merchant account or a line of cred-
it.
    "Always remember," says Berry, "that your home-based busi-
ness is supposed to be a business, not a hobby. Plan it like
a business and you'll get the benefits of being in business."

                          -30-
```

Lead

Name the oldest civilization in North America. If your anthropological information is such that you pinpointed the Aleut peoples of Alaska, you are both well informed and correct.

Ending

"Intellect and knowledge, technical skills, helpfulness, and concern for the truth are still the hallmarks of Aleut culture," observes

EXHIBIT 8.9   Feature Story, Version B

<u>Build Business Plan with Bricks for Solid Home-Based Success</u>

Just like the pigs' houses in "The Three Little Pigs," business plans will get blown down if they aren't built right. "The best business plans are built of three types of solid bricks: specificity, realism, and simplicity. Otherwise, they fall down," says Tim Berry, internationally known planning expert and principal author of Business Plan Pro™, a leading business-planning software.

The big bad wolf is the real world. It gets in the way of completing and using a plan, according to Berry. The best way to succeed in a home-based business is to build a brick foundation and maintain the plan's structure with follow-up.

Start with specifics. Does the plan set concrete, measurable objectives? For example, a specific percent sales increase or gross margin is measurable; statements like "being the best" or "optimizing customer satisfaction" are not measurable. Fill your plan with names and dates. Every business activity needs a person in charge whose work depends on the activity's success or failure. Assign real responsibilities to real people, attaching names, deadline dates, and budgets for later follow-up. "Even if you're a one-person business," Berry stresses, "assign tasks so you can track yourself."

The second brick is realism. Are the forecasts and expenses realistic? A company that has steadily sold $50,000 per year and is growing at 10 percent per year should not expect to sell $200,000 next year. When business plans are based on common sense, the results can be tracked. Also, no one will feel obligated to achieve the objectives if they seem unattainable. To develop objectives, check with similar businesses of the same type or look at the company's past results.

The third brick is simplicity. "This is a business plan, not a doctoral thesis," explains Berry. "Don't show off." A simple plan can be grasped immediately and is easy to track and update. Stick to the main points, explain them simply, and summarize well.

When a plan is built with the right bricks, the business is off to a good start. But Berry cautions plan writers to revisit the plan every month. "Compare your planned results to the actual results and follow up on any changes. Make revisions as needed and continue to manage." "What you want in the end," Berry says, "is results, not just a plan. Your brick foundation will get you there."

-30-

Connecticut anthropologist Laughlin. Such virtues are valuable assets, ever more useful as the 21st century approaches, and the bedrock on which the best that is Aleut may find permanence and continuity. (Richard C. Davids for *Exxon USA*)

- Setting the scene in the lead/referral ending:

EXHIBIT 8.10 Feature Story: APC's Answer Man

The lead paragraph incorporates many of the basic elements of a news-type lead, including who, what, where, and how. It also delays the discovery of the topic until the second sentence by setting the scene first.

The second paragraph is the "bridge" from the lead to the body of the story. It begins with one factual statement and ends with another.

Paragraphs 3 through 6 follow a sort of chronological order based on the construction of the new building, and provide background information.

APC's Answer Man

You might have noticed, if you've been in the new headquarters building at Associated Products Corporation long, a rather harried figure dashing madly up and down the halls. That man with the worried expression is Dave Martin. Dave, in a sense, is the ombudsman for APC's new building. He's the man who fields all the complaints, large and small, that have to do with everything from desk positioning to major malfunctions.

Dave's official title reads: Manager, Headquarters Facilities and Services. This constitutes a promotion for Dave, who was Manager, Technical Services. It also constitutes quite a lot of "heartburn."

The job was almost a matter of evolution for Dave, who became associated with the project through working with Bob Allen, Project Manager for the new building. Dave continually found himself involved with planning of space allocation, since this was a natural carryover from his former job. He cites the speed at which the building was completed as one of the major factors for his almost sudden immersion in the project.

An undertaking of this magnitude usually takes years to complete. The space layout itself, which usually takes six to eight months, took only six to eight weeks. Dave and the planners worked night and day setting up seating arrangements for each department. These arrangements had been approved by each department weeks before but had to be thoroughly scrutinized by the architects and planners before implementation.

Dave realizes, of course, that not everyone is going to be completely happy with his or her particular arrangement, but no major changes can be made until after the first of the year. There are several reasons for this. "The move itself will take up to 60 days to complete," says Dave, "during which time furniture will constantly be arriving." According to Dave, each piece has been designated for a particular spot in the new building, and last-minute changes would only serve to further confuse what will doubtless be a confusing move as it is.

Telephones have already been assigned to particular individuals and can't be moved, and the special ambient lighting fixtures built into the desks provide light for a specific

-more-

Lead

For one emotion-filled moment on July 28, when the Olympic torch is lit atop the Los Angeles Memorial Coliseum, this sprawling California city will be transformed into an arena of challenges and champions. But that magic event, shared with two billion television viewers around the world, will mark more than the beginning of the XXIII Summer Olympic Games.

grouping of furniture. Moving a desk would mean disrupting the lighting scheme for a particular area, which would affect more than just one person. All of these factors lead Dave to stress acceptance of the new floor plan, at least for the time being. According to Dave, psychological adjustment to new surroundings normally takes about 30 days. A great number of complaints handled prior to that time are likely to be adjustment oriented. Those are the complaints he would like to avoid initially.

Dave's new position will have him on the fourth floor as part of the Industrial Relations Department, where he will be in charge of the expanded reproduction facilities as well as Office Services, which handles supplies, PBX operation, mail service, and messenger service.

Dave is going to be monitoring almost every aspect of the new building. He will handle the janitorial contract, the plant contract (yes, Virginia, there will be greenery inside too), and snow removal. As Dave says, "If the building has a problem during the day, I'll hear about it first." Dave's only concern right now is that he will receive too many complaint calls like, "I don't want to sit next to Joe," or, "I can't see the window from here." With all of the major problems involved in a move of this magnitude (by the way, he's also in charge of getting everybody into the building), Dave doesn't need to hear the "personal" problems each employee is bound to have.

So, if you see this man with the harried look in his eyes rushing around the halls of APC's new headquarters building, have a heart. Remember that Dave, like a modern-day Atlas, bears the weight of six floors on his shoulders. Just say "Hi," give him a smile, and learn to live with your new desk for a while.

-30-

Paragraphs 7 and 8 come back to the subject (focusing on the human angle) and expand on position and point of view.

The closing paragraph refers to the opening paragraph as a technique for gaining closure.

Ending

For GTE employees worldwide, perhaps some of that special thrill can be shared by just watching the Games on television, and knowing that whenever gymnastics, fencing, water polo, volleyball, yachting, or tennis are televised, those images and sounds will have passed through the hands of 425 fellow employees—GTE's Team at the Olympics. (Bill Ferree for *GTE Together*)

- An anecdotal lead/summary and referral ending:

Lead

In 1737, Benjamin Franklin wrote in the *Pennsylvania Gazette* of an auroral display so red and vivid that some people thought it was a fire and ran to help put it out.

Ending

Although the effects of auroral activity on the lower levels of the earth's atmosphere are more apparent, the effects on the upper atmosphere are not, and we are only now beginning to understand them. With more understanding, we may eventually view the aurora with a more scientific eye, but until that day comes, it still remains the greatest light show on earth. (Tom Bivins for *National Bank of Alaska Interbranch*)

Common Types of Features

Although several standard types of feature articles are appropriate for magazines and newsletters, the most common is the **profile.** The profile is most typically a feature story written specifically about a person, a product or service, or an organization or some part of it. It literally profiles the subject, listing facts, highlighting points of interest, and—most important—tying them to the organization. Regardless of the subject of your article, you are writing for a specific organization, and the article must have some bearing on it—direct or indirect.

The Personality Profile. *Personality profiles* are popular because people like to read about other people, whether these people are just like them (so they can easily relate) or very different (so they can aspire or admire). Of course, a personality profile should do more than just satisfy human curiosity; it should inform the reader of something important about the organization itself by putting it in the context of a biographical sketch. For example, this lead was written for a brief profile on an award-winning engineer:

> When Francis Langly receives the Goodyear Medal this spring, it will represent the symbolic crowning of a lifetime of dedication to the field of chemistry. Awarded by the Rubber Division of the American Chemical Society, the Goodyear Medal is the premier award for work in the field of specialty elastomers—an area that Langly helped pioneer. When Langly makes his medalist's address to the gathering in Indianapolis in May, his comments will be a reflection of almost 50 years of innovation and development, which began in 1938 when he joined Rogers Experimental Plastics Company as a research chemist.

What does this profile say about the organization? It implies, for one thing, that the company is obviously a good one to have such a well-respected person work for it for so long. A profile like this calls attention to the merits of the organization by calling attention to someone who has something to do with it—or, in some cases, to someone who benefits from its services or products. Consider the following lead:

> Guy Exton is a superb artist. His oils have hung in galleries all over the country. But, for nearly five years, he couldn't paint anything. In order to paint, you typically need fingers and a hand, and Guy lost his right hand in an auto accident in 1983. But now, thanks to a revolutionary new elastomer product developed by Rogers Experimental Plastics Company (REP), Guy is painting again. He can grip even the smallest of his paintbrushes and control the tiniest nuance through the use of a special prosthetic device designed by Medical Help, Inc., of Franklin, New York. The device, which uses REP's "Elastoflex" membrane as a flexible covering, provides minute control of digits through an electromechanical power pack embedded in the wrist.

One of the most common types of personality profiles is the *Q & A (question and answer) format.* This style typically begins with a brief biographical sketch of the person being interviewed, hints at the reason for the interview, and sets the scene by describing the surroundings in which the interview took place. For the remainder of the piece, speakers are tagged *Q* or *A.* Sometimes the interviewer is designated with the publication's name (for example, *The Corporate Connection* might be shortened to *CC*). Likewise, the interviewee might be designated by his or her last name.

The *descriptive narrative* tells the story of the individual being profiled from a second-person point of view. Naturally, quotes from the subject may be included, but sometimes a successful profile is simply a biographical sketch and won't necessarily need them. The profile in Exhibit 8.11 is a mixture. Although there are some brief quotes, most of the profile is simple biography.

The Product or Service Profile. A *product* or *service profile* describes it in a way that is unusual in order to draw attention to the product and the organization. This is often done in subtle ways. For example, the personality profile on the artist Guy Exton is really a way of mentioning a product. Clearly this doesn't detract from the human-interest angle, but it does accomplish a second purpose (probably the primary purpose), which is publicity. The same techniques you use in other article types can be used in profiling products.

The Organizational Profile. In the *organizational profile,* an entire organization or some part of it is profiled. The organizational profile and the personality profile are accomplished in much the same way, except that you need to interview a number of key people in the unit you are profiling in order to obtain a complete picture of that unit. The profile in Exhibit 8.12 looks at a department within a large corporation.

EXHIBIT 8.11 Personality Profile

A Lifetime of Service

When Francis Langly receives the Goodyear Medal this
spring, it will represent the symbolic crowning of a lifetime
of dedication to the field of chemistry. Awarded by the Rubber
Division of the American Chemical Society, the Goodyear Medal
is the premier award for work in the field of specialty elastomers—an area that Langly helped pioneer. When Langly makes
his medalist's address to the gathering in Indianapolis in
May, his comments will be a reflection of almost 50 years of
innovation and development, which began in 1938 when he joined
Rogers Experimental Plastics Company as a research chemist.

Born in Brooklyn, New York, in 1915, Langly received his
BA in chemistry and his Ph.D. in organic chemistry from
Cornell in 1939. His first position at REPC was in the
Chemical Department at the Experimental Station near
Ravenswood, Vermont. At the outset of World War II, he was
working on the synthetic rubber program addressing the prob-
lem of an adhesive for nylon tire cord for B-29 bomber tires.
These studies eventually culminated in the development of the
vinyl pyridine adhesives so widely used today.

Langly's background in organic chemistry led to his transfer to the Organic Chemicals Department at the Johnson
Laboratory in Stillwater, Oklahoma, where he discovered the
first light-fast yellow dyes for cotton; and during the next
10 years, he led the task force that developed dyes for the
new synthetic fibers that were fast becoming a mainstay of
American fashion.

From his work in dyes, Langly moved on to work in fluorine
chemical research. The small research team he headed is credited with the discovery of a family of new elastomers. The
team at that time had what Langly calls "a very special business in fluorine chemicals," but no solid applications yet for
these quickly developing products. Langly and his group knew
that they had something distinctly different and new in the
field of elastomers. To an inventor, of course, the invention
comes first. It didn't seem to trouble him that there

-more-

Editorial Considerations for Display Copy

Display copy, from an editorial viewpoint, includes headlines, subheads,
captions, and pull quotes. Each of these elements has to be written for best
effect. Ideally, each should contribute to the article to which it refers by
adding to, elaborating or amplifying on, or drawing attention to information already presented in the article.

```
was little or no market at that time for these new products.
"There was no surprise in development," Langly says. "We
understood the properties of the products we were developing
and were sure that markets would eventually open up."

     Chief among these early fluorelastomers was Axon, a poly-
mer that could resist extremely high temperatures, toxic chem-
icals, and a broad range of fluids. Other products, however,
were gathering attention in industry and defense, and the com-
pany was eager to market these already-accepted materials. In
fact, the Axon project was sidetracked in the early 1950s when
it was thought that the Langly research team could be better
utilized in work on an already existing product. In a way,
this turned out to be a profitable diversion. Although the
proposed research turned out to be a dead end, a small pres-
sure reactor system that had been designed to build EP rub-
bers was converted to make fluoropolymer and used as a pilot
plant to produce Axon.

     According to Langly, "you rarely have a chance to fill a
vacuum with something entirely new." And Axon was entirely
new. The Air Force had been searching for some time for a
product that could withstand very low and very high tempera-
tures and was impervious to oil for use as engine seals on
jet aircraft. Axon fit the bill perfectly. The Air Force
quickly adopted it for use in jets, and the product went com-
mercial for the first time in 1959.

     When interest in space led the United States into the space
race in the late 1950s, Axon gained another and larger mar-
ket for use in rocket engine seals. Because of its ability to
seal against "hard" vacuum, Axon was one of the first rubbers
that could be used in space.

     As the markets for Axon continued to expand—to automotives,
industry, and oil exploration uses—Langly progressed through
a series of promotions. When the Elastomer Chemicals
Department was formed in the mid-1960s, he was transferred to
corporate headquarters in Freeport as Assistant Director of
Research and Development.

     Until his retirement in 1979, Langly continued to develop
his interest in the field of elastomers. To date, he has 35

                              -more-
```

Writing Headlines. Headlines for newsletters and magazines are similar; however, there are some exceptions. First, some definitional differences: A *headline*, strictly speaking, is for news stories, while a *title* is for features. For example, a headline for a news story on a new product might read like this:

New software will "revolutionize education" says APC president

Now, contrast that headline with the following title:

patents issued in his name and some 15 publications. In the 25 years since the birth of Axon, Langly has seen the product grow to its present status as the premium fluoroelastomer in the world with a new plant recently opened in Belgium providing the product for a hungry European market.

But Langly numbers the discovery and development of Axon as only one in a long line of accomplishments attained during his half-century of work in the field of chemistry. Since his retirement, he has remained active in the field, working in art conservation, developing new techniques for the preservation of rare oil paintings. In a year and a half of work with the City Museum in New York, he set up a sciences department for the conservation of paintings. He is currently scientific advisor for the Partham Museum in Baltimore. He continues to consult, working closely with industry. He gives expert testimony at court trials involving chemicals. And, he has given a speech before the United Nations on rubber.

Yet Langly remains low key about his accomplishments and his current interests. "I'm just trying to keep the fires going," he says. Despite this modesty, it is apparent to others that when Francis Langly receives the Goodyear Medal this year, it will represent not a capstone but simply another milestone in a lifetime of service.

-30-

Talking to the past—Learning about the future

The headline tells something about the story, so that even the casual reader can glean some information from reading it alone. The title, on the other hand, entices the reader or piques his or her interest. For purposes of the following discussion, however, I will use *headline* to indicate both types. To begin with, then, a basic rule for writing headlines is: *Use headlines for news articles and titles for feature articles.* And, as with all writing,

EXHIBIT 8.12   Organizational Profile

APC's Legal Department

Sitting behind a cluttered desk, boxes scattered around the office—some still unopened—is the new head of Associated Products Corporation's Law Department, Ed Bennett. Ed is a neat man, both in appearance and in speech. As he speaks about the "new" Law Department, he grins occasionally as though to say, "Why take the time to interview someone as unimportant as a lawyer?" That grin is deceiving because, to Ed and the other attorneys who work for Associated Products Corporation (APC), law is serious business.

Questions of law are rarely debated around APC. According to Ed, when something is not legal, it simply is not legal. No vote is taken by anyone; no decision needs to be arrived at. For this reason, "house counsel" (those attorneys who work for and in companies rather than for individuals) are often thought to be against all suggestions—paid to say no to projects or suggestions. This isn't so, says Ed. "It just so happens that a number of things that people wish to do must meet certain requirements. In most cases," he says, "it's not a question of 'you can't do it' but rather a matter of 'you have to do it this way.'"

According to Ed, this often puts the bearer of such news in an awkward position—much like the messenger who brings the Chinese emperor bad tidings and has his head cut off for his efforts. It is a lot better in Ed's mind to make the adjustments to a particular project now than to wait until they can no longer be made and find out that the entire project is unworkable.

In APC's Law Department, each attorney handles a specific area dealing with particular projects. Like many of the other departments in APC, Law is experiencing a period of transition. Consequently, specific areas of assignment are only tentative. Still, the four-man legal staff now employed by APC is specialized to the extent that each member has an area of expertise in which he or she works a majority of the time.

Dennis Silva, newly arrived at APC from work with the state, is involved primarily with local and state government

-more-

try to be clear. If your headline or title confuses the readers, they won't read on.

Remember, whether headline or title, it should grab the reader's attention and make him or her want to read the article. It should be informative and brief. Here are some guidelines that will help you in constructing good headlines:

matters. Gary Williams is involved primarily in contractual
matters, often between APC and other large companies. Keith
McGowan has been handling research and certain other issues
frequently dealing with the federal government.

Ed, just recently elected Vice President and General
Attorney, describes his role as that of a player-coach. Aside
from his specific responsibilities, he must also present the
legal overview of the company's actions and accept the consequences of his advice. "Along with responsibility comes
accountability," he says.

Ed, who has been with APC for nearly two years, was assis-
tant center judge advocate at Walter Reed Army Medical Center
prior to coming to APC. He received his Juris Doctor from the
University of Pennsylvania Law School and graduated from the
College of William and Mary. Ed also served as a judge advocate officer at the U.S. Army Headquarters, Fort Dix, New
Jersey, from 1982 to 1985.

Together with the three other attorneys, Ed helps comprise
a relatively small department. Despite its size, it may well
be one of the most important functions within the company.
"The myriad legal and regulatory requirements, particularly in
a business like this, create a jungle," Ed says. "It is impossible to get to the other shore of this particular river by
rowing in a straight line. There are crosscurrents and tides
with the wind blowing from a hundred different directions."

The metaphor may be mixed, but the point is clear.
According to Ed, the various state and federal regulations
governing our operations are by no means consistent. Neither,
frequently, are the goals of the company as expressed by the
input of each of the departments. Consequently, it is also the
responsibility of the Law Department to make uniform, or parallel, the various desires of the company.

"The end is always the same, though," says Ed. "It is not
to turn out neat legal briefs which, though often well
researched and executed, are not useful if a manager can neither understand nor conform to them. It is to strike a balance between our own professional conscience and the utili-
tarian nature of the work."

-more-

• **Keep them short.** Space is always a problem in any publication. Be
aware of column widths and how much space that sentence-long headline you are proposing will take up. Every column inch you devote to
your headline will have to be subtracted somewhere else. Headlines
don't have to be complete sentences, nor do they have to be punctuated unless they are complete sentences.

"Of course," says Ed, "we'd like to spend six months on each item, carefully researching it, but by then we have lost the element of timeliness, which is often equally important."

The people who make up the Law Department are, in the highest sense, professional. In fact, they have a professional responsibility quite separate from the company. Every attorney is a member of a bar association and thus has imposed upon him the Code of Professional Responsibility unique to his profession. "We are not exempted," says Ed, "simply because we are 'house counsel,' from the dictates of that code." Thus, their advice has to be correct, or as correct as it can be under prevailing circumstances. All of APC's attorneys are members of at least one bar and some are members of up to four.

The role of APC attorneys is similar to that of "outside" attorneys in that they represent the company in legal matters. But APC's Law Department does more than that. It not only represents the company when it gets into difficulty, but expends a great deal of time and effort in keeping the company out of difficulty. To that end, the house counsel of APC must maintain sufficient contact with the company, its people, and its activities in order that it may render timely advice and thus prevent difficulties.

In a way, the modern attorney is still much like his medieval predecessor, who, hired to represent his client on the field of combat, used every honorable device in his power to win. Perhaps the armor and shield have been replaced by the vested suit and briefcase, but the same keen edge that decided many a trial-by-combat is still very much apparent. Never draw down on attorneys. They are still excellent swordsmen.

-30-

- **Avoid vague words or phrases.** Your headline should contribute to the article, not detract from it. Cute or vague headlines that play on words should be left for entertainment publications like *Variety* (famous for its convoluted headlines). Don't use standing heads for recurring articles such as "President's Message" or "Employee Recognition." It is better to mention something of the article's content in the headline, such as "Packaging Division wins companywide contest."

- **Use short words.** A long word in a headline often has to be hyphenated or left on a line by itself. You can always come up with an alternative that is shorter.

Writing Subheads and Crossheads. Subheads are explanatory heads, usually set in a smaller type (or italics), that appear under the headline. For example:

> **ACME buyout impending**
> *Statewide Telecom makes takeover bid*

In most cases, a headline is sufficient; however, there are times when a rather lengthy subhead is necessary, especially if the headline is brief or cryptic, such as in the following example:

> **'A drama of national failure'**
> *A best-selling author talks about reporting on AIDS*

Subheads should be used sparingly, if at all, and only for clarity's sake. **Crossheads** are the smaller, transitional heads within an article. You shouldn't need them in a typical newsletter article. About the only time they might be useful is in a longer article—perhaps a newsletter devoted to a single subject or a magazine article (and, as we will see in Chapter 9, in brochures and flyers as well). Crossheads should be very short and should simply indicate a change in subject or direction. Most writers use crossheads in place of elaborate transitional devices. Space is always a consideration, and using a crosshead instead of a longer transitional device may save you several column inches.

If you do use crossheads, make sure that more than one is warranted. Like subpoints in an outline, crossheads don't come solo. Either delete a single crosshead, or include another one.

Writing Captions. Captions, or **cutlines,** are the informational blurbs that appear below or next to photographs or other illustrations. They are usually set in a smaller point size. Like headlines, they should contribute to the overall information of an article, not detract from it.

Keep captions brief. Make sure they relate directly to the photograph. (The best captions also add information that may not be included in the article itself.)

If your caption is necessarily long, make sure it is clear. If you are naming a number of people in a photo, for example, establish a recognizable order (clockwise from the top, right to left, from the top, from the left, etc.).

Captions, like headlines, should not be vague or cute. You simply don't have enough space to waste developing that groaner of a pun.

Writing Pull Quotes. Pull quotes are relatively new to newsletters. Traditionally a magazine device, they draw a reader's attention to a point within an article. They almost always appear close to the place in the article from which the quote is taken.

Pull quotes don't have to be actual quotes, but they should at least be an edited version of the article copy. Pull quotes usually suggest themselves. If you have a number of good quotes from an interviewee, you can always find a good one to use as a pull quote. Or, if you simply want to stress an important point in an article, use it as a pull quote.

Pull quotes are useful both as editorial and as design elements. Editorially, a pull quote draws attention to your article by highlighting an interesting quote. As a design element, a pull quote can create white space or fill up unused space left over from a short article. If, for instance, you have several inches left over on your page, simply add a pull quote to the middle of the article in the length you need to take up the extra space (see Exhibit 8.13). A good pull quote can be as long or as short as you want and still make sense. It can span several columns, be constrained to a single column, head the page, appear in the center of a copy-heavy page, or help balance some other graphic element on the page.

Remember: A good pull quote reflects the best your article has to offer; a mundane pull quote is wasted space.

Editing Your Articles ———————

Feature articles probably get—and deserve—the most editing of the various types of writing discussed in this book. Length has something to do with it, but more than that: It's the freewheeling attitude of some article writers (especially novices) that contributes the most to this need. Since many writers of basic company publications end up dealing with pretty dry topics, an assignment to do an article for the house magazine might be seen as an invitation to creativity. This usually leads, in turn, to a looser style, wordiness, and lack of organization. Whatever the reason, even the best-written article can benefit from intelligent editing.

A quick word here about the term *intelligent editing*: This implies that you are being edited by someone (or yourself, if you're doing the editing) who knows about writing—both grammar and style. Unfortunately, as many of us who have worked on in-house publications for years know, editors often are chosen because of their position within the organizational hierarchy (or the obligatory approval chain) and not for their literary talents. One of the best (if perhaps a little cynical) rules for dealing with "inexpert" editing is to ignore about 80 percent of it. You quickly get to recognize what is useful to you and what is not. Basically, editing that deals with content balance and accuracy is usable; most strictly "editorial" comment is not. A vice president's penchant for ellipses or a manager's predilection for using

EXHIBIT 8.13   Pull Quotes

Lorem ipsum,Dolor sit amet, consectetuer adipiscing elit, sed diam nonummy nibh euismod tincidunt ut laoreet dolore magna aliquam erat volutpat. Ut wisi enim ad minim veniam, quis nostrud exerci tation ullamcorper suscipit lobortis nisl ut aliquip ex ea commodo consequat.

"From the opening baton to the last, lingering note, this season will be a winner."

Duis autem vel eum iriure dolor in hendrerit in vulputate velit esse molestie consequat, vel illum dolore eu feugiat nulla facilisis at vero eros et accumsan et iusto odio dignissim qui blandit praesent luptatum zzril delenit augue duis dolore te feugait nulla facilisi.
Lorem ipsum dolor sit amet, consectetuer adipiscing elit, sed diam nonummy nibh

Lorem ipsum,Dolor sit amet, consectetuer adipiscing elit, sed diam nonummy nibh euismod tincidunt ut laoreet dolore magna aliquam erat volutpat. Ut wisi enim ad minim veniam, quis nostrud exerci tation ullamcorper suscipit lobortis nisl ut aliquip ex ea commodo consequat.

"From the opening baton to the last, lingering note, this season will be a winner."

Duis autem vel eum iriure dolor in hendrerit in vulputate velit esse molestie consequat, vel illum dolore eu feugiat nulla facilisis at vero eros et accumsan et iusto odio dignissim qui blandit praesent luptatum zzril delenit augue duis dolore te feugait nulla

Lorem ipsum,Dolor sit amet, consectetuer adipiscing elit, sed diam nonummy nibh euismod tincidunt ut laoreet dolore magna aliquam erat volutpat. Ut wisi enim ad minim veniam, quis nostrud exerci tation ullamcorper suscipit lobortis nisl ut aliquip ex ea commodo consequat.

"From the opening baton to the last, lingering note, this season will be a winner."

Duis autem vel eum iriure dolor in hendrerit in vulputate velit esse molestie consequat, vel illum dolore eu feugiat nulla facilisis at vero eros et

As a design element, a pull quote can be used to take up space on a page. The normal restrictions for trapped white space don't apply here as the increased white space can be used as a point of emphasis. Notice that the extra white space falls below the pull quote.

which instead of *that* are strictly stylistic preferences (and often ungrammatical). In many cases, even if you do ignore these obligatory edits, these same "editors" won't remember what they said when the final piece comes out. A guideline for most experienced writers is to try to avoid being edited by noneditors. If you can't, at least see how much you can safely ignore.

As for editing yourself, there are several methods for cutting a story that is too long, even if you don't think you can possibly do without a single word:

- Look at your beginning and end to see if they can be shortened. Often we write more than we need by way of introduction or closing when the real meat is in the body of the article.

- If you used a lot of quotes, cut the ones that are even remotely "fluff." Keep only those that contribute directly to the understanding of your story.

- Are there any general descriptions that, given later details, may be redundant? Cut them.
- Are there any details that are unnecessary given earlier general descriptions? Cut them. (Be careful not to cut both the general description and the details.)
- Are there any people who can be left out? For instance, will one expert and his or her comments be enough, or do you really need that second opinion?
- Finally, look for wordiness—instances in which you used more words than you needed. This type of editing hurts the most, because you might have struggled over that wording for an hour.

Your goal is to get the article into the size you need without losing its best parts or compromising your writing style. Exhibit 8.14 shows how some of these guidelines can be applied.

KEY TERMS

downward communication   subhead

upward communication   crosshead

style sheet   caption

feature style   cutline

profile   pull quote

EXERCISES

1. Bring into class two of the following six types of newsletters: association, community, institutional, publicity, special interest, or self-interest. Be prepared to discuss the subject, target audience, and "look" of your chosen newsletters.

2. Bring in what you consider to be one well-designed newsletter and one "ugly" newsletter. Be prepared to discuss why you like or dislike each of them.

3. Pick a straight news story from a newspaper. Write down what additional information you would need to know to make it a feature. Also, develop a feature lead for the story.

4. Bring in a house magazine for analysis. From reading the publication, determine its audience and purpose. Assess its strengths and weaknesses, both editorially and graphically.

5. Look through your local newspaper for any stories you think might have been generated by publicity. Bring in the stories and be prepared to talk about the publicity value of the story versus its news value to the publication in which it was printed.

EXHIBIT 8.14   Sample Edited Article

DGA Wins UL Certification

   The sign on the door reads "Grade 'A' UL Central Station."
To the people at Dallas General Alarm (DGA) and to the hundreds of businesses and homes they protect, this means the
availability of some of the best alarm and intrusion detection systems in the country. In fact, almost every improvement made at DGA over the past few years has had as its goal
the attainment of UL certification.

   In 1924, Underwriters Laboratories, Inc., began offering
a means of identifying burglar alarm systems that met acceptable minimum standards. The installing company can apply for
investigation of their services and, if found qualified, may
be issued UL certification.

   To the customer, this certification can mean a large reduc-
tion (sometimes up to 70 percent) in insurance premiums,
depending on the exact grade and extent of the UL-approved
service used.

   However, Dallas General Alarm doesn't sell only UL service.
"We sell and lease our systems on the merit of the system and
the particular need of the customer," says Dave Michaels,
Director of Quality Control for DGA. "Of course, those who do
have the UL Grade 'A' system installed can usually pay the
extra cost entailed with the savings they make on insurance
alone."

   What makes this Grade "A" system so effective that insurance companies charging sometimes thousands of dollars a year
in coverage are willing to cut 40, 60, or even 70 percent off
their premiums?

   "The UL people are really tight on their standards," says
Michaels. "They conduct a number of 'surprise' inspections of
DGA on a regular basis. If we fall down in any of their
requirements, we get our certification cancelled."

   DGA has its own tight security system consisting of television monitors on all doors and verbal contact with people
entering their offices. The central control room is always
manned and locked. A thick glass window allows the operators

                              -more-

The next four para-
graphs, although provid-
ing additional informa-
tion, can be cut without
loss to the overall information impact of the
story because they deal
with details we can get
along without. Given
enough space, however,
we would opt to leave the
story intact.

6. Visit an organization of your choosing (for-profit or not-for-profit)
    and ask about the trade publications the employees read on a reg-
    ular basis. Write a short paper outlining the organization, its prod-
    ucts or services, the names of the trade publications its employees
    read most often, and why you think these publications are impor-
    tant to the organization. If possible, obtain a copy of one of these
    publications to bring to class for discussion and analysis.

on duty to check personally all people entering the premises. Other UL requirements are extra fireproofing for the building itself and a buried cable containing the thousands of telephone lines used to monitor the various alarm systems that run out of the building. The cable is unmarked, preventing the adventurous burglar from cutting it and thus disabling the hundreds of systems served by DGA.

The 1,000-plus customers who either lease or buy alarm or detection systems from DGA range from some of the biggest businesses in Dallas to private residences. In addition, all of the schools in the Dallas area are monitored from the DGA central station against break-ins and vandalism.

The monitoring devices, located at the DGA central control, vary from a simple paper tape printout to actual voice communication with the premises being protected. For instance, the card-key system used by Atlantic Richfield Company allows access to certain areas through the use of a magnetic card inserted into a slot in the door. Access is forbidden to those lacking the proper clearance, and the number and times of the attempted accesses are printed out at the DGA central station.

By far the most impressive system is the Hyper Guard Sound System, which allows the central station operators actually to listen into a building or home once the system is activated. If the building is entered, the sound-sensitive system is activated, causing an alarm to go off at the DGA central station. By the use of microphones installed on the premises, the DGA operators can then determine the presence of an intruder. The owners, of course, sign in and out verbally when they open and close. Most of these customers also carry the special "holdup" feature of this system, which allows them to trigger, unnoticed, an alarm in the event of a robbery.

"We tried out a lot of other sound-activated systems," says Michaels, "but the 'Hyper Guard' made by Associated Products Corporation is the best I've ever seen." Michaels says that the Hyper Guard system is probably 20 times more

-more-

> Whatever you do, don't edit out the purpose for writing the article in the first place. In this case, it's mention of a product in the next two paragraphs.

7. Locate both a product profile and a personality profile. Outline each profile, noting how it is written and the order of presentation of facts. Include both the lead and the ending of the profiles as the first and last items on your outlines.

sensitive than most other brands DGA has tried. "And, in our business, sensitivity is a key component of a successful detection."

Once an alarm is received from any of the hundreds of points serviced by DGA, it is only a matter of seconds before security guards, police, ambulance, or fire department are notified and on their way. DGA maintains direct, no-dial lines to all of these agencies.

DGA currently contracts with Smith-Loomis, which dispatches two or three security guards to each of DGA's calls. "Our average response time is under four-and-a-half minutes," says Dave Michaels. "Of course, we often have to wait for the owner to show up to let us in." Michaels says that if DGA keeps a key to the premises, another 10 percent often can be taken off on insurance premiums because it allows a faster response time and a higher apprehension rate. "Recently, we got two apprehensions in three alarms at a local pharmacy," he says. "We roll on every suspicious alarm. UL only allows one opening and one closing time per business unless prearranged," says Michaels. "This way, we know exactly when there should be nobody on the premises."

DGA offers a number of different systems. Some respond to motion and some to sound. There are systems with silent alarms and systems with on-sight alarms fit to frighten the toughest intruder. DGA also handles smoke- and heat-detection systems. But, the key to a UL Grade "A" certified system, says Michaels, is the central control. "That's the added factor in a Grade 'A' system," he says. "We know immediately when something has occurred, and we respond."

Frank Collins, president of Southwestern Gemstones, Inc., has had his Grade "A" system since September. "I was robbed last year of over $400,000 worth of merchandise," he says, "and I was uninsured. That won't happen again." Collins is impressed with his system.

From his office in the Calais Building, Collins can watch everyone who enters his showroom via television monitor. A telephone allows visitors to identify themselves from outside

-more-

The next two paragraphs are a good example of an extra character who can be deleted without substantial loss to the story. Although this kind of testimony adds credibility to any story, in this case the story is about DGA, and their spokesperson actually provides the first-person credibility needed for the purpose—which is to get one of the products mentioned.

the front door before entry. The showroom has an impressive array of precious gems and gold and a great many antique art objects, frequently handmade turquoise and silver pieces. "I got the complete works," Collins says, "audio sensors, motion sensors, TV monitors, everything," resulting in a good-sized cut in his necessarily high insurance premiums.

For the many high-risk businesses served by Dallas General Alarm, the UL Grade "A" system seems to be the answer.

"We don't expect more than a couple of hundred customers for the UL system over the next few years," says Dave Michaels, "but that's all right. Our customers know their needs, and they know that they can't get a better system for the price." Collins smiles. "For the three or four dollars a day this system costs, they couldn't even afford a guard dog."

-30-

## CHAPTER 9

BROCHURES, FLYERS, AND PRINT ADVERTISING

In this chapter you will learn:

- How to plan, write, and design a brochure.

- How to plan, write, and design flyers and posters.

- How to plan, write, and design corporate print advertising.

It might seem odd to those already familiar with public relations writing that brochures, flyers, and print advertising are all included in one chapter; however, there is some method to my madness. All of these pieces are composed of nearly identical elements: *brief, sales-oriented copy* presented in *a limited space* with *heavy use of visuals*. Because of these similarities, and because they also share a common script format based on their similarities, I have chosen to address brochures, flyers, and print ads as a package.

Brochures

Like newsletters, brochures are often written and designed by the same person. This is not universally true, of course, but in many a nonprofit agency or small office a single person is put in charge of "making" a brochure. It is my belief that this particular medium unites design and copy in a unique and nearly inextricable way. The following discussion, therefore, includes a bit about brochure design as well as writing.

Most brochures are used to arouse interest, answer questions, and provide sources for further information. Even when used as part of a persuasive campaign, brochures are seldom persuasive in themselves; rather, they are support pieces or part of a larger media mix. Brochures can serve as stand-alone display-rack literature, as a component of a press kit, or as part of a direct-mail packet. The length of a brochure varies enormously, with the amount of information to be imparted being the key factor. Most brochure copy is abbreviated, however; longer copy is best suited to other formats such as booklets or pamphlets. Also be aware that odd-sized brochures will probably be more expensive to produce because printers will have to make special adjustments to their equipment to accommodate you.

Brochures usually are formed of a single sheet of paper folded one or more times. The folded brochure often is pocket-sized, but it doesn't have to be—part of the fun of designing a brochure is choosing its size and number of folds. Although writing for a brochure implies that you already know what size and shape the finished product will be, you can also write first and then determine the size and shape that fits your copy. As with any in-house publication, you can work it either way, fitting copy to design or design to copy. You should take the approach that works best for you, though you may need to cut costs by trimming your copy, or accommodate mandatory information by expanding it.

Planning Your Brochure

Before you begin to write, you need to plan your brochure and determine exactly what your message is and how it can best be presented. Who is your intended audience? Are you trying to inform or persuade? Is a brochure the best medium for your message? Your format and your style must match your audience's expectations and tastes.

Know Your Intended Audience. In addition to following the procedures discussed in Chapter 2 for knowing your intended audience, begin by assuming that your audience is seeking or processing an abbreviated amount of information. Most readers understand that brochures aren't intended to provide long, involved explanations.

There are three other audience-centered questions you should take into consideration before you begin writing for your brochure:

- **Is your audience specialized or general?** If your audience is specialized and familiar with your subject, you can use the trade language or jargon familiar to them, no matter how technical it might be. For example, in a brochure on a new chemical product (a copolyester, let's say) you can deal with durometer hardness, temperature-related attributes, resistance to pollutants and weather, and stress characteristics. None of these concepts should be new or surprising to a specialized audience of chemical engineers or designers who use polymers. On the other hand, if you are writing a brochure for a lay audience, you will have to deal in lay terms, or generalities.

  Here are two examples of a piece on an imaginary copolyester— one for a technical audience (engineers) and one for a less specialized audience (retailers of a manufactured product made from the raw product):

  Technical
  The results of laboratory testing indicate that AXON 11Æ polyester elastomer is resistant to a wide variety of fuels including leaded and unleaded gasoline, gasohol, kerosene, and diesel fuel. With a hardness range of 92A to 72D durometer, tests show the most fuel-resistant type of copolyester to be the 72D durometer, with the other family types also showing an impressive amount of fuel resistance.

  General
  AXON 11Æ polyester elastomer offers design potential plus for applications in a variety of industries. On the toughest jobs, AXON IIÆ is proving to be the design material of the future. Its unique properties and flexibility in processing make it applicable in areas previously dependent on a range of other, more expensive, products.

- **Are you persuading or informing?** If you are persuading your audience, you can use the standard persuasive techniques covered in Chapter 3, including emotional language, appeal to logic, and association of your idea with another familiar concept. As with print advertising, the tone of the brochure (whether persuasive or informative) is set in the introductory headline. For example, here are two cover titles or headlines from two brochures on graduate programs in journalism. The first is persuasive and the second informative:

Persuasive

Is one graduate program in journalism better than all the others? Yes.
The University of Northern Idaho.

Informative

Graduate studies in journalism at the University of Northern Idaho.

Regardless of your intent, the brochure copy should always be clear on what you expect of your audience. If you are trying to persuade, state what you want the reader to do—buy your product, invest in your stock, vote for your candidate, support your bond issue. Persuasion only works if people know what it is you want them to be persuaded about.

• **How will your audience be using your brochure?** Is the brochure intended to stimulate requests for information on a topic for which detailed information can be obtained in another form? Will it urge readers to send for more information? Is it meant to be saved as a constant reminder of your topic? Many health-oriented brochures, for example, provide information meant to be saved or even posted for reference, such as calorie charts, vitamin dosages, and nutrition information. If your brochure is designed to be read and discarded, don't waste a lot of money on printing. On the other hand, if you want it to be saved, not only should you make the information valuable enough to be saved, but also the look and feel of the brochure should say "don't throw me away." The same is true of any publication. Newspapers, by their inexpensive paper and rub-off ink, say "read me and then throw me away," while a magazine like *National Geographic* says "throw me away and you would be trashing a nice piece of work."

Determine Your Format. **Format** refers to the way you arrange your brochure—its organizational characteristics. As with everything else about brochures, format can go two ways: you can fit format to your writing or you can fit your writing to a predetermined format. For instance, if you are told to develop a Q & A (question and answer) brochure, you will have to fit both writing and design to this special format. On the other hand, if you are writing a persuasive piece, you might decide to go with a problem-solution format, spending two panels of a six-panel brochure on setting up the problem and three on describing the solution (the sixth panel is reserved for the cover).

Some organizational formats work well in brochures, some don't. Space organization (up to down, right to left, east to west), which can work well in book form or in magazine articles, doesn't seem to fit in a brochure. Neither does chronological organization. The reason for this may be the physical nature of the brochure itself. Magazine and book pages are turned, one after the other, and each page contains quite a lot of information. A brochure demands a more concentrated effort, one that is less natural than leafing through pages. Because each panel is limited in space, development has to take place in "chunks." Organizational formats that require continuous, linked development or constant referral to previous information aren't suited to brochures. The sole exception would be brochure points that are numbered, which, by definition, are sequential if not chronological.

More common formats for brochures include: question and answer or FAQ (frequently asked questions), problem-solution, and narrative (storytelling). Pick a format that is suited to your topic and then design your brochure to suit your format. Creative brochure design is part of the fun of working with this type of publication.

Position Your Brochure. Positioning refers to placing your piece in context as either part of some larger whole or as a standout from other pieces. Is your brochure to be used as part of a larger communication package (a press kit, for instance), or is it meant to be a stand-alone piece? If it is part of a larger package, then the information contained in the brochure can be keyed to information elsewhere in the package. If it is a stand-alone piece, it will need to be fairly complete—and probably longer. Knowing how your brochure fits into a larger communications program helps you to position it properly.

If your brochure is part of a larger program, you also need to be sure your writing style mimics the style of the overall package. Obviously, this doesn't mean that the brochure should read like a magazine because it is packaged with a magazine, but it should resemble the companion pieces as closely as possible. If the other pieces are formal, the brochure should be formal; if they are informal, the brochure should be also. The key is consistency.

Decide on Length. Succinctness is an art. Almost all writers are able to write long, but very few can write short without editing down from something originally longer. Your information will probably be edited a number of times to make it as spare and succinct as possible, because short copy is the ideal for brochures—for space limitations; in order to leave enough white space for aesthetic value; for type size considerations (for example, a brochure for senior citizens must utilize a fairly large typeface); or for cost considerations. Whatever the reason, you must learn to write short and edit mercilessly.

The brochure in Exhibit 9.1 builds a brief image of a new company and sets out both its needs and its benefits to the community of which it is becoming a part. While the copy itself looks brief in its laid-out form, it is actually longer than it looks due to the utilization of a relatively small type size.

The brochure in Exhibit 9.2 is not only larger in format but also contains a considerably greater amount of copy than that in Exhibit 9.1. The brochure in Exhibit 9.1 was not written to present a capsule image; rather, it was developed to answer, in some detail, a very important question concerning the effects of electromagnetic fields. Specialty, single-use brochures such as this are ideal for explaining hard-to-understand concepts.

The key to editing brochure copy is to realize exactly how much your reader needs to know about your subject. If you include too much in a piece designed merely to attract attention, you may lose your readers. On the other hand, if you don't provide enough basic information, you may never pique their interest. Although some edited elements may in fact influence the final decision-making process, they may not be important in the awareness stage of the adoption process. Once you have decided on the purpose of your brochure, writing and editing become a much easier job.

Fitting It All Together

Whether you write for a specific size or you fit the size to the amount of information you have (especially if your boss simply can't live without that detailed explanation of how beneficial your new widget is to Western technology), your copy will have to fit the unique characteristic of the brochure: the number of folds.

Brochures are designated by how many folds they have. A *two-fold*, a sheet with two creases, has six panels—three on one side and three on the other. A *three-fold* has eight panels, and so on. Each fold adds two or more new panels. Although some very interesting folds have been developed, the usual configuration consists of panels of equal size (see Exhibit 9.3).

Each panel in a brochure may stand alone—that is, present a complete idea or cover a single subject—or may be part of a larger context revealed as the panels unfold. Either way, in the well-designed brochure, careful attention is paid to the way the panels unfold to ensure that the information is presented in the proper order. Good brochures do not unfold like road maps, but rather present a logical pathway through their panels (see Exhibit 9.4).

Research indicates that the first thing a reader looks at in a direct mail package is the brochure. The last thing is the cover letter. Exactly how you present the brochure may determine whether it gets read or gets thrown away.

EXHIBIT 9.1   Brochure Copy for a Short Brochure

This brochure features eight panels. Panels 2, 3, 4, and 5 are the "inside" of the brochure and panels 6, 7, 8, and 1 (the cover) are the "outside."

(Continued)

(Continued)

Panel 2

Panel 3

Panel 4

Panel 5

EXHIBIT 9.2   Brochure Copy for a Longer Brochure

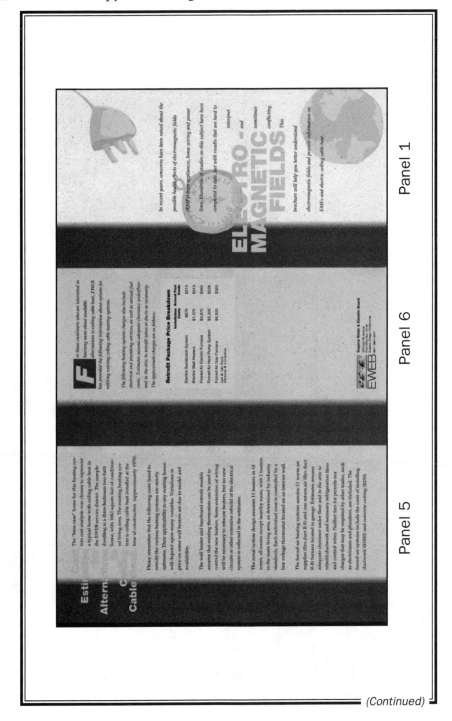

Panel 1

Panel 6

Panel 5

(Continued)

(Continued)

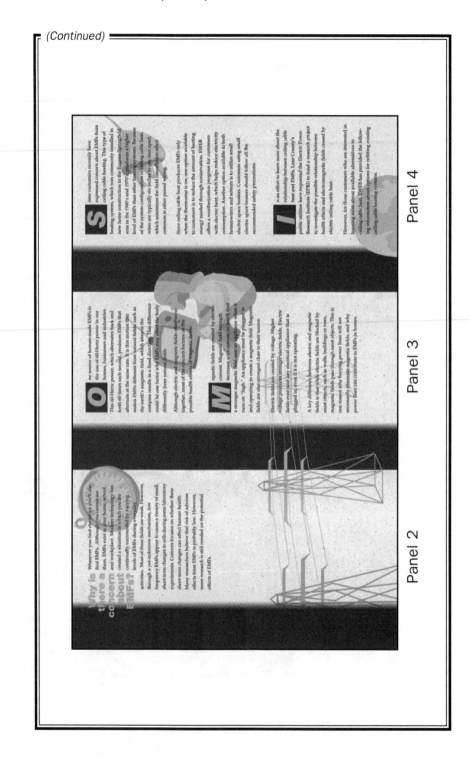

Panel 2

Panel 3

Panel 4

EXHIBIT 9.3   Typical Brochure Folds

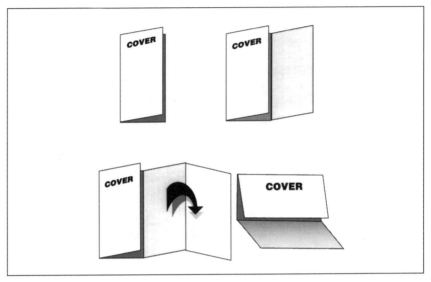

Order of Presentation. The first step is to establish where the front panel is and where the final panel is. The first panel, or front cover, need not contain any information, but it should serve as an eye-catcher that draws the reader inside. It should employ a *hook*—an intriguing question or statement, a beautiful photograph, an eye-catching graphic, or any other device that will get the casual peruser to pick up and read the complete brochure.

If you begin your printed matter on the front cover, the headline or title becomes very important. Most informational brochures use a title simply to tell what's inside. After all, most people looking for information don't want to wade through a lot of creative esoterica. A brochure headline should be to the point. Headlines that tell the reader nothing (called *blind headlines*) are of no use in a brochure. For example:

Reaching for the stars?

Is this headline for a product (maybe telescopes)? A service (astrology)?

In the Air Force, you can reach for the stars!

Now both the intent and the sponsor are clear. For the information-seeking reader, a blind headline might work; however, if you really want to be sure—and if you want to pick up the browser as well—avoid them.

The second panel, at least in a two-fold brochure, is the first panel of the inside spread. Its job is to build interest. The opening section should explain the purpose of the brochure and refer to the title or headline. This is the *bridge*. It is usually copy heavy and may contain a subhead or

EXHIBIT 9.4   Brochure Logic

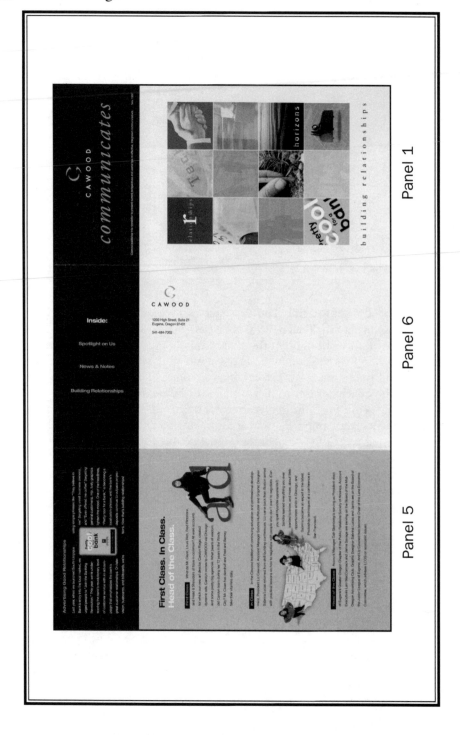

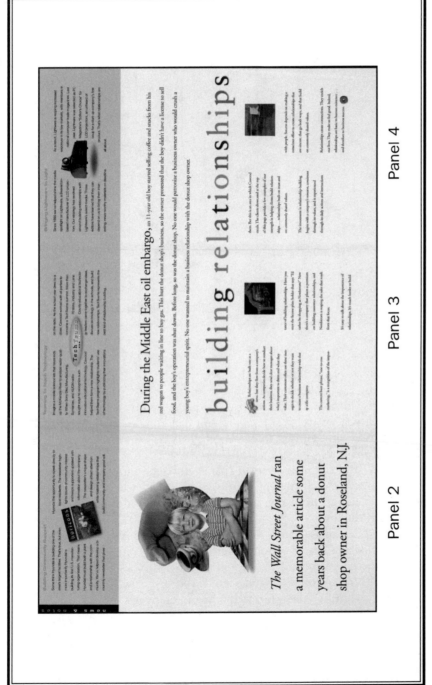

building relationships

During the Middle East oil embargo, an 11-year old boy started selling coffee and snacks from his red wagon to people waiting in line to buy gas. This hurt the donut shop's business, so the owner protested that the boy didn't have a license to sell food, and the boy's operation was shut down. Before long, so was the donut shop. No one would patronize a business owner who would crush a young boy's entrepreneurial spirit. No one wanted to maintain a business relationship with the donut shop owner.

The Wall Street Journal ran a memorable article some years back about a donut shop owner in Roseland, NJ.

Panel 2

Panel 3

Panel 4

EXHIBIT 9.5 Traditional Brochure Fold

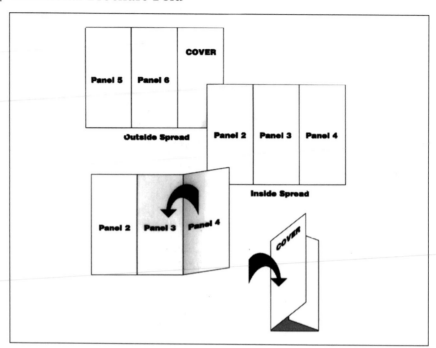

The standard two-fold folder places the cover on the far right panel of the outside spread. Panel five (inside panel four) folds in first. This traditional fold requires two "unfolds" to access the inside spread—the cover and panel five; however, panel five may or may not be intended as part of the inside spread. More often, it follows panels two through four, yet it appears as the first panel seen when the folder is opened.

crosshead (explained below). In fact, panels may be laid out around crossheads. But make sure the reader knows which panel follows which. Never let your copy run from panel to panel by breaking a sentence or a paragraph—or (worst of all) a word—in half. Try to treat each panel as a single entity with its own information. This isn't always possible, but it's nice to strive for.

The rest of the inside spread (panels three and four) carries the main load. It may be constructed to present a unified whole with words and graphics bleeding from one panel to the next, or the panels may retain their individuality.

The back panels (panels five and six) serve various purposes. Panel five may be used as a teaser or short blurb introducing the inside spread, or it may be incorporated into the design of panel two (especially useful since this panel is often folded in and seen as you open the front cover). It may also simply continue the information begun on panels two, three, and four. Panel six may be left blank for mailing or contain address information. It doesn't usually contain much else.

Most of us are used to seeing two-folds folded so that the far right panel (inside panel four and outside panel five) is folded in first with the far left panel (outside panel one and inside panel two) folded over it (see

EXHIBIT 9.6   Nontraditional Brochure Fold

The standard two-fold folder is redesigned here, placing the cover in the center of the outside panel. This allows panel two to fold inside. Outside panel two (inside panel three) folds inside, becoming the first copy panel seen when the folder is opened. Panel six folds over it to become the back (or mailer). This presents the center outside panel as the cover and sets up two "unfolds" to get to the inside spread; however, there is no doubt that panel two (even though it is folded inside) is the first panel to be read. This fold alleviates the "panel five" problem of the traditional fold.

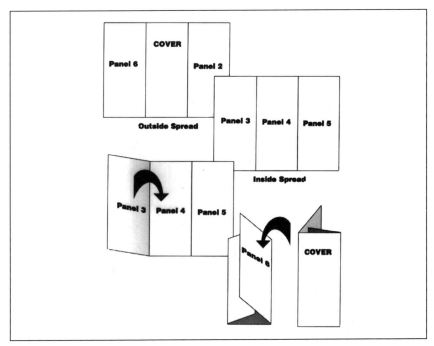

Exhibit 9.5). But this layout has always presented problems. For instance, what do you put on panel five? It is the first panel you see when you open the cover, yet it is technically on the back of the brochure. You can use it as a teaser, or simply as the informational panel that follows the inside spread. Or, you can experiment with the fold (see Exhibit 9.6). So much depends on the presentation of your information, and because they are folded, brochures are among the hardest collateral pieces to present properly. If readers are even slightly confused, you have lost them.

Crossheads. Crossheads, or subheads, should be used liberally in a brochure. They help break up copy and give your brochure a less formidable appearance. Studies have shown that copy formed into short paragraphs broken by informative crossheads gives the reader a feeling that he or she can read any section independently without being obligated to read the entire piece. Although in some instances this may be self-defeating, reading one pertinent paragraph is often better than reading none; and, if you run your copy together in one long, unbroken string, you're going to limit readership to a hardy few. Additionally, your brochure will look better with the increased white space crossheads can add, and white space encourages readership as well.

Copy Format. As you create your brochure, you may have to present the copy to others for approval. It helps to place it into a format that conveys the look of the finished product. The best way to show someone how a finished piece will look is to mock it up; however, copy often must be approved prior to any mock-up, so indicating headlines, visuals, and copy blocks in the order in which they appear is an important visual aspect of the brochure copy format. This type of format is like the script for a play, which traditionally describes visual action that takes place along with dialogue or monologue. Remember reading those Shakespearean plays in school?

> ACT I
> SCENE I   *Elsinore. A platform before the castle.*
>   [FRANCISCO *at his post. Enter to him* BERNARDO]
> BERNARDO   Who's there?
> FRANCISCO   Nay, answer me: stand, and unfold yourself.

This play script sets the scene, introduces the players, and indicates dialogue. Using a brochure "script" accomplishes much the same thing, as Exhibit 9.7 shows. Visuals (the scene) are described, and copy (dialogue) is indicated. If a visual change is indicated, it appears in the spot in which it would appear in the finished piece, with copy interrupted to account for the visual—much like a scene change is indicated in a script. Indicating headlines and visuals this way will help you to formalize your thoughts if you are doing the entire brochure yourself, and will enhance continuity between the writer and the designer if they are different people.

Producing a script is as far as most writers go; however, if you work for a small firm or nonprofit agency, you may be solely responsible for producing collateral pieces from writing to layout. Remember: You can write first and then develop a length and size to fit your editorial needs, or you can limit your copy to a preset design and size. Either way, you have to be aware of copyfitting requirements. Once you know how much you must write, stick to your guns. If you find that you have written more than will fit your original design concept, you can increase the number of folds and, thus, the number of available panels, or you can edit your copy to fit the original design.

If your supervisor isn't clamoring for every ounce of information you can provide in 93.5 square inches of space, stick with editing your copy. The best brochures are almost always the short ones.

Flyers ──────

Flyers are a quick way to disseminate information, even to large audiences, cheaply. A flyer is typically a single sheet of paper, usually letter-size, printed on one or both sides. A flyer is most often photocopied but is sometimes printed if slickness is important.

EXHIBIT 9.7   Brochure Copy Format

```
"Phone Fraud"
Three-fold folder
Attorney General

PANEL 1
HEADLINE:        WE THOUGHT YOU'D LIKE TO KNOW ABOUT (graphic
                 splits line here) PHONE FRAUD
VISUAL:          Stylized graphic of telephone
SUBHEAD:         A consumer guide to your rights and obliga-
                 tions when dealing with telephone sales


PANEL 2
SUBHEAD:         WHAT IS PHONE FRAUD?
COPY:            We've all been asked to purchase something or
                 donate to a cause over the phone.

                 Most of the people who contact us represent
                 legitimate firms that use the telephone to
                 sell quality goods and services or to raise
                 money for worthy causes.

                 However, there are companies that are involved
                 in telemarketing fraud. According to the
                 Federal Trade Commission, telemarketing fraud
                 is the use of telephone communications to pro-
                 mote goods or services fraudulently. And this
                 can cost you money!
VISUAL:          Cartoon drawing of telephone receiver
SUBHEAD:         WHAT ARE THEY TRYING TO SELL YOU?
COPY:            Fraudulent sales callers try to sell us every-
                 thing from vacations and time-share condomini-
                 ums to vitamins and magazine subscriptions.
                 They say they represent film clubs, vacation
                 resorts, charities, magazine and book clear-
                 inghouses, and even churches. Sometimes they
                 want money sent to them directly, or sometimes
                 they just want your credit card number.

                          -more-
```

Flyers can be folded, but this is most often done only for mailing purposes. Usually, they are distributed flat, because the most common form of flyer dissemination is still by hand. In fact, the term "flyer" refers to the rapidity with which they can be delivered—historically by children running through the streets handing them out.

Flyers are handed out on street corners, at entrances to events, and practically anywhere large numbers of people gather. Flyers are distributed in employee mailboxes and door-to-door. They are pinned on

```
                                (This is especially dangerous because they can
                                charge any amount they want with your number.)
        SUBHEAD:                WHAT DO THEY SAY TO YOU?
        COPY:                   Although  fraudulent  sales  callers  may  have
                                vastly different products or services to sell,
                                there  are  frequently  similarities  in  their
                                "pitches." These pitches often sound very pro-
                                fessional. Sometimes you are even transferred
                                from person to person to make it sounds more
                                like  a  business  setting.  Do  the  following
                                lines sound familiar?

                                • "You've been specially selected to hear
                                  this offer!" (How was the selection
                                  process made?)
                                • "You'll get a wonderful prize if you
                                  buy . . . ." (How much is this prize
                                  worth?)
                                • "You have to make up your might right
                                  away . . . ." (They make it seem like
                                  this is a now-or-never opportunity.)
                                • "It's free—you just have to pay the
                                  shipping and handling!" (If they get
                                  only $7.00 shipping and handling per
                                  person and can con 100 people into paying
                                  up front, they make $700!)
                                • "But first, I'll have to have your credit
                                  card number to verify . . . ." (To verify
                                  what and why?)

        PANEL 3
        SUBHEAD:                WHAT HAPPENS THEN?
        COPY:                   If it is a fraudulent sales call, you sometimes
                                actually  receive  the  merchandise—but  it  is
                                often  overpriced,  of  poor  quality,  or  a  cheap
                                imitation.


                                            -more-
```

bulletin boards and office doors. In short, flyers are one of the most useful—and one of the most ubiquitous—forms of information dissemination around.

Unlike brochures, good flyers are laid out like good print ads, or sometimes, depending on the amount of information needed, like a good newsletter page. But, like a brochure, the copy is written and the graphics designed to work together to bring the reader's attention directly to the message being imparted. The same script format is used, therefore, for flyers and posters as for print ads and brochures.

```
                    Or, if you've been asked to invest in some-
                    thing, it may turn out to be nonexistent.

                    Or, you find out the worthy cause you donated
                    to only got a tiny part of your actual dona-
                    tion while the caller got the bulk of it.

                    Or, unauthorized charges start appearing on
                    your credit card bills.

PANEL 4
SUBHEAD:            HOW CAN YOU PROTECT YOURSELF?
COPY:               1. First of all, always find out who is call-
                       ing and who they represent. Ask how they
                       got your name. Ask who is in charge of the
                       company or organization represented. Get
                       specific names and titles. Ask for the
                       address and telephone number of the firm
                       calling you. Be extremely cautious if the
                       caller won't provide that information.
                    2. Be cautious if the caller says an invest-
                       ment, purchase, or charitable donation
                       must be made immediately. Ask instead that
                       information be sent to you.
                    3. Be wary of offers for free merchandise or
                       prizes. You may end up paying handling
                       fees greater than the value of the gifts.
                       And don't ever buy something just to get a
                       free prize.
                    4. If you're interested in the offer, ask for
                       more information through the mail. Also
                       ask if it's possible to obtain the names
                       and numbers of satisfied customers in your
                       area.
                    5. If you're not interested in the offer,
                       interrupt the caller and say so. Remember,

                               -more-
```

Tips on Writing for Flyers

When writing for flyers, keep in mind how much information you need to impart versus how much space you have to work with. In most cases, you have a considerable amount of space—the same space as a standard brochure with none of the restrictions that panels impose. This leaves plenty of room for creativity.

If you have a lot to say, consider using a newsletter- or magazine-style approach to layout. Divide the page into columns and work within those borders with both words and graphics. Use subheads to break up the copy

```
                              part of the caller's job is to talk
                              without pause so you can't ask them
                              questions. Don't be afraid to interrupt.

         PANEL 5
         SUBHEAD:             WHAT DO YOU DO IF YOU'RE VICTIMIZED
         COPY:                Report the facts to:

                              Financial Fraud Section
                              Department of Justice
                              240 Cottage Street S.E.
                              Salem, Oregon 97210
         KICKER:              REMEMBER, YOU HAVE RIGHTS. DON'T BE VICTIM-
                              IZED BY TELEPHONE FRAUD!

         PANEL 6
         HEADLINE:            HOW TO RECOGNIZE PHONE FRAUD AND WHAT TO DO
                              ABOUT IT, FROM THE STATE OF OREGON ATTORNEY
                              GENERAL'S OFFICE

                                        -30-
```

and plenty of bulleted items for clarity. You might also mimic print-ad layout by using one of the common layouts mentioned later in this chapter.

Choose your graphics carefully and for full impact. Only the most striking graphics should appear on flyers, since you usually have only one shot to capture attention. Why? Because you are competing with dozens of other information pieces just like yours for attention.

If you have only a little to say (maybe an announcement of an event), then use full-impact language—as in advertising. Get readers' attention with a big headline and striking graphic. Make them pay attention to your copy, brief though it may be.

EXHIBIT 9.8   Poster and Flyer

Seen here is a one-shot poster produced for a special event. It was placed in a heavy traffic area for maximum exposure. Next to it is a simple black-and-white flyer, which was widely distributed.

The main selling points of a good flyer are its ease of production, the easy way it lends itself to creativity, and its relative inexpensiveness.

Flyers often can accompany posters as a cheaper support device. The example in Exhibit 9.8 shows a 34-by-22-inch poster and an accompanying flyer. Unless you have a lot of money to spend on full-color posters, you might try a single poster to grab attention and flyers to add the message repetition needed to keep attention going.

A Quick Word About Posters

The only real differences between posters and flyers are size and cost. While most flyers are "down and dirty" in terms of cost, posters are usually more costly for a number of reasons. First, they are larger—anywhere from 11 by 17 inches to several square feet in size. And, although some are in black and white, most posters are in color. The most common use for posters is announcements. They have historically heralded plays, movies, gallery openings, rallies, and other special events. They have called us to arms and called us to save the planet. Posters are incredibly useful communication devices; however, their prohibitive costs have usually limited their usefulness to public relations.

A resurgence of sorts began about 15 years ago with corporations realizing their use in the workplace to keep employee morale up. Since that time, posters have proliferated in some corporations and businesses (although by no means all). Their usefulness depends on the purpose to which they are being put. The most useful employee posters seem to be those designed with information in mind. Exhibit 9.9 shows two examples from a poster series developed to alert employees of educational benefits.

Advancements in computer-printing techniques have allowed even small-run posters (fewer than would be cost-effective using traditional printing techniques) to be produced. Exhibit 9.10 shows a 22-by-34-inch "one-shot" poster (only one was run) printed on a large-format ink-jet printer. It is full color and still cost only forty dollars to run. Traditional printing methods, such as offset printing, simply wouldn't allow for the printing of a single poster.

Print Advertising ━━━━━━

For writers, there can be no truer proving ground than the print ad. Aldous Huxley once remarked that trying, through words on paper, to sell something to someone who doesn't want to buy it is the hardest task a writer can set himself. The fact of the matter is, most print ads don't get read at all. Readers have a tendency to skip over ads that they find of no immediate interest. While television, and radio to an extent, play to "captive" audiences, not so a magazine or newspaper. Gone are the devices used by the electronic media to interest the reader. In print advertising, there are no catchy music scores or flashy moving images, no slick camera angles or intriguing sound effects—only the printed word and the overall effect of layout and design. Print advertising is not a waste of time, however; on the contrary, it offers the reader the luxury of perusing at leisure.

EXHIBIT 9.9   Informational Posters

This series of posters was designed to inform employees of special educational benefits for their children and themselves.

(Continued)

Put on your thinking cap

If you've got big ideas but a little savings account, you may want to contemplate a *ConSern* loan. Through an arrangement between Weyerhaeuser and the U.S. Chamber of Commerce, you can get from $1,500 to $25,000 per academic year at a low interest rate with no prepayment penalty. *ConSern* loans are unsecured (you don't need collateral) personal loans that can be used at accredited universities, colleges and secondary schools. *They are available to you and all your family members, and you can apply at any time.* All loans have a 15 year repayment plan and, for college, you may defer payment on the principal for up to 4 years. Interested? Talk to your HR manager or call *ConSern* directly at 1-800-767-5626. Look for more information in the September issue of *Benefacts*.

▲ Weyerhaeuser

EXHIBIT 9.10 One-Shot Poster

As such, print can be most effective as a vehicle for information too complex or lengthy for television or radio.

Public relations practitioners do not usually spend a great deal of time writing for product or service advertising; however, corporate America spends billions of dollars a year in advertising aimed not at selling products but at creating or enhancing image (known as **corporate advertising**). And this means that more and more PR writers are responsible for producing ad copy. There is also a trend in public relations toward a more complete integration with other communication functions. Marketing, advertising, and public relations all share common goals when it comes to the organization in which they work. Flexibility is the key. Being able to produce copy for corporate advertising is just another aspect of being a complete public relations writer.

Writing Print Advertisements

Corporate advertising falls into three basic categories: public interest, public image, and advocacy advertising.

- **Public interest advertising** usually provides information in the public interest such as health care, safety, and environmental interests. Magazine ads encouraging vaccinations for children that are "brought to you by" insurance companies are an example of this approach. Likewise, TV commercials for "heart-healthy" eating habits sponsored by Blue Cross/Blue Shield are corporate ads done in the public interest. Public interest advertising in the form of PSAs, or public service announcements, are typically placed for free if the sponsoring organization is a verifiable tax-exempt, not-for-profit agency. All other profit-making organizations must pay regular advertising rates.

- **Public image advertising** tries to sell the organization as caring about its employees, the environment, the community, and its customers. Unlike the public service ad, the public image ad always focuses on the company and how it relates to the subject. Ford Motor Company's "Quality is Job 1" series focused primarily on employees and not products. Phillip's *Petroleum* magazine ads on preserving wetlands is another example.

- **Advocacy advertising** presents a definite point of view. This may range from political to social, and positions, by inference, the company as an involved citizen of the community or the nation. While not many organizations are willing to stick their necks out in advocacy advertising, some, notably Mobil Oil in the 1970s and 1980s, take a more aggressive approach to issues. Mobil's famous "Fables for Our Times" and lengthy editorial-style ads in *The New York Times* and a variety of upscale consumer magazines made them the most visible of all the oil companies for nearly 20 years. Their sponsorship of public television is now legendary.

The object of corporate or institutional advertising is not usually to sell a product or service but rather to promote an idea or image. All forms of corporate advertising are, in fact, image advertising because in each the organization is projecting an image of itself as concerned, caring, and involved. Image advertising has become as important to most organizations as product advertising, and most major advertising agencies now handle as much image advertising as sales promotion.

While the focus may vary according to the type of ad being produced, the format for all corporate print advertising is generally the same. To begin with, print ads are composed of three primary elements: headline, visual, and copy.

Headlines. Like the news release, the print advertisement has to be sold on its appearance, but in this case the audience is the public, not the media. To the writer, this means that the reader has to be hooked in some way into reading the ad. The best place to start is the beginning.

Aside from an eye-catching visual, nothing attracts a reader like a good headline. Recent research indicates that the headline is often the only thing read in a print ad. And David Ogilvy, in his classic book *Ogilvy on Advertising,* says that "on the average, five times as many people read the headline as read the body copy."

Headlines come in all shapes and sizes and need be neither long nor short to be effective. What they do need to be is interesting. Consider the following headlines gathered from a number of consumer magazines.

YOUR DYING IS YOUR RESPONSIBILITY.
   —The Hemlock Society

THE WAY SOME OF US PERCEIVE AIDS, YOU WOULD THINK YOU COULD GET IT BY JUST TOUCHING THIS PICTURE.
   —Pediatric AIDS Foundation

FOR 50 YEARS, TEXACO HAS BEEN HAVING A LOVE AFFAIR WITH THE MOST PASSIONATE WOMEN.
FOR 50 YEARS, TEXACO HAS BEEN ASSOCIATING WITH THE MOST VILLAINOUS CHARACTERS.
FOR 50 YEARS, TEXACO HAS BEEN SUPPORTING THE MOST HEROIC MEN.
FOR 50 YEARS, TEXACO HAS BEEN YOUR TICKET TO THE MET.
(A series of small ads placed in the upper right-hand corner of succeeding pages)
   —Texaco

Research conducted by Starch INRA Hooper, an advertising research firm, concludes that what the headline says is of more importance than its form or design. However, inclusion of the following elements was found to increase readership:

- A headline addressing the reader directly.
- A headline referring to a specific problem or desire.
- A headline offering a specific benefit.
- A headline offering something new.

Of course, not all readers will be interested by all headlines. Print ads, like other forms of communication, are intended for a target public. A print ad for the preservation of bald eagles by the Sierra Club may not get much readership among nonconservationists (or poachers). All good headlines, however, have certain attributes in common:

- They should be specific. Try to avoid vague phrases or references that mean little or nothing to your reader.
- They should be believable. If you make them appear unbelievable, you should do so only in an effort to entice the reader into reading further.
- They should be simple. A good headline sets forth one major idea. The time to elaborate is in the body of the ad, not the headline.

There are several ways to construct your headlines to help them attract readers:

- Introduce *news value* into your headline. News invites readership. Any time your ad can appear newsworthy, your readership will increase. The headline, "Why reforming our liability system is essential if America is to succeed in overseas markets," appeared on a two-page ad by AIG. Headlines such as these appear as lead-ins to articles and appeal to readers who are interested in informative advertising.
- Target your message by using a *selective headline* that pinpoints the exact public you are trying to reach. An ad run by Metropolitan Life featured a small child on crutches and the headline, "If you forget to have your children vaccinated, you could be reminded of it the rest of your life." This headline obviously appeals to its target audience—parents—but it might or might not appeal to people with no children.
- The *testimonial approach* features a firsthand quotation. "Rock the boat!" is the headline on one of a series of ads featuring firsthand employee testimonies about Texaco and its products. This ad features a chemist talking about innovation. A testimonial headline is particularly useful if spoken by a celebrity. Many nonprofit agencies now utilize the

talents of celebrities to sell ideas. Paul Newman speaks out against nuclear weapons, Charlton Heston speaks on behalf of the nuclear deterrent, and numbers of celebrities urge us to become foster parents or pen pals to underprivileged children.

- The *curiosity headline* invites the reader to read further in order to answer a posed question. "Do we really want to return to those good, old-fashioned days before plastics?" comes from an ad on recycling from Amoco.

- The *command headline* orders the reader to do something. "Make a life or death decision" refers to the right to die and is from a series of single-column magazine ads from the Hemlock Society. In most cases, this type of headline isn't actually commanding you to do something; it is simply suggesting that you think about it.

Of course, there are other types of headlines used less often than these, but most fall into one of these categories. Remember: The headline is the hook. Write a good headline, and half your job is already done.

Visuals. You don't absolutely have to have a visual in a print ad, although most of us are used to seeing one. Many good advertisements have been carried off with words only. For instance, Chase Manhattan Bank once ran an ad with a very large headline comprised of a single word: "WOLF!" The rest of the ad, run without a visual, spoke of the necessity of "crying wolf" occasionally in order to draw attention to the vanishing capital situation in the United States today.

If you do decide that you need a visual, make it a good one. (The ad in Exhibit 9.11, for example, uses visuals effectively.) The choice of visual is not always the prerogative of the writer. In most cases, that part is taken care of by the art department or agency; however, every writer of print advertising has something in mind when creating an ad. It is virtually impossible to come up with snappy copy without having something visual in mind. It is your job to communicate your ideas for visuals to the people who will be charged with producing the final ad. You don't have to be an artist—all you need to do is provide a rough sketch (a *thumbnail*) and a narrative description of the visual with the ad copy. The headline, visual, and body copy should work together to make a single point.

Body Copy. Good body copy is hard to write. Don't let anybody tell you otherwise. You can bet the best examples of good ad copy are the ones that took the most time, effort, and revision. Good body copy is easy to spot, too. It uses a minimum of adjectives and relies heavily on nouns. It uses verbs to keep things moving along. Most of all, it follows a logical order of presentation.

EXHIBIT 9.11   Effective Visuals in an Ad

Much like brochure copy, good advertising body copy begins with a bridge from the headline (an expansion of the headline idea), continues with the presentation of major points, and ends with a recapitulation of the main point, a call for action (overt or implied), or both. Sometimes, a device known as a *kicker* is used to reiterate the message of the headline. A kicker is usually a slogan or a headline-type phrase coming at the end of the body copy. Consider this ad (written by a student) concerning nuclear waste disposal:

BURYING THE MYTH ABOUT NUCLEAR WASTE IS TOUGHER THAN BURYING NUCLEAR WASTE.

One of today's biggest misconceptions is that nuclear waste can't be disposed of safely. This just isn't true. With today's technology, we can safely bury nuclear wastes deep underground, imprisoning them in a series of safeguarding barriers designed so that even if one should fail, the waste would still be contained. Nuclear waste disposal can be as safe as taking out the trash. It simply requires good sense. So please, bury the myth, and we'll bury the waste.

Notice, first of all, that the headline is interesting and plays on the term "burying" to designate both the disposal of nuclear waste and the disposal of a misconception. The lead sentence in the body copy elaborates on the headline by explaining exactly what "myth" is referred to. A presentation of the main points follows the lead sentence and explains how technology helps ensure safety. The ad wraps up with a kicker and a call for action. All of the components necessary for a successful ad are present.

Notice, too, that the copy is limited. As Hamlet said, "Brevity is the soul of wit." This is especially sage advice for the ad copywriter. Unfortunately, not all public relations advertising can fit so neatly into so few words. It is the nature of public relations to be informative. This often requires detail of the kind that can only be presented in the print media and at length. Longer public interest ads—often running to one or more pages—can provide detailed explanations and will be read, but only by those intensely interested in the topic. Others, not interested enough to read through an entire ad of this type, might still skim it for highlights or, at the very least, appreciate the fact that the sponsoring agency felt that the issue was important enough to spend money advertising it.

Aside from logical order of presentation, there are some basic guidelines that will help you to write good body copy:

- **Stick to the present tense when possible.** This will make your message seem timely and active.

- **Remember that you are speaking to one person.** Unlike television and radio ads, which reach a mass audience simultaneously, print is read by one person at a time. Use a familiar voice. Use personal pronouns. Involve the reader. Say "we" or "our" instead of "the company" or "the industry." Make the readers understand that you are one of them.

- **Use the active voice.** Don't say, "A proposal was made whereby nuclear waste can more effectively be disposed." Say instead, "We've proposed a new method for disposing of nuclear waste."

- **Use words that are familiar to your readers, but don't talk down to them.** Assume they know something about your subject but are looking to your ad to increase their knowledge. If you use a necessarily difficult word or phrase, explain it. Remember: Readers like to think that the people explaining or giving advice are smarter than they are, but not a whole lot smarter.

- **Although the average sentence length for ease of readability is about 16 words, vary your sentence length for variety.** Varying paragraph length, too, will lend your ad an appearance of readability. Many readers who do not have time to pore over long, unbroken passages will read shorter paragraphs. To this end, subheads and crossheads are useful to point to especially informative passages.

- **Use contractions.** People talk that way, so why not write that way—as if you were speaking to them. An exception would be the contracted form of *there is—there's*. The contraction reads awkwardly and is too often used ungrammatically instead of *there are*.

- **Always punctuate properly, even in headlines.** Think about what punctuation does. It makes the reader pause and denotes a change or variance in emphasis. Stay away from exclamation points and try not to use ellipses, called "leaders" in broadcast jargon.

- **Avoid clichés and try not to use vague words or phrases.** People like to feel that they understand you.

- **Never say anything controversial that you don't back up with facts or evidence.** Unsupported statements will hurt your credibility.

Formatting Print Ads

As with brochures and flyers, print ads are most often produced out-of-house—in fact, probably more so, since most writers don't understand the intricacies of laying out print ads. However, it doesn't take an artist to conceptualize a print ad. And even if you're working with a designer, you still need to know how the entire ad is going to look *before* you write it.

Ad Copy Format. Print ads, like other forms of public relations writing, require the proper format for presentation. Most print ads, however, will not be sent directly to the media as mere copy but rather as complete, ready-to-be-published (camera-ready) pieces. Nevertheless, it is necessary to format your ad copy so that the agency or department handling the assembly of the final product understands what you are trying to do.

Fortunately, the format for ad copy is similar to other formats such as brochures, posters, and direct-mail pieces. It is easily adapted to any form of copywriting that requires a mixture of headlines, visuals, and text. The key is to make sure you designate all of the elements clearly at the left-hand margin so that a reader can see what element of the ad he or she is reading at the time (see Exhibits 9.12 and 9.13).

EXHIBIT 9.12   Print Ad Format

```
Pacific Rim Investments
"Interesting Times" full-page ad

GRAPHIC:        Silhouette of mountains with clouds rising
                above them. Headline is written as follows
                over the clouds.
HEADLINE:       The Ancient Chinese had a saying . . .
                "May you live in interesting times."
                Some people interpret it as a blessing . . .
                Others, as a curse.
COPY:           The question is, how do you see it? We here at
                Pacific Rim Investments would like you to see
                it as a blessing. That's the way we look at
                it. After all, the future is always uncertain,
                to a greater or lesser degree. And the past is
                over and done with. There's nothing we can do
                about that. So our "times" are right now.
                Today.

                We want you to see these "times" as a chal-
                lenge, not a threat. For that reason, we've put
                together a small booklet outlining all the
                positive things we see every day . . . the
                things we think you should come to see as
                blessings. Things like: healthy children,
                solid marriages, renewed faith, increased
                understanding of our fellow human beings, a
                growing concern for our environment . . . those
                kinds of things.

                We don't want to appear to be Polyannas, but
                we think there are a lot of opportunities for
                optimism in today's world. All you have to do
                is look for them.

                If you'd like a free copy of our "Guide to
                Interesting Times," just call us toll-free at
                800-555-8749 and we'll send it to you free of
                charge. Just one more thing to be thankful for.
                After all, interesting times are only what you
                make of them.

                              #####
```

Ad Layouts. Some public relations writers, especially those in limited-budget nonprofit organizations, find themselves in sole charge of some forms of advertising and must design ads as well as write the copy for them. It is best to know how to proceed before you're assigned the task. Even if you don't lay out your own ads, it's a good idea to become familiar with the

EXHIBIT 9.13 Print Ad Layout

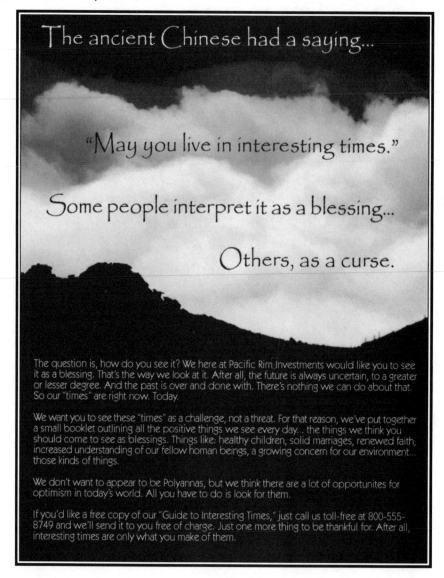

The ancient Chinese had a saying...

"May you live in interesting times."

Some people interpret it as a blessing...

Others, as a curse.

The question is, how do you see it? We here at Pacific Rim Investments would like you to see it as a blessing. That's the way we look at it. After all, the future is always uncertain, to a greater or lesser degree. And the past is over and done with. There's nothing we can do about that. So our "times" are right now. Today.

We want you to see these "times" as a challenge, not a threat. For that reason, we've put together a small booklet outlining all the positive things we see every day... the things we think you should come to see as blessings. Things like: healthy children, solid marriages, renewed faith, increased understanding of our fellow human beings, a growing concern for our environment... those kinds of things.

We don't want to appear to be Polyannas, but we think there are a lot of opportunites for optimism in today's world. All you have to do is look for them.

If you'd like a free copy of our "Guide to Interesting Times," just call us toll-free at 800-555-8749 and we'll send it to you free of charge. Just one more thing to be thankful for. After all, interesting times are only what you make of them.

most common ad formats so that as you write, you can conceptualize exactly how your copy will fit into the finished product. The following represent the most common print ad formats in use. The formats are also illustrated in Exhibit 9.14.

- The *picture window* layout format is probably one of the most popular styles for print ads. The visual dominates this format and usually takes up the top or bottom two-thirds of the page. Normally, the headline is a single line followed by body copy in two or three columns.

- The *copy-heavy* format places the emphasis on the copy rather than on the visual. For messages that are complex in nature and require detailed explanation, this is one of the best formats to use. In corporate advocacy advertising, copy-heavy ads are very common.

- *Silhouette,* or *copy fit,* usually has the copy "wraparound" an open (as opposed to framed or bordered) piece of art. Copy fit takes an expert in typesetting. This isn't something a beginner will normally feel comfortable with, but a good copyfit ad can exude an air of unity that may not be found in other layouts.

- The *Mondrian* layout format is named after the Dutch artist who developed the style. This style is, again, not for the beginner. Mondrian divides the ad space into rectangles of various sizes into which headlines, copy, and visuals are placed. Balance is the key here.

- *Frame,* or *donut,* refers either to framing copy with a visual or framing a visual with copy. If the perimeter is open at either the top or the bottom, the layout is sometimes called *horseshoe.*

- *Circus* is definitely the domain of graphic designers. It takes an expert to balance this layout well. This format often utilizes both framed and silhouetted visuals along with copyfit body copy and numerous subheads.

- *Multi-panel,* or *cartoon,* is exactly what it says. In this format, the panels are usually of equal size. Sometimes the panels tell a sequential story. Multi-panel does not always have to frame each picture in the sequence. Some multi-panel layouts use a series of open or silhouetted visuals—often a repeated image that changes gradually as it progresses.

- Finally, the *type specimen* format relies on the effect of a special or enlarged typeface in place of or as the primary visual element. Again, it takes an expert designer or typographer to handle a type specimen design.

Remember: While advertising is theoretically the domain of the advertising agency, don't be fooled into thinking that all advertising is out of your hands. Public relations practitioners do an increasing amount of image advertising, and you would best be prepared to think and write like an advertising account representative while retaining your special abilities in persuasion and publicity.

EXHIBIT 9.14   Ad Formats

Picture Window Format

Copy Heavy Format

MONKEY SHINES.

THAT'S WHAT THEY USED TO CALL IT WHEN YOU PLAYED AROUND. NOW THEY JUST CALL IT STUPID.

Lorem ipsum,Dolor sit amet, consectetuer adipiscing elit, sed diam nonummy nibh euismod tincidunt ut laoreet dolore magna aliquam erat volutpat. Ut wisi enim ad minim veniam, quis nostrud exerci tation ullamcorper suscipit lobortis nisl ut aliquip ex ea commodo consequat. Duis autem vel eum iriure dolor in hendrerit in vulputate velit esse molestie consequat, vel illum dolore eu feugiat nulla facilisis at vero eros et accumsan et iusto odio dignissim qui blandit praesent luptatum zzril delenit augue duis dolore te feugait nulla facilisi.

Lorem ipsum dolor sit amet, consectetuer adipiscing elit, sed diam nonummy nibh euismod tincidunt ut laoreet dolore magna aliquam erat volutpat.

Lorem ipsum dolor sit amet, consectetuer adipiscing elit, sed diam nonummy nibh euismod tincidunt ut laoreet dolore magna erat volutpat. Duis autem vel eum iriure dolor in hendrerit in vulputate velit esse molestie consequat, vel illum dolore eu feugiat nulla facilisis at vero eros et accumsan et iusto odio dignissim qui blandit praesent luptatum zzril delenit augue duis dolore te feugait nulla facilisi.

Silhouette Format

Mondrian Format

Which of these is used in a non-contact sport?

Lorem ipsum,Dolor sit amet, consectetuer adipiscing elit, sed diam nonummy nibh euismod tincidunt ut laoreet dolore magna aliquam erat volutpat. Ut wisi enim ad minim veniam, quis nostrud exerci tation ullamcorper suscipit lobortis nisl ut aliquip ex ea commodo consequat. Duis autem vel eum iriure dolor in hendrerit in vulputate velit esse molestie consequat, vel illum dolore eu feugiat nulla facilisis at vero eros et accumsan et iusto odio dignissim

SafeSports: A United Way Member

(Continued)

(Continued)

WHAT MAKES BATH TIME SO MUCH FUN?

Lorem ipsum,Dolor sit amet, consectetuer adipiscing elit, sed diam nonummy nibh euismod tincidunt ut laoreet dolore magna aliquam erat volutpat. Ut wisi enim ad minim veniam, quis nostrud exerci tation ullamcorper suscipit lobortis nisl ut aliquip ex ea commodo consequat. Duis autem vel eum iriure dolor in hendrerit in vulputate velit esse molestie consequat, vel illum dolore eu feugiat nulla facilisis at vero eros et accumsan et justo odio dignissim qui blandit praesent luptatum zzril delenit augue duis dolore te feugait nulla facilisi.

Lorem ipsum dolor sit amet, consectetue r adipiscing elit, sed diam nonummy nibh euismod tincidunt ut laoreet dolore magna aliquam erat volutpat.

Lorem ipsum dolor sit amet, consectetuer adipiscing elit, sed diam nonummy nibh euismod tincidunt ut laoreet dolore magna aliquam erat volutpat. Duis autem vel eum iriure dolor in hendrerit in vulputate velit esse molestie consequat, vel illum dolore eu feugiat nulla facilisis at vero eros et accumsan et justo odio dignissim qui blandit praesent luptatum zzril delenit augue duis dolore te feugait nulla facilisi.

Lorem ipsum dolor sit amet, consectetuer adipiscing elit, sed di

nonummy nibh euismod tincidunt ut laoreet dolore magna aliquam erat volutpat. Ut wisi enim ad minim veniam, quis nostrud exerci tation ullam corper suscipit lobortis nisl ut aliquip ex ea commodo consequat.

Lorem ipsum dolor sit amet, consectetuer adipiscing elit, sed diam nonummy nibh euismod tincidunt ut laoreet dolore magna aliquam erat volutpat. Duis autem vel eum iriure dolor in hendrerit in vulputate velit esse mole stie consequat, vel illum dolore eu feugiat nulla facilisis at vero eros et accumsan et justo odio dignissim qui blandit praesent luptatum zzril delenit augue duis dolore te feugait nulla facilisi.

Lorem ipsum dolor sit amet, consectetuer adipiscing elit, sed diam nonummy nibh euismod tincidunt ut laoreet dolore ma gna aliquam erat volutpat. Ut wisi enim ad minim veniam, quis nostrud exerci tation ullamcorper suscipit lobortis nisl ut aliquip ex ea commodo consequat. Duis autem vel eum iriure dolor in hendrerit in vulputate velit esse molestie consequat, vel illum dolore eu feugiat nulla facilisis at vero eros et accumsan et justo odio dignissim qui blandit praesent luptatum zzril delenit augue duis dolore te feugait nulla facilisi.

The Family Safet

Frame Format

Circus Format

What about soccer socks?

Do they really need them?

Lorem ipsum,Dolor sit amet, consectetuer adipiscing elit, sed diam nonummy nibh euismod tincidunt ut laoreet dolore magna aliquam erat volutpat. Ut wisi enim ad minim veniam, quis nostrud exerci tation ullamcorper suscipit lobortis nisl ut aliquip ex ea commodo consequat. Duis autem vel eum iriure dolor in hendrerit in vulputate velit esse molestie consequat, vel illum dolore eu feugiat nulla facilisis at vero eros et accumsan et justo odio dignissim qui blandit praesent luptatum zzril delenit augue duis dolore te feugait nulla facilisi.

Lorem ipsum dolor sit amet, consectetue r adipiscing elit, sed diam nonummy nibh euismod tincidunt ut laoreet dolore magna aliquam erat volutpat.

Lorem ipsum dolor sit amet, consectetuer adipiscing elit, sed diam nonummy nibh euismod tincidunt ut laoreet dolore magna aliquam erat volutpat. Duis autem vel eum iriure

LOST IN SPACE?

LET US HELP YOU FIND YOUR WAY HOME.

 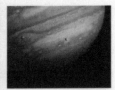

Astronomy Online

Multi-panel
Format

Type Specimen
Format

Silence is Golden

That's why we're offering our introduction to meditation free to the first 200 people who call us.

Lorem ipsum,Dolor sit amet, consectetuer adipiscing elit, sed diam nonummy nibh euismod tincidunt ut laoreet dolore magna aliquam erat volutpat. Ut wisi enim ad minim veniam, quis nostrud exerci tation ullamcorper suscipit lobortis nisl ut aliquip ex ea commodo consequat. Duis autem vel eum iriure dolor in hendrerit in vulputate velit esse molestie consequat, vel illum dolore eu feugiat

KEY TERMS

format

positioning

corporate advertising

public interest advertising

public image advertising

advocacy advertising

EXERCISES

1. Bring in a brochure for class discussion. Answer the following questions in writing prior to class discussion:

   • What is the stated purpose of the piece? Who is its intended audience?

   • Is the purpose of the piece clear from the cover or first page?

   • Does the first paragraph of copy support or refer to the headline or title of the piece?

   • Does the visual (or key design element) reinforce the message?

   • Does the piece make use of subheads or other graphic dividers?

   • Is there a clear and logical flow of information throughout the piece?

   • Do you think there is enough, too little, or too much information?

   • In what context and to what end do you think the piece was produced?

   • What do you think about the design and layout of the piece? How could it be improved?

2. Find what you consider to be an "ugly" brochure. Using the existing copy, redesign the brochure for more effective presentation. If you have access to computer design software, use it. If not, develop a brochure script detailing the new design along with edited copy.

3. Working in teams of three to five, come up with an idea for a poster encouraging students to spend more time studying. Consider both visuals and copy as well as headlines, layout, and design. Sketch out or otherwise create a draft composition (comp) of your poster for class discussion. In addition, produce a script following the chapter guidelines.

4. Bring in a copy of an ad designed to influence opinion about an organization (not its products or services). Be prepared to discuss the placement of the ad, the chosen publication, and the audience it is intended for.

5. Design an ad for your school or college, selling it as a great place to get an education. Hit heavily on its strengths (location, educational reputation, etc.). Use the standard ad format for writing the ad up, including notations for any graphics. Also include a rough idea of the ad layout.

## CHAPTER 10

TELEVISION AND RADIO

FOR IMMEDIATE RELEASE

In this chapter you will learn:

- The methods for reaching broadcast audiences.

- The basic concepts of television production.

- How to write scripts for television production.

- How to produce an effective television PSA.

- How to write public relations material for radio.

- How to get your radio PSAs on the air.

Broadcasting is pervasive. Since the advent of radio, people have become more and more dependent on the broadcast media for their information and entertainment. Today, more than ever before, the public views the world through the window of television. The average American family spends more than six hours a day watching television, and, according to recent research, they find it the most credible news source by a wide margin. Radio reaches more people each day than any other medium, with more than 500 million radios in American homes and cars.

For the public relations practitioner, utilization of these two powerful and influential media is often restricted. While approximately 90 percent of the nonadvertising content of print media is informational, 90 percent of the nonadvertising content of broadcast media is entertainment. There is simply very little time available for news-related items. Radio usually airs news, but often in an abbreviated format. Each of the 30-minute network television news shows has only 22 minutes of actual news, which would fill about one-quarter of the front page of a daily newspaper. And while cable news has greatly expanded over the past 10 years, it is devoted almost exclusively to national and international news, leaving very little opportunity for the local public relations practitioner.

There are some obvious advantages to using the broadcast media, however. Most obviously, they reach millions of people each day. Moreover, television and radio involve their audiences more than print does, and can be highly memorable. People tend to react more personally to broadcast than they do to other media. Think of the influence television celebrities have on the youth of today. Consider the power of national newscasters such as Peter Jennings or Dan Rather in influencing opinion. Even local newscasters display a certain amount of charisma. Why would local events such as fund-raisers try so hard to get them as hosts otherwise? Think of all the times you've seen local radio announcers as "talent" on television commercials. All of this speaks to the power of broadcast celebrity status and the power of broadcasting to influence.

Reaching Broadcast Audiences

Although getting public relations material aired on network radio and television is difficult, local broadcast media offer some avenues for the experienced practitioner. There are five basic methods for the public relations writer to reach broadcast audiences: news releases (covered in Chapter 6), video news releases, radio and television tapes and actualities, interviews and talk shows, and corporate advertising or public service announcements.

Video News Releases

Video news releases (VNRs) are a fairly new phenomenon. Originally, they were simply prepackaged publicity features meant to be aired on local, regional, or national television. Now they have become staples of many local news shows searching for time-filling informational pieces.

The entertainment industry was among the first to recognize the potential in producing its own videos for publicity purposes. For example, the publicity department for a new motion picture might produce a tape that includes collages of footage from the film in varying lengths, special "behind the scenes" looks at production, and interviews with key stars. Each of these segments has both an A and B sound track. The A sound track contains both music and voiceover, while the B sound track contains music only. The varying lengths allow a TV station to air a segment suited to its particular time requirements. The choice of sound tracks allows the station to drop in its own announcers' voices to give the piece a local feel.

It is in local television that VNRs are most successful. Filling an hour with local news is sometimes difficult for programmers, and program managers are constantly seeking out "fillers" to plug 30-, 60-, or 90-second holes in newscasts. In fact, some polls show more than 75 percent of all TV stations regularly use VNRs.

Organizations and their PR agencies and departments have been quick to capitalize on this opportunity. The key is to produce fillers in various lengths that have certain news value yet are not time bound. This way, stories can be produced, packaged, and mailed to stations around the country with no fear that the news will be old before it is received. Medialink, a New York-based company (www.medialinkworldwide.com), developed the nation's first dedicated video newswire and has become a leading distributor of VNRs, with Medialink wires in over 600 television newsrooms around the United States. This type of distribution network allows organizations to get even the most time-sensitive news on the air soon enough to be effective. For example, a company can stage an important news conference, tape interviews and visuals from the event, combine this with pre-produced or stock footage of the company, and send it out via satellite all over the country in a matter of hours.

There are some problems with this infant publicity vehicle, however. A major criticism in the news industry is that much of what is packaged as video "news" releases is really advertising in disguise. This may be true, in part—VNRs are an excellent means of plugging a product by wrapping it in a soft news format. The same thing, of course, has been done for years in product-oriented articles for trade publications; the difference is that VNRs are being sent to mainstream media outlets that deal in hard news, not product publicity. The old advertising adage, "buyer beware," should hold here. Alert journalists should always be aware of the publicity angle inherent in any sort of release—print, video, or otherwise. On the PR side, practitioners won't gain any media support by deliberately disguising product plugs as hard or soft news. The best approach is to tag clearly any VNR as to its sponsor and content and let the media do the gatekeeping.

How you write for a video news release depends on the format of the release. Taped press conferences and the like should follow a straight news format, as should straight news print releases. Features should follow feature style. Most of the techniques discussed below also apply to writing for VNRs. Simply be aware of the format and target media, and conform to their accepted styles. Remember, as with all other media, the broadcast media will accept only that which fits their needs and format.

Radio and Television Tapes and Actualities

Radio and television rely heavily on taped actualities in covering the news. An **actuality** is simply a firsthand account, on tape, of a news event. Actualities lend credibility to any newscast. They may feature newspeople describing the event or interviews with those involved in the event, or they may simply provide ambiance or background for a voice-over.

Rarely will the public relations writer be in the position to provide a finished actuality to a radio or television news program. Most of the time, he or she will act as the intermediary or spokesperson for the organization. Or, the public relations practitioner may arrange a taped interview with another company spokesperson, typically outside of the public relations department. In some cases, the medium may be interested enough to send out a reporter or news team to cover an event firsthand. In that case, the public relations practitioner usually acts as liaison, arranging the schedule and making sure that everything is in order for the taping.

Interviews and Talk Shows

Local radio and television stations often have talk shows or other vehicles for which information about your organization is suitable. These shows are usually listed in media directories (see Chapter 5) or can be gleaned by contacting the station personally and asking. The public relations practitioner, here again, usually acts as liaison, arranging the interview for a spokesperson, getting preparatory materials together, and making sure the spokesperson gets to the interview or talk show on time. As the media specialist, you may also be called on to coach the spokesperson or even write his or her responses (see Chapter 5 for media interview tips).

Corporate Advertising and Public Service Announcements

As was discussed in Chapter 9, the object of corporate advertising is not usually to sell a product, but rather to promote an idea or image. Realizing that profit-making organizations don't usually need free airtime, the

Federal Communications Commission (FCC) requires them to purchase time for their ads, even if the messages presented are in the public interest.

Like corporate public interest advertising, the **public service announcement (PSA)** is aimed at providing an important message to its target audience. However, unlike corporate advertising, even that done in the public interest, the PSA is reserved strictly for nonprofit organizations—those that qualify as nonprofit under federal tax laws. Nonprofits may air their public service announcements for free.

Remember that public service announcements and image advertising, while different under the law, are identical in format and style. They are both an attempt to sell something, whether it's a product, an idea, or an image. What follows is applicable to both.

Writing for Television

Broadcast messages, whether paid-for advertising or PSAs, are called **spots.** Producing a complete television spot is usually beyond the expertise of the public relations writer and is best left to professional film and video production houses. Many practitioners, however, prefer to write their own scripts, so a knowledge of the proper form is essential.

A good script tells the director, talent, or anyone else reading it exactly what the spot is about, what its message is, and the image it should convey. In a well-written script, virtually nothing is left to the imagination. A good working knowledge of film and video techniques is also necessary if you are to be able to visualize your finished product and transmit that vision to someone else. Before beginning a script, therefore, you need to become familiar with some basics of television production and the language of script writing.

Basic Concepts of Television Production

Television spots are produced either on film or videotape. Because both formats involve similar aesthetics, a discussion of one will serve to cover both. Television spots, and all commercials and programs for that matter, are composed of a series of scenes or camera shots joined together by transitions. A scene usually indicates a single locale, so a 30-second commercial might be composed of a single scene that is in turn composed of several camera shots. Or, a 30-minute program might be composed of many scenes composed of many camera shots. These scenes and shots are joined by transitional devices, usually created by switching from one camera to another (a form of on-the-spot editing), or in the case of a single-camera production that is edited later, by switching from one kind of shot to another. The script tells the director, camera operators, and talent what sort of composition is required in each shot.

Camera shot directions are scripted in a form of shorthand. The most common designations are described below. For our purposes, we will assume that the shots are of a person:

- *CU* or *close-up*—A shot that takes in the neck and head but doesn't extend below the neck.
- *ECU* or *extreme close-up*—A much tighter version of the CU, usually involving a selected portion of the person, such as the eyes.
- *MS* or *medium shot*—A shot that takes in the person from about the waist up.
- *Bust shot*—A shot of a person from the bust up.
- *LS* or *long shot*—A shot of the entire person with little or no room at the top or bottom of the screen.
- *ELS* or *extreme long shot*—A shot with the person in the distance.

There are variations on these basic shots, such as MCU (medium close-up), MLS (medium long shot), two-shot (a shot of two people), three-shot (a shot of three people), etc. When designating shots in scripts, you just need to be in the ballpark—you don't have to have it down to the millimeter. Whatever you write in your script may ultimately be changed by the artistic collaboration between the director and the camera operators.

Camera shots are accomplished in one of two ways: by movement of the optical apparatus (or lens) or by movement of the camera itself. The most common designations for lens movement are *zoom in* and *zoom out*. Physical movements generally are scripted for studio productions in which cameras can be moved about in order to accommodate certain shots. However, the following terms also are applied to scripts in general to indicate certain camera effects that can be accomplished by cameras either handheld or mounted in other ways, such as on rails or booms:

- *Dolly in/out*—Move the camera in a straight line toward or away from the object.
- *Truck right/left*—Move the camera right or left, parallel to the object.
- *Pan right/left*—Move the camera head to the right or left.
- *Tilt up/down*—Move the camera head up or down.

Each of these movements creates a different optical effect, and each will impart a different impression to the viewer. Dollies and trucks, for instance, impart a sense of viewer movement rather than movement of the object being filmed or taped. In other words, the camera becomes the viewer. This type of shot is frequently called *point of view (POV)*. Pans and tilts appear as normal eye movement, much as if the viewer were moving his or her eyes from side to side or up and down. Remember that the camera is actually the eyes of the viewer limited by the size of the screen.

Transitions are the sole domain of the director and editor. In the case of a studio production, such as a live talk show, the director and technical director work together—the director giving transitional directions, and the technical director following those directions by electronically switching between the cameras. Transitions in field productions and single-camera productions are taken care of in post-production editing through a cooperative effort between the director and the editor. The following are the most-used transitions:

- *Cut*—An instantaneous switch from one shot to another.
- *Dissolve*—A gradual replacement of one image with another.
- *Wipe*—A special effect in which one image is "wiped" from the screen and replaced by another. This was used extensively in silent movie days and in adventure films of the 1930s and 1940s.
- *Fade*—A gradual change, usually to or from black designating either the beginning or end of a scene.

Other shorthand notations are specific to audio directions. The most common are:

- *SFX* or *sound effects*—Anything from crashing cars to falling rain.
- *SOF* or *sound on film*—The sound source is the audio track from a film.
- *SOT* or *sound on tape*—The sound source is the audio track from a videotape or audiotape.
- *SIL* or *silent film*—No sound has been added or has occurred ambiently.
- *Music up*—Signifying that the volume of the music bed is raised.
- *Music under*—Signifying that the volume of the music bed is lowered, usually to allow for narration.
- *Music up and out*—Usually designating the end of a production.
- *VO* or *voice-over/voice only*—Indicating that the speaker is not on camera.
- *OC* or *on camera*—Indicating that the speaker or narrator can be seen. This is usually used when the speaker has been VO prior to being OC. In other words, it indicates that he or she is now on camera.

Writing for the Eye

When you write for television, you write for the eye as well as the ear, which means that you have to visualize what you want your audience to see and then put that vision on paper. Your image must be crystallized into words that will tell others how to re-create it on tape or film.

In order to end up with the best possible script, you must begin with an idea. Try to think in visuals. Take a basic concept and try to visualize the best method for presenting it to others. Should you use a studio or film outdoors? Will you use ambient sound or a music background? Will you have a number of transitions or a single scene throughout? Answering these questions and others will help you conceptualize the television spot.

Scripting for Television

Writers typically produce three types of scripts for a television production: script treatments, shooting scripts, and accompanying scripts. The writer must also choose a style for the television spot, time the script appropriately, and cut the script to the fit the length of the spot.

Script Treatments

Once you have a basic idea of what you would like to say, the next step is to write a **script treatment.** This is a narrative account of a television spot. It is not written in a script format but may include ideas for shots and transitions. The key is to keep it informal at this point—there will be plenty of time to clean it up in later drafts. Exhibit 10.1 is a treatment for a promotional ad for a documentary to be shown on television.

Shooting Scripts

The next step is to sharpen your images in a **shooting script,** which will ultimately be used by the director to produce your spot (see Exhibit 10.2). As you work through what will inevitably be several drafts, you should include all of the information necessary for a complete understanding of your idea; remember, your goal is to get to a final product that is finished enough to be used by your director. You should begin to flesh out camera shots, transitions, audio (including music and sound effects), narrative, acting directions, and approximate times. Here are some guidelines that will help you as you move through your shooting script:

1. Open with an attention-getting device—an interesting piece of audio, an unusual camera shot, or a celebrity. The first few seconds are crucial. If your viewers are not hooked by then, you've lost them.

2. Open with an establishing shot if possible—something that says where you are and intimates where you are going. If you open in a

EXHIBIT 10.1   Script Treatment

```
"IDITAROD"
30 second promo
Treatment

Opening shot of dog team against setting sun across long
stretch of tundra. Cut to flashes of finish-line hysteria—dogs
running, racers' faces frozen or exhausted, stretches of open
ground, trees, checkpoints, etc., perhaps terminating at
starting gun. Images continue under narration.

Voice-over: WHAT MAKES SOME PEOPLE SPEND LITERALLY AN ENTIRE
YEAR TRAINING BOTH THEMSELVES AND THEIR DOGS, OFTEN WITH
HEARTBREAKING RESULTS? WHAT DRAWS A PERSON TO DOGSLED
RACING? IS IT A MYSTIQUE UNIQUE ONLY TO ALASKA, OR IS IT SOME-
THING COMMON TO ALL PEOPLE AT ALL TIMES?

Cut to close-up of winner of last year's Iditarod race . . .
exhaustion . . . joy . . . satisfaction. Zoom-in to freeze-
frame of face.

Voice-over: JOIN US FOR A TWELVE-HUNDRED MILE RACE ACROSS
ALASKA WHEN NATIONAL GEOGRAPHIC PRESENTS "IDITAROD: THE RACE
ON THE EDGE OF THE WORLD."

NGS logo . . . super day and time.
```

classroom, for instance, chances are you are going to stay there. If
you jump too much, you confuse viewers.

3. If you open with a long shot, you should then cut to a closer
shot, and soon after, introduce the subject of the spot. This is
especially applicable if you are featuring a product or a celebrity
spokesperson.

4. Vary shot composition from MS to CU throughout, and somewhere
past the midpoint of the spot return to an MS then to a final CU

EXHIBIT 10.2 Shooting Script

PRODUCTION: A.P.P.L.E 9/17 Revised   Page 1 of 33

PRODUCER: University of Alaska Media Services

VIDEO	AUDIO
ELS mountain range, AERIAL	(ambient sounds of birds)
Camera PANS range, descends through wooded area, zeroing in on the edge of a grassy clearing.	(sound of wind)
DISSOLVE to LS grassy clearing	
Colorful objects can be made out scattered within the clearing.	
DISSOLVE to MLS grassy clearing	NARRATOR: ALASKA'S LAND IS PRETTY COMPLEX AND UNDER-STANDING IT CAN BE COMPLI-CATED. THERE ARE A FEW BASIC
At ground level, camera slowly PANS across objects and stops on box labeled "nonrenewable resources."	THINGS, HOWEVER, THAT YOU SHOULD KNOW SO THAT WHEN THE TIME COMES FOR YOU TO MAKE DECISIONS ABOUT LAND, YOU
DISSOLVE to MS mime	CAN MAKE GOOD ONES.
Camera PANS as mime enters scene and approaches box.	
DISSOLVE to CU mime and box	YOU SHOULD KNOW ABOUT RESOURCES: RENEWABLE AND NONRENEWABLE.
FREEZE-FRAME as mime starts to open box.	

#####

and a *superimposition (super)* of a logo or address. A super involves placing one image over another.

5. Don't call for a new shot unless it adds something to the spot. Make your shots seem like part of an integrated whole. Be single-minded and try to tell only one important story per spot.

Although a director will feel free to adapt your script to his or her particular style and to the requirements of the production, you should leave as little as possible to the imagination.

EXHIBIT 10.3   Accompanying Script

PRODUCTION: Iditarod DATE: 9/17/94   Page 1 of 1

PRODUCER: Northstar Associates

VIDEO	AUDIO
Open on LS dogsled racing into setting sun.	(National Geographic music up)
Series of quick CUTS of finish line excitement, checkpoints, racing, and scenery.	
Narration begins as series of shots of winning team flash by.	NARRATOR: WHAT MAKES SOME PEOPLE SPEND LITERALLY AN ENTIRE YEAR TRAINING BOTH THEMSELVES AND THEIR DOGS, OFTEN WITH HEARTBREAKING RESULTS? WHAT DRAWS A PERSON TO DOGSLED RACING? IS IT A MYSTIQUE UNIQUE ONLY TO ALASKA, OR IS IT SOMETHING COMMON TO ALL PEOPLE AT ALL TIMES?
Quick series of CUs and MSs of racer.	
PAN of faces in crowd at finish line.	
CUT to CU of winner's face showing joy and exhaustion.	
FREEZE-FRAME of face MATTED on magazine cover.	JOIN US FOR A TWELVE-HUNDRED MILE RACE ACROSS ALASKA WHEN NATIONAL GEOGRAPHIC PRESENTS "IDITAROD: THE RACE ON THE EDGE OF THE WORLD."
SFX logo.	
SUPER station air date.	(music up and out)

#####

Accompanying Scripts

The **accompanying script** is the version sent with the taped spot to the stations that will run it (see Exhibit 10.3). It is written on the assumption that the shooting script has been produced as it was originally described. The accompanying script is stripped of all but its most essential directions. It is intended to provide the reader with a general idea of what the taped spot is about and is to be used only as a reference for broadcasters who accept the spot for use.

It is customary to send out taped spots in packages that include a cover letter explaining what the package is, a form requesting the receiver to designate when and how often the spot is used, and an accompanying script for each spot. Sometimes a storyboard also is sent with an abbreviated frame-by-frame summary of the major points, both audio and video, of the spot.

Choosing a Style

The two styles most common to television spots are talking heads and slice-of-life. In a **talking heads spot,** the primary image appearing on the television screen is the human head—talking, of course. This style is often chosen for reasons of cost—a talking heads spot is relatively cheap to produce—but it can be very effective. Exhibit 10.4 is an example of a script for a talking heads spot.

Talking heads spots often are criticized for being boring or unexciting, but this does not need to be the case. The key is to make what is said forceful and memorable while at the same time introducing enough camera movement and varied shot composition to make the video image visually interesting. By incorporating the simplest of camera movements into your scripts, you can hold the attention of the audience long enough to impart your verbal message. With this in mind, read through Exhibit 10.4 again and notice how closely the subtle camera movements are tied to the verbal message.

As its name implies, the **slice-of-life spot** sets up a dramatic situation complete with a beginning, middle, and end (see Exhibit 10.5). In the slice-of-life spot, the focus is on the story, not the characters. The message is imparted through an interesting sequence of events incorporating, but not relying on, interesting characters. Slice-of-life spots usually use a wide variety of camera movements and post-production techniques, such as dissolves and special effects. Although this type of spot often is shot with one camera, the effect is one of multiple cameras due to the post-production process. Slice-of-life spots may be more difficult to produce than talking heads spots, but they are just as easy to script.

Timing Your Script

How do you know when you have written a script that will end up running 30 or 60 seconds on the television screen? Timing a script isn't easy and requires a certain amount of "gut feeling." The best way to time a script is to read through what you have written as if it were already produced. Always exaggerate your delivery—people usually talk faster than you think they do. Pause for the music, sound effects, and talent reactions. You also need to simulate movements as if they were occurring on screen. If

EXHIBIT 10.4   Talking Heads Spot

The American Tuberculosis Foundation
1212 Street of the Americas
New York, N.Y. 00912

"Your Good Health"
30-Second TV Spot   Page 1 of 1

VIDEO	AUDIO
Open on CU of young woman's face against a neutral background. She is smoking.	NARRATOR: (VO) YOU KNOW THE DANGERS OF CIGARETTE SMOKING.
Woman looks unconcerned. She takes another puff as narrator talks.	SMOKING CAUSES HEART DISEASE, EMPHYSEMA, AND CANCER. BUT DON'T STOP BECAUSE YOU MIGHT DIE FROM IT.
Pull back to MS to reveal child of about four years old looking up at her.	STOP SMOKING BECAUSE SOMEONE YOU LOVE MIGHT DIE FROM IT. WHEN YOU SMOKE AT HOME, YOUR CHILDREN BREATHE THE SAME
Child covers his mouth and coughs.	CANCER-CAUSING SMOKE YOU DO . . . AND THEY DON'T HAVE ANY CHOICE. THEY CAN'T
Slow zoom to CU woman, still holding cigarette. Looks concerned.	DECIDE TO QUIT SMOKING. BUT YOU CAN. IF YOU WANT TO STOP SMOKING, WRITE US. WE'LL SEND YOU A FREE PROGRAM THAT WILL HELP YOU STOP IN 30 DAYS.
Fade to black, super address.	REMEMBER, SOMEONE YOU LOVE CARES ABOUT YOUR GOOD HEALTH.

# # # # #

your script calls for the talent to walk up a classroom aisle, for instance, walk the equivalent distance while you read the narrative. This type of "live action" walk-through will give you a ballpark idea of how long your script will be when finally shot.

Remember, the director will ultimately make the adjustments necessary to fit your script into the required time slot, but it's always in your best interest (as far as your reputation as a writer is concerned) to be as close as possible.

EXHIBIT 10.5   Slice-of-Life Spot

Institute for Higher Education
Box 1873
Washington, D.C. 19806

"Payoff"
60-Second TV Spot   Page 1 of 3

VIDEO	AUDIO
Open on MLS large crowd shot, city street, people walking. We see a young man in front of crowd as it stops at crosswalk.	(Music up: "You've Earned Your Chance")
Continue MLS as light changes and crowd crosses.	"THE CITY'S HOT. THE DAY'S BEEN LONG, BUT YOU'VE BEEN OUT THERE HANGING ON.
ARC LEFT and AROUND as young man crosses street and FOLLOW shot behind him as he reaches other side.	
CUT TO MLS as young man stops in front of building, checks address on slip of paper in his hand, and enters.	THE FACES START TO LOOK THE SAME, YOU WONDER IF THEY KNOW YOUR NAME.
CUT TO MS young man as he rushes to squeeze into elevator.	THERE'S ONE MORE SHOT BEFORE YOU'RE THROUGH.
CUT TO MCU young man looking uncomfortable in crowded elevator. He looks to right and left as others ignore him.	YOU KNOW YOUR TIME IS COMING DUE. IT'S YOUR TURN NOW, YOUR DUES ARE PAID.
CUT TO MS of elevator doors opening as young man exits, looks both ways and turns screen left.	YOU'VE EARNED YOUR CHANCE, YOU'VE MADE THE GRADE."

-more-

Cutting Your Script

Cutting a script means understanding the message you want to impart, and then making sure that it is still intact after editing. It may sound obvious to say that a 30-second spot is half the length of a 60-second spot, but 30 seconds lost out of a 60-second spot can result in the deletion of a lot of

```
"Payoff"                                        Page 2 of 3
60-Second TV Spot

VIDEO                              AUDIO
_____

CUT TO MS of young man paus-
ing before door, checking
number, and entering.

                                   (Lyrics end, music under)

CUT TO MLS young man enter-
ing front office. Secretary
is seated at desk and
glances up as he enters
room.

CUT TO CU secretary's face.       SECRETARY: MAY I HELP YOU?

CUT TO CU young man's face.       MAN: YES. I'M HERE FOR AN
                                  AP-POINTMENT WITH MR.
                                  ALDRICH.

CUT TO 2-SHOT secretary and       SECRETARY: YOU MUST BE MR.
young man.                        ROBINSON. MR. ALDRICH IS
                                  EXPECTING YOU. I'LL LET HIM
                                  KNOW YOU'RE HERE. WHY DON'T
                                  YOU HAVE A SEAT. I'M SURE
                                  HE'LL BE RIGHT WITH YOU.

Follow MS young man as he
seats himself. He picks up a
magazine and begins to read.

VCUT TO MCU young man as he       ANNOUNCER: YOU'VE PREPARED
glances at office door.           FOR THIS MOMENT FOR FOUR
                                  YEARS. NOW IT'S PAYOFF TIME.
CUT TO CU young man's face        YOU'RE CONFIDENT AND POL-
exuding confidence.               ISHED. YOU'VE GOT A COLLEGE
                                  EDUCATION AND THE TRAINING
                                  YOU NEED TO GO WHERE YOU
                                  WANT TO GO AND TO DO WHAT

                         -more-
```

valuable setup and development time. That 10 seconds you took to pan slowly around the classroom scene now has to go. What do you do instead? Here are some guidelines for cutting your script:

1. Always begin with the longer script. It is easier to cut down than to write more.

2. Look first at the opening and closing sections to see if you can eliminate long musical or visual transitions or fades.

"Payoff"   Page 3 of 3
60-Second TV Spot

VIDEO   AUDIO
_____   _____

                                 ANNOUNCER (CONT.): YOU WANT
                                 TO DO IN LIFE. YOU HAD THE
                                 INSIGHT AND THE DRIVE TO
                                 BETTER YOURSELF THROUGH
                                 HIGHER EDUCATION, AND NOW IS
                                 THE MOMENT YOU'VE WAITED
                                 FOR.

CUT TO MLS as office door   INTERVIEWER: MR. ROBINSON?
opens and interviewer steps   I'VE BEEN LOOKING FORWARD TO
out to shake young man's   MEETING YOU. I'VE GOT TO
hand.   TELL YOU—YOU'RE JUST THE
                                 KIND OF PERSON WE'RE LOOKING
CUT TO CU interviewer's   FOR. WE'VE GOT A LOT TO TALK
face.   ABOUT.

CUT TO CU young man's face,
smiling.

CUT TO MEDIUM 2-SHOT as two   ANNOUNCER: MAKE YOUR DREAMS
men chat.   A REALITY. GO TO COLLEGE.
                                 EDUCATION PAYS OFF. FOR MORE
                                 INFORMATION, WRITE:

LOSE   focus   and   SUPER   INSTITUTE FOR HIGHER EDUCA-
address.   TION
                                 BOX 1873
                                 WASHINGTON, D.C. 19806

                                 (Music and lyrics up)

FOCUS on MEDIUM 2-SHOT as   YES, YOU'VE EARNED YOUR
two men enter office and   CHANCE, NOW GIVE IT ALL
close door behind them.   YOU'VE GOT.

                    # # # # #

3. Next, check for long dissolves or other lengthy transitions within the body of the script to see if these can be replaced with shorter transitional techniques such as cuts, or eliminated altogether.

4. See if you can eliminate minor characters. Cutting a character with only one or two lines will save you a lot of time.

5. See if you can eliminate any narrative assigned to your major spokesperson. Leave only the key message, slogan, any necessary

EXHIBIT 10.6   Edited Slice-of-Life Spot

```
Institute for Higher Education
Box 1873
Washington, D.C. 19806

"Payoff"
30 Second TV Spot                              Page 1 of 2

VIDEO                           AUDIO
```

VIDEO	AUDIO
Open on LS young man entering front office. Secretary is seated at desk and glances up as he enters room.	
CUT TO CU secretary's face.	SECRETARY: MAY I HELP YOU?
CUT TO CU young man's face.	MAN: YES. I'M HERE FOR AN APPOINTMENT WITH MR. ALDRICH.
CUT TO 2-SHOT secretary and young man.	SECRETARY: YOU MUST BE MR. ROBINSON. MR. ALDRICH IS EXPECTING YOU. I'LL LET HIM KNOW YOU'RE HERE. WHY DON'T YOU HAVE A SEAT. I'M SURE HE'LL BE RIGHT WITH YOU.
Follow MS young man as he seats himself. He picks up a magazine and begins to read.	ANNOUNCER: YOU'VE PREPARED FOR THIS MOMENT FOR FOUR YEARS. NOW IT'S PAYOFF TIME. YOU'RE CONFIDENT AND POLISHED. YOU'VE GOT A COLLEGE EDUCATION AND THE TRAINING YOU NEED TO GO WHERE YOU WANT TO GO, AND DO WHAT YOU WANT TO DO IN LIFE.
CUT TO MCU young man as he glances at office door.	
CUT TO CU young man's face exuding confidence.	

```
                         -more-
```

contact information—and enough narrative transition to allow for coherent development.

6. Finally, try out the cut-down version on someone who hasn't seen the longer version to make sure it flows and makes sense.

Read Exhibit 10.6, the 30-second version of the slice-of-life spot in Exhibit 10.5. Notice what was left out and what remains. Is the message still clear? Did the story lose anything in the cutting?

"Payoff"
30 Second TV Spot   Page 2 of 2

VIDEO   AUDIO

CUT TO MLS as office door opens and interviewer steps out to shake young man's hand.	ANNOUNCER (CONT.): YOU HAD THE INSIGHT AND THE DRIVE TO BETTER YOURSELF THROUGH HIGHER EDUCATION, AND NOW IS THE MOMENT YOU'VE WAITED FOR.
CUT TO CU interviewer's face.	INTERVIEWER: MR. ROBINSON? I'VE BEEN LOOKING FORWARD TO MEETING YOU. I'VE GOT TO TELL YOU—YOU'RE JUST THE KIND OF PERSON WE'RE LOOKING FOR. COME IN. WE'VE GOT A LOT TO TALK ABOUT.
CUT TO 2-SHOT as both enter office and shut door behind them.	ANNOUNCER: MAKE YOUR DREAMS A REALITY. GO TO COLLEGE. EDUCATION PAYS OFF. FOR MORE INFORMATION, WRITE:
SUPER address on door.	INSTITUTE FOR HIGHER EDUCATION BOX 1873 WASHINGTON, D.C. 19806

# # # # #

Effective Television PSA Production ————

Before we move on to radio production, here are some tips that may enhance your chances of getting your public service announcement (PSA) on the air:

- Keep your PSAs simple. Covering one or maybe two points in 30 seconds is the best you should shoot for; any more will simply dilute your message. It's usually best to stick to one point and repeat it in several different ways.

- This also means fewer scenes. Although a soft-drink commercial may have the money and energy to jump through 30 scenes in 30 seconds, such a frenetic pace doesn't suit most PSAs. Don't take the chance of confusing your audience.

- Work from the general to the specific. A problem–solution format is usually best. Tell or show your audience the problem and then how it can be solved. Don't dwell on the problem, though; it'll turn off your audience.

- Demonstrations work well in the visual media. Show how your service works or what you want people to do.

- Always start with something interesting. Remember: You only have a few seconds to hook your audience. After that, they'll simply tune you out.

- Use testimonials when appropriate. People who are directly involved in your work, especially those being helped by it, can be very effective spokespersons. Don't avoid ordinary people. If they know what they're talking about, they can be much more effective than a celebrity who doesn't.

- In fact, avoid celebrities altogether unless they are or can be made to appear to be really involved in your cause. Using celebrities simply because of their celebrity status can be self-defeating. Your audience may remember them but not your message.

- On the other hand, if you are lucky enough to attract someone who is well known and who believes in what you are doing, you can create a memorable spot.

- Unless you have attracted a practiced professional, avoid stand-ups if possible. A stand-up is basically one person delivering your message. Unless you have a superb speaker—one who can really engage an audience with just a voice and a direct gaze—stay away from this approach. Also, make sure that whoever you pick can deliver your message sincerely, from a sound understanding of what you do and represent. Your audience will know if the message rings false.

- If you've got something interesting to show, however, use voice-over. It's ultimately better to show something other than just a face. In many cases, celebrities are easily identifiable by their voices or can identify themselves at the end of the spot. In fact, some celebrities would rather do just a voice-over because it saves them time and they don't have to go through all the preparation it takes to be seen on television.

- If you decide to show your phone number, address, or Web address on the screen, keep it up long enough for viewers to write it down—

usually at least eight seconds. Remember all those handy gadget commercials—"but wait, there's more!"? They read their phone numbers so many times you can recite them by heart. That's what you have to do, too.

- On the other hand, if it's not really important to have people call or write you—for instance, if your goal is to motivate people—you may not need a phone number or address at all. Decide what the purpose of your spot is, and leave out anything that doesn't contribute directly to that purpose, even if it's your phone number.

- In the same vein, if you do superimpose information on the screen, make sure what is being seen by your viewers is also being talked about. If it's a written message or an address, your audio should be reading it at the same time.

- Viewers won't listen if they are watching something that doesn't match what's being said. For example, a few years ago a famous national news anchor produced a piece on a presidential candidate that showed him stumping the country, smiling, and delivering his message of hope and good cheer. However, her voice-over lambasted the candidate for avoiding the issues and merely wrapping himself in the flag. She received a phone call the next day from the candidate's press secretary thanking her for the excellent coverage. "But, didn't you get it?" she said. "I spent nearly three minutes berating your candidate for avoiding the issues." "Do you think anyone was listening to you?" he replied. "All they were seeing were the great images of my candidate you put up for them to watch." In other words, if what you're saying doesn't match what you're showing, most people will go with what you're showing.

- If you must use music, use good music, either written and performed specifically for your spot or paid for from a commercial source. Be sure to match the feel of your music to your message.

Writing for Radio ━━━━━

The radio spot, like the television spot, must be absolutely clear in order to be understood—both by the listener and by the broadcaster who will be airing it. Remember from Chapter 6 that radio scripts are written for the ear. As such, you must be clear and simple, reducing ideas to their essence.

Radio may be the most flexible of media because it can rely on the imagination of the listener to fill in visuals. In radio, it is possible to create virtually any scenario that can be imagined by the audience. With the appropriate sound effects, you can have elephants perform on stage or lions in your living room; you can position yourself in the middle of the Amazon jungle or on the highest mountain peak. Radio spots are also much cheaper to produce than television spots and can be changed on much shorter notice. Lengths of radio spots vary. While television spots are typically either 30 or 60 seconds in length, radio spots can run anywhere from 10 to 60 seconds and any length in between. The standard lengths for radio spots are:

10 seconds, or about 25 words.

20 seconds, or about 45 words.

30 seconds, or about 65 words.

60 seconds, or about 125 words (not as common as the other lengths).

Types of Radio Announcements

Radio announcements are typically of two types: spot announcements and "as-recorded" spots. The simplest type of radio spot is the **spot announcement,** which involves no sound effects or music bed and is meant to be read by radio station personnel. This type is usually sent in a package of two, three, or four spots and can be general in nature, geared to a specific program, or tied to some specific time of the year or holiday.

Like television scripts, radio scripts must be uniformly formatted. Although most stations will transfer the information from a spot announcement to a 3-by-5-inch card for ease of handling, you should always send your spots on standard bond paper. Some other rules include:

1. Head up your spot with the name of the originating agency and its address and telephone and fax numbers. Include a contact name.

2. Title your spot and give the length at the beginning, not the end.

3. Because spot announcements are never more than one page in length, you may be able to get more than one per page. The standard is usually five or six 10-second spots per page; two 30-second spots per page; and one 60-second spot per page. As with news releases, end all spots with #####.

4. For ease of reading, type all radio spots in upper case, double-spaced. Talent directions, if there are any, should be upper and lowercase in parentheses.

Because spots are typically written as a series, it is necessary to develop a theme that will carry over from spot to spot. This is best accomplished by the use of key ideas and phrases, repeated in each spot. The concepts and ideas should be such that they can be developed more fully as the spots increase in length and time.

The spots in Exhibits 10.7, 10.8, and 10.9 employ some standard methods for creating a cohesive series. Whenever you produce a series of

EXHIBIT 10.7   Live Radio Spot #1

American Tuberculosis Foundation
1212 Street of the Americas
New York, N.Y. 00912

"YOUR GOOD HEALTH": 10 SEC. LIVE RADIO SPOTS

THE AMERICAN TUBERCULOSIS FOUNDATION AND THIS STATION CARE
ABOUT YOUR GOOD HEALTH. DON'T SMOKE . . . SOMEONE WHO LOVES
YOU WANTS YOU TO QUIT.
# # # # #

(station call letters) AND THE AMERICAN TUBERCULOSIS FOUNDA-
TION CARE ABOUT YOUR GOOD HEALTH. IF YOU SMOKE, TRY TO STOP.
IF YOU'RE THINKING OF STARTING, THINK TWICE.
# # # # #

SMOKING NOT ONLY HARMS YOUR LUNGS, IT HARMS THE LUNGS OF THOSE
AROUND YOU. SOMEONE YOU LOVE WANTS YOU TO QUIT. THE AMERICAN
TUBERCULOSIS FOUNDATION CARES ABOUT YOUR GOOD HEALTH.
# # # # #

IF YOU'RE THINKING OF STARTING TO SMOKE . . . THINK TWICE.
SMOKING HARMS YOU AND THOSE YOU LOVE. THE AMERICAN TUBERCU-
LOSIS FOUNDATION AND THIS STATION CARE ABOUT YOUR GOOD HEALTH.
# # # # #

GOOD HEALTH MEANS TAKING CARE OF YOURSELF. DON'T START SMOK-
ING. AND IF YOU ALREADY SMOKE . . . TRY TO STOP. SOMEONE YOU
LOVE CARES ABOUT YOUR GOOD HEALTH. A MESSAGE FROM (station
call letters) AND THE AMERICAN TUBERCULOSIS FOUNDATION.
# # # # #

---

spots, they should reflect a continuity of theme and message. Ask yourself
these questions about the spots:

1. What is the underlying theme or concept throughout the spots?
2. How is this theme carried out from spot to spot?
3. What key ideas and phrases are repeated in all the spots?

Notice that the longer spots in Exhibit 10.7 elaborate on the theme in some way. The shorter spots, especially the 10-second spots, are the basic message—often only the phrase or idea that will be repeated in the longer spots. The longer spots, particularly the 60-second spot, can take time for development and enumeration of points barely mentioned in the shorter versions.

Unlike the television spot, radio spots come not only in different lengths but in different formats as well. Television spots are rarely written to be read by a television announcer as a drop-in or time filler. The radio spot, on the other hand, can be prerecorded, utilizing many of the same techniques as television—sound effects, music beds, multiple talent, sound fades and dissolves, and changes in scenes. Of course, these effects are more difficult to pull off when you are restricted to audio only, but the challenge is in the trying.

As-recorded spots are produced by the originating agency and are ready to be played by the stations receiving them. They are usually sent in the format used by the particular stations or on reel-to-reel tape, which will probably be transferred to the proper station format. As with television spots, an accompanying script is sent along with the standard cover letter and response card.

As-recorded radio spots differ in format from television scripts but contain much of the same information. However, if you are basing your radio spots on already produced or written television spots, you will need to transfer the video cues to audio cues. For instance, if you are using a celebrity spokesperson who is easily recognizable on your video spots, she will have to identify herself on radio. Scene setting, which can be accomplished easily enough on video, will have to be taken care of verbally or through sound effects for radio. Consider the example in Exhibit 10.10 to see how a radio spot sets the scene.

How to Get Your PSAs on the Air ——————

The best way to ensure your radio spots get on the air is to follow each media outlet's guidelines for PSAs to the letter. Ask each media outlet for its guidelines. If an outlet doesn't have them in writing, ask for a verbal explanation. Some of the things you should look for in these guidelines are as follows:

- Find out the deadline. The media are deadline oriented. If you don't work within their deadlines, they won't run your PSA. Find out what their deadlines are, and plan as far ahead as you can.

- Most stations typically run shorter spots—usually 30 seconds. Find out what lengths they will run, and produce in that length.

- Submit rough versions of your scripts or ideas to the stations if time permits. Ask for their advice to make sure your needs meet theirs.

EXHIBIT 10.8   Live Radio Spot #2

```
American Tuberculosis Foundation
1212 Street of the Americas
New York, N.Y. 00912

"YOUR GOOD HEALTH": 30 SEC. LIVE RADIO SPOTS

DO YOU SMOKE? IF YOU DO, DO YOU REMEMBER WHEN YOU STARTED?
MAYBE YOU WERE A TEENAGER AND YOUR FRIENDS THOUGHT IT MADE
THEM LOOK "ADULT." WHATEVER THE REASON, SMOKING ISN'T GROWN
UP ANY MORE . . . IT'S JUST PLAIN STUPID. THE AMERICAN TUBER-
CULOSIS FOUNDATION AND THIS STATION WANT YOU TO KNOW THAT
SOMEONE YOU LOVE CARES ABOUT YOUR GOOD HEALTH. WE WANT YOU TO
HAVE THE CHANCE TO ACT LIKE A GROWN UP. IF YOU'D LIKE TO STOP
SMOKING,WRITE US. OUR ADDRESS IS:

THE AMERICAN TUBERCULOSIS FOUNDATION
BOX 1892
NEW YORK, NEW YORK 00911

                    # # # # #

WHEN YOU SMOKE, YOU'RE NOT JUST HURTING YOURSELF, YOU'RE HURT-
ING THOSE AROUND YOU . . . AND MAYBE EVEN SOMEONE YOU LOVE.
THE AMERICAN TUBERCULOSIS FOUNDATION WANTS YOU TO KNOW THAT
YOU CAN QUIT. WE'VE DEVELOPED A PROGRAM THAT WILL HELP YOU
STOP SMOKING IN 30 DAYS, AND WE'LL SEND YOU THAT PROGRAM FREE.
ALL YOU HAVE TO DO IS WRITE US AT:

THE AMERICAN TUBERCULOSIS FOUNDATION
BOX 1892
NEW YORK, NEW YORK 00911

WE CARE ABOUT YOUR GOOD HEALTH.

                    # # # # #
```

- Find out whether any of the stations will produce your spots for you. Some will, if you provide the script and it suits their needs. Look especially for cosponsorship opportunities through which the station can publicize its involvement with you.

- Be careful, though. Competing stations may not want to run spots produced by a rival station, especially if you use that station's "personalities." However, if a station merely produces your spots for you, find out if you can then run those on other stations.

EXHIBIT 10.9   Live Radio Spot #3

```
The American Tuberculosis Foundation
1212 Street of the Americas
New York, N.Y. 00912

"YOUR GOOD HEALTH": 60 SEC. LIVE RADIO SPOT

SMOKING CAUSES HEART DISEASE, EMPHYSEMA, AND CANCER. BUT DON'T
STOP SMOKING JUST BECAUSE YOU MIGHT DIE FROM IT. STOP SMOK-
ING BECAUSE SOMEONE YOU LOVE MIGHT DIE FROM IT. THAT'S RIGHT
. . . SECOND-HAND SMOKE IS A PROVEN CONTRIBUTOR TO HEALTH
PROBLEMS IN NONSMOKERS. WHEN YOU SMOKE AT HOME, YOUR CHILDREN
BREATHE THE SAME CANCER-CAUSING SMOKE YOU DO . . . AND THEY
DON'T HAVE ANY CHOICE. THEY CAN'T DECIDE TO QUIT SMOKING. BUT
YOU CAN. IF YOU WANT TO STOP SMOKING, WRITE US. WE'LL SEND
YOU A FREE PROGRAM THAT WILL HELP YOU STOP IN 30 DAYS. WRITE:

THE AMERICAN TUBERCULOSIS FOUNDATION
BOX 1892
NEW YORK, NEW YORK 00911

(repeat address)

REMEMBER, SOMEONE YOU LOVE CARES ABOUT YOUR GOOD HEALTH.

                        # # # # #
```

- Find out when each station is most likely to run PSAs. Although it might be best for you to get your message out during the Christmas season, the stations will probably be inundated with similar requests. You'll find that most stations have more available airtime following major holidays.

Remember: Broadcasting (and cable) still reach more people than any other medium. The proliferation of cable channels has multiplied your

EXHIBIT 10.10 As-Recorded Radio Spots

Northwest Library Association
1342 Placer Ave.
Seattle, Wash. 98901

"Werewolf" 30 Sec. PSA—As Recorded

(sfx: sounds of wind, howling, and footsteps running)

WOMAN: DID YOU HEAR THAT? IT SOUNDED LIKE A WEREWOLF!
MAN: DON'T WORRY. WE'RE SAFE.

(sfx: loud sound of bushes rattling and sudden snarling)

WOMAN: (very frightened) IT IS A WEREWOLF! WHAT ARE WE
            GOING TO DO?
MAN: (reassuringly) I TOLD YOU NOT TO WORRY. I HAD
            PLENTY OF GARLIC ON MY PIZZA TONIGHT, REMEMBER?
WOMAN: (sarcastically) I CERTAINLY DO.
WEREWOLF: (in terror) GARLIC! (screams)

(sfx: sounds of rapidly retreating footsteps and howling fading into distance)

WOMAN: (relieved) HOW ON EARTH DID YOU KNOW THAT GARLIC
            WOULD FRIGHTEN A WEREWOLF AWAY?
MAN: I READ IT IN A BOOK AT THE PUBLIC LIBRARY.
WOMAN: (sarcastically again) AND DID THIS BOOK EXPLAIN
            THE EFFECTS OF GARLIC ON YOUR DATE?
MAN: WHOOPS . . .
ANNCR: YOU'D BE SURPRISED WHAT YOU CAN LEARN AT YOUR PUB-
            LIC LIBRARY. GIVE READING A TRY . . . IT MAKES
            GOOD SENSE.
MAN: (voices fading as couple walks away) OH, COME ON
            CAROL, IT SAVED OUR LIVES DIDN'T IT . . . I'LL
            CHEW SOME GUM . . . I'LL BRUSH MY TEETH. . . .

                        # # # # #

---

opportunity for placement while further segmenting your audience for you.
Don't automatically discount broadcast and cable because of costs. As this
chapter has shown, there are ways to cut costs and still use the medium to
its fullest advantage. Explore those avenues. It can only help your chances
of being heard—and seen.

KEY TERMS

video news release (VNR)

actuality

public service announcement (PSA)

spot

script treatment

shooting script

accompanying script

talking heads spot

slice-of-life spot

spot announcement

as-recorded spot

EXERCISES

1. Monitor television programming for a two- or three-hour period. During that period, ascertain the number of public relations-oriented commercials/PSAs you see. Be careful not to select pure product advertising. Answer the following questions:
   - If the spot or spots are PSAs, who is the sponsor?
   - Can you determine the producer (for example, Advertising Council)?
   - Is the producer different from the sponsor?
   - If the spot or spots are legitimate commercials, are they image-oriented, public interest, or issue-oriented?

2. Contact a radio or television station news or program director and ask for the station's policy regarding the placement of PSAs. Present a report on the public service editorial policies of that station.

3. Write a 30-second script featuring a seated spokesperson asking for support for the United Way of Anytown, U.S.A. The appeal should be primarily to parents to support a new pediatric clinic to be built with UW support.

4. Write a 30-second script featuring two celebrities (of your choice) in which they endorse a "support cancer research" theme.

5. Tape a television commercial or PSA. Transcribe it in writing. Rewrite the TV spot as a 30-second radio spot, taking care to convert the visuals into verbal cues in the transition.

## CHAPTER 11

SPEECHES AND PRESENTATIONS

In this chapter you will learn:

- The types of speeches and their uses.

- The modes of delivery for speeches, and how they differ.

- How to prepare, write, and deliver a speech.

- How to handle a Q & A session.

- How to use presentation materials to accompany a speech, and why.

Speechwriting is putting words into someone else's mouth—and that's not an easy task. It requires an intimate knowledge of the person you are writing for. You need to know his or her style of speaking, body language, tone of voice, speech patterns, and, most important, personality. When you write a speech, you become the person you are writing for, and, to an extent, that person will become you at the moment he or she begins to speak your words.

Thus, speechwriting is a truly collaborative effort. It requires the absolute cooperation of all parties involved. Think of famous speeches you have heard or read: Patrick Henry's "Give me liberty or give me death," Winston Churchill's "Blood, sweat and tears," John F. Kennedy's "Ask not what your country can do for you," and Martin Luther King's "I have a dream" are a few examples. Often, famous speeches such as these were written by the speakers themselves, but just as often, they were collaborative efforts by the speakers, professional speechwriters, and others with valuable input into the process. As in all forms of public relations writing, everybody has something to say about what you write.

Whether you are preparing speeches for others or for yourself, this chapter serves as a good introduction. First we will talk about how to prepare, write, and deliver an effective speech or presentation and how to handle question-and-answer sessions. In the last section, we will discuss using audiovisual materials as support.

Types of Speeches

The public relations speech is as varied as the purposes to which the speech will be put. In fact, speeches are usually classified by purpose:

- A speech to *inform* seeks to clarify, instruct, or demonstrate.
- A speech to *persuade* is designed to convince or influence and often carries a call to action.
- A speech to *entertain* covers almost everything else, including celebrations, eulogies, and dinner speeches.

The type of speech you use will be determined largely by the topic and the audience. The method of delivery and the degree to which the speech relies on audiovisual aids also will depend on these factors.

Modes of Delivery

There are four basic modes of speech delivery: extemporaneous, impromptu, scripted, and memorized. For extemporaneous and impromptu speeches, the public relations writer is responsible primarily for the research and compilation of information, usually in outline form. The speaker then studies the notes carefully and is (theoretically) prepared to speak knowledgeably and fluently on the topic. Speeches delivered from script or from memory can be written entirely by the public relations writer.

For all modes of speaking, once the speech is prepared the primary responsibility of the public relations practitioner is to coach the speaker. This means, of course, that you must know how to give a good speech yourself. If you don't—and many public relations people don't—find someone who can and have that person coach the speaker. This often means hiring outside professionals to do the job, which may be costly, but in the long run may be well worth the effort and expense.

Preparing and Writing the Speech ————

Preparation is the most important element in any type of speech or presentation. Although some of us are able to speak "off the cuff," it is a dangerous habit to get into. Think of the politicians who have lost elections because of candid "off-the-record" remarks or unwise ad libs. It is extremely important that you prepare in advance everything you will say and do during a presentation. Don't leave anything to chance.

The "nuts and bolts" of an effective presentation include:

- Specific purpose.
- Clear understanding of your audience.
- Well-organized ideas.
- Adequate support.
- Effective delivery.

Specifying Your Purpose
Keep two important principles in mind here. First, the speech should be results oriented. Think of the effect you want it to have on the audience. Decide whether you want your audience to be persuaded, informed, or feel entertained by your presentation.

Second, the purpose of your presentation should be the basis for all the other decisions you make. This means that the way you organize your ideas, the kind of audiovisual support materials you use, even the way you deliver the presentation, will hinge on why you are giving it in the first place.

Analyzing Your Audience
Your presentation is given for your listeners. Even if you think it is the best presentation you have ever given, it will have failed if it doesn't affect them.

Analyze the occasion: What is the reason this group is together at this time, and what do they expect to hear from you?

Analyze the people: What experience and knowledge about the subject do they bring to your presentation? What is their attitude toward the subject? Toward you?

Organizing Your Speech

Good organization lets your audience know that you know what you're talking about. A seemingly confused speaker loses credibility and wastes valuable time. No one will sit still for long—especially if you're not making sense. And the only way to make sense is to be organized.

It is worth repeating that the best way to organize a speech is to think of its purpose. Use that purpose as the basis for deciding what goes in your speech, how you structure it, what data you present, even for deciding your style or wording.

Here is a typical speech format:

Introduction
- Attention-getter—Tell people why they should listen.
- Establish rapport—Create a bond with your audience. Show them what you have in common.
- Preview—Tell people what they are going to hear.

Body/discussion
- Main points, arranged logically (usually in order of importance).
- Data supporting each main point.

Conclusion
- Review—Summarize the key points the audience has heard.
- Memorable statement—Create a desired "frame of mind" that will stay with the audience.
- Call for action (if applicable).

Building a speech is like building anything else: You've got to have a solid foundation. It helps if what you build has a look of continuity, coherence, and completion. No one likes a structure that looks haphazard or loosely constructed. For speechmakers, a solid structure implies a solid idea.

You can see from this outline that in speeches, it pays to be repetitious. Tell people what you are going to do, do it, then tell them what you have done.

Most writers find it easier to work on the body of the presentation first, before thinking up a snappy introduction and conclusion.

The body of a speech may be developed in a number of ways:

- **Chronological**—Organized by time. For example, cover this year's events first, then next year's.

- **Spatial**—Organized by direction. For instance, talk about your company's development as it moved from the East Coast across the nation to the West Coast.

- **Topical**—Organized by topic. Cover one set of ideas that are related to each other, then move on to the next set of related ideas.

- **Cause and effect**—Organized by need/fulfillment. Describe "what we need" and then "how to get it."

- **Problem/solution**—Organized by question/answer. Describe the problem and then the solution, or vice versa.

Pay attention to how you word the main points you want to make. Work for parallelism, balance, and good transitions between main points. (Notice how the five types of organization described above begin with parallel openings. Notice, too, that they are balanced in both length and sentence structure.)

With the body of the presentation in hand, tackle the introduction. A good introduction is relevant to the audience and occasion, involves the audience personally, positively disposes them toward your presentation, and stimulates them.

A good introduction does not begin with the phrase, "Today I want to talk to you about . . . ," nor does it necessarily include a joke. Good introductions can be questions, unusual facts, good examples, stories, illustrations, metaphors, analogies, or any one of a number of other devices.

Once you have an attention-getting introduction, you can work on the conclusion of your speech or presentation. The conclusion should summarize or reiterate the main points of your presentation ("tell them what you have done"). Finish with a memorable statement that makes the purpose of the speech clear and positions the audience firmly on your side. If your speech is intended to persuade, you will also make a call to action—for example, to join the group you are pitching, or to call their local congressional representative about the issue you have just raised.

One of the best ways to organize a speech is to develop a summary sheet. Include at least the following information:

- **The audience:** What are the ages, educational backgrounds, and demographic characteristics of the audience members? How big is the audience?

- **The purpose:** Are you trying to inform, persuade, reinforce attitudes, or entertain? Complete the phrase, "After listening to my speech, audience members will. . . ."

- **Organization of the speech:** Is it chronological, spatial, topical, cause and effect, or problem solving?

- **Supporting materials:** What statistics, quotations, case histories, analogies, hypothetical illustrations, and/or anecdotes do you have to support your claim?

- **Purpose of introduction and conclusion:** How will you gain interest, create a need for listening, summarize, and call for action?

- **List of visual aids:** Which media will you use (slides, computer presentation, flip charts)? What content (words, charts and graphs, etc.)? How will visuals be integrated into speech (during, following, support only, or stand-alone?

For a complete sample summary sheet, see Exhibit 11.1.

Supporting Your Ideas

The detail or support you use to fill out your presentation must be sufficient to ensure that your listeners know precisely what you mean but should not be so overwhelming that you lose your audience in minutia.

Your support must be relevant to your listeners. If it makes no sense to them you will fail to get their attention, gain their good will, or persuade them to your view. For example, if you are writing a speech that intends to persuade the audience to give money to your nonprofit organization, you would want to include some concrete examples about how their money will be used—a pledge of $5 per month will deliver 100 hot lunches to shut-ins—but you don't need to detail the exact costs of each meal.

Use any kind of support that is appropriate to your purpose and ideas. Facts and statistics are almost mandatory for many business presentations, and examples and illustrations can often make those hard numbers "come alive." Quotations from a source your listeners respect can add proof that what you are saying is true. Analogies and metaphors can often be used to make concrete that which is abstract by bringing the abstraction down to human terms. Preachers use these two devices all the time. Remember, use enough support and detail to do the job—but no more.

Delivering Your Speech

Finally, you are standing in front of your listeners (assuming you are the speech- or presentation-giver). Now it is your job to make your ideas come alive. The secrets of effective delivery are thorough preparation and lots of practice. You cannot deliver a presentation effectively if you don't know what you want to say. That requires preparation. And the only way you can become a fluent speaker is to practice. There is no shortcut!

EXHIBIT 11.1

Summary Worksheet

Preliminary Questions

    I. What are the expectations of this audience?

    Toward me?

    Toward my topic?

    Toward this specific situation (are there any extenuating circumstances that should be considered)?

    II. How do I expect my audience to be affected by my presentation? Will the general purpose of my presentation be to inform, persuade, reinforce certain ideas, entertain?

    The specific thesis: After listening to my speech, the audience will . . .

The Body of the Speech

    III. What is the best structure to follow, given I and II above? Should my presentation be arranged chronologically? Spatially? Topically? By cause and effect? By problem-solution?

    The structure I have chosen is the best in this particular situation because . . .

    IV. What are the three or four main points suggested by the specific structure?

    A.

    B.

    C.

    D.

    V. How will I support the main points? Will I use statistics, examples, analogies, case studies, direct quotations?

    A will be supported by:

    B will be supported by:

    C will be supported by:

    D will be supported by:

    VI. How should I adapt my language and word choice to suit audience expectations?

    To what extent should I use jargon and "buzz words"?

    To what extent should I be conscious of defining certain words?

(Continued)

(Continued)

VII. Should I use any visual aids?
      What should be visualized?
      How should it be visualized?
      Why should it be visualized?

VIII. How should I introduce the speech?
      Why should my audience listen to this message?
      How will my audience benefit by listening to me?
      How can I make my audience want to listen?
      My audience should listen to me because . . .

IX.   How should I conclude the speech?
      How do I relate the conclusion to the main points I have covered?
      In conclusion . . .

OK. You are thoroughly prepared and well practiced. Now you must stand up and do two things. First, stick to what you have practiced. Don't get distracted. Don't "throw away" your prepared presentation for an impromptu effort. Second, keep your eyes on your audience. Look at them. Watch their reactions to what you say. Don't get engrossed in your script. In fact, try not to use a script at all; use an outline or brief notes instead.

Also, don't get engrossed in your audiovisual material. Watch the audience, not the screen. Even if you are using 35mm slides in a darkened room, look out at your audience. You won't be able to see them well, but it is important that they get the feeling you can.

Another piece of advice: Look relaxed, even if you aren't. Smile, frown, move your arms, look around the room at everyone. Try to feel as though you are in the middle of a lively conversation with a group of friends. It will do wonders for your delivery.

Handling the Q & A Session ━━━━━

Anticipation is the key to successful question-and-answer (Q & A) periods. If you're the type of speaker who has to have everything written out in advance, then Q & A is not for you. You need to know whether you can handle thinking, analyzing, and speaking off the cuff before you "throw yourself to the lions." The best hedge against blowing a Q & A session is practice. It's advisable to have someone who is familiar with the topic you cover in your presentation work with you on possible questions in advance.

That way, you have at least some idea of what to expect when you face the real thing. The following advice will help you when you do:

- Repeat the question or paraphrase it in your own words.
- Make sure you understand the question before answering it. Seek clarification if necessary.
- Don't lie, fabricate, or distort information. If you don't know the answer, say so—but don't appear flustered. Offer to find the answer and get back to the questioner. Confidence breeds credibility.
- Refer to any visual aids that will help you answer the question.
- Be concise—don't give another speech.
- Don't allow a questioner to take you on a tangent. Stick to the main points of your speech.
- Don't allow an individual questioner to monopolize the Q & A session.

Using Presentation Materials ━━━━

We live in a visual society today. Most of us watch TV or go to the movies. Our magazines and newspapers are more and more visually oriented. And, increasingly, we spend a lot of time "surfing the Internet." While the Internet still hasn't taken full advantage of melding visuals and words, it has come a long way, and it is fast becoming one of the most integrated media available to communicators. With all this focus on visual appeal, it's hard for a speech or presentation audience to maintain attention, even with the most persuasive of speakers, without something to look at. Used as integrated components of a speech, audiovisual materials can help keep the audience's attention and add valuable information.

Audiovisual support should be for impact—to develop audience interest and hold attention. Use it for effectiveness—to help your listeners remember more, longer. Don't use it simply because it is there. Use it only if it enhances your presentation. If you do use audiovisual support:

- Be sure it adds to your presentation.
- Don't let the support control the presentation. Your ideas must come first.
- Be sure to rehearse the presentation with the audiovisual materials. Learn how to use them.
- Don't talk to the visuals, talk to the audience.
- Talk louder—you are competing with the visuals for audience attention.
- Stand clear—remember, visuals must be seen to be useful.

Preparing Presentation Materials

The most common support materials used with speeches are visual-only support materials such as graphs, diagrams, photographs, and handouts; and audiovisual support materials such as videotapes, slides, and multimedia programs. The advent of software programs such as Adobe Persuasion (now out of print) and Microsoft PowerPoint has ushered in a new age of audiovisual presentation. These programs, and others like them, combine the traditional support of slides with an entirely new element: motion. Now, instead of using charts and graphs on posterboard, a videotape, and a slide show, you can prepare all of these support materials in one place.

In the past, it took a lot of work and a pretty hefty investment in equipment just to add dissolves to your slide show (two projectors and a dissolve unit, at least). Today, you can add not only dissolves, but fades, wipes, and myriad other effects to your slide show just by pressing a few computer keys. You can also add music, moving images (captured video, for instance), and voices—all digitized and implanted into your slide show. And now, with the latest projection technology, these shows aren't even limited to your computer screen. They can be projected onto screens rivaling those at your local theater (they also cost about as much as your local theater's).

While the technology has drastically changed, the rules for developing a good slide presentation haven't. A good slide show should add zip and clarity to information that may otherwise be dull. It requires that you be well organized, know your audience, and follow a few simple rules:

1. **Define your objective.** Be sure you know what you want to accomplish, what changes you want to take place in your listeners, and what behavior you want to affect.

2. **Analyze your audience.** Are they lay people or experts? Do you aim for the "lowest common denominator"? The middle? The top? The more you know about your audience, the easier it is to make that decision.

3. **Work from an outline when creating your visual presentation.** Don't replicate everything you are going to say. Keep it to a concise summary of the major points and supporting materials needed to reach your objective with this audience.

4. **Decide what mood or treatment you want.** A light, humorous treatment may mean cartoons and a comic narration. Are you going to threaten? Cajole? Be low-key? Mood makes a difference in how you use color and pacing.

5. **Write a script, if you plan to use one.** This will include all of the details not reflected in your visual presentation.

6. **Plan your slides:**

- Convert material originally designed for publication to slide format. *Hint:* You can scan this material and insert it into your slides as needed. In my experience, most of the presentation software accepts PICT format best, and images saved in PICT format typically take up less memory. Also, if you're projecting directly from a computer, or showing your slide presentation on your computer, you don't need the highest resolution. Scan your images at no greater than 100 dots per inch (dpi).

- Use a series of slides or charts, disclosed progressively, to build up complex ideas. *Hint:* If you have a long list of subpoints spread among several slides, be sure to use the same header on each slide so your audience remembers what your major point is.

- Keep all copy and symbols simple and legible. Projected letters should be at least two inches high and one-half inch wide. What this means to you is that your type size shouldn't be any smaller than 18 points or it won't be legible. *Hint:* Use sans-serif type and keep it mostly bold. Serif type tends to be harder to read when projected.

- Make all copy on slides short and to the point. Include no more than 15 or 20 words or 25 or 30 pieces of data per slide. Again, remember to keep the type size legible.

- Keep slides simple and bold. Limit each slide or chart to one main idea.

- Use charts and graphs rather than tables. Tables almost always look complicated and confusing.

- Use variety in layout, color, charting, and graphics for change of pace. *Hint:* Don't use more than one slide background per slide show. Presentation software includes a dizzying selection of background templates. Pick one and stick to it for your entire presentation. *Second hint:* Pick uncluttered backgrounds and dark colors for use with light-colored lettering. Uncluttered backgrounds allow you more space to work, while light letters against dark backgrounds are easier to read.

- Avoid mathematical formulas or equations on slides.

- Keep photographs uncluttered.

- Keep moving. Leave slides up only long enough for the audience to read. Remember: The slides are there to supplement and support your words and ideas, not take your place. *Hint:* Most presentation software allows for manual or automatic mode. In most cases, you'll want control of the speed yourself using the manual mode. Only use automatic if your slide show is designed to run unaccompanied as a stand-alone display.

- Enlist the aid of a competent audiovisual specialist. While the new programs aren't all that difficult to learn, your presentations can still benefit from someone trained in visual design.

7. **Edit your slide presentation.** Ask yourself the following questions:
   - Are all major points covered?
   - Does the content of each slide fit the narration?
   - Are all slides legible?
   - Are colors and visuals bold and effective?
   - Does each slide depict one idea only?
   - Is there good continuity from slide to slide?
   - Does the program add up to form a visually coherent and pleasing presentation?

8. **Rehearse, rehearse, rehearse.**

9. **Prior to your presentation time, visit the room where you will be making the presentation to make sure the projector is there and in working order.** Run through your program to make sure all is as you want it. *Hint:* Computer compatibility is still a problem, especially between electronic projectors and laptop computers. Ideally, you would have your own portable setup. If you don't, meet with the computer technician in charge of the facility where you will be presenting and make sure everything works before the curtain goes up.

10. **Slide programs are almost always given in darkened rooms.** The only other light may be the one on the lectern you use. The new computer projection units aren't any brighter than the old slide projectors. That means you must make a special effort to force yourself to look out into a blackened room at people you may be unable to see. Don't lose eye contact with them, because they can see you just fine. Remember: A slide show is an accompaniment. *You're* the real show.

See Exhibit 11.2 for sample computer-generated slides.

Scripting for Audiovisuals

Scripts employing visual accompaniment are formatted similarly to television scripts, with visuals on the left and narration on the right. No matter whether you are writing for a live presentation accompanied by visuals or a self-contained presentation that will run automatically with narration already added, the technique of scripting is the same. A script includes everything you are going to say, not just an outline of your visuals. Unless you (or your presenter) have done this particular presentation a number of

EXHIBIT 11.2   Computer-Generated Slides

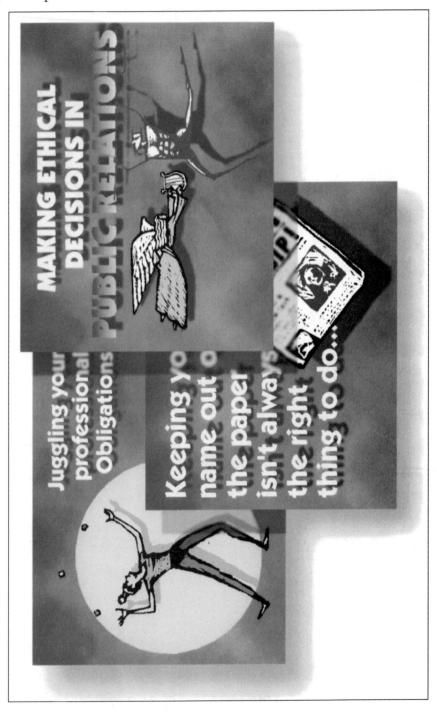

times or are very good at *prompted extemporaneous speaking* (using visuals as reminders), you'll probably need a script.

The audiovisual script should be easy to follow. Visuals appear exactly opposite their audio counterparts, often with numbers corresponding to the slide placed within the script narration to indicate the exact point at which the slide will be changed.

The major difference between audiovisual scripts and television scripts is length: Slide presentations are usually longer with fewer visual changes. To keep them lively, count on changing slides every five to ten seconds. Much depends on the type of presentation. For instance, if you are presenting the annual budget report, you might be severely limited as to the type and number of slides shown. If the slide contains written information, gauge the amount of time it will take to read it by reading it aloud. If you are dealing strictly with visual images, then the five- to ten-second time allotment should be just about right The new technology allows for a number of special effects that can alleviate some of the boredom of static slides (points popping on the screen one at a time, graphics moving in and out, etc.). Just don't overdo the movement.

Exhibit 11.3 is a slide/tape presentation that accompanies a fund-raising appeal to corporate sponsors from a major university. See if you can discern where best to place the slides within the narration. What do you see as the theme or focus of this first page? Can you tell who the intended audience is from the tone and focus?

EXERCISES

1. Prepare a brief presentation about your school or college, selling it as a great place to get an education. Hit heavily on its strengths (e.g., location, educational reputation). Use the format presented in this chapter for combining words and visual aids. If you have access to presentation software, develop your full audiovisual support that way. Try developing a support slide show and a full, stand-alone presentation.

EXHIBIT 11.3 Slide Script

Society for Needy Children   Contact: Lucille Bevard
4240 Welxton Ave.   Day Phone: 555-8743
Newhope, Minn. 78940   Night Phone: 555-9745

SNC FUNDRAISER NETS $75 THOUSAND   FOR IMMEDIATE RELEASE

:90 Seconds
Tape Roll (SIL)

A little girl stood for the first time today to receive a new teddy bear and a check for $75,000 from the Society for Needy Children. Eight-year-old Mary Patterson accepted the check on behalf of the children at the St. Mary Martha's Children's Hospital. The money represents the culmination of a year-long fund-raising drive by the Society. The money is earmarked for a new ward to be devoted exclusively to the treatment of crippling diseases in children. One of the first beneficiaries will undoubtedly be little Mary, who has been disabled by congenital arthritis since birth. Along with her new teddy bear, Mary and the other children at the hospital will be using a new physical therapy center that was donated through a matching grant from the Friends of St. Mary Martha's. Hospital Administrator Lois Shelcroft says that the check and the new therapy center are just the first step . . .

(SOT: Shelcroft :20)

(CUT TO SHELCROFT INSERT OUTRO: ". . . continue next year.")

The next fundraising drive, scheduled to begin in September, will provide money for a new lab.

# # # # #

## CHAPTER 12

DESIGN, PRINTING, AND DESKTOP PUBLISHING

FOR IMMEDIATE RELEASE   In this chapter you will learn:

- What design is, and why it is important in communication, particularly public relations publications.

- The principles of design.

- How to choose the appropriate typeface, ink, paper, and printing process for a publication.

- What desktop publishing is, and how it has changed the design and printing process.

- How to work well with a printer.

Design is central to the success of any communication. In fact, most designers would go so far as to suggest that design is just as important an element of a publication as writing. Don't get me wrong: If your writing stinks, graphic cartwheels and high-design acrobatics won't cover up the smell. But the point must be made that good design attracts and holds readership, while bad design repels and discourages it. If you don't get them in the tent, they won't see the show.

Like it or not, we read externally first and internally second. That is to say, we judge publications not only by their covers, but by their overall visual appearance as well. Design provides an outward structure upon which we further communicate our messages, sell our soap, project our images, inform our publics, and otherwise hang our corporate hats. Although most companies pay plenty of attention to the design of their ads, packaging, logos, and other images, they often lose sight of design's importance when it comes to their publications.

But make no mistake. Whether the publication is internal (a newsletter, benefits folder, or employee recruitment kit) or external (a brochure, annual report, or company magazine) its design requires careful planning. Without structure, visual thought, and order, a publication will not get the attention it deserves. No matter how well written and carefully edited your message may be, readers will pass over poorly designed print materials. It's as simple as that.

For these reasons, then, we need to spend some time talking about design. As a public relations writer, you must understand and be able to use basic design principles. Second, you need to develop a design vocabulary, so that you can communicate clearly with designers, printers, and other publication professionals. Third, you must know how the eye moves through a page (so you can direct and redirect visual traffic) as well as understand how to attract and hold readers. Finally, you need to comprehend the "parts of sight" as clearly as you know the parts of speech.

Design: What It Is and
Why It Might Be Greek to You —————

Before venturing further, we need to define what we mean by **design.** Essentially, design is the act of bringing order to whatever surrounds us. It is planning and organizing physical materials and shaping and reshaping our environment to accommodate specific needs. There's nothing particularly mysterious about design, but many of us are intimidated by it.

For one thing, few of us have had much visual education. That looms especially ironic when you consider how much our learning and survival depend upon sight. Think about it: With few exceptions, our verbal literacy is learned, broadened, and specialized through vision—i.e., through reading and writing skills. We study letters, words, spelling, vocabulary, grammar, syntax, style, writing, and literature. Grammar is apt to be central to our language studies from third grade through our first year of college. Writing begins before we start our formal education and runs fully through all the years of our education. Visual studies, however, tend to end somewhere between the second and third grades when crayons are either thrown or taken away.

Another reason why we underestimate the impact of design is the effortless nature of sight itself. Our eyes are designed to receive and process lines, shapes, textures, colors, intricate spatial relationships, and other complex visual information almost instantly. So long as we keep our eyes open, we don't run red lights, fall down stairs, open the wrong end of a soda can, or trample people. That sight works so easily is both good and bad. Good in that our visual sense operates automatically, is well greased, and complete beyond our wildest dreams. Bad in that we take it for granted and often assume that to have sight is to have visual literacy. Of course, this is no more the case than to assume that speaking a language is the same as reading and writing that language.

It should come as no surprise, then, that design seems foreign to most of us. It enjoys its own vocabulary, grammar, syntax, composition, and meaning. Additionally, it possesses a unique literature, history, and heritage—one that, in fact, precedes written language. But, happily, acquiring this new visual "language" is considerably less painful than the average root canal procedure. Let's get started.

Designing Public Relations Materials ——————

Do different print formats require different design approaches, principles, and strategies? More simply stated, do you design differently for different formats? Well, yes and no. Or, as Winnie the Pooh might say, it all depends.

There is a set of design principles that applies to whatever we create, regardless of format, medium, intent, or audience. In each instance, we plot a visual course that becomes the blueprint for our publication's architecture. And although publication formats vary, just as buildings differ, they possess similar structural principles—just as skyscrapers, shopping malls, museums, and homes have some characteristics in common. Publications, like buildings, employ a structural plan that mixes serious pragmatic and aesthetic concerns while providing a sound framework and foundation.

But every publication deserves a good design that takes into account its format, medium, intent, and audience (see Exhibit 12.1). For example, the exaggerated vertical *format* of a brochure presents a set of spatial concerns much different from those of a poster. The brochure's long, relatively small, and narrow area is arranged in a series of panels—of equal or

EXHIBIT 12.1   Hyundai Newsletter

The Hyundai newsletter, *Horizons,* folds down to an 8½-inch square by folding it first vertically, then horizontally. This provides for an eight-page newsletter with an intriguing design.

unequal size—that can be folded two, three, or more times, vertically or horizontally. These properties make the brochure's continuity and sequence especially important. A poster, on the other hand, presents a single "face" to its reader and is, therefore, designed much more like a print ad with a point of emphasis for entry and a series of "guides" leading the reader through the integrated communication.

The *medium* also brings its own eccentricities and needs to the design. While an annual report may bear a strong resemblance to a magazine—and the best ones seem to— it requires special care to design a report that communicates with its many audiences while conforming to exacting SEC requirements that prescribe everything from logistics to point size. Designing a poster that will be read from across a room by a moving audience—or that may itself be moving—presents a different challenge. The point is that the medium brings its own unique eccentricities and needs to the design.

Intent also figures squarely into the design formula. Let's assume that a company has had a financially disastrous year. While it can easily afford a full-blown, four-color report with portraits of smiling CEOs in three-piece suits, perceptive company planners might decide that a more austere approach is warranted. Or, perhaps due to a corporate takeover or a major image overhaul, a company decides to completely reposition itself and court a changed or new audience. To do so, it redesigns everything from newsletter to logotype. Simply put, your purposes affect the look and structure of what you publish.

Finally, bear in mind something that should be obvious at all times: All publications should be designed with their *audience* in mind. Too often we forget the audience by neglecting to notice that it has changed dramatically or is in the process of a major change. Or, we're so insulated that we don't measure what we publish by the most important touchstone—our consumers. Nothing like a sudden decline in readership for the company newsletter to alert an editor to potential problems.

Principles of Design ─────

Most of us don't pay much attention to a design when everything is correctly ordered. In fact, the average person seldom sees design in anything at all. We read newspapers daily without noticing the skeletal framework that orders the headlines, photography, graphics, text, and other style elements of a page. And we raise our wineglasses to toast without realizing that the stems are designed to keep our hands from warming the wine. But the best design is like that: it exists but doesn't call attention to itself. As a friend once remarked, "A good designer doesn't design for design's sake. The best design serves its purpose, period—without calling attention to itself."

While there are a number of basic design principles, most public relations writers can get by well enough if they understand only an indispensable few. These are balance, proportion, sequence, emphasis, and unity. Other design choices facing the PR writer involve grids, alignment, and typefaces. We'll discuss these issues, too.

Balance

Most of us intuitively understand balance—at least to the extent that we notice immediately if something is out of balance. As children, we seemed to just know that if the person on the other end of the teeter-totter was bigger than us, we had to sit closer to the end to counterbalance their weight. In a way, we might say that balance is natural to human beings. We seek it in our lives, our budgets, and in the way we view the world. The very fact that we walk upright (at least most of the time) suggests that we understand balance somewhere deep in our genetic programming.

In its simplest form, **balance** as it relates to design means that what is put on one side of a page should "weigh" as much as what is on the other side. All the elements you place on the page have weight, even the white space you leave by not placing elements. Size, color, degree of darkness—all play a part in balance.

There are two ways to achieve balance. The easiest is the *symmetrical approach*. To balance symmetrically means to place exactly the same amount of weight in exactly the same positions on either side of the page (or spread). Symmetrically balanced pages tend to appear more formal and can be used to impart a non-verbal conservatism to your layout. The *asymmetrical approach* is generally more interesting. The technique involves shifting weight on one side of a page or spread to balance the opposite side (much like in the teeter-totter example). For instance, if a two-page spread has a big photo near the gutter (the center line of a two-page spread) on one side of the layout, you can achieve balance by placing a smaller picture closer to the outside edge of the opposite page (see Exhibit 12.2). This arrangement works with all elements of varying weight, including white space. An asymmetric layout appears less formal than its symmetric counterpart.

When you increase the number of elements on a page or spread, you increase the difficulty of working with symmetrical balance. It is difficult, for instance, to ensure that all your photos will be the same size, all your illustrations roughly the same shape, or all your headlines the same length (especially if you want to emphasize a story over others on the page). In fact, we are almost forced into asymmetry on most layouts unless we plan carefully for the opposite effect.

For the beginner, there are several ways to check whether your layout is balanced, all based on looking at it from an altered perspective. For one, you can squint at your layout. The blurring attained through narrowing

EXHIBIT 12.2 Balance

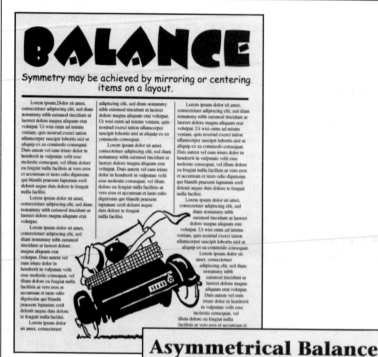

The easiest way to achieve balance is through pure symmetry. Place identically weighted elements on either side of the center axis of the page. Symmetry can also be affected by centering objects. Asymmetry, on the other hand, requires more practice to achieve. The fundamental rule in asymmetric balance requires visualizing your layout as a teeter-totter. Balance the objects on either side of your vertical axis according to weight and distance from the fulcrum.

your eyes tends to block out the light areas and bring the darker areas of your layout to the forefront. You can also turn your layout upside down or look at it in a mirror. Both of these methods provide you with an opposite view, and, thus, a new look at your layout. Balance, or lack of it, will jump out at you almost immediately.

Proportion

We tend to think of proportion in terms of comparison. For instance, a picture on a page is bigger or smaller than another picture on the page, or it is the largest element on the page in comparison to the other elements. Thus, **proportion** is a measure of relationship in size. It helps to show one object's relationship to other objects in your layout. For example, articles and their accompanying pictures, cutlines, and pull quotes typically will form a proportional whole in relationship to the rest of the page. Or the space that separates articles from one another may be greater than that which separates the elements within an article. We use proportion to tell us what belongs with what on a page.

Our sense of proportion has, or should have, a parallel in nature. Pythagorus, the Greek mathematician and philosopher, noticed this over 2,000 years ago when he suggested that the most pleasing proportion is based on a roughly 2 to 3 ratio. In Pythagorean terms, the lesser dimension in a plane figure is to the greater as the greater is to the sum of both. Using the 2:3 ratio, 2 is to 3 what 3 is to 5. Get it?

Fortunately, there is a simpler method of explaining the concept. Think of a page of typing paper. It is 8½-by-11 inches—roughly, a 2:3 ratio. In other words, it has an asymmetric proportion rather than a 1:1, symmetric proportion. For designers, this means avoiding dividing a page into halves, or any increment of a 1:1 ratio, such as 4:2 or 6:3. Not that this rule has to be religiously followed, but it does add visual interest to your layout. A layout based on halving the page is more formal, more constrained.

A more practical—and easier—method of working with a page layout is the **rule of ground thirds.** This method requires that you divide a page into thirds, and that you balance the page using a two-thirds to one-third ratio. You've probably already noticed that two-thirds is roughly equivalent to three-fifths, the Greeks' favorite aspect ratio. This two-thirds to one-third ratio is commonly used in newsletter layout, but is most often apparent in print advertisements in which a large graphic image takes up two-thirds of the page, while the copy takes up the other third.

Don't get the idea that you have to group two-thirds of your elements into two-thirds of every page. This ratio can be achieved in a number of ways. For instance, you can have a page two-thirds full and one-third empty. Or you can have a page that is two-thirds empty and one-third full (although your boss might think this a little wasteful). Exhibit 12.3 shows a page that is two-thirds occupied by a headline and text and one-third occupied by a photo.

Sequence and Emphasis

When we look at a page, we tend to move from big elements to smaller elements, dark areas to lighter areas, colored elements to black-and-white elements, bright colors to muted colors, and unusual shape to usual shape. As shown in Exhibit 12.4, proper **sequence,** or order, of the elements on your layout will literally lead your readers through your page.

Emphasis has to do with focusing your readers' attention on a single element on a page. This is what you want them to see first, and is usually where you want them to start interpreting your page. We emphasize elements by assigning them more optical weight than other items on the page. These emphasized elements are larger, darker, more colorful, oddly shaped. They draw the readers' attention first among all the other items on the page (see Exhibit 12.5).

There are a number of simple techniques that, if used properly, will show your readers exactly where to look first and where to go from there. And while the following guidelines below are meant specifically for newsletter layout, they can be adapted to many other types of layout as well:

- **All elements.** Elements placed high on the page will gain emphasis; elements placed at or near the bottom will have less emphasis. Placement near or at the center of the page will also gain emphasis, especially if used in conjunction with another form of emphasis such as color or size. The left side of a page or the left page of a two-page spread has priority over the right. On the other hand, the outside margins of a two-page spread (the left margin of the left page and the right margin of the right page) are focal points as well.

- **Headlines.** For heavier emphasis, place headlines at the top or near the center of the page. The eye naturally falls in these areas. Additional emphasis can be gained by using a larger point size or stretching the headline over more than one column width. Typical options, then, are one-column heads in a smaller point size, heads of more than one column in a smaller point size, one-column heads in a larger point size, and heads of more than one column in a larger point size.

  Depending on the number of columns you are working with and the range of point sizes you choose, the degrees of emphasis are many. Keep in mind, however, that you should vary headline size by no more than a few basic increments. For example, if minor heads are set at 18 points, major heads should not be larger than 24 or 30 points. This closeness in point size adds to the unity of your design. The rare exception might be the major headline on the front page of your

EXHIBIT 12.3   Proportion

PROPORTION

Means filling your page in a 2 to 3 ratio

Proportion is achieved by using the Greek principle of "ground thirds." In this example, the headline and copy take up approximately two-thirds of the page while the picture occupies the other third.

Dolore magna aliquam erat volutpat. Ut wisi enim ad minim veniam, quis nostrud exerci tation ullamcorper suscipit lobortis nisl ut aliquip ex ea commodo consequat. Duis autem vel eum iriure dolor in hendrerit in vulputate velit esse molestie consequat, vel illum dolore eu feugiat nulla facilisis at vero eros et accumsan et iusto odio dignissim qui blandit praesent luptatum zzril delenit augue duis dolore te feugait nulla facilisi.

Lorem ipsum dolor sit amet, consectetuer adipiscing elit, sed diam nonummy nibh euismod tincidunt ut laoreet dolore magna aliquam erat volutpat.

Lorem ipsum dolor sit amet, consectetuer adipiscing elit, sed diam

nonummy nibh euismod tincidunt ut laoreet dolore magna aliquam erat volutpat. Duis autem vel eum iriure dolor in hendrerit in vulputate velit esse molestie consequat, vel illum dolore eu feugiat nulla facilisis at vero eros et accumsan et iusto odio dignissim qui blandit praesent luptatum zzril delenit augue duis dolore te feugait nulla facilisi.

Lorem ipsum dolor sit amet, consectetuer adipiscing elit, sed diam nonummy nibh euismod tincidunt ut laoreet dolore magna aliquam erat volutpat. Ut wisi enim ad minim veniam, quis nostrud exerci tation ullamcorper suscipit lobortis nisl ut aliquip ex ea commodo consequat.Lorem ipsum dolor sit amet, consectetuer adipiscing elit, sed

newsletter. You might go all the way to 36 points, but be sure that your headline doesn't then conflict with and lessen the impact of your banner or nameplate.

- **Articles**. Place lead articles at or near the top of the page. Also place "continued" articles (known as *jumped articles*) at or near the top. Since continuation lines (e.g., "continued from page 1") are usually small, you can still emphasize another article on the same page as a

EXHIBIT 12.4 Sequence

SEQUENCE

Dolore magna aliquam erat volutpat. Ut wisi enim ad minim veniam, quis nostrud exerci tation ullamcorper suscipit lobortis nisl ut aliquip ex ea commodo consequat. Duis autem vel eum iriure dolor in hendrerit in vulputate velit esse molestie consequat, vel illum dolore eu feugiat nulla facilisis at vero eros et accumsan et iusto odio dignissim qui blandit praesent luptatum zzril delenit augue duis dolore te feugait nulla facilisi.

Lorem ipsum dolor sit amet, consectetuer adipiscing elit, sed diam nonummy nibh euismod tincidunt ut laoreet dolore magna aliquam erat volutpat.

Lorem ipsum dolor sit amet, consectetuer adipiscing elit, sed diam nonummy nibh euismod tincidunt ut laoreet dolore magna aliquam erat volutpat. Duis autem vel eum iriure dolor in hendrerit in vulputate velit esse molestie consequat, vel illum dolore eu feugiat nulla facilisis at vero eros et

accumsan et iusto odio dignissim qui blandit praesent luptatum zzril delenit augue duis dolore te feugait nulla facilisi.

Sequence means leading your rader throught your pages by the use of visual cues.

Lorem ipsum dolor sit amet, consectetuer adipiscing elit, sed diam nonummy nibh euismod tincidunt ut laoreet dolore magna aliquam erat volutpat. Ut wisi enim ad minim veniam, quis nostrud exerci tation ullamcorper suscipit lobortis nisl ut aliquip ex ea commodo consequat.

Lorem ipsum dolor sit amet, consectetuer adipiscing elit, sed diam nonummy nibh euismod tincidunt ut laoreet dolore magna

aliquam erat volutpat. Duis autem vel eum iriure dolor in hendrerit in vulputate velit esse molestie consequat, vel illum dolore eu feugiat nulla facilisis at vero eros et accumsan et iusto odio dignissim qui blandit praesent luptatum zzril delenit augue duis dolore te feugait nulla facilisi.

Lorem ipsum dolor sit amet, consectetuer adipiscing elit, sed diam nonummy nibh euismod tincidunt ut laoreet dolore magna aliquam erat volutpat. Ut wisi enim ad minim veniam, quis nostrud exerci tation ullamcorper suscipit lobortis nisl ut aliquip ex ea commodo consequat.

In this example, the large photo in the upper-left corner draws your eye naturally to the starting point (helped by our natural inclination to look there anyway). The headline, natural column flow, pull quote, and the final photo all lead you to the exit point at the lower right of the layout.

jumped article by working with the headline. By using boxes and tint blocks, you can emphasize an article by setting it off from other elements on the page. Also, dividing your page into ground thirds and placing an emphasized article in either portion by itself will get it attention.

• **Graphics.** Larger photographs and other graphic devices impart greater emphasis, no matter where they are placed. Smaller elements

EXHIBIT 12.5   Emphasis

Emphasis
Means creating a focal point for your layout

Dolore magna aliquam erat volutpat. Ut wisi enim ad minim veniam, quis nostrud exerci tation ullamcorper suscipit lobortis nisl ut aliquip ex ea commodo consequat. Duis autem vel eum iriure dolor in hendrerit in vulputate velit esse molestie consequat, vel illum dolore eu feugiat nulla facilisis at vero eros et accumsan et iusto odio dignissim qui blandit praesent luptatum zzril delenit augue duis dolore te feugait nulla facilisi.

Lorem ipsum dolor sit amet, consectetuer adipiscing elit, sed diam nonummy nibh euismod tincidunt ut laoreet dolore magna aliquam erat volutpat.

Lorem ipsum dolor sit amet, consectetuer adipiscing elit, sed diam nonummy nibh euismod tincidunt ut laoreet dolore magna aliquam erat volutpat. Duis autem vel eum iriure dolor in hendrerit in vulputate velit esse molestie consequat, vel illum dolore eu feugiat nulla facilisis at vero eros et accumsan et iusto odio dignissim qui blandit praesent luptatum zzril delenit augue duis dolore te feugait nulla facilisi.

Lorem ipsum dolor sit amet, consectetuer adipiscing elit, sed diam nonummy nibh euismod tincidunt ut laoreet dolore magna aliquam erat volutpat. Ut

wisi enim ad minim veniam, quis nostrud exerci tation ullamcorper suscipit lobortis nisl ut aliquip ex ea commodo consequat.

Lorem ipsum dolor sit amet, consectetuer adipiscing elit, sed diam nonummy nibh euismod tincidunt ut laoreet dolore magna aliquam erat volutpat. Duis autem vel eum iriure dolor in hendrerit in vulputate velit esse molestie consequat, vel illum dolore eu feugiat nulla facilisis at vero eros et accumsan et iusto odio dignissim qui blandit praesent luptatum zzril delenit augue duis dolore te feugait nulla facilisi.

Lorem ipsum dolor sit amet, consectetuer adipiscing elit, sed diam nonummy nibh euismod tincidunt ut laoreet dolore magna aliquam erat volutpat. Ut wisi enim ad minim veniam, quis nostrud exerci tation ullamcorper suscipit lobortis nisl ut aliquip ex ea commodo consequat. Duis autem vel eum iriure dolor in hendrerit in vulputate velit esse molestie consequat, vel illum dolore eu feugiat nulla facilisis at vero eros et accumsan et iusto odio dignissim qui blandit praesent luptatum zzril delenit augue duis dolore te feugait nulla facilisi.

Lorem ipsum dolor sit amet, conse ctetuer adipisc ing elit, sed diam nonummy

Using strong graphics, color, unusual shapes, or large type will all indicate to your readers where you want them to look first; however, this may not mean you want them to start reading there. Although emphasis can be used to establish sequence, it can also be used simply to draw attention to something, with the understanding that the reader should then know where to look to begin reading. In this example, that entry point is established by the headline.

placed at the top or bottom of the page can also gain emphasis. A small photo, for example, placed at or near the bottom of a page might help balance a large headline placed at the top of the page.

Again, graphic elements should follow the general restrictions of your *grid* (the number of columns you are using). Thus, a three-column grid will allow photos of one, two, or three columns in width. Remember, too, that the darker the graphic element, the more emphasis it will have. This applies to boxed articles and tint blocks as well (see Exhibit 12.6).

- **White space**. White space is not usually thought of as an element of emphasis. Rather, it is usually an element of *contrast*—that is, it is used to emphasize something else, not draw attention to itself. The one rule to remember when using white space is, don't surround it with other elements. White space should be pushed to the outside of your pages, not the inside. And on a two-page spread, the only white space between the two pages should be the gutter. Wide side margins, heavy drops (the amount of white space at the top of a page), or uneven bottoms all add contrast. The creative use of white space will add an air of affluence to your publication and make it look more sophisticated. Too much white space, on the other hand, will make a newsletter look like its editor ran out of stories. Remember that white space is weighted just like any other design element. Using it effectively requires a lot of practice.

Unity

Unity is one way of providing readers with a whole by drawing relationships among its various parts. This means that body type and headline type should be compatible. Photos should be either all black-and-white or all color. The layout should be all formal or all informal. In other words, unity is the creation of a recognizable pattern.

Perhaps the best way to gain unity of design has more to do with an overall look, a unifying design (see Exhibit 12.7). Following are some basic guidelines for gaining unity in your publication:

- Stick with one or two typefaces. You can gain a lot of variety by simply changing size and weight and working with the various forms that any one particular typeface offers. For example, some faces come in light, text, regular, bold, black, and ultra, not to mention the italic versions of all these variations. Two typefaces should be plenty.

- Use justified type for a formal look, unjustified type for an informal air. To increase the formality of unjustified type, just increase the hyphenation. This will make your lines less ragged on the right and thus more formal.

- Use rules (lines), tint blocks, and boxes for more formality; eliminate them for informality.

- Use top and bottom "anchors" (lines or strips of color) for more formal layouts.

- Make sure all illustrations are of the same type. If you are using cartoons, stick with cartoons throughout. If you're using pen and ink

EXHIBIT 12.6   Tint Boxes

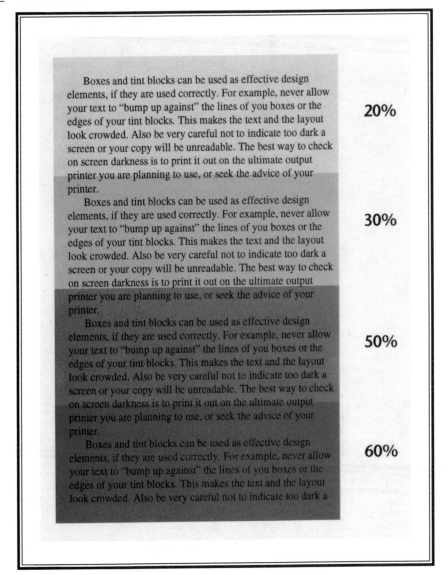

Boxes and tint blocks can be used as effective design elements, if they are used correctly. For example, never allow your text to "bump up against" the lines of you boxes or the edges of your tint blocks. This makes the text and the layout look crowded. Also be very careful not to indicate too dark a screen or your copy will be unreadable. The best way to check on screen darkness is to print it out on the ultimate output printer you are planning to use, or seek the advice of your printer.

20%

Boxes and tint blocks can be used as effective design elements, if they are used correctly. For example, never allow your text to "bump up against" the lines of you boxes or the edges of your tint blocks. This makes the text and the layout look crowded. Also be very careful not to indicate too dark a screen or your copy will be unreadable. The best way to check on screen darkness is to print it out on the ultimate output printer you are planning to use, or seek the advice of your printer.

30%

Boxes and tint blocks can be used as effective design elements, if they are used correctly. For example, never allow your text to "bump up against" the lines of you boxes or the edges of your tint blocks. This makes the text and the layout look crowded. Also be very careful not to indicate too dark a screen or your copy will be unreadable. The best way to check on screen darkness is to print it out on the ultimate output printer you are planning to use, or seek the advice of your printer.

50%

Boxes and tint blocks can be used as effective design elements, if they are used correctly. For example, never allow your text to "bump up against" the lines of you boxes or the edges of your tint blocks. This makes the text and the layout look crowded. Also be very careful not to indicate too dark a

60%

When using tint boxes, take care that your type will read well over the percentage screen you've chosen. Top to bottom are 20, 30, 50, and 60 percent screens.

illustrations, stick with them. Too much variance in artwork will lend an air of confusion to your publication.

- Increase white space for a more informal look. The same goes for the use of larger graphics, especially those that are unboxed.

EXHIBIT 12.7   Unity

Unity means using compatible elements in your layout (type, artwork, photos, design, etc.). The best way to lose unity is to combine too many disparate elements in a single layout. In this simple brochure layout, only three typefaces are used (headline, subhead, and body copy), along with a single illustration style. This gives the piece a unified design.

Grids

As already noted, a **grid** is another term for the columns used in a layout. While the use of grids is most common to newsletter, annual report, and magazine layout, they also can be valuable for complex brochures and flyers as well as ad layouts.

For publications such as newsletters, the most common formats are three- and four-column layouts. Both are quite flexible, with three-column being more appropriate for smaller formats and four-column for larger. The more columns you have, the narrower they will have to be and the smaller your type needs to be to accommodate the column width.

If you're just beginning, try a basic three-column grid for all your pages. The column width is enough to give you a readable type and to use graphics in legible sizes. The basic rule of laying out a newsletter is to use the columns as your grid and lay all your elements out (in our three-column grid) in one-, two-, and three-column widths. Exhibit 12.8 shows an example.

Alignment

Alignment refers to the way your copy is arranged in relation to column margins. The two most typical alignments are *flush left* (sometimes called *ragged right*) and *justified*. Flush left copy is getting to be quite common for newsletters, some in-house magazines, and other types of publications. It imparts a less formal look, involves less hyphenation, and takes up more space.

Justified copy looks more formal, is more hyphenated, and takes up less space. However, when using justified copy, keep in mind that the width of your columns severely affects word spread. The narrower your columns, the more your words will separate from one another in order to maintain justification. Computers allow for minute adjustments to word and letter spacing to help correct this spread, but the best way to avoid it is to keep your columns at the average or maximum width for your type size.

There are other alignment possibilities, as well, such as *flush right* and *centered*. Flush right copy should be avoided because it is difficult to read. However, it is sometimes useful for very brief text blocks such as pull quotes that appear in outside left margins. Centered body text should always be avoided. Centered headlines are not in fashion these days, although centered pull quotes are still found quite a bit.

The best idea is to pick either flush left or justified for your body copy and not to deviate. Stick with flush left for headlines. Use either flush left or justified for pull quotes and captions. (See Exhibit 12.9.)

Type and Typefaces

Type is the generic term for the lettering used in printing, while **typeface** refers to the nearly limitless alphabets and ornaments available as type. **Font** is the classification within a given typeface, such as bold or italic. The array of type and typefaces you can choose from is truly bewildering. But if you learn a few basics now, that array can be narrowed down to just a few choices for you and your public relations material.

EXHIBIT 12.8   Three-Column Layout

As you can see, all the elements on these two pages conform to the three-column grid. Not only do the headlines and text fit within one column, but the illustrations are also designed to fit either one or two columns. Try not to use fractions of columns, which will make your layout look jumbled.

EXHIBIT 12.9   Text Alignment

What's the difference between a therapist, psychologist, psychotherapist, psychiatrist, and counselor? If you don't know, you're among the millions of people who are confused about the multi-tiered mental health counseling field.

The Public Relations Student Society of America (PRSSA) at the University of Oregon has been retained by the Association to develop a program of information that will better define the various roles contained under the umbrella term "mental health counselor." Jamie Weiskoff, regional director of AMHCA says that the confusion seems to stem from a misconception over what constitutes a "counselor."

What's the difference between a therapist, psychologist, psychotherapist, psychiatrist, and counselor? If you don't know, you're among the millions of people who are confused about the multi-tiered mental health counseling field.

The Public Relations Student Society of America (PRSSA) at the University of Oregon has been retained by the Association to develop a program of information that will better define the various roles contained under the umbrella term "mental health counselor." Jamie Weiskoff, regional director of AMHCA says that the confusion seems to stem from a misconception over what constitutes a "counselor."

What's the difference between a therapist, psychologist, psychotherapist, psychiatrist, and counselor? If you don't know, you're among the millions of people who are confused about the multi-tiered mental health counseling field.

The Public Relations Student Society of America (PRSSA) at the University of Oregon has been retained by the Association to develop a program of information that will better define the various roles contained under the umbrella term "mental health counselor." Jamie Weiskoff, regional director of AMHCA says that the confusion seems to stem from a misconception over what constitutes a "counselor."

Notice that the justified text (top) takes up less space than the flush left text (center). The flush right text (bottom) is nearly impossible to track (move from end of one line to the beginning of the next).

The first thing to know is how to classify type. Let's start with the most general, and useful, classification for publication purposes. First of all, type is measured in **points** (in type, this is a vertical measurement). There are 72 points in one inch. Imagine trying to designate 11-point type in inches and you know why printers have traditionally used a different scale. Small type, up to 14 points, is called **body type.** Type that is 14 points and above is called **display type** (normally used in headlines). Most typefaces come in both body and display sizes; however, there are subtle differences between the sizes. The best way to choose type is to look at a complete alphabet in all the sizes and weights you are going to be using and check out the differences for yourself. Look for straight or curved serifs, for example, or whether the loops close or are left open on certain letters. Most of these distinctions boil down to a matter of taste. Only you know which is best for your job.

Next, type can be broken down into five other, fairly broad categories: blackletter, script, serif, sans serif, and italic. For our purposes, we'll look at just the last three. Exhibit 12.10 shows samples of each typeface.

- **Serif.** Most **serif typefaces** are distinguished by a variation in thick and thin strokes, and by *serifs*—the lines that cross the end strokes of the letters. Serif type can be further broken down into *romans* and *slab*, or *square serif*, faces. Romans have the traditional thick and thin strokes, while slab serif faces have relatively uniform strokes and serifs. Serif faces usually are considered easier to read, especially in body type sizes.

- **Sans serif.** **Sans serif typefaces** are without serifs (*sans*, from the French, meaning "without"). They are usually, but not always, distinguished by uniformity of strokes. They usually impart a more modern look to a publication, especially if used as display type. Setting body type in sans serif is unwise because the uniformity of the strokes tends to darken your page and makes for difficult reading. There are some exceptions. Optima, for example, has some variation in stroke and reads fairly well in smaller sizes. Additionally, Stone Sans, a new face designed by Sumner Stone of Adobe Systems, makes excellent use of thin and thick strokes.

- **Italics.** Some typographers don't consider italics a separate category of type because most typefaces today come with an italic version. However, true Roman italic versions of many typefaces are completely different from their upright versions. Since the advent of desktop publishing, editors have had the option of italicizing a typeface with a simple keystroke. This method typically only slants the existing face; it does not always create a true italic version of that typeface. Only by selecting a typeface that has been designed specifically as an italic do we get true italics. Because they are slanted, italics tend to impart an informality and speed to your message. On the other hand, also because of the slant, they are more difficult to read and should be used for accent only.

Just as a point of interest, italic refers only to a version of a serif face. A slanted version of a sans serif typeface is called *oblique*. Like italics, true obliques are designed as separate fonts (a complete alpha-

EXHIBIT 12.10   Type Samples

Serif Type

Times

Serifs are the small lines that cross the end strokes of the letters in serif type. Roman serifs have the traditional thick and thin strokes.

Lubalin

Square or slab serifs have fairly uniform thicknesses of both the letter strokes and their serifs.

Sans Serif Type

Helvetica

In this example of sans serif type (Helvetica), notice the uniformity of stroke width. This is characteristic of most, but not all, sans serif type.

Optima

Optima is one of several sans serif typefaces with some interesting variation in strike width. This variation (along with a hint of serifs) tends to make the face more readable.

Italic/Oblique Type

Type Type

There is quite a bit of difference between a true italic face (Goudy italic) left, and a slanted version of the upright face, right. Type designers would just as soon you didn't distort their original typeface designs.

Type Type

Sans serif typefaces don't have italic versions per se. Instead, they have obliques. Like italics, obliques are specifically designed to be set at a slant. They are not simply slanted versions of the upright face.

bet, number series, and set of punctuation points and miscellaneous marks) and are not simply the original face at a slant.

If you are typesetting or desktop publishing your publication, then you will have to select typefaces. Following are some of the most common questions regarding that selection:

- **Can I use just one typeface?** Yes. The safest route to take is to stick with one typeface. Using a single face lends your written material unity and consistency. Pick one that comes in as many variations as possible—style, weight, size, and width.

Most typefaces come in *regular* and/or *light* versions. These are sometimes called *book* or *text*. They also come in *upright* (roman) and italic (or oblique, if the typeface is sans serif). In addition, they may have *demibold* and *bold* versions in both upright and italic or oblique (these versions may be called *heavy* or *black;* or heavy and black versions may be in addition to bold). And the demibold and bold versions may come as *extended* and/or *condensed* (referring to the width of the letters).

The greater the variety available, the more flexibility you have in a single typeface. For example, you could use the regular version for body type, the bold version for headlines, and the regular italic version for captions, pull quotes, and subheads (in different point sizes).

- **Can I use more than one typeface?** In spite of the fact that you may have access to a type library of 20 or more faces, try to limit yourself to no more than two different typefaces in a publication, and make sure they don't conflict with each other. This is the most difficult part of using more than one face. Here are a few guidelines to remember:

  - If your body type is serif, try a sans serif for headlines. Two different serif faces will probably conflict with each another.

  - If you are using a light body type (as opposed to its regular version), use a regular or demibold headline type. You don't want your headline weight to overpower your text weight.

  - Above all, don't pick your type just by looking at a type chart. Have a page set, complete with body copy and headlines, to see for yourself whether your two faces are going to harmonize.

- **Where do I go to select type?** If you are working on a computer, you probably have 20 or so typefaces that come with either your system software or your layout software or both. In addition, you can easily add anywhere up to 400 or 500 choices, depending on the sophistication of your desktop-publishing system. Stick with a small array of type. It's easier and saves a lot of frustration in the long run. If all you have is Times Roman, use it. If you have Times Roman and Helvetica, use Times for the body copy and Helvetica for the headlines. If you have access to a larger type library on your computer, explore your options by experimenting with several combinations, printing out a page with each one.

Don't forget to try several different point sizes for body copy. There can be a great deal of variation in readability between 12-point Times and 12-point Palatino, as well as between 12-point Palatino and 10-point Palatino, for example.

Also, be aware that your type will look different when printed on different printers. Decide which printer you're going to use to print your final camera-ready copy and check its print quality against your type choice. Typefaces with thin serifs may not print as well on a dot-matrix printer as on a laser printer, or as well on a laser printer as on an imagesetter. Bold or heavy faces (especially if condensed) will tend to clog and fill on dot-matrix and laser printers but will print cleanly on an imagesetter. If you don't have access to different typefaces on your computer, ask your printer for samples of type set in copy blocks and as display type. Most printers can provide you with more than just a type chart.

Working with Printers ─────

The relationship between the writer-designer and printer should be a symbiotic one; however, both of you will probably have to work at it for a while until you get comfortable with the relationship. The trick to working successfully with printers is to know what you are talking about—there's no substitute for knowledge. You have to know a bit about the printing process in order to get along with your printer. Every writer can tell you horror stories about printers who, after seemingly understanding exactly what you want, proceed to print exactly what they want. This is not to say that it is hard to get along with printers. It simply means that you have to know what you want and be able to explain it in printer's terms. I recommend that you try out several printers and work with those who not only give you the best deal, but who also are willing to give you good guidance. This is not an easy process, but it does pay off in a lower frustration factor in the long run.

It used to be that printers took over as soon as you handed them your copy. These days, however, it's just as likely that you've not only written the copy, but also designed the piece and laid it out before you ever talk with a printer. You no longer have to go through a typesetter, for instance. However, most printers can still desktop publish your piece for you if you don't know how. And while you can often even download your work directly to a printer's file server, it is still wise to speak with them in person first in order to avoid the almost inevitable hardware and software incompatibilities.

For example, does the printer carry the typefaces you use in your publication? If not, can you legally supply them or do you have to "print" your publication to a Postscript file, thus imbedding all the fonts in the publication itself? Do you know how to print to a Postscript file? Do you even know what a Postscript file is? You're probably beginning to get the picture. No matter how sophisticated we may get, for the foreseeable future we will still be relying on printers for much of what we need in the way of finished product.

In addition, printers can be an invaluable aid in selecting printing methods, papers, inks, bindings, and so on. Even the seemingly simple process of picking a paper can be mind numbing. There are literally thousands of papers available for printing and an unlimited number of ways you can size, fold, and otherwise decorate your printed product. Just remember: You can get what you want if you know how to ask for it.

Printing Processes

Many writers simply entrust the choice of printing method to the printer. Although there are a number of printing processes available to you, probably the two you will have most contact with will be offset lithography and quick printing or quick copying. Most collateral pieces and many newsletters are simply offset printed, which is one of the fastest and cheapest methods to get good-quality printing today. Quick-print and quick-copy methods will usually result in a loss of quality. Other, more detailed printing jobs, such as embossing or special paper shapes, may require specialty printing. Be advised that specialty printing is costly. Make sure that you are willing to bear the extra cost before you decide on that gold-foil stamp on the cover of your new brochure.

Offset Lithography. The most common printing process used today is **offset lithography.** This process is based on the principle that oil and water don't mix. During the printing process, both water and ink are applied to the printing plate as it revolves. The nonprinting area of the plate accepts water but not ink, while the image, or printing, area accepts ink but not water. It is named *offset* printing because the plate isn't a reverse image as in most printing processes; instead, as shown in Exhibit 12.11, the plate transfers its right-reading image to an offset cylinder made of rubber (which reverses the image), and from there to the paper. Because the plate never comes in contact with the paper, it can be saved and used again and again, saving cost on projects that have to be reprinted periodically—unless, of course, you make changes.

Most public relations documents are printed using offset lithography. It is relatively inexpensive compared to other processes, and it results in a high-quality image. Although small press runs of 1,000 or less can be made using offset lithography, it is especially cost-effective for larger runs, because presses are capable of cranking out hundreds of copies a minute.

Quick Print and Quick Copy. The quick-print or quick-copy process involves two methods of reproduction.

Quick print involves a small cylinder press using paper-printing plates. The plates are created using a photoelectrostatic process that results in a raised image created with toner (much like the toner used in photocopy machines). This raised image takes the ink and is imprinted directly onto the paper.

EXHIBIT 12.11 Offset Printing

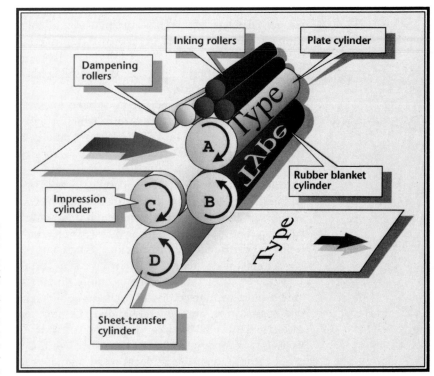

Offset gets its name from the indirect, "offsetting" printing process, in which the printing plate's image is "offset" to a rubber blanket that puts the ink on the paper. Notice how the type and image go from right-reading to reversed to right-reading again.

Quick copy used to mean exclusively xerography; however, many of the newer quick-copy setups, such as Xerox's Docu-Tech, don't use this now-familiar process at all. Instead, these machines (literally computers) use laser technology to print. The result is a rapid-print method that is not limited to black-and-white, like xerography, but can present a wide range of grays. This is a great boon to newsletter editors who use a lot of photographs, for example (anyone who has ever photocopied a photograph knows how bad the quality can be). The larger model photocopiers used in this process can rapidly produce multiple copies in sizes up to 8½-by-17 inches.

Neither of these processes is useful for two-color work, but both are inexpensive and fast. If you are going to use photocopy, reserve it for rush projects or those that won't suffer from single-color xerography. Be aware, also, that there can be major differences between photocopiers, and even between copies run on the same machine. A copier that ran your last job beautifully may not repeat the same quality the next time if the toner hasn't been changed recently. Don't be afraid to ask for a test print of your most difficult page to make sure the blacks are really black and there is no fade-out on any part of the page.

Choosing Paper

Paper choice is one of the most important aspects of producing effective public relations documents, particularly a collateral piece such as a brochure. Your choice of paper may determine whether your brochure is picked up and read, whether it lasts more than one or two days before it falls apart, or whether it even works well with your chosen type style, graphics, and ink color.

When choosing a paper, you will need to consider three major criteria. First, does the paper suit the use to which it will be put? In other words, does it have the right look, feel, color, durability, and so on? Second, how much does it cost? Third, are you using a laser printer?

Suitability. In judging the suitability of your paper choice to your job, you must first determine the nature of your information. Some pieces, such as flyers or announcements, are printed on relatively cheap and lightweight stock and are meant to be thrown away soon after reading. Others need to be more permanent. A brochure outlining company benefits to employees, for example, is one that probably will be kept and used over and over again. It will need to be on a heavier and more durable stock. A company magazine printed in four-color will need a durable paper that will take constant opening, closing, and general handling without tearing because the publication will probably be passed on to other readers. A flyer announcing this weekend's company picnic, on the other hand, can be printed on a lightweight stock because it is meant to be read and discarded quickly.

Aside from durability, three other factors need to be considered in judging the suitability of your paper: weight, texture, and color.

- **Weight.** Papers come in various weights. Weight is determined by taking 500 sheets of the paper and weighing it. Although a heavier weight usually indicates a thicker stock, it doesn't have to. One 25-pound bond paper may be thicker than another; likewise, one 60-pound book paper may be lighter and less durable than another. The best way to judge weight versus thickness is to personally handle the paper for each type of stock. Most printers have hundreds of samples of paper stock and can help you select the weight and thickness you want for your job. As a general rule, stick with text weights for newsletters and magazines and heavier, or cover, stocks for magazine covers and brochures.

- **Texture.** Texture is also an important consideration when choosing a paper. Heavily textured paper may impart a feeling of quality or a feeling of roughness, depending on the paper stock and the method of manufacture. Basically, papers break down into two broad categories for texture: matte-finish and coated stock. *Matte finish paper* ranges from a paper with a rather smooth but nonglossy surface to heavily textured paper. *Coated stock paper* refers to any paper that is "slick" or "glossy." Again, the range is considerable. Photographs often reproduce better on coated stock, which is what most magazines use. On the other hand, using a matte stock will soften the color and give a photograph an entirely different feeling. Some heavily textured stocks may not take ink well but may be perfect for foil stamping or embossing. The best way to tell if your idea will work on a certain texture stock is to ask the printer, look at some samples, and come to an informed decision.

- **Color.** Paper color has to complement all the other graphic elements of your collateral piece—typeface, ink color, photographs, and artwork. It will also set the mood of your piece. Color preference is a very personal matter. Remember, however, that you are producing pieces to be read by certain target publics who may or may not like your color choice. Thus, to an extent, color choice is a matter of gauging your intended audience's reaction to a particular color. Research has shown, for instance, that business people will not respond to questionnaires printed on hot-pink paper (not much of a surprise). They will respond well to beige and various shades of white, but respond very little to pale blue and green. All colors carry connotations for most people. You need to stay away from outrageous combinations and any color you think might not get the response you want from your information piece.

Cost. The determining factor in your paper choice may well be cost. Don't despair, though, just because your budget may be limited. Paper comes in thousands of weights, colors, and textures; one of them will fit your cost restrictions. Also remember that a few extra dollars on a good grade of paper may well pay off in the long run by impressing your readership.

Paper for Laser Printing. Some papers are made specifically for laser printers, and some papers definitely should be avoided. Ask yourself three questions when you pick laser printer paper:

1. Will the laser copy be used as a finished piece or for reproduction?
2. Does the paper say what you want it to say? In other words, what is its look and feel?
3. Does the paper run well in your printer?

Keeping in mind the paper specifications presented earlier, the following guidelines should help you select the proper paper for your needs and your printer:

- Brighter paper reproduces well on laser printers. (This doesn't mean whiter paper; there are varying degrees of brightness even among white papers.) Brighter papers are also good for reproduction masters. In fact, several manufacturers make papers specifically for laser printer output that will be used for reproduction. Also, because it's hard to predict the degree of darkness of your printer, the brighter the paper, the more contrast you are likely to have between the print and the paper. In general, avoid colored paper; however, some interesting effects can be obtained with lighter colors such as gray and beige.

- Stay away from heavily textured paper. The heavier the texture, the more broken your type will look, because it will be harder for the toner to adhere to the paper's surface. Texture also affects any large, dark areas such as screens and display type. Some texture, like that found in bond paper and linen stock, is fine. The trick here is to experiment.

- Avoid heavy papers weighing 90 pounds or more (like cover stock), unless you enjoy removing jammed paper from your printer. On the other hand, extremely light papers, such as onion skin, may stick to the rollers or jam as they feed into the printer. Don't experiment much here. Just settle for a text-weight paper (generally around 60 pounds) and consign the choice of cover paper to your commercial printer.

- Use a fairly opaque paper, especially if the laser-printed copy is to be your final version. If you use a paper with high opacity, be sure it isn't also heavily textured.

- Don't expect heavily textured papers to retain their texture. Unlike off-set presses, laser printers flatten the paper as it moves through the printer. In most cases, any texture will be lost.

- By the same token, don't use embossed or engraved papers in your laser printer because they might jam the mechanism and will flatten out anyway.

- Make sure your paper is heat-resistant. Because laser printers work in temperatures of around 4000° F, certain letterhead inks may melt or stick and any metal or plastic will certainly ruin your printer. Above all, don't use acetate in your laser printer unless it has been specifically designed for your particular printer.

Choosing Ink

Choosing an ink can be a nightmare for the novice. Even the most experienced designers often have a short list of their favorite inks. Inks come in virtually limitless color combinations. And each color will be affected by the paper it is printed on—coated paper will result in brighter colors while matte finish paper will soften the color. The texture of the paper also affects ink color, as does using colored paper.

There are no easy ways to learn what inks to use. The best way for a beginner to choose an ink is to look at other work done using the same ink/paper combination. Also, obtain a copy of the Pantone Color

Matching System® (PMS). It's really just a color sample book, like the ones you see when you pick out a house paint, but it is the most commonly used system among printers and designers. You'll be amazed at the variety of colors available to you. Don't be embarrassed, however, to stick to the basic colors to begin with. They are usually the safest to work with. Your printer will usually have a Pantone book you can use while there. Pantone's address is on the sample book. Just write them and ask about obtaining your own copy.

If you don't want any surprises, ask to see samples of work your printer has done using different papers and inks. Most printers take great pride in their work and will be more than happy to share it with you.

Color brings an added dimension to any publication, whether it's as simple as a second color to help accent, unify, or dress out a publication, or as complete as full color. To use color effectively, you should have a rudimentary understanding of how the different color processes operate. The two most common are spot color printing and process color printing.

Spot Color Printing. Spot color printing (also known as **two-color printing**) is the placement of a second color (black, or whatever the primary inking color, being the first) in a publication. (Note that in printing, black is counted as a color.) Unless you're using a multicolor press, applying the second color means an additional press run. That translates to more ink, materials, handling, press time, and money.

In two-color printing, two sets of printing plates are made, one for each color run. Often, a designer will use the black (or other first color) for the type and use the second color for the art and graphic highlights—such as dropped-initial letters. This also means that you have to create two originals, one for the black plate and one for the second color. This is not an easy process for most people and is usually left to a designer or printer. Check with your printer first and see what their requirements are for two-color printing.

Process Color Printing. Process color printing (also known as **four-color printing**) is used for reproducing full-color artwork or photography. This illusion of full color is accomplished by optically mixing the three primary colors—yellow, red (actually magenta), and blue (called cyan)—along with black. Four-color plates are shot through a screen to reduce solid areas to printable, graduated dot patterns. Because each color is shot through a slightly different angle screen, the screened halftone of each blends through the overlaid dot patterns.

During printing, each color is applied separately, one plate at a time and one color atop the others. The quality of this four-color overprinting method largely depends upon the quality of the original work, the quality of the cameras, plates, and printing press used, and upon the skills and professionalism of those who operate the equipment. Process color is best left to your printer to handle for you. As always, ask in advance.

Binding

With binding, as with everything else, if you want to know what to expect, ask your printer, and seek out samples on your own. Basically, there are two types of binding: the kind used for relatively thin publications such as magazines and pamphlets, and the kind used for thicker publications such as books. We'll discuss only those most applicable to public relations output here.

Regardless of what you are binding, it will probably be organized into signatures. **Signatures** are groupings of pages printed on both sides, usually 16 to a signature, but sometimes fewer, as long as they're in multiples of four (pages printed for binding are usually printed four to a two-sided sheet of paper).

After signatures have been collated, they may be bound. Among the most common bindings that public relations people are likely to use are *saddle stitching, perfect binding,* or *spiral binding.* Most quick printers can do saddle stitching and spiral binding; however, only larger printers will be able to do perfect binding. More traditional forms of binding, such as *case binding* (for hardcover books), are reserved for publications you want to last longer than you.

Swipe Files

One of the best ways to tell your printer what you want is to show them an example. A **swipe file** is a collection of your favorite pieces done by other people or companies. They will help you a great deal with design, layout ideas, and writing style, as well as with communicating your ideas to printers. You may find a particular brochure, for instance, that is exactly the right size and design for the information piece you want to produce. You may decide to use similar paper, ink color, or even design. Most graphic artists, designers, and printers use ideas generated from a variety of sources. Don't plagiarize your source, however, and don't steal the artwork right off the source brochure. Be careful to differentiate between emulation and plagiarism. If you do decide that you must "borrow" directly from another piece, obtain permission from its originator in advance of the publication of your piece.

Keep a swipe file of samples to show your printer. If you find a piece that you would like to emulate, show it to the printer to get an idea of how much it will cost to produce. The printer can tell you what the typeface is and whether your copy will fit in that size, as well as the paper stock and weight, ink color, and mechanical specifications—all of which will affect the price. For the beginner, a sample is worth a ten-thousand-word explanation.

Preparing Computer Layouts for Printing

The final stage of layout is the *mechanical,* the finished camera-ready layout that goes to the printer. The computer has revolutionized this process. If you are diligent, exact, and working with a limited range of graphics, you can present your printer with a mechanical in one piece—with no pasted-up parts. Computer imagesetters, such as the Linotronic, print out your layouts onto paper exactly as you have designed them, ready to be shot into printer's negatives. You can even go directly to negative film from an imagesetter, saving the cost of shooting negatives from a positive mechanical—but only if you are completely satisfied with your layout.

Assuming you are working in black-and-white, there are several ways to construct your mechanical:

- You can have it run entirely off an imagesetter, either from your computer disks or through a network or telephone line hookup. This requires that all of the elements on your mechanical be computer-generated: word-processed text and display type; borders, boxes, and rules produced in your page-layout program; photos scanned, cropped, and sized in either a photo manipulation program (such as Adobe PhotoShop) or right in your layout program; illustrations created in a paint, draw, or illustration program and imported or placed in your layout program; and any color separations already performed by your software.

- You can run the basic mechanical (text, display type, rules, and boxes) on an imagesetter and have photos and art shot separately and stripped into the negative before the printing plate is made. If you don't have a scanner or access to electronic clip art, this is probably the closest you'll get to having the whole thing done in one step. Even at this level, the savings in typesetting and paste-up alone are worth it.

- You can run your mechanical on a laser printer at either of the above two levels. This assumes you either don't have access to an imagesetter, or you don't feel that the extra quality is needed for your particular publication. Some very nice newsletters and brochures can be offset printed directly from laser-printed mechanicals. Most office-quality laser printers are capable of printing to plain paper at anywhere from 300 to 1200 dots per inch (dpi) resolution.

    An imagesetter can print either to resin-coated paper positives or directly to right-reading film. Printing to film greatly enhances resolution, especially of scanned photographs, because it eliminates one step in the printing process—the shooting of negatives from camera-ready copy. When imagesetting directly to film, always ask for a proof prior to final printing.

Preparing Print Orders

The most important interface between the desktop publisher and the printer is when the print order is submitted. Following are several sets of suggestions for getting your publication out of your computer and onto paper:

In General. Always call your printer in advance to see how they can meet your publishing needs. Find out:

- If they support your computer platform (Macintosh or Windows).
- If they can use your fonts, have their own versions of the fonts you used, or accept only PostScript files.
- If you can download directly to the printer or if you have to bring your work in on disk.

When you submit your material, include the following:

- The name and version (3.0, 5.4, etc.) of the software application you used to create your publication.
- File names under which your publication is stored.
- Hard copy of the publication (if you've laid it out already).
- Kind of output desired (imagesetter, laser printer, offset lithography).

Regarding Photos and Artwork. If you do not include your artwork and photos directly in your file and require that the printer either mechanically or digitally work with your graphics, observe the following guidelines:

- Photos and artwork should be cropped and marked with the finished size, either a percentage of the original or the final image dimensions.
- Place crop marks in margins of photos and artwork. If there are no margins, then tape it to a larger sheet and indicate crop marks.
- Use a felt-tip pen to put instructions on backs of photos. Marks made by graphite pencil or ballpoint pen can leave impressions on the face of the photo that reproduce. Avoid putting paper clips or staples on photos.
- Keep photos and artwork free of dirt, glue, wax, and other foreign material.
- If you mark instructions near artwork or copy, it is best to use light-blue pencil or pen.
- Avoid rolling maps, charts, or artwork into tubes. Keep these items flat if possible.

- Find out in advance the maximum sizes that can be handled by your printer's reproduction equipment.
- Find out the maximum sizes that their digital scanners can accommodate.

Proofs.

- Read proofs carefully and mark corrections plainly so they can be seen easily; a red pencil or pen is best. Use standard proofreader's marks.
- Avoid changes on bluelines (the final printer's proof) unless they are essential. Changes at this stage are costly because the plate (if it is to be offset printed) has already been made.

A Word on Desktop Publishing ───────

Anyone who assumes the responsibilities of writing and laying out a publication for an organization has a lot to learn. The availability of desktop-publishing software and hardware designed specifically to augment those tasks has made the job, if not easy, at least manageable by a single person. What once had to go through the traditional writing, editing, typesetting, paste-up, and printing processes can now be done in fewer steps and with the involvement of fewer intermediaries. While it may be true that a desktop-publishing system won't make you an instant designer, it does provide the writer, editor, and designer with more tools to better accomplish their respective jobs. Without the knowledge and experience gained through a study of the basics of writing, editing, and design, however, even the best hardware and software won't help you.

The greatest benefit of desktop publishing to the public relations writer is that it allows you to control your own output, right down to the printing. Its greatest drawback is that it allows you to control your own output, right down to the printing. In other words, desktop publishing's greatest asset is also its greatest deficit, and you are the deciding factor. Unless you become skilled at not only writing and editing but also layout and design, the complete benefits of desktop publishing may never be realized for you. But that's OK. What you really need to do is to realize exactly what you can do, what you are willing to learn to do, and how much you can afford to spend to get it all done. Remember, everybody has to begin somewhere, and, fortunately for us, there is a wealth of programming to fit every need.

Ultimately, your final, printed publication is going to determine how successful your desktop-publishing system is—and a lot of that success depends not on your hardware and software, but on you. You are the final ingredient in this system. Your energy, talent, interest, and organizational abilities will be the final determinant in the success or failure of your ads. Truthfully, you can get by on a lot less than you think you can if you possess the right attitude and the requisite abilities. Fancy hardware and expensive software only enhance and streamline a process you should already have down to a fine art.

The fact is that many excellent publications are still laid out the "old-fashioned" way. Nothing substitutes for being able to accomplish the task this way. Don't get the wrong idea: Computers have made and are continuing to make a tremendous difference in publishing. But always remember that the multithousand-dollar system you sit down in front of every day is only a tool. The system doesn't make you an artist, just as sitting in front of a typewriter doesn't make you a writer. Dedication, hard work, and talent do.

Take a hard look at your layouts and ask yourself a few questions:

- Are your layouts already the best they can be without the addition of desktop publishing? If they are, you probably already know the basics and are ready for desktop publishing. If they're not, why not? Will the technology help the look or simply add to the clutter? Be honest. Don't expect desktop publishing to give you something you don't already possess.

- What, exactly, do you expect desktop publishing to add to your layouts or the process of developing them? Again, if you're looking for an answer to your design problems, check out your own abilities first. On the other hand, if you're expecting the technology to streamline the process and save you some money, it probably will.

- Will the savings you accrue be offset by the cost of the system? It takes a lot of savings in typesetting to counterbalance a $25,000 investment.

- Are you willing to take the time needed to make you an expert on your system? If you aren't willing to become an expert, you're wasting your money. Anyone can learn the basics (or just enough to cause trouble), but if you're serious about desktop publishing, you'd best dedicate yourself for the long haul. Be prepared to immerse yourself in the process, the programs, and the machinery. The more you know, the more streamlined the process becomes.

Above all, don't set yourself up for frustration. Realize the limitations of your system and of desktop publishing in general. Understand how it works and why it does what it does. You don't have to become a "computer nerd" to gain a fairly complete understanding of your hardware and software. The more you know, the less frustrated you'll be when something does go wrong. Most of the frustration of working with computers comes from not knowing what's happening in software or hardware problem situations. Keep those technical support hotline numbers close at hand and use them. Don't be afraid to ask questions, but read your manuals first so you'll know what to ask.

Finally, take it all with a grain of salt. A computer is just a tool of the trade. Misuse it, and your shortcomings will become apparent to everyone who looks at your work. Use it wisely, and it will show off for you.

KEY TERMS

design	type	quick print
balance	typeface	quick copy
proportion	font	spot color printing
rule of ground thirds	point	two-color printing
sequence	body type	process printing
emphasis	display type	four-color printing
unity	serif typeface	signature
grid	sans serif typeface	swipe file
alignment	offset lithography	

EXERCISES

1. Find one example each of the following design principles shown in action:

   balance (symmetric and asymmetric)
   proportion
   emphasis
   sequence
   unity

   Your example can be any printed piece including brochures, newsletters, print ads, posters, flyers, etc. Be prepared to discuss your choices and how they reflect these design principles.

2. Pick a brochure or newsletter that you like particularly well. Take it to two different printers and get printing estimates from each. Assume that you will be reprinting the piece exactly as it is now printed—same paper, ink, color, etc. You will be running 1,000 copies. Ask the printer to include the cost of folding in the estimate. Tell the printer that you will bring the piece to them on computer disk fully laid out. Take notes on what each printer asks and what they say they can and can't do for you. Be especially mindful of anything you didn't know you needed until you talked to the printer, and make a list of those items you'd need to confirm prior to actual printing.

## CHAPTER 13

THE DIGITAL MEDIA

FOR IMMEDIATE RELEASE

In this chapter you will learn:

- How to compose on a computer, both on your own and in collaboration with others.

- What intranets are, and how they are used for internal corporate communication.

- What the Internet is, and how corporations use it to communicate with external publics.

- How to write for Web sites.

Although scientists may disagree, I believe that the two greatest boons the computer has granted us are word processing and desktop publishing. Of course, that's from a public relations writer's perspective.

Back in the dark ages, public relations writers used typewriters (this was right after carving in stone became unsatisfactory because of too many last-minute changes). Typewriters, as you may recall, evolved from click-clicking mechanical monsters to electronic marvels over the course of about 100 years. Following the advent of the personal computer, it only took about 10 more years for typewriters to become completely obsolete. Today, if they use them at all, most people use typewriters only to type envelopes—another job rapidly being taken over by more advanced computer printers.

Typewriters, of course, were a vast improvement over having to write everything by hand, and they did mimic typesetting, which made reading a good deal easier. But editing? That was another story entirely. At first you had to erase with a very rough little instrument designed, apparently, to tear typewriter paper to shreds. Then there was something called "erasable bond paper," but its surface was so slick that the paper seemed to erase on its own much of the time. Next came typewriter correction fluid. But the fluid looked awful, and you could never get it off your hands. Finally, there was "correcting ribbon" for electric typewriters, which literally lifted the letters right off the page.

All of this may seem like an odd and long-winded preamble to a chapter on writing with and for the digital media, but we need to realize that the greatest benefit of computers in our end of the business is that we no longer have to erase, paint over, or lift off anything! While this may seem obvious to many of you, those of us who actually remember typewriters in all their manifestations breathe a prayer of thanks to the wizards of science every time we sit down to compose a press release. Those of you who don't remember will just have to take my word for it!

This chapter is about how to write both on and for the computer—how to use this marvelous tool to your greatest benefit, and how to write public relations material intended to be published on a digital site.

Writing on a Computer

Personal computers and word-processing software allow us to manipulate words in all sorts of ways—ways that would have been unimaginable on a typewriter. Words can be put down faster, corrected almost as fast, rearranged, reorganized, counted, parsed, and printed, to name a few of the advantages. I'm not going to waste your time here recommending word-processing software. There are far too many good ones on the market for you to go too far wrong. Just remember to match your software to your needs. Most of the big word-processing packages include rudimentary layout and graphic insertion capabilities, which is fine if you don't know how to use a basic desktop publishing program. However, at this point, even the most sophisticated word-processing program doesn't come close to being as flexible as a basic layout program. So pick one that is good at writing, not layout.

You'll need a program that is easy to understand yet can carry out complex jobs such as outlining, page numbering, bulleting, indenting at various levels, moving text rapidly, font changing and stylizing, spell checking, and word counting. For me, these are the basic requirements. Some writers have special needs, such as an online thesaurus, the ability to insert or design tables and charts, mail merge, macro design, and so on. Just remember: Unless you really want to become a designer (and add to your workload), stick with writing—which means stick with a program that handles writing well. If you don't need all the bells and whistles, don't pay for them.

For those of us who learned to write in other ways—on a typewriter or by hand—computer writing is very different. For all the reasons stated above, writing on a computer is easier. That doesn't make it necessarily better, however. Remember what I said at the beginning of this book: Good writing is good writing. No piece of software will make you a good writer, just as relying on a spell checker won't make you a good speller—or make up for your being a bad one. With that caveat in mind, let's look at some ways to get the most out of computer writing.

On Your Own

Most writers are solitary by nature and generally prefer to work alone, and computers have made working alone more congenial than ever. A computer seems to do some of the work for you. As I am typing this now, my software is noting misspellings as I go along. Even a solitary writer sometimes has the feeling that he or she is collaborating with someone else. Under most circumstances, I would suggest therapy; however, all writers need a little help occasionally, and the interactive nature of software today provides much of that help automatically. This often gives you the illusion of having a partner. The trick is not to let it go to your head literally. You're still in charge, no matter how smart your computer seems to be. You're still the writer; it's the tool.

Take advantage of this marvelous tool in the following ways as a lone writer.

Brainstorming. Computers have made brainstorming incredibly easy. Of course, nothing substitutes for your creativity, but computers can help stimulate that creativity. Try these tricks:

- **Freewrite.** In other words, write without giving a thought to grammar, spelling, or logic. Take an idea and simply write about it—stream of consciousness. This was possible prior to the computer, obviously, but a computer makes working with your freewriting much easier in the organizing and editing stages. Freewriting tends to stimulate creativity, but don't get in the habit of thinking that it's a substitute for good writing. It's just an exercise.

- **Blind write.** Another easy trick to try is to write blindly. Turn down your monitor's brightness and write without looking at what you are saying. This reduces the tendency all writers have to edit as we go along. It may take several attempts before you become comfortable with this technique, but it can produce some interesting results.

- **Use your swipe files.** All good writers and designers keep swipe files. For designers, these are pieces that spark your imagination and present you with a design idea that you can mimic (see Chapter 12). For writers, a swipe file contains all the pieces we have written in the past. Ideally, they are on computer disks and properly labeled so that we can find them. You'd be amazed how much "boiler plate" you can borrow from other pieces you have written and adapt to your current needs. That company intro you wrote for the open house brochure two years ago can now be used in your backgrounder or your annual report. All you need to do is create the transitions between the old material and the new. A word of caution here: Be sure not to "borrow" from someone else's writing, unless it is company property. This is not called "borrowing" by the courts; it's called "plagiarism." If something has been written for your organization by someone else and you want to use it, just make sure it is yours to use, free and clear. Typically, if it was done for your organization, it is company property, even if it was written by a freelancer.

- **Start a "phrase" file.** For want of a better word, I've used *phrase*. This used to be an old poet's trick. Every poet comes up with lines that can't be used in the poem he or she is currently working on. Sometimes a line may have sparked the idea for the poem itself, but when the poem is finished, the line no longer seems to fit. In any event, poets catalogue these lines or phrases for use in future poems. Similarly, your file could contain a number of headings composed of either phrases that were never used or phrases that bear repeating. For example:

  - *Headlines or titles.* These could be anything from book titles to headlines from newsletters or magazines. If possible, try to further categorize them by topic.

  - *Leads or intros.* Include good leads from news releases, feature stories, etc. Even if the subject is different, a good construction or an apt turn of phrase can be used again. The same type of file could be created for good endings.

- *Quotes.* There's nothing like a good quote. I've got hundreds of quotes catalogued by author and by subject. Thousands of quotes are now available in an instant on the Internet. Either way, these quotes are handy for speechwriting or feature stories. Just remember to attribute them to the right source. For instance, I was recently notified via e-mail—by someone I'd never met—that a biblical quote I'd used on a Web site was not from Ezekiel but from Daniel. Nothing like publicly embarrassing yourself, especially if you're a writer.

- **Catalogue your ideas.** Catalogue your best ideas, used and unused. Looking at this list regularly will help stimulate your creativity. That idea you discarded last month may be just the right thing today.

- **Browse the Internet.** It's amazing how many good ideas you can get simply from browsing. Some of my best work has come from the hours I used to spend wandering the library aisles. Today, much the same thing can be accomplished without ever having to leave your desk chair. (Of course, you don't burn nearly as many calories.) Just sign on the Internet, pick a search topic, and browse. Download anything that interests you, remembering that this, too, is copyrighted material. Also remember that you have a job to do, and surfing the Net can be addictive. I've found that setting aside an hour a day for surfing, and sticking to it, keeps my productivity steadier.

Writing. At some point, you have to stop brainstorming and start writing. Here again, the computer can prove invaluable. You should become familiar with some of the following techniques:

- **Use layout and publishing tools to organize.** This refers to the ability of most programs to move words, sentences, and paragraphs with ease by simply highlighting and moving them with the mouse or by cutting and pasting. The more sophisticated programs allow for the rearrangement of entire pages, sections, or chapters. This is perhaps the greatest benefit of using a computer to compose. Organization is the key to all good writing, and a computer makes reorganization a snap. As you move things around, don't leave the original words or paragraphs in their original places. In other words, cut them and reposition them. Don't copy them. If you copy them, you'll soon have redundancy everywhere you look. If you're not sure where to put material you've cut out, put it into a separate file by splitting your screen. Be sure to save this file in case your computer crashes. You can also use the "strike through" function included in most word-processing programs. This visually indicates text that may be edited out at a later time.

- **Take advantage of multitasking.** Most computer platforms utilize windows that allow multitasking, enabling you to work with multiple documents simultaneously. Most programs also indicate how many windows you have open at any one time and allow you to switch from one to the other with relative ease. This makes copying and pasting among documents extremely easy. Just remember not to *cut* from other documents to your master, just *copy*, leaving the other documents intact. Don't open more than three documents at a time or use the "window shade" function some platforms support to "roll up" documents you are not currently working on. Having more than three documents open requires a mental juggling act that usually ends in confusion.

Proofreading and Editing. Whether you're doing your own editing or someone else is working with you, you're going to want to proofread your work. You don't want to look *too* bad to your editor or to fellow writers. Here are some tips for using your computer to help you.

- **Use proofreading tools.** Most software programs, and even some design programs, come with spell checkers. Word-processing software also comes with grammar checkers, thesauruses, word counters, and, sometimes even readability checkers. I always use a spell checker and often a word counter, especially for magazine articles that have to be a certain length. I rarely use a grammar checker because I don't believe it can substitute for a good grasp of grammar, and it is wasted on good writers who don't usually make egregious errors in that department anyway. But don't rely on your spell checker to catch everything. As already mentioned, they don't catch all errors and they often flag things that aren't problems at all. Be even more cautious with grammar checkers. If you feel you have to use one, your job as a writer may be in jeopardy.

- **Check your organization.** Take a last-minute stroll through your piece to check for organizational problems. If you find any, correct them by using the methods discussed above. Also make sure each paragraph reflects a single idea or subject. Read with your cursor as a pointer. If you come to a point within a paragraph at which ideas have changed, just position the cursor and hit "return."

- **Use "search and replace."** If you do find an error that you suspect might have been repeated elsewhere, or if you decide to substitute another word or phrase for one you've used throughout, use your "search and replace" function to make the changes. You can also use this function as an editing tool. For example, if you are compiling a lengthy document with a number of references to illustrations or charts, you might have to wait until your graphics are assembled to insert text references (e.g., "see Exhibit 9.1"). You can enter these references into your text in advance by inserting a character that you can search for later when your exhibits are in order. For example, using brackets as a search character usually works because most of us only use them for editorial comment anyway. Or you could enter a string of characters that wouldn't normally appear in writing, such as ?????.

- **Change typeface or size.** By simply enlarging your font size or changing typefaces, your written piece takes on a new look. This new look may help you spot mistakes more easily. In most cases, this sort of temporary change doesn't disturb your formatting. Bullets in one typeface will usually be bullets in another. These formatting options are part of the program itself and not generally typeface-dependent.

In Collaboration

T. S. Eliot's famous poem *The Waste Land* was twice the length in draft form as in its final published form. In fact, by some accounts, it was unfathomable. Eliot's friend and editor, Ezra Pound, cut the work nearly in half, thereby ensuring that Eliot would become recognized as one of the finest poets in the English language. We'd all like to have editors like that, of course; however, we more often benefit as much from simple collaboration. Here again, the computer can be extremely useful. Let's look at some of the ways you can use your computer to collaborate with other writers and with editors:

1. **Real-time collaboration.** This can be accomplished in a number of ways. If you share a local area network (LAN) with your collaborators, you can literally work online with them, in real time. It's possible, and not all that annoying, to write together by "trading" phrases, rewriting each other's work, and reordering points, all without actually laying eyes on each other (unless you have video capabilities on your computer and like to see who you're talking to). This sort of collaboration requires solid teamwork and a willingness to let others contribute to your work as it is being created. There is an old poetry game in which each person makes up a stanza of a poem, the final poem being a linked chain of all the contributed stanzas. Collaborative writing in real time is something like this game.

2. **On-line collaboration.** This is roughly the same as the method described above except that you don't work in real time. Instead, you submit your drafts to a fellow writer or an editor sharing the same network as you, and he or she returns your work along with suggestions or edits keyed right into the text.

3. **E-mail.** This is perhaps the slowest of the online methods, especially if you are communicating with someone outside your LAN. However, it beats waiting days or weeks for your work to be edited and turned around in the regular mail. E-mail also requires that you have compatible software in order to download attached files. Otherwise, your text has to be included in the mail message itself—a bit clumsy, to

say the least. The book you are reading now was rewritten and edited by e-mail, saving weeks of time. The editor and I sent our revisions back and forth to each other, then the editor sent each completed chapter to the publisher in Chicago, all via e-mail—the only part of the book sent by regular mail was the artwork.

If you decide to use this method, make sure you understand who is responsible for the final draft. That person must see to it that all edits and corrections are made and the piece is ready to go to its final destination. Date all drafts, file them according to some logical scheme (don't put multiple drafts in the same folder), and purge those that are out of date. Nothing is more confusing than trying to remember which draft included the latest information. Don't rely on the computer dating that is automatic with your system. You may have actually put that new piece of information into yesterday's draft and mistakenly opened an older one today. This error will redate your old draft, making it seem newer than the later one. And don't store your work on more than one computer. Instead, use disks to move files around.

Writing for the Computer ———————

Recent changes in technology have allowed organizations to reach out to their constituencies in ways never before imaginable. The computer has not only spawned word processing and desktop publishing, it has also allowed us to make major changes in our communications and our modes of delivery. Additionally, technology has expanded the scope of both internal and external communications beyond that of traditional media. The role of everything from the news release to the corporate magazine has been broadened by the ability to turn what was once a static delivery system into interactive communication. Nowhere has this change been more apparent then in employee communications.

Employee Communications: Intranets

As mentioned in Chapter 8, employee communications such as newsletters and magazines have gone through an evolutionary process, resulting in publications that are less focused on entertainment and more focused on information. However, recent research has shown that employee publications alone don't seem to provide all the information that employees need and want, especially during times of change. In addition, the employee publication has traditionally been considered a one-way form of communication in that it does not provide the opportunity for employees to ask questions of—or provide feedback to—their employers. New technology has changed not only the speed at which information can be delivered to employees, but it has also allowed for a range of interactivity not available to print media. For our purposes, the most relevant of these technologies is company intranets.

The development of the Internet and the World Wide Web in the last several years has, in many ways, revolutionized the way people communicate with each other, as well as how they access information. Through the Internet (which we will discuss in more detail shortly), information can be shared electronically all over the globe. An *intranet* is essentially an internal version of the Internet. In the last few years, organizations have discovered the potential for developing intranets that enable their employees to access information within the confines of the organizational walls that can be used to help them with their jobs.

From a technical standpoint, an intranet is similar in design to the World Wide Web. Documents are organized into home pages that contain information on a particular subject, often punctuated with graphics or audio. The type of information available on an intranet can be determined by management, or, in some cases, by the employees themselves, who might design their own home pages. At the most sophisticated level, an intranet can provide employees with access to information about an organization's financial data, daily news updates, customer profiles, sales figures, and meeting minutes.

One of the added benefits from an employee communications perspective is that an intranet allows for greater interaction between employees as well as between employees and management. This offers an opportunity for employees to provide feedback to one another and to their supervisors. The intranet at U.S. West's Englewood, Colorado, location, for instance, includes an online chat room—an interactive "location" that enables the company's employees to have conversations with each other via computer. Other examples serve to demonstrate how readily organizations are to adopt these new, and seemingly successful, approaches to communication:

- Hewlett-Packard began an ambitious program in 1991 to change the style of employee communications. As a result, electronic communications have almost completely replaced print publications at H-P. The organization has developed an intranet that enables employees to access a variety of information. For example, employees might be sent general announcements via e-mail that direct them to sites on the intranet where they can get more specific details. A daily news service sent through this intranet provides 15 to 20 news stories a day about the company, the business climate, and the world in general.
- Silicon Graphics, Inc., based in California, has an intranet called "Silicon Junction," where employees can access a monthly newsletter (also available in print), a quarterly magazine featuring articles about employees, and general news releases about the company.

- Another California-based company, Levi Strauss, employs nearly 38,000 people worldwide. Historically, the company has used a number of traditional methods of communicating with its employees. More recently, however, it has switched over to electronic media, prompted in large part by employee interest. The company now has an online employee publication and a news service.

- Over the past several years, AT&T has shifted the focus of its employee communications from a program dominated by print communications to one whose emphasis is primarily on electronic communications. Its intranet offerings include a daily news service called "AT&T Today," which features news items, information about competition, benefits materials, and an electronic letters-to-the-editor department through which employees can express their opinions and concerns. An electronic management publication is also sent out to district managers.

Communicating with Other Publics: The Internet

In addition to the changes in delivering news releases (covered in Chapter 6), the most obvious example of using new technology to communicate with external publics is the Internet.

The Internet, which stands for "interlocking networks," is a large computer network that links several already established computer networks together with a common language. The result is a sharing of information over vast distances with the ease of dialing a phone. What once took days, weeks, or even months to accomplish now takes only minutes. Just as an intranet can be used to enhance employee communications, the Internet can be used to better meet the demands of external publics.

A quick tour of corporate Web sites will "net" you a rather complete picture of an organization's mission, products, and services (and how to purchase them if the site is retail); economic situation; investment opportunities; frequently asked questions (FAQs); and myriad other topics. Primarily, such sites serve two sometimes mutually exclusive purposes: retail sales and/or image building. Of course, most public relations writers would be more concerned with image-building sites.

Designing a Web Site. Public relations writers often are both designers and writers for other information pieces—newsletters, brochures, etc.—and they are just as likely to be called upon to design their company's Web site. Thus, it is important that you understand the basic premises behind Web sites and be able to contribute to them. It is not my intention to discuss the details of Web site construction here, but rather simply to point out some generalities that will help you get started.

While the computer screen doesn't replicate the printed page exactly, many of the techniques used in print layout are still valid for Web site design. Some critics counter that this is exactly the problem: Computers shouldn't attempt to replicate print. (Many people believe that television made the same mistake in replicating radio programming and not exploring its full potential as a visual medium.) For the foreseeable future, however, people will continue to react to computer screen layout the same way they react to the printed page. As such, a Web site should be designed to attract, hold, and guide the inquiring reader (or viewer)—just like any other vehicle used for the dissemination of information. Keep in mind, however, that as the technology develops and as more and more users gain sophistication, "reading" Web sites will continue to evolve. We already see the first generation of users who are familiar with the language and the structure of the Web as a whole and are quite capable of navigating its congested waters with ease. This "expertise" should not deter you, though, from constructing a site that is readable by all who use it, not just the Web sophisticates.

The single biggest obstacle in designing a readable Web site is clutter. There is a great temptation with Web sites, as with any other publication, to overstate your design. Surf several corporate sites and you will immediately notice differences. Retail locations often sell advertising to allied companies in the form of animated banners and other links. While this may help to support the cost of maintaining a Web site, it adds decidedly to the clutter. For instance, outdoor outfitter REI has a vivid and eye-catching Web site (www.rei.com), but the clutter makes it difficult to find what you are looking for. Web sites devoted to company image and information usually keep to the simpler formats, understanding that you must guide in order to inform. Since its inception, the Saturn car company has spent millions of dollars on company image, and that concern is reflected in the company's Web site (www.saturn.com).

Here are some very basic tips for getting the most out of your Web site:

1. **Begin with a goal.** What is your Web site's "mission"? Is it to inform, persuade, sell, open two-way communication?

2. **Develop an outline.** Write down, in order, what you would like to include in your Web site. Remember: the term *Web site* refers not only to your home page but also to any local links (links within your site). You might want to make each major heading a separate linked site (see Exhibit 13.1).

3. **Decide what you want to include on your home page.** This is your introduction. Keep it simple and to the point. Many home pages consist of opening remarks with links to more complex information. Remember not to clutter this most important first contact point.

4. **Rough out a basic design for your home page.**
   - *Keep it simple.* In my opinion, the best designs are still the simple ones, the ones that incorporate the basic principles of design. Despite all the talk about nonlinear thinking, we still view layout

EXHIBIT 13.1   Web Site Outline

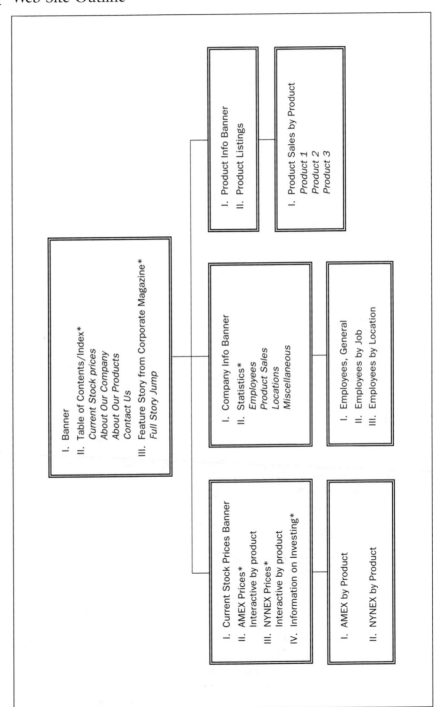

It is best to design your outline in the form of a chart, much like an organizational chart, with connections shown from site to site. This can become fairly large and complex very quickly, proving the old advertising acronym, KISS: "Keep It Simple, Stupid."

in a linear fashion: left to right, top to bottom. And we still need the same visual cues to lead us. You really can't go wrong if you stick with the basic design rules laid out in Chapter 12.

- *Avoid going with the latest "cute" device.* For example, how many Web sites have you seen with annoying little animation pieces on them moving through a set range of motion and then repeating it endlessly? Waving flags, jumping frogs, runners, you name it—they all detract rather than enhance. This is like the use of "novelty" type in print publications—avoid it at all costs.

- *Include an index or table of contents on your home page.* These are located typically across the top or down the left margin of the page. Each entry should be a link to one of your other outline points. It is also advisable to repeat this index at each site connected to your home page as a common reference point.

- *Use graphics wisely.* Visuals are undoubtedly one of the strengths of the computer in all its forms. Though the computer was once thought of as merely a word processor (or number cruncher), its ability to integrate sight, sound, and motion now makes it a leading vehicle for communication. As with any other element, however, graphics can be overused. Again, avoid clutter. Use only the best graphics and make them central to your layout. Follow the advice found in Chapter 12 on the uses of emphasis and sequence as you lay out your page. Use video only if you feel it is absolutely indispensable to your communication effort. While movies on the computer screen are certainly novel to most of us, they are also difficult to play (software requirements vary), and they use an incredible amount of memory. Remember, the more slowly your page runs, the less patient your reader/viewer becomes.

5. **Integrate graphics and copy carefully.** As with print publications, use visuals to break up heavy copy. While the Web effectively accommodates a lot of copy, reading from a screen can be tedious. That's why so many people still download text from Web sites rather than read it online. Try not to go on too long without some graphic interruption relief.

6. **Keep introductory material brief.** Although you may include lengthy written pieces in your site, introductions to that material should be brief. They should stand out the same way headlines stand out in print publications (of course, you may use headlines as well to draw attention to material).

7. **If possible, make your successive pages consistent with your home page design.** For example, repeat your index on each page in the same location. Use the same background, or "wallpaper," for each page. And be sure to include links back to your home page and to the top of the current page at regular intervals—especially if the page is long.

8. **Keep it simple.** I know, I've already said this. This time, however, it means keep the level of complexity in your overall site down. Too much information is just as deadly as not enough. Limit the number of links you use and make them as clear and as logical as possible. One of the greatest dangers of Web site design is that your readers/viewers will be distracted from their purpose (and from yours). Set an agenda and make sure everything on your Web site has some bearing on it. If it doesn't, don't include it. This also goes for those courtesy links to similar sites. Do you really want your readers to "jump" to another location? Knowing the siren song of the Internet, I wouldn't bet on them returning any time soon.

Exhibit 13.2 shows how all of these guidelines come together in a well-designed home page.

Writing for Web Sites

Here is where you probably think you're going to find the secret to digital success. Wrong. My advice? Use the formats and styles outlined elsewhere in this book (including this chapter) when you write for the Internet. A news release is still a news release. A feature is still a feature. Ad copy is still ad copy. A FAQ section is just a Q & A. You get the idea.

The most glaring difference seems to be the huge amount of "chatter" on the Internet. Fortunately, this is mostly confined to chat rooms and e-mail; however, a casual perusal of Web sites will quickly alert you to the inability of many site owners to write or, seemingly, express themselves in a coherent manner. The lesson is this: Don't succumb to the temptation to be chatty. Public relations writing is professional writing, even on the Internet. Follow the rules of good writing no matter what vehicle you are using, and you can't go wrong.

In a recent online editorial for *E&P Interactive* (part of the *Editor & Publisher* Web site at www.mediainfo.com), Steve Outing reviews Crawford Kilian's book *Writing on the Web* (International Self-Counsel Press, due out in 1999). Kilian offers some sage advice for those who are already engaged in that dubious activity. First, he cites well-known Internet guru Jakob Nielsen as saying that Web readers read 25 percent more slowly than print readers. Kilian concludes that "if we read 25 percent slower on screen, then perhaps we owe our readers 25 percent less text."

Although he cautions that Web site writing rules should be taken with a grain of salt because they are constantly evolving, here are Kilian's six general principles about writing for the online medium:

1. Web writing requires orientation, information, and action. That is, provide background information and navigation aids; provide the information itself; and provide a way for a reader to respond.

EXHIBIT 13.2   Well-Designed Home Page

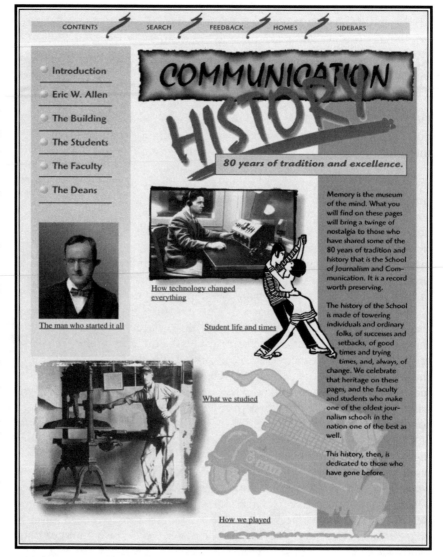

While at first glance this Web page may seem to be eclectic, there are a number of direct and indirect visual design clues to lead the viewer to appropriate points on the page. The top of the page shows a quick list of links, including contents (repeated on the left-hand bar), search options (for keyword searches), feedback opportunities (for e-mail response), links to other home pages, and sidebars. Notice how the eye is drawn first to the headline, then downward, either to the introduction flowing to the right or to the various graphics scattered in a "Z" pattern down the page. The table of contents, of course, can also be the starting point. Remember, also, that not all of this page will be seen on a computer monitor. Viewers will have to scroll down to see the entire page.

2. Web writing should be understandable at first glance.

3. Web writing should be the least you can possibly present to effectively deal with the subject. Excess information is a disservice to the Web reader.

4. Web writing displays a positive attitude to problems. Even if dealing with a negative topic like some injustice, offer the reader something constructive to do to deal with the injustice (taking advantage of the interactive nature of the online medium).

5. Web writing presents facts and ideas in terms of the reader's advantage. A smart Web writer seldom uses "I" and "we" and often uses "you" and "your."

6. Web writing displays correctness, clarity, and consideration—correct organization, format, names, addresses, spelling, and grammar; appropriate language, proper tone, concision, coherence, and consideration of the reader's needs.

Do these rules sound familiar? They should. They are basically what this book is all about, and they pretty much bolster my long-held argument that good writing is good writing, no matter where you read it.

Kilian also reminds us that we need to know our target audience. Are they sophisticated about the topic? If so, we can use jargon common to the subject; if not, we must avoid using potentially confusing terms. Similarly, some audiences will need a more straightforward design with easy "signposts" leading them from one place to the next, while other, more sophisticated audiences may respond easily to a more complex design. For instance, look again at Saturn and REI's home pages and notice how much simpler Saturn's links choices are compared with REI's. As with any other publication, suit your design to your audience.

The most prominent message that Outing promulgates in his review is that we shouldn't let technology drown out the message. Much as design that is done just for the sake of design will probably deter the serious seeker of information, a technologically stunning Web site may actually hinder the task of communicating successfully. The warning is well timed. I increasingly counsel students who are whizzes at Web site design, but who still can't write a coherent paragraph, on their job prospects. Sadly, they continue to believe that knowing the technology is all they need.

Remember: The difference between writing *for* a Web site and writing *on* the computer is that the computer is a writing tool, just like a typewriter or a pen, while a Web site is a communication vehicle, just like a newsletter. A well-written piece of communication is what you get paid to produce as a public relations writer. Ultimately, you will be judged by how well you write.

EXERCISES

1. Write a one- or two-page collaborative piece on the public relations topic of your choice with a classmate or co-worker. Be prepared to discuss the process—how you communicated, how it worked (or didn't), how it differed from writing alone, etc.

2. Locate two Web sites, one retail-oriented and one image-oriented. Using Kilian's rules for writing on the Web as your guide, critique the sites and make suggestions for their improvement.

## CHAPTER 14

THE BASICS OF GRAMMAR

FOR IMMEDIATE RELEASE

In this chapter you will learn:

- How to distinguish among the parts of speech.

- How to achieve variety in sentences and clauses

- The correct use of case.

- How adjectives and adverbs qualify meaning.

- How to ensure proper agreement.

- How to avoid dangling constructions.

- How to write using parallel structure.

- Proper use of punctuation and mechanics.

- How to improve and check your spelling.

Writing is a technical skill as well as an art and, as such, it demands a thorough understanding of grammar. Unfortunately, most of us still have some rather uncomfortable memories of grammar lessons in either grade school or high school. And some of us believe that we can write intuitively, without any formal knowledge of grammar. This is a dangerous idea, because it leads to a false sense of security and often a misunderstanding of the basic rules of grammar.

The simple fact is that those who know and understand grammar are better writers than those who don't. Obviously, no one wants to start at the beginning of a grammar text and wade all the way through it in order to gain a better understanding of how to use a comma. The following brief discussion of grammar is offered as a shortcut.

This is not a definitive text. It is merely a collection of helpful hints and a few guidelines that will set you on the right track. The key, of course, is recognizing when you need help. As a public relations writer, you will never want for editors who point out your errors, even though some are no better at grammar than you are. It is in your best interest to learn the rules and use them. Writing without a knowledge of grammar is like falling into the water without a knowledge of swimming—in either case, your chances of surviving in the medium are slim.

AP Style or English Grammar? ━━━━━━

Before we begin our explanation of the mechanics of the language, a bit needs to be said about the differences between what follows here (and in Chapter 15) and AP style. *The Associated Press Stylebook and Libel Manual* has been the journalists' bible for far longer than most of us can remember. All journalists and editors know it by heart. It is widely used as a guide to writing straight news and, to some extent, news-oriented features. You can see its vestiges in *Time* and *Newsweek,* and it is still very much alive on the front page of your local newspaper. AP style was developed originally for newspaper writing, and its conventions were set to encourage ease of reading and consistency among the various media publishers. Because of the nature of news writing and the need to move from the written word to the typeset page quickly, many standard style conventions were altered. For example, italics were virtually eliminated from typeset copy (not from headlines), because it was easier to set type in upright, or Roman, than to switch to italics. And while the setting of italics is now virtually painless, the convention still stands.

The key is to know when you need to use AP style and when you don't need to. Basically, use AP style when you're writing anything that goes to a media outlet, especially news releases. News articles for news magazines should also follow AP style, as should those for newsletters that are journalistic in style. However, brochure copy needn't be AP style, nor should any other piece not specifically meant to mimic a journalistic style of writing. In other words, there is a time and a place for AP style. Use it then and stick with common English usage the rest of the time.

What follows, both here and in the next chapter, is based on accepted English usage and not on AP style. It is in your best interest to obtain a copy of the *AP Stylebook* and look it over. If you are in the business of producing news releases on a regular basis, you need to have more than just passing familiarity with it.

Parts of Speech ━━━━━━

The **parts of speech** are simply the categories in which words belong. Most words are classified in three ways:

- By their *grammatical function* (such as *subject, object,* etc.).
- By their *grammatical form* (such as the *-s* form added to the end of plural nouns).
- By their *meaning* (such as the names of things, as in the case of *nouns,* or statements of action, as in the case of *verbs*).

No matter what category we place words in, some of them will end up as more than one part of speech. Take the word *place,* for instance:

As a noun
This advanced version of PSO-1 will certainly take the *place* of older compounds in plastics manufacturing.

As a verb
In a startling move, John Rivers, mayor of Edmonton, has decided to *place* his hat in the ring for the governor's race.

As a modifier
Place settings of plastic spoons were totally inappropriate at the company picnic, considering that roast beef was being served.

Parts of speech are categorized according to what they do. The following groups represent the basic parts of speech in English.

Nouns
Nouns are words that name a person, place, or thing. Subjects of sentences are usually nouns, as are objects of verbs and prepositions. Notice the nouns in the following sentence:

Associated Products *Corporation* (APC) of *Syracuse, N.Y.,* today announced a joint *venture* to educate American *schoolchildren* in the *uses* of *computers*.

Keep in mind that although most nouns form the plural by simply adding -*s*, some, such as *sheep* and *women*, are irregular.

Pronouns

Pronouns substitute for nouns, but in order to understand exactly what noun a given pronoun is substituting for, we have to look for its **antecedent,** the preceding noun to which the pronoun refers. Can you spot the antecedent in the following sentence?

> Tom said that *he* was going out for a while, but *he* left no forwarding address or indication when *he* would return.

In this sentence, it is clear that the pronoun *he* refers to the antecedent, *Tom*.

Indefinite pronouns (*everybody, anybody, someone*) do not refer to particular persons or things and therefore take no antecedent. These, like *one* in the following sentence, refer to whoever takes the action.

> *One* would have to be a fool to come to work dressed for the warm weather outside when the air conditioner still insists it's winter.

Verbs

Verbs are action words, as we were told so many times in grade school; but what they really do is make a statement about the subject of the sentence. For public relations writers, choosing the right verb tense is important. For instance, stating that the president of APC "has announced" an important project has a different effect on readers than saying he "announced" an important project. Both use a past tense form, but the first is more immediate. The nuances are subtle, but they are definitely there.

The following tenses are the most common for regular verbs:

- *Present tenses* express actions that are happening now or that are habitual. The *simple present tense* might most commonly be used in print ad copy.

  > Associated Products Corporation *Announces* a Breakthrough in Educational Software.

  The *present progressive tense* uses a *present participle* (the -*ing* form). This implies immediacy and is not generally used in press releases because it would imply the action is taking place right now.

> James L. Sutton, a native of Deerborn and president of Associated Products Corporation of Syracuse, New York, *is announcing* the development of a new educational software line as we speak.

Present perfect tense indicates an action carried out before the present and completed in the present. It can also be used for an action that was begun in the past and continues in the present.

> James L. Sutton, a native of Deerborn and president of Associated Products Corporation of Syracuse, New York, *has announced* the development of a new educational software line.

This tense is the perfect choice for some press releases because it implies immediacy, yet ties the action to the past. It has the benefit of being nonspecific and doesn't call for the inclusion of a date.

- *Past tenses* express actions that took place in the past.

> James L. Sutton, a native of Deerborn and president of Associated Products Corporation of Syracuse, New York, *announced* the development of a new educational software line at a two o'clock press conference today (May 25).

Again, note that the use of the past tense in this lead is followed by a specific time. *Past perfect tense* expresses actions completed before other past actions occurred. Compare the use of the past perfect and the simple past tense in this press release lead:

> James L. Sutton, a native of Deerborn and president of Associated Products Corporation of Syracuse, New York, *had announced* the development of a new educational software line just before he *announced* his resignation from the company.

- *Future tenses* express an action that will occur in the future.

> James L. Sutton, a native of Deerborn and president of Associated Products Corporation of Syracuse, New York, *will announce* the development of a new educational software line at a two o'clock press conference today (May 25).

A specific time is called for here too.

The *future perfect tense* indicates actions that will be completed before a specified future time.

> James L. Sutton, a native of Deerborn and president of Associated Products Corporation of Syracuse, New York, *will have announced*

the development of a new educational software line before he
resigns.

Clearly, some of these tenses are more common in public relations
writing than others. The point, however, is that they each impart a special
nuance to your writing and should be chosen with care.

Adjectives and Adverbs

Adjectives and adverbs are the modifiers. **Adjectives** modify nouns or words
acting as nouns, and **adverbs** modify other adverbs, adjectives, verbs, and
most other words. We will look in detail at these parts of speech later on.

Prepositions and Conjunctions

Prepositions and conjunctions are used to connect parts of a sentence. A
preposition usually relates a noun, pronoun, or phrase to some other part
of the sentence.

The ancient cities *of* Sodom and Gomorrah have long since vanished *from* these
shores. (*Cities* is related to *Sodom and Gomorrah; vanished* is related to *shores.*)

Sitting *behind* a cluttered desk, boxes scattered *around* the office—no lights
on—is the new head of the Law Department. (*Sitting* is related to *desk; boxes*
is related to *office*).

A **conjunction** is used to join words, phrases, or clauses together. In
using conjunctions, never forget that these simple words carry meanings of
their own as well as show relations between the sentence parts that they
connect.

The project is a joint effort of the National Education Association *and*
Associated Products Corporation of Syracuse, New York. (*And* joins the
NEA with *APC.*)

The Lincoln High School graduate has been chief systems engineer *since*
1974, *but* he says the new project has given him a rare opportunity to
work with designers outside the computer field. (*Since* links the first
clause with a specific date; *but* joins two main clauses.)

Sentences and Clauses ━━━━━

Words are the basic units of written English. Good writers string these units
together to form coherent clauses, which in turn form complete sentences.
The type (and therefore the complexity) of sentence we write depends on
the type and combination of clauses we choose to make up the sentence.

Independent Clauses

Independent clauses, sometimes called *main clauses,* always have a subject and a verb and make a statement independent of the rest of the sentence. A sentence always has one independent clause, and sometimes it has more than one.

There are several frequently used words that serve to separate independent clauses. These are called *coordinating conjunctions.* The most common coordinating conjunctions are *and, but, so, for, yet, or, nor.* A comma is usually used before a coordinating conjunction separating independent clauses.

> A recent study shows that students between the ages of 7 and 14 have the ability to acquire computer skills readily, *yet* many schools do not have computer teaching facilities.

> The program is designed to benefit a small segment of the public, *but* the public relations "fallout" will be apparent for years.

Conjunctive adverbs, like coordinating conjunctions, join complete clauses that are linked by a common idea. And, like coordinating conjunctions, they possess meanings of their own. Make sure that you are using the correct conjunctive adverb for your transition—one that indicates the relationship between the clauses. The most common conjunctive adverbs are:

accordingly	however
also	likewise
besides	moreover
consequently	nevertheless
else	otherwise
furthermore	then
hence	therefore

> The announcement came as a complete shock to those present; *consequently,* few questions were asked. (*Consequently* implies that the second clause is a result of the first clause.)

> There are many possible excuses for not getting to work on time; *however,* John chose to say he had been kidnapped by terrorists and was released only an hour ago. (*However* indicates that what happened in the second clause happened in spite of what happened in the first clause.)

Subordinate Clauses

Subordinate clauses, sometimes called *dependent clauses,* contain ideas that are less important than those in the independent clause. A subordinate clause relies on an independent clause for meaning and is frequently introduced by a *subordinate conjunction* such as:

although	unless
as	until
because	when
how	where
though	whether

Subordinate clauses also act as parts of speech (adjectives, adverbs, nouns). The sentence must contain an independent clause or it will not be a complete sentence.

When he arrived . . . (Subordinate clause, but not a sentence.)

When he arrived, the meeting was already underway. (Subordinate clause followed by an independent clause, thus a sentence.)

The meeting was already underway when he arrived. (Same here, except that the subordinate clause is positioned last.)

Sentences are classified by the number of subordinate or main clauses they contain. The basic sentence classifications are: simple, compound, complex, and compound complex.

A **simple sentence** has a single main clause:

You can do something to help save the whales.

A **compound sentence** has two or more main clauses:

You can do something to help save the whales, and you can earn money doing it.

A **complex sentence** has a main clause and one or more subordinate clauses:

By doing something to help save the whales, you can also earn money.

A **compound-complex sentence** contains two or more main clauses and one or more subordinate clauses:

If you do something to help save the whales, you can earn money and they can continue to live in peace.

Case ————

Case is used to indicate the function of nouns and pronouns in a sentence. For instance, in the sentence "He gave me a week's vacation," the *nominative case* form *he* indicates that the pronoun is being used as subject; the *objective case* form *me* shows that the pronoun is an object; the *possessive case* form *week's* indicates that the noun is a possessive.

Personal pronouns (*I, you, he, she, it*) have different forms for the nominative, possessive, and objective cases. The following table will help clear up the differences.

	Nominative	Possessive	Objective
SINGULAR			
First Person	I	my, mine	me
Second Person	you	your, yours	you
Third Person	he, she, it	his, her, hers, its	him, her, it
PLURAL			
First Person	we	our, ours	us
Second Person	you	your, yours	you
Third Person	they	their, theirs	them

Probably the most troublesome use of case involves the *relative pronoun who*. In both the singular and plural forms, *who* is the nominative case, *whose* is the possessive case, and *whom* is the objective case.

Nominative

Use the *nominative case* to indicate the subject of a verb. In formal English (which usually means anything you write short of a personal memo or note), try to adhere to the following rules:

1. Use the nominative case of the pronoun after the conjunctions *as* and *than* if the pronoun is the subject of an understood verb.

   > Hoffman obviously felt that they were better off than *he* (was). (*He* is the subject of the verb *was,* which is understood.)

2. Use the nominative case for the subject of a clause even when the whole clause is the object of a verb or preposition. (Compare this rule to the use of the objective case discussed later.)

   > Sutton has stated that he will give a bonus to *whoever* accomplishes the task first. (*Whoever* is the subject of the verb *accomplishes* in the clause of which it is a part.)

3. Use the nominative case of the personal pronoun after forms of the verb *be* (*is, are, were, have been*). This is a tough rule to follow, however, because even good speakers these days tend to use less formal forms. In this instance, it is usually permissible to be more informal, especially when a contraction is involved. Let the expectations of your audience be your guide.

> *Formal*
> It was I. I thought it was he. It was not we.
>
> *Informal*
> It's me. I thought it was him. It wasn't us.

4. Use the nominative case following the infinitive *to be* when the infinitive has no expressed subject. Again, the informal form is commonly used instead.

> *Formal*
> I would not want to be he.
>
> *Informal*
> I would not want to be him.

Possessive

Most nouns have a common form that is changed to show possessive by simply adding *'s*, as in *worker/worker's*. In the *possessive case*, *'s* should be used with nouns that are animate objects. For inanimate objects, use the *of* construction.

> *Sutton's* leadership has inspired a number of workers in their creative endeavors.
>
> The value *of the dollar* has increased dramatically over the past month.

Objective

The *objective case* is particularly troublesome for some writers. Following a few basic rules should iron out the difficulties:

1. Use the objective case for the object of a verb, verbal (gerunds and participles), or preposition.

> *Whom* did you see about the irregularity in your typewriter? (*Whom* is the object of the verb *see*.)

I saw *him.* (*Him* is the object of the verb *saw.*)

Visiting *them* was the highlight of the convention. (*Them* is the object of the gerund *visiting.*)

Two of *us* were reprimanded for being late this morning. (*Us* is the object of the preposition *of.*)

Whom does he want to nominate for president? (*Whom* is the object of the infinitive *to nominate.*)

As a contrast, consider this sentence:

Who do you suppose convinced him to run? (*Who* is the subject of the verb *convinced,* which has the object, *him.*)

2. In formal English, *whom* is always used in the objective case; however, informal English permits the use of *who.* We have become so used to using *who,* it is now difficult to switch to *whom* in formal writing. Again, think of the expectations of your audience.

   Formal
   Whom are you seeing this morning?

   Informal
   Who are you seeing this morning?

3. One of the more confusing constructions is the use of the objective case after the conjunction *and.*

   They found *Sheila and me* locked in an embarrassing grip behind the filing cabinet. (Not *Sheila and I. Me* is the object of the verb *found.*)

   You must choose between *him and me.* (Not *he and I. Him* and *me* are both objects of the preposition *between.*)

4. After the conjunctions *than* and *as,* use the objective case only if it is the object of an understood verb.

   This company needs him more than *me.*

By using the objective case, the sentence is understood to mean "This company needs him more than it needs me." If we were to use the nominative case, the meaning of the sentence would be altered:

This company needs him more than I (need him).

Adjectives and Adverbs ━━━━━

Adjectives and adverbs are words that qualify meanings. Without them, descriptive writing would be impossible. Consider the following sentence:

Sutton is a *neat* and *energetic* man who speaks *glowingly* of his *latest* project.

Remove the adjectives and adverbs and you are left with:

Sutton is a man who speaks of his project.

The key to the proper use of adjectives and adverbs in public relations writing is to avoid overusing them. The more adjectives and adverbs you use, the less credible your writing becomes.

Sutton is an excruciatingly neat man who speaks in absolutely glowing terms of his latest project.

Adjectives are words that modify nouns or noun substitutes. Never use an adjective to modify a verb, another adjective, or an adverb.

Wrong
She was *terrible* upset when he spilled coffee on her new dress. (*Terrible* is an adjective and thus cannot modify *was upset*.)

Right
She was *terribly* upset when he spilled coffee on her new dress. (*Terribly* is an adverb.)

She jumped *very* quickly to her feet when he spilled the coffee. (*Very* is an adverb modifying the adverb *quickly*.)

There are two basic types of adjectives: descriptive and limiting. *Descriptive adjectives* name some quality of an object, such as a white house, a small car, or a worn carpet.

Limiting adjectives restrict the meaning of a noun to a particular object or indicate quantity. There are five kinds of limiting adjectives:

Possessive: My suit; *their* office.

Demonstrative: This suit, *that* office.

Interrogative: Whose suit? *Which* office?

Articles: A suit; *an* office; *the* office.

Numerical: One suit; *second* office.

Nouns as Adjectives

Sometimes a noun can be used as an adjective. It is advisable to avoid this use, other than in such commonplace uses as *horse* race, *theater* tickets, or *show* business.

When you do use a noun as an adjective, make sure that you are using the proper form of the noun:

Wrong

The *Taiwan* plant opened on schedule in October.

Right

The *Taiwanese* plant opened on schedule in October.

Linking Verbs

One of the most confusing areas of adjective/adverb usage comes when we have to deal with linking verbs. *Linking verbs* connect the subject of the sentence with the subject complement (the word that modifies the subject).

The most common linking verbs are *be, become, appear,* and *seem.* Others pertain to the senses, such as *look, smell, taste, sound,* and *feel.* Modifiers that follow linking verbs refer back to the subject and should be in the form of an adjective and not an adverb.

Joan looks *pretty* today. (*Pretty* modifies *Joan.*) Joan looks *great,* but she sounds *bad.* (*Great* and *bad* both refer to *Joan.*)

One of the most common errors is "I feel badly" in place of the correct form, "I feel bad."

Wrong

I felt badly about the loss of your mother.

Right

I felt bad about the loss of your mother.

The selection of an adjective or adverb as a modifier will alter the meaning of your sentence. Use an adverb after the verb if the modifier describes the manner of the action of the verb.

The man looked *suspiciously* at her. (The adverb *suspiciously* modifies the verb *looked.*)

The man looked *suspicious.* (The adjective *suspicious* modifies the subject *man.*)

In the first example, the verb *looked* expresses action and must be modified by an adverb. But in constructions like "He looks tired" or "He feels well," the verbs serve not as words of action, but as links between the subject and the adjective.

The choice of an adjective or an adverb thus depends on whether or not the verb is being used as a linking verb. Ask yourself whether you want to modify the subject or the verb—and be careful not to alter the meaning of your sentence.

Degree or Quantity

Adjectives and adverbs also show degree or quantity by means of their positive, comparative, and superlative forms.

- The *positive form* expresses no comparison at all: *slow, quickly.*

- The *comparative form* permits a comparison between two (and only two) nouns by adding *-er* or the adverb *more* to the positive form of the word: *pretty, prettier; rapid, more rapid.*

- The *superlative form* involves a comparison between three or more nouns by adding *-est* or the adverb *most* to the positive form: *pretty, prettiest; rapid, most rapid.*

As a general rule, most adjectives and a few one-syllable adverbs form the comparative and superlative forms with *-er* and *-est.* Two-syllable adjectives often offer a choice, as in *lovelier, loveliest* and *more lovely, most lovely.* Adjectives and adverbs of three or more syllables usually use *more* and *most* (*more assiduous,* not *assiduouser*).

Some adjectives and adverbs are absolute in their meaning and can have no comparison. These are words like *final, unique, empty, dead,* and *perfect.* However, you may imply that something is *not quite empty* or *not quite perfect* by using the adverb *nearly,* as in "This flower is *more nearly perfect* than the other."

Agreement ——————

Subject/Verb

What's wrong with the following lead?

> The National Education Association (NEA), in cooperation with the Associated Products Corporation (APC), are cosponsoring a program that is designed to educate schoolchildren about computers.

The verb *are cosponsoring* doesn't agree with the subject, *the National Education Association*. The problem is that the writer has mistakenly assumed a compound subject, which normally requires a plural verb form. In this sentence, *Associated Products Corporation* is the object of the prepositional phrase *in cooperation with*. A singular subject requires a singular verb, and a plural subject requires a plural verb.

The following types of constructions often cause trouble in subject–verb agreement:

1. When words or phrases come between the subject and the verb, the verb agrees with the subject of the sentence, not with the noun in the intervening expression.

   Wrong
   The first two hours of the day *was* boring.

   Right
   The first two hours of the day *were* boring.

2. When a sentence has a singular pronoun, the singular pronoun takes a singular verb.

   Wrong
   Everyone involved in the transfer *think* that APC made the right move.

   Right
   Everyone involved in the transfer *thinks* that APC made the right move.

3. A sentence that has two or more subjects joined by *and* always uses a plural verb.

   Wrong
   Both the IRS and Associated Products *considers* the agreement fair.

   Right
   Both the IRS and Associated Products *consider* the agreement fair.

   However, when the parts of the subject refer to the same thing, the verb form is singular.

   Right
   His editor and friend *recommends* that he pursue a career other than writing. (Assumes that the editor and friend are the same person.)

Right

His editor and friend *recommend* that he pursue a career other than writing. (Assumes that the editor and friend are two different people.)

Right

My husband and lover *was* there to help me.

Wrong

My husband and lover *were* there to help me. (Unless, of course, they are two different people.)

4. In a sentence that has two or more subjects joined by *or* or *nor*, the verb agrees with the subject nearest it.

   Wrong

   Neither the board members nor the CEO *were* there.

   Right

   Neither the board members nor the CEO *was* there.

5. In a sentence with a *collective noun* (*assembly, committee, jury, mob, herd*), a singular verb should be used to indicate that individual members of the group are acting collectively.

   The committee *has reached* a consensus.

   If you wish to emphasize the individual actions of a collective group, add a plural noun and make the verb plural.

   The committee members *have returned* to their offices.

6. In a sentence with a *predicate noun* (one that usually follows the verb but says something about the subject), the verb agrees with its subject, not the predicate noun.

   Wrong

   Status and pay *is* reason enough for most corporate climbers.

   Right

   Status and pay *are* reason enough for most corporate climbers. (*Reason* is the predicate noun.)

Antecedents

An antecedent is a word or group of words referred to by a following pronoun. The following general rules apply to the selection of the correct pronouns for agreement:

1. Use a singular pronoun to refer to antecedents such as:

any	man
anybody	neither
anyone	one
each	person
either	somebody
every	someone
everybody	woman
everyone	

   Everybody held *his* breath as the ball dropped, signifying the new year had begun.

   Each of the participants brought *his* own expertise to bear on the problem.

   The problem with sentences such as these is that the use of *he* as a pronoun will probably be construed as sexist. The use of *he* or *his* to denote a group of unspecified gender composition is a delicate one. There are basically three ways to avoid this most common use of sexist language. One is to use a *he or she, him or her* construction.

   A public relations person can get ahead if he or she works hard.

   Another is to recast the sentence in the plural, making sure the pronoun is also plural.

   Public relations people can get ahead if they work hard.

   The most common mistake made in this construction is to leave the noun antecedent singular while changing the pronoun to a plural.

   A public relations person can get ahead if they work hard.

   Finally, the pronoun can be deleted altogether.

   A public relations person can get ahead by hard work.

2. With a collective noun as an antecedent, use a singular pronoun if you are considering the group as a unit. If you are considering the individual members of the group separately, add another noun to indicate individual actions.

   The *committee* has finished its work for the day.

The *committee members* have decided to finish their work for the day.

3. If two or more antecedents are joined by *and,* use a plural pronoun to refer to them. If two or more singular antecedents are joined by *or* or *nor,* use a singular pronoun to refer to them. If one of two antecedents joined by *or* or *nor* is singular and one plural, make the pronoun agree with the antecedent nearer to it.

> Jack and Jim have finished *their* work.
>
> Neither Jack nor Jim has finished *his* work.
>
> Neither the department head nor the secretaries have finished *their* work.

Faulty Pronoun References

Faulty references of pronouns frequently present problems. The answer is to avoid sentences in which there are two possible antecedents for a single pronoun.

Unclear
Jack told Carl that he was ungrateful. (Is *he* Jack or Carl?)

Clear
Jack said to Carl, "You are ungrateful."

Clear
Jack confessed to Carl that he was ungrateful.

Also avoid the indefinite use of *they, you,* and *it.*

Informal
In smaller offices, they do not have great problems of communication.

Formal
In smaller offices, the problems of communication are not great.

Informal
In some states you are not permitted to walk against traffic.

Formal
Some states do not permit pedestrians to walk against traffic.

Informal
It says in the newspaper that Monday will be warmer.

Formal
The newspaper says that Monday will be warmer.

Dangling Constructions ━━━━━━

A **dangling construction** is one in which the second clause in a sentence does not logically modify anything in the first, although it seems to at first glance. Most people will, however, understand the sentence despite the dangling construction.

Two of the most common types of modifiers are participles and gerunds. These parts of speech are called *verbals* and are words that are derived from verbs but are normally used as nouns or adjectives. Verbals often cause trouble because they look like verbs; however, they can act only as modifiers or as nouns. They can never, by themselves, transmit action.

A **participle** is the form of a verb that ends in *-ing* in the present form and in *-ed* or *-en* in the past form. A participle can act as an adjective.

Perspiring heavily, the man ran wild-eyed into the oncoming truck. (*Perspiring* is an adjective modifying *man*.)

When using participles as adjectives, make sure that they relate to noun or a noun substitute; otherwise, there is nothing to modify and dangling construction results.

Dangling participle
While hunting in the woods, several deer were shot. (This means, literally, that several deer were hunting in the woods.)

Corrected version
While hunting in the woods, we shot several deer.

Dangling participle
The afternoon passed quietly, watching the words on the screen of the word processor scroll slowly by. (This means, literally, that the afternoon watched the word processor.)

Corrected version
She passed the afternoon quietly, watching the words on the screen of her word processor scroll slowly by.

A **gerund** is the form of a verb that ends in *-ing*. The gerund is always used as a noun.

Taking your medicine is better than avoiding the consequences of your acts. (*Taking* is a noun and the subject of the sentence.)

One of the most common problems with verbals is that we often think we are using a gerund (as a noun and therefore as the subject of a sentence) when we are really using a participle (which requires a subject).

Gerund as subject
Reading a good novel is a thoroughly engrossing experience.

Dangling participle
Reading a good novel, time passed quickly. (This means that time was reading the novel.)

Corrected version using a gerund
Reading a good novel causes time to pass quickly. (The subject of the sentence is *reading a good novel*.)

Corrected version using a participle
While reading a good novel, Tom didn't realize that time was passing so quickly. (*Reading* modifies *Tom*.)

Parallel Structure ━━━━━

Another common problem for writers is handling parallel structure correctly. In a sentence that has **parallel structure,** each of the phrases and clauses is structured in the same way. This helps keep the meaning of sentences clear.

Notice the correct use of parallel structure when the elements in a sentence are joined by a coordinating conjunction:

Wrong
Bob likes working late and to take charge of everything.

Right
Bob likes working late and taking charge of everything.

Or
Bob likes to work late and to take charge of everything.

Wrong
Ginny is bright, with a quick wit, and has a college degree.

Right
Ginny is bright, shows a quick wit, and has a college degree.

Or
Ginny is bright, with a quick wit and a college degree.

In sentences that make comparisons, parallel structure is sometimes difficult to achieve. Make sure that you complete all comparisons. This often can be done simply by repeating a word or two.

Wrong

He is as tenacious, if not more tenacious, than I am.

Right

He is as tenacious as, if not more tenacious than, I am.

If you read the first sentence without the parenthetical comparison, you'll see that it doesn't make much sense.

He is as tenacious than I am.

Now read the corrected version the same way.

He is as tenacious as I am.

Another common mistake is to leave out one of the terms of the comparison. This can alter the meaning of a sentence.

Wrong

I admire her more than Jane.

Right

I admire her more than Jane does.

Or

I admire her more than I admire Jane.

In some sentences, the meaning may be drastically altered by omitting a necessary word.

Wrong

Mr. Grant helps around the office by filing and making coffee. (Does Mr. Grant file coffee?)

Right

Mr. Grant helps around the office by filing and by making coffee.

Difficulties also arise in sentences that use *and/who* or *and/which* clauses.

Wrong

They bumped into Marge at the top of the stairs, an unlit passageway at best and which is dangerous at worst.

Right

They bumped into Marge at the top of the stairs, which is an unlit passageway at best and which is dangerous at worst.

The second *which* can be left out as long as the first is present. Another option might be:

They bumped into Marge at the top of the stairs—an unlit passageway at best, and dangerous at worst.

The correlatives *either/or, neither/nor, not only/but also, both/and,* and *whether/or* require parallel constructions.

Wrong

You are either late or I am early. (This makes the adjective *late* parallel with the clause *I am early.*)

Right

Either you are late or I am early. (Now we have two parallel clauses.)

Wrong

Philbert not only has been understanding to his secretary but also to his wife. (A verb parallel with a preposition.)

Right

Philbert has been understanding not only to his secretary but also to his wife. (Two parallel phrases.)

Larger elements also need to be parallel. This is especially important in writing where lists or bulleted items are used. It is necessary that all items in a series be kept parallel. Note the following problems with parallel structure:

In using the following program, we have set certain long-range objectives. These include:

- Informing children of the voting process.
- Increasing voter participation in the future.
- Increasing voter understanding in the future in the home as well as in the classroom.
- Promote patriotism by having people become involved in the U.S. government.
- Promote teaching of the governmental processes in schools and in the home.

The problem is that the first three items begin with gerunds and the last two begin with verbs. Change the last two to gerund forms (*promoting*) and the structure is parallel. The following lists show other parallel structure problems.

General Goals:

- Gear programs to specified target audiences.
- Program elements to be evaluated.
- Design a program that is easy to use and understand and is interesting.
- Testing of all elements by target audiences.

The problem here is that two of the items begin with verbs, one begins with a gerund, and one begins with a noun. To correct this structure, the second item should read, "*Evaluate* program elements," and the fourth item should read, "*Test* all elements by target audiences."

Some notable economic/financial highlights of 1983 were:

- Increased GNP of approximately 6.2 percent (fourth quarter to fourth quarter).
- A drop in unemployment from 10 percent to 8.2 percent by year-end—Inflation (C.P.I.) of approximately 4.0 percent (December to December).
- Corporate profits up approximately 15 percent on average and still rising.
- Strong U.S. dollar.

By converting each of the items to a phrase beginning with a noun, we would achieve parallel structure. Thus:

- An increased GNP....
- A drop in unemployment ....
- A rise in corporate profits ....
- A strong U.S. dollar.

Related to parallel structure is the problem of **mixed construction.** The most common error results from shifting from one verb tense to another or from one "person" or "voice" to another in pronoun references.

Mixed

My secretary told me she *would* type the letter for me as soon as she *can* get to the word processor.

Fixed

My secretary told me she *would* type the letter for me as soon as she *could* get to the word processor. (or *will/can.*)

Mixed

People are always making mistakes. You could avoid most of them by thinking before you act.

Fixed

We are always making mistakes. We could avoid most of them by thinking before we act.

Mixed

A man (or male of the species) is a complex being, and he is quite territorial. They are constantly on the alert for competitors.

Fixed

A man (or male of the species) is a complex being, and he is quite territorial. He is constantly on the alert for competitors.

Punctuation ────

Internal punctuation is possibly the most complex area of grammar because it is so open to interpretation.

Internal punctuation marks indicate the relationship of elements within a sentence. In English, five punctuation marks are used for this purpose: commas, semicolons, colons, dashes, and parentheses. Using these marks correctly requires adherence to certain rules. The only options are those that allow the writer nuances in meaning. For example, consider this unpunctuated sentence:

Woman without her man is an animal.

Now, place two commas setting off *without her man* as a parenthetical element and you have:

Woman, without her man, is an animal.

Place a period setting off *woman* as a statement, make *without her* an introductory phrase, and you have:

Woman. Without her, man is an animal.

As you can see, punctuation is important to meaning. How well we punctuate may mean the difference between being understood and being misunderstood.

Commas

The simplest reason for using a **comma** is to indicate a pause. Commas are most commonly used to separate independent clauses joined by a coordinating conjunction.

> I was tied up all morning with work, and I had a meeting just before lunch.
>
> Marvin could not make it to the ten o'clock meeting, but he sent his secretary to take notes.

The only exception to this rule is when one or both of the clauses are very short.

> Just ask me and I'll go.

If in doubt, use a comma. It is better to use punctuation than to leave it out and possibly cause confusion.

Don't mistake a compound *subject* for a compound *sentence*, however. A compound subject does not require a comma.

> Both the obnoxious tasting potato salad and the equally horrible hot dogs were provided by the company food service crew.

Commas also are used to separate introductory clauses and phrases from a main clause.

> When he saw the approaching storm, he quickly ran to the cellar and locked himself in.
>
> In an office of so many functions, she remains functionless.

The comma may be omitted, however, after very short introductory clauses or phrases unless this omission may lead to misunderstanding, as in the following examples.

> *Unclear*
> After dark streets in the poorer section of town begin to empty.
>
> *Clear*
> After dark, streets in the poorer section of town begin to empty.
>
> *Unclear*
> When you return gifts will be waiting for you under the tree.
>
> *Clear*
> When you return, gifts will be waiting for you under the tree.

Commas are used to set off transitional expressions such as *for example, on the other hand, in fact,* or *second.* Normally, these expressions occur at the beginning of the sentence and are followed by a comma.

> In fact, Jones was so intoxicated that he couldn't even sign his name.
>
> For example, the number of schools receiving aid under the new computer loan program has doubled in the past six months.

Commas also separate items in a series (usually called a *coordinate series).*

> Eudora spoke haltingly, quietly, and quickly.
>
> The woods are quiet, dark, and deep.
>
> It is a dark, dank, foreboding place to work.

There is an option in this case. Many people always include the final comma after the *and* in a coordinate series (called the *serial comma).* Others always leave it out. It's up to you, of course, but remember to leave it in if there is any chance of confusion.

> Perry used his windfall to purchase a number of new items including an automobile, a new television, some antique books and furniture. (Was the furniture antique too?—if not, insert a comma.)

Remember to group items joined by *and* and to separate these groupings by commas.

> Perry used his windfall to purchase a number of new items including an automobile and tires, a new television and VCR combination, and a remodeled sailboat.

Use a comma to separate *coordinate adjectives* (adjectives that all modify the same noun). A good guideline is that if you can insert *and* between the adjectives without altering the meaning, use commas.

> He sat behind a large, black, metal desk and smiled his best Cheshire Cat smile. (All adjectives modify *desk.* Removing the comma after *black* would make *black* modify *metal.* The difference may be subtle, but it is there.)

All coordinate adjectives refer to the noun they precede. If one or more of the adjectives refers to another adjective in the series, don't separate it with a comma from the adjective to which it refers.

> It was a dark red house. (The house wasn't dark. It was a dark shade of red.)

Set off nonrestrictive elements with commas; do not set off restrictive elements with commas. A *nonrestrictive element* is a word or group of words that is a supplement to, rather than an integral part of, the basic word or group of words it modifies. If the word or phrase can be omitted without changing the meaning of the sentence, it is nonrestrictive and must be set off by punctuation. If the word or phrase cannot be omitted without impairing the sense of the sentence, it is a *restrictive element* and must not be set off.

> Bank employees, who are highly paid, can afford vacations to the Virgin Islands. (Here, *who are highly paid* applies to all bank employees and is therefore nonrestrictive.)
>
> Bank employees who are highly paid can afford vacations to the Virgin Islands. (Here, *who are highly paid* applies only to some bank employees and is therefore restrictive.)

It's appropriate here to mention two words—*that* and *which*—that often cause some confusion. The key to understanding exactly when each should be used is knowing whether they represent a restrictive or nonrestrictive element within the sentence: *That* is the restrictive or defining pronoun, and *which* is the nonrestrictive or nondefining pronoun.

> The copier *that* is broken is on the third floor. (Indicates which copier we are talking about.)
>
> The copier, *which* is broken, is on the third floor. (Indicates some additional information about the copier in question.)

A good general rule is that if the phrase can be set of with a comma without changing meaning, use *which*. When speaking of people, always use *who*.

> That crowd from the Marketing Department, *who* are on the third floor, just barricaded themselves in the lounge. (*Who* refers to the people from marketing who are forming this particular crowd, not the entire department.)
>
> That crowd from the Marketing Department, *which* is on the third floor, just barricaded themselves in the lounge. (*Which* refers to the whole department.)
>
> That crowd from the Marketing Department *that* is on the third floor just barricaded themselves in the lounge. (*That* refers to a specific Marketing Department among several.)

Semicolons

Semicolons are normally used as substitutes for commas when a relationship exists between two clauses yet the ideas are strong enough to appear almost as separate sentences. Semicolons can be used in place of commas to separate main clauses joined by a coordinating conjunction, especially when the clauses already contain commas.

> Joan, the best writer at the magazine, won the journalist of the month award; but Anne, Becky, and Ruth were all given honorable mentions.

Semicolons also should be used to separate main clauses not joined by a coordinating conjunction, especially if the two clauses show a strong relationship of ideas.

> Fred is a total nerd; every day he proves it more.

Never join sentence elements of unequal grammatical rank with a semicolon. Always make sure both clauses are main clauses.

> *Wrong*
> Fred is a total nerd; although he is sincere.

> *Right*
> Although he is sincere, Fred is a total nerd.

Use a semicolon to separate main clauses joined by a conjunctive adverb.

> John was late for work this morning; however, he brought doughnuts.
> Dr. Howard has published several works over the past 10 years; therefore, he is considered an authority.

Colons

Colons are overused in most writing. The **colon** is used most appropriately to separate two main clauses, the second of which amplifies the first.

> On the door of the men's room was posted a sign: Off limits due to bifunctional overload. (Note that the first word of a complete sentence following a colon may be capitalized or not—one of the few options in the correct use of grammar.)

The most common use of the colon is as a means of introducing a list.

Sales of the "Gaftex" plastic elbow have increased as follows:

- 20 percent in January.
- 30 percent in May.
- 10 percent in July.

A colon should not be used, however, to introduce a list that is an object of an element in the introductory statement.

> A number of new applications have been discovered, including automotive, industrial, aerospace, refined foods, and retail sales.

Dashes and Parentheses

Dashes and parentheses are used in place of commas to either add or subtract emphasis. They are used to set off parenthetical expressions that abruptly interrupt the structure of the sentence. The choice of which marks to use is entirely up to you. Most writers, however, use **dashes** to set off statements that they wish to emphasize, and **parentheses** to set off less emphatic statements.

> *Emphatic*
> The bottom line—as the boss often said—is the bottom line.

> *Less Emphatic*
> The bottom line (as the boss often said) is the bottom line.

> *No Emphasis*
> The bottom line, as the boss often said, is the bottom line.

Dashes can also be used to prevent confusion when commas might lead to a misreading.

> *Confusing*
> Two women, Jane and Myrna, run the entire department from the confines of a small office on the third floor. (This could be misread [and there is always someone who will misread it] to mean four women—two unnamed and Jane and Myrna.)

> *Clear*
> Two women—Jane and Myrna—run the entire department from the confines of a small office on the third floor.

When using parentheses, make sure to include any punctuation that normally would be used in the sentence without parentheses.

> Because she went to lunch early (nine o'clock), she was docked one hour's pay.

If the matter within parentheses is a complete sentence, place a period within the parentheses.

Whatever the reason, Fred chose not to attend. (He frequently pulls this maneuver.)

Don't confuse brackets with parentheses. **Brackets** are used to set off editorial corrections or explanations within quoted matter. They are sometimes necessary (but only rarely) to set off another item from an item already set off by parentheses.

The letter opened, "Dear Fiends [sic] and Romans."

He [the manager of public relations] spoke at great length and with something less than aplomb.

The bottom line (as the boss [Mervin Smirks] often said) is the bottom line.

Quotation Marks

Quotation marks are almost always used properly. What are misused are the punctuation marks placed either inside or outside the quotation marks. In the United States, internal punctuation, such as commas, is placed inside the quotation marks.

"There is no use in working today," he said.

Periods are also placed inside quotation marks.

According to Tom, "Work is the only true medicine for depression."

Colons and semicolons, however, should be placed outside the quotation marks.

According to Tom, "Work is the only true medicine for depression"; however, Tom is frequently wrong.

Place a dash, question mark, or exclamation point inside the marks when it applies only to the quotation. Place it outside the quotation marks when it applies to the whole statement.

He said, "Will I see you tomorrow?"

Did he say, "I'll see you tomorrow"?

Do not place a punctuation mark after the quotation marks if another punctuation mark has been used inside the quotation marks.

The program, entitled "Johnny can learn to read!" will be available to most of the country this fall. (Normally, you would be required to put a second comma after the parenthetical element; but, in this case, that would leave you with three punctuation marks. The comma can be eliminated without disturbing the message.)

Apostrophes

The **apostrophe** is used to denote several different things. For example, use an apostrophe to indicate the omission of letters or numbers.

can't

the summer of '42

Contractions always use an apostrophe to indicate where letters have been omitted. Thus, *don't* is the contracted form of *do not;* the apostrophe indicates where the *o* has been omitted from *not*. The same is true in contractions such as *wouldn't* (*would not*), *I've* (*I have*), and *we'd* (*we had*).

One of the most common grammatical mistakes in the English language is the use of an apostrophe in the possessive form of *its*.

Wrong

The magazine was new, but it's pages were torn.

Right

The magazine was new, but its pages were torn.

The only form of *its* that uses an apostrophe is the contracted form of *it is—it's*.

Wrong

Its been a long, hot summer.

Right

It's been a long, hot summer.

Another common mistake (thankfully relegated to advertisements and signage) is exemplified by *rock 'n' roll:* The *'n'* is a contraction for *and,* thus requiring two apostrophes.

Use an apostrophe to form the plurals of letters, numbers, and words used as words.

Cross your *t*'s and dot your *i*'s.

Count to 10,000 by *2*'s.

Don't use so many *and*'s when you write.

Don't use an apostrophe before the *s* indicating decades, however.

1960s

1980s

the '90s (notice the apostrophe indicating missing digits.)

Use an apostrophe to indicate the possessive form of a word. Place it before the *s* in the singular form and after the *s* in the plural form.

The boss's desk was absolutely spotless. (Only one boss.)

The bosses' desks were absolutely spotless. (Many bosses.)

Hyphens

The **hyphen** is a useful punctuator, but it is often confused with the dash when typed on a typewriter. (Most computers have both a dash and a hyphen.) On a typewriter, two hyphens (--) equal one dash (—).

Use a hyphen for compound words that are not yet accepted as single words. Many of the words we accept today as being single, unhyphenated words started as two separate words and then became compound words joined by a hyphen.

base ball → base-ball → baseball

The only accurate way to determine whether a word is hyphenated or not is to check a recent edition of a dictionary.

Use a hyphen to join two or more words that act as a single adjective before a noun. Don't hyphenate two adjectives if they follow the verb.

Arthur is a well-known philanthropist, which is amazing considering that he only makes $10,000 a year.

That Arthur is a philanthropist is well known.

Omit the hyphen when the first word is an adverb ending in *-ly*.

He managed to glue the entire typewriter back together using quick-drying cement.

He managed to glue the entire typewriter back together using quickly drying cement.

Use a hyphen to form compound numbers from 21 through 99 and to separate fractions.

twenty-nine

two-thirds

Use a hyphen with the prefixes *self, all, ex,* and the suffix *elect.*

> self-important
>
> all-conference
>
> ex-mayor
>
> president-elect

And use a hyphen to avoid ambiguous or awkward combinations of letters.

> *belllike* should be *bell-like*
>
> *recreate* means "to enjoy leisure time"; *re-create* means "to create anew."

Mechanics ━━━━━

There are several areas we haven't touched on yet that serve to complete this discussion of grammar. They are the use of italics, capitalization, and numbers.

Italics

Before computer typesetting (which is what you do every time you write on a computer), italics were indicated by underlining. When marking up copy for typesetting in the days before computers, editors would simply underline anything that was to be set in italics. Anyone setting type would then understand that underlining meant "set in italics" and set it properly. Today, of course, we can "set" our own italics. When to set it, however, is an interesting question.

Italics are a tricky business for the public relations writer. When writing news releases, for instance, the public relations writer has to act as, and follow the guidelines of, a journalist. According to the *Associated Press Style Book and Libel Manual,* for instance, there are several rules for using italics. For example, AP style does not allow for italics for the titles of books, records, and newspapers. It would have you place these in quotation marks. *The New York Times* thus becomes "The New York Times." And, for magazines, *Newsweek* would become, simply, "Newsweek."

The tricky part is that AP style is anything but consistent and is intended largely for journalists and, as public relations writers, there are times when we have to write in acceptable journalistic style. However, most public relations writers probably spend as much, or more, time writing copy for items that will be printed (house magazines, newsletters, brochures, etc.) as they do writing releases for the print media. In the long run, it will probably be to your benefit to become familiar with both AP style and accepted standard usage for italics.

The following rules, therefore, reflect standard English grammar usage—not AP style—for italics and use of quotation marks for publications:

1. Use italics (underlining) to indicate the titles of complete publications.

    The New York Times

    Time magazine (The entire name of the magazine is *Time*, not *Time Magazine*.)

    The Sun Also Rises (Note that the movie version of this book would also be set in italics.)

2. Use quotation marks to indicate a chapter from a book, an article in a newspaper or magazine, or a cut from a compact disc (the title of each would be in italics, as it is a complete publication).

    The article "I Was a Teenage Corporate Executive" appeared in the June issue of *Forbes*.

    Billy Joel has had several number one hits, including "Keeping the Faith" from his album *Innocent Man*.

3. Italicize letters, words, and numbers used as words.

    Your *r*'s look very much like your *n*'s.

    When you use the word *dedicated*, exactly what do you mean?

4. Use italic to add stress or emphasis to certain words, but don't overuse it.

    I was speaking of *your* bad habits, not mine.

Capitalization

Capitalization also can be tricky unless you adhere to some basic rules:

- First of all, capitalize proper nouns and common nouns used as proper nouns.

    Specific persons, races, and nationalities
    William, Mary, American, Asian

    Specific places
    Dallas, Iran, Peoria

Specific organizations, historical events, and documents
Democratic National Committee

Taft-Hartley Act

Civil War

NAACP

- Capitalize titles when they precede a proper noun:

    Professor Wilson

    Dr. James Arlington

    President Bill Clinton

- When titles follow a name, capitalize them only if they represent a title and not a job description.

    John Smith, President, Bank of the North

    John Smith, the president of the Bank of the North, was conspicuously absent from the meeting.

- Capitalize common nouns when used as an essential part of a proper noun.

    University of Delaware (Not in "The university was overrun with bigots.")

    General Motors Corporation (Not in "The corporation stands to lose millions this year.")

- An exception is usually made for state and federal governments.

    The state encompasses some three million square miles. (Speaking of the state as a landmass.)

    The State refused to reinstate voting rights to over 400 criminals. (Speaking of the state as a government.)

    The federal government ran roughshod over the territory for over 40 years.

- Capitalize geographic locations when they refer to the locations themselves and not to a compass direction.

    The Northeast is seriously overcrowded yet maintains a vast amount of virgin forest.

    If you travel northeast from here, you are bound to come to a fast-food restaurant.

Numbers

Numbers are a sticky subject. Different style and grammar books approach numbers in a variety of ways. Probably the best method to use is laid out in *The Associated Press Stylebook*. What follows is a distillation:

1. Spell out all numbers from one through nine. The numbers 10 and above should be written as numerals. There are, of course, exceptions:

   - Spell out numbers at the beginning of sentences, regardless of the size of the number. (This doesn't apply to dates.)

     Forty people attended the meeting, which was held in a closet-sized room.

     1986 is going to be a good year.

   - Spell out numbers that represent rounded figures or approximations.

     About two or three hundred members were in attendance.

     He was obviously in his nineties.

   - Spell out fractions.

     one-fourth

     two-thirds

     seven-eighths

   - Spell out numbers preceding a unit-of-measure modifier containing a figure.

     five 9-inch toothpicks

     seven 1/2-inch pieces of plastic

2. Use figures to represent numbers in the following cases:

   - When numbers below 10 appear in the same sentence but refer to the same general subject as larger numbers.

     Melissa sent out for 3 sandwiches, 20 cups of coffee, and 4 small bags of pretzels, but she wanted them within five minutes. (The number five does not refer to the same general subject and so does not have to be written as a numeral.)

   - When numbers refer to parts of a book, they should be figures.

     Chapter 2, page 75, paragraph 4

• When numbers precede units of time or measurement, they should be written as numerals.

3 x 5 card

9 o'clock or 9:00

15-yard penalty

Spelling ━━━━━━

Spelling is a problem for many of us. We simply cannot spell. Part of the problem is our language. English, historically, is made up of many languages: Latin, French, Dutch, German, and many others. Often there seems to be no logic to the way words are spelled in English.

For instance, the letter *a* can have many different phonetic sounds, as in *ran, air, day, papa,* or *lathe.* On the other hand, different combinations of letters are often sounded alike: *rec(ei)ve, repr(ie)ve, rep(ea)l.* There seems to be no logical reason for the difference in the sound of *c* in *citizen* and *cat* or the *g* in *regal* and *regency.* Some letters don't seem to belong in the word at all as in *i(s)land, recei(p)t,* and *de(b)t.* And then there are the words for which pronunciation would seem to be impossible if we hadn't grown up knowing the difference: *through, bough, trough, though.*

Of course, knowing all this doesn't help the chronic poor speller. Knowing that *sight* comes from Anglo-Saxon, *site* from French, and *cite* from Latin doesn't help us unless we spell by context and recognize the differences in meanings of these words.

For the problem speller, there is, however, some hope. That hope lies in correct pronunciation, recognition of differences in meanings and spellings, and memorization of some of the rules of spelling.

Correct Pronunciation

Correct pronunciation can act as an invaluable aid to spelling. Many words are commonly mispronounced, leading to misspelling. The following list is by no means exhaustive, but it does contain some of the most often mispronounced words.

arctic	disastrous	nuclear
athletics	grievous	prejudice
boundary	incidentally	quantity
candidate	interest	temperature
cavalry	irrelevant	veteran
comparable	mathematics	
desperate	mischievous	

Note that some of these words have more than one pronunciation. If you have trouble spelling them, you should cultivate the pronunciation that helps you with spelling.

Many words in English sound alike but are spelled differently. These are called *homonyms,* and the spelling must be derived from the meaning within the sentence.

ascent = a climb	assent = to agree
all ready = everyone is ready	already = by this time
all together = as a group	altogether = entirely
altar = a place of worship	alter = to change
capital = governing city, or wealth	capitol = a building
council = an assembly	counsel = to advise
bare = stripped or naked	bear = to carry, or a stuffed Teddy
course = a path or way	coarse = rough textured
complement = that which completes	compliment = praise
principal = chief or most important	principle = a belief or rule
stationery = writing paper	stationary = not moving
weather = the elements	whether = if

Spelling Rules

Unfortunately, the only way for many of us to improve our spelling is to memorize the rules. This may sound impossible, but knowing some of the rules that pertain to your particular area of weakness can aid you immeasurably.

1. Write *i* before *e* except after *c,* or when sounded like *a* as in *eighty* or *sleigh:*

belief	neighbor
ceiling	receive
deceive	thief
feign	vein
field	

   Naturally, there are some exceptions: *financier, species, fiery, weird.*

2. When using prefixes, add the prefix to the root of the word without doubling or dropping letters:

   *dis*appear

   *dis*satisfaction

   *un*necessary

3. Drop the final *e* before a suffix beginning with a vowel but not before a suffix beginning with a consonant:

care + ful = careful   fame + ous = famous

come + ing = coming   ride + ing = riding

entire + ly = entirely   sure + ly = surely

In some words, keep the final *e* to keep a *c* or *g* soft before an *a* or *o*:

change + able = changeable

courage + ous = courageous

notice + able = noticeable

Again, there are some exceptions: Some words that take suffix *-ful* or *-ly* drop the final *e*:

awe + ful = awful

due + ly = duly

true + ly truly

And some words taking the suffix *-ment* drop the final *e*:

acknowledge + ment = acknowledgment

judge + ment = judgment

4. The final *y* is usually changed to *i* except before a suffix beginning with *i* (usually *-ing*):

cry + ing = crying   funny + er funnier

happy + ness = happiness   hurry + ied = hurried

hurry + ing = hurrying   study + ing = studying

5. Double the final consonant before a suffix that begins with a vowel when a single vowel precedes the consonant, and the consonant ends an accented syllable or a one-syllable word:

format + ed = formatted (*a* is a single vowel preceding the final consonant, but the word is accented on the first syllable.)

sad + er = sadder (*a* is a single vowel preceding the final consonant, and the word is one syllable).

stoop + ing = stooping (The word is one syllable, but the final consonant is preceded by two vowels.)

6. Sometimes, adding a suffix like *-ity, -ation,* or *-ic* can help you spell the base word by showing you the pronunciation:

similar   similarity

moral   morality

symbol   symbolic

grammar   grammatical

The bottom line is that good spelling can become a habit. Once you have learned to spell a word correctly, you shouldn't have any more trouble with it. Nevertheless, here are some steps that might help you to spell troublesome words and prevent you from using ingrained misspellings:

1. Look closely at a word that is giving you trouble and say it to yourself, taking care to pronounce it carefully and correctly.

2. Divide the word into syllables, taking care to pronounce each one.

3. Try to visualize the correct spelling before you write the word.

4. Write the word without looking at the correct spelling.

5. Then look the word up to see if you spelled it correctly. If you did, cover the word and write it again. Write it one more time just to be sure you have it down. If you've written it correctly all three times, chances are you won't have any more trouble with it in the future. If you had some problems with any one of the three writings, go over the word again starting with step one.

6. Finally, make a list of words that give you trouble. Go over the list frequently using the above method until you have eliminated them one by one. If you are a chronic misspeller, this can seem an almost never-ending job, but it is well worth the effort.

KEY TERMS

parts of speech	case
noun	dangling construction
pronoun	participle
antecedent	gerund
indefinite pronoun	parallel structure
verb	mixed construction
adjective	internal punctuation marks
adverb	comma
preposition	semicolon
conjunction	colon
independent clause	dash
subordinate clause	parentheses
simple sentence	bracket
compound sentence	quotation mark
complex sentence	apostrophe
compound-complex sentence	hyphen

THE BASICS OF STYLE

FOR IMMEDIATE RELEASE

In this chapter you will learn:

- When to use formal and informal language and jargon in your writing.

- How to be as exact and creative as possible in your word choice.

- How to vary sentence length and construction to add interest to your writing.

- How to build transitions within and between paragraphs.

- How to organize and plan your writing.

Why study style? The problem is, not many of us learned to write the way we do in school—instead, we learned on the job, picking up bad habits as well as good ones and having those habits further ingrained by people who couldn't put words together much better than we could. That's why it's important to pause for a few moments and check our writing style to see if we have acquired any bad habits that we should correct.

That's the purpose of this section: to help you understand some of the accepted methods of "good" style and to apply those methods to your personal writing style. I don't want you to change an already good writing style. What I would like to give you is an increased awareness of how to change those things you would like to change while leaving the good parts intact. I've tried to make this section as painless as possible by providing you with the most appropriate areas of style in the most abbreviated way.

Working with Words ——————

How we use words has a huge impact on the success of our message, so choosing just the right words is of critical importance.

Formal vs. Informal

All of us think we know how to use a dictionary. It's part of every writer's library, right? The problem is that a lot of people don't use their dictionaries to check the meanings and spellings of the words they use. This leads, of course, to misinterpretation of written materials by readers.

One of the biggest problems in using dictionaries is deciding whether or not a word is appropriate in context. For instance, a word that might be entirely appropriate in informal English might not be appropriate in formal English. Dictionaries can be of some help. Most provide guidance in selecting the right word. For instance, a dictionary might label the word *swipe* as a colloquial or informal alternative to *steal* or *plagiarize*. You wouldn't want to use it in a formal business letter.

This brings us to our first rule: Avoid using informal words in formal writing.

Informal
It seems that Mr. Jordan swiped the information on the new plastic widget from a brochure he found in his files.

Formal
It seems that Mr. Jordan plagiarized the information on the new plastic widget from a brochure he found in his files.

It's usually safe to assume that if a word is not labeled as informal in your dictionary, it is considered to be in general usage and therefore formal.

For the public relations writer, contractions (which are usually considered informal usage) can be useful. Frequently, you can take on a familiar tone with your target audience by using contractions. For strictly formal documents, however, it is still a good rule to write out the complete word or phrase instead of its accepted contraction. Words like *can't, won't,* and *isn't* should be written out as *cannot, will not,* and *is not.*

Jargon

All industries have their jargon, or specialized vocabulary. Banks call certificates of deposit "CDs," journalists call paragraphs "graphs," police call a record of arrests a "rap sheet," and highly technical industries develop an entire dictionary of shorthand notations. Jargon should not be used for external information pieces unless they are to be read only by experts in the field. For internal pieces, jargon is usually acceptable. For the lay reader, use jargon only if you are able to explain it in lay terms. It is wise to follow this procedure unless you are sure that your jargon has become accepted general usage.

When jargon becomes cumbersome, it overrides meaning. What we commonly refer to as "legalese" and "bureaucratese" is really an overuse of jargon. The result is ambiguity.

Jargon
Do not discharge your mechanical device releasing its base-metal projectile until such time as the opposing force has decreased the distance between your two positions to a point allowing visual recognition of the delineation between the ocular components of the aforesaid opponent and recognition of the opaque, globular housing thereof.

General
Don't fire until you see the whites of their eyes.

Words like *impact* and *input* have now become jargon to many industries. They sound "trendy" to many people and give them a false sense of belonging to a select group of "experts."

Jargon
I have asked Ms. Pomeroy to *input* the latest cost figures so that we may have the results by 4:00 this afternoon. (A noun misused as a verb.)

General
I have asked Ms. Pomeroy to *enter* the latest cost figures so that we may have the results by 4:00 this afternoon. (A verb used correctly.)

Jargon

The severe downturn in the economy has negatively *impacted* our industry. (A noun misused as a verb.)

General

The severe downturn in the economy has negatively *affected* our industry. (A verb used correctly.)

Did you recognize any other use of jargon in the above examples? What are they, and how would you change them to a more general style?

In your efforts to write clearly and concisely, remember that the object of written communication is to communicate. In other words, don't "fuzzify."

Exactness

Exactness is an art. Most of us tend to "write up" when we assume a formal style. But when we "write up," we lose precision. What we should strive for is clarity, and clarity can be achieved most easily by using exact words. Most of our writing is read by people who know something about us and what we do, but we cannot always assume that to be the case.

Denotative and Connotative Meanings. One way to avoid confusion is always to use words whose denotative meanings most closely match those understood by our audience. The **denotative meaning** of a word is its "dictionary" meaning and, of course, the best way to determine that is to look the word up. The first example following uses the wrong word.

Wrong

The employees were visibly effected by the president's speech. (*Effect* means result.)

Right

The employees were visibly affected by the president's speech. (*Affect*, in this case, means emotionally moved.)

Wrong

As a manager, Marvin was fine; but as a human being, he had some severe problems dealing with sex differences among his department members. (*Sex* usually refers to biological differences or the act itself)

Right

As a manager, Marvin was fine; but as a human being, he had some severe problems dealing with gender differences among his department members. (*Gender* has become the accepted term for the differences in roles related to the total experience of being either male or female.)

Connotative meanings are those meanings your audience may associate with words in addition to or instead of their dictionary meaning. Connotation is the result of automatic associations your audience makes when interpreting certain words. For example, you may intend the word *dog* to mean a four-footed, warm-blooded animal of the canine species. To audience members whose past associations with dogs have been positive, a picture of a particularly friendly dog may pop into mind. For some who may have had negative experiences—such as being bitten by a dog—the association may be entirely the opposite of what you intend. Although there is no way to guard against all such associations, there are certain words or phrases that you should avoid as being too vague in connotation to be useful to you as a communicator.

Think of the different connotative meanings for words such as *liberal, conservative, freedom, democracy, communism,* and *patriotism.* Words with multiple connotations may not be the best words to select if you are striving for exactness.

Some words or phrases may have little or no connotation, such as *place of birth.* The denotative meaning of this phrase is clear, but there is little connotative meaning. However, if we replace the phrase with the word *hometown,* not only does the denotative meaning become clear, but the word also gains a definite connotative meaning—usually a positive one.

Specific Words vs. General and Abstract. Exactness requires that you be specific. When we read something that has been written in general, nonspecific terms, we can't help but feel that something is being left out—perhaps on purpose.

General words are indefinite and cover too many possible meanings, both denotatively and connotatively. Specific words are precise and limited in definition.

General	Specific
car	Honda Accord LX
people	Delawareans
animal	cat
precipitation	rain

Abstract words deal with concepts or ideas that are intangible, such as *freedom* or *love.* Use these words, but make sure that they are not open to misinterpretation.

"Enjoy the freedom of 7-Eleven!" (Does *freedom* mean that you pay lower prices, can shop 24 hours a day, have ample parking, preserve the American way each time you shop there, or what exactly?)

One of the parts of speech affected the most by inexactness is the adjective. A number of adjectives are extremely general and impart little or no additional meaning to a noun, thus negating their function.

General

Marisa, please take this report to word processing and tell them it's a rush job. (Show me something that isn't a rush job!)

Specific

Marisa, please take this report to word processing, and tell them we need it by 3:00 this afternoon. (Now word processing has a specific deadline.)

Keep It Fresh. At one time, all expressions were original; however, today we're frequently stuck with many trite or overworked expressions or clichés. The problem with these is that they may be entirely overlooked by your reader, who has probably seen them a thousand times.

Trite

Nine out of ten times Harcourt is wrong in his instant analysis of a problem.

Better

Most of the time Harcourt is wrong in his instant analysis of a problem.

Trite

Harcourt is claiming that his latest plan is a viable option in controlling employee absences.

Better

Harcourt is claiming that his latest plan is a solution to the problem of employee absences.

Public relations writing, like many other forms of writing, including journalism, has developed certain stock expressions that some might consider to be clichéd. Many of these, however, are acceptable shortcuts that aid understanding.

John Smith, *a native of* Chicago . . .

Or

Chicago *native* John Smith . . .

Generally, these semantic shortcuts impart the correct meaning without being vague or appearing trite. Other phrases have become clichéd through overuse and have consequently lost their meaning.

The head of programming says this new product will keep APC *on the cutting edge*. James Sutton, president of Associated Products Corporation, *announced today* (May 25) the release of a new line of plastic widgets.

The key is to recognize trite, overused expressions and clichés and understand when they can be useful and when they can hurt your message. Remember, good writers avoid worn-out words and opt instead for fresh usage.

Wordiness

Being too "wordy" is a habit that most of us fall into at one time or another. Perhaps, as was mentioned, we once thought it meant we were writing in a formal style. Actually, the opposite is true. Formal English should be no more wordy than informal English. In fact, it should be even more precise because it is formal. As a writer, you will find that the best way to eliminate wordiness is through editing. You probably already have more editors than you need, but your best editor is still you. You can eliminate a lot of shuffling of papers up and down the channels of communication for approvals if you perform some surgery early on. When you edit, strike out the phrases and words that add no additional information to your work, and clarify with precise words.

First draft
I would appreciate it if you would set up a meeting for sometime in the late afternoon, midweek, for our next, important get-together.

Revised draft
I would appreciate it if you would set up a time sometime late Wednesday afternoon for our next meeting.

Final draft
Please set up a 3:00 meeting for next Wednesday.

First draft
We would like to attempt to schedule our very next company picnic to be held in or around the city of Wilmington in order to facilitate transportation by employees to the site.

Revised draft
We want to schedule our company picnic in Wilmington to make it easier for employees to attend.

Of course, you don't want to be brief to the point of abruptness, but you can see what exactness can do in the editing process. The key is to make sure that all important information is covered in enough detail to be useful to the reader.

Unfortunately, we often overclarify in an attempt to make our messages understood; however, much of what we write is simply redundant or not needed for clarification.

> The in-basket is completely full. (How can it be incompletely full?)
>
> Johnson has come up with a most unique design for dismantling the employee pension fund. (It's either unique or it's not—*most* adds no meaning.)
>
> The meeting date has been set for March 31, the last day of the month. (The final phrase is redundant.)

Emphasis

Organization of words within a sentence, sentences within paragraphs, and paragraphs within a larger work is key to clear writing style. We typically organize based on the importance or weight assigned to these words, paragraphs, or larger elements. By placing them in a prescribed order, we give the thoughts they represent emphasis.

Following are some of the standard methods for gaining emphasis:

- Place the most important words at the beginning or end of the sentence.

  Unemphatic
  There was a terrific explosion in the photocopy room that shook the whole building. (*There* is an unemphatic word in an important position.)

  Emphatic
  A terrific explosion in the photocopy room shook the whole building.

- The end of a sentence is also a strong position for emphasis.

  Unemphatic
  I know Tom was the one who stole the stapler.

  Emphatic
  I know who stole the stapler—Tom.

- Increase emphasis by arranging ideas in the order of climax. Rank items in a series by order of importance, building from the least important to the most important.

Jill was abrasive, lazy, undedicated, and generally ill-equipped to deal with her co-workers. (In this case, *ill-equipped* is used to sum up Jill's other attributes.)

Watch out for an illogical ranking of ideas. If done unintentionally, this could cause some unwelcome hilarity, as in the following example.

Because of his brief exploration of the casinos, Jerry became morose, despondent, melancholic, and lost $12.

- Gain emphasis by using the active rather than the passive voice. The active voice indicates that the "doer" of the action is the most important element in the sentence; the passive indicates the "receiver" is the most important.

  Unemphatic
  Not much is being done by the employer to defray health benefit costs.

  Emphatic
  The employer is not doing much to defray health benefit costs.

  Unemphatic
  The study, accomplished by the Finance Department, showed a sharp decline in quarterly earnings.

  Emphatic
  The Finance Department's study showed a sharp decline in quarterly earnings.

- Add emphasis by repeating key words or phrases. Such repetition not only adds emphasis but often serves as a memory stimulant.

  I am afraid that these negotiations gave rise to false hopes, false indications of changes that may not occur, and false expectations on the part of management as to its ability to fulfill false promises.

- Add emphasis by balancing sentence construction. Balanced structure occurs when grammatically equal elements are used to point to differences or similarities. The usual construction is one in which two clauses contain parallel elements.

Knowing the health hazards and still smoking is freedom of choice; not knowing and smoking is victimization.

Working here is boring; not working here is unemployment.

Working with Sentences ━━━━━━━

Unvarying sentence length creates monotony, and monotony creates disinterested readers.

The key to good style is to vary sentence length. Don't string together short, choppy sentences if they can be joined to form more interesting compound sentences.

Monotonous

Harvey walked into the office. He sat down. He began to type on his 1923 Underwood. It was the typewriter with the black metal carriage. Harvey hated typing this early in the morning. He was never fully awake until at least 10 o'clock.

Varied

Harvey walked into the office, sat down, and began to type on his 1923 Underwood with the black metal carriage. He hated typing this early in the morning, since he was never fully awake until at least 10 o'clock.

Notice that related ideas are linked as compound sentences. Linking unrelated ideas is an easy mistake and sounds silly.

Harvey walked into the office, sat down, and began to type on his 1923 Underwood. It was the typewriter with the black metal carriage, and he hated typing this early in the morning. (What does his typewriter having a black metal carriage have to do with Harvey's dislike for early-morning typing?)

Be careful, however, not to make your sentences too long. Short sentences are easier to read. A guideline for determining proper sentence length is to keep sentences down to about 16 words long. Naturally, you're not going to count each word you write, but you get the idea. Shorter sentences in the context of longer ones can also increase emphasis, as in the following examples:

I have discovered that the content employee is dedicated, remains on the job longer, suffers fewer illnesses, creates fewer problems, and rarely complains. In short, he or she is productive.

I understand. You have a number of assignments due simultaneously, your secretary is out sick, your copier is broken, and you cannot get an outside line. I still need it now.

Another easy method of preventing monotony is to alter the beginnings of your sentences. In other words, don't always write in the subject–verb–object order. One of the best ways to vary this order is to use a subordinate clause first:

Because of his dislike for early-morning typing, Harvey never showed up at work prior to 10 o'clock.

Starting out early, Harvey walked two blocks at a brisk pace, then collapsed.

Before you start on that report, come into my office for a little chat.

And don't forget—beginning a sentence with a conjunction is perfectly acceptable.

Remember, though, that even conjunctions have meanings and usually infer that a thought is being carried over from a previous sentence.

Not only was Harvey later than usual, he was downright tardy. And I wasn't the only one to notice. (Implies that the information is being added to the previous thought.)

Not only was Harvey later than usual, he was downright tardy. But I was probably the only one who noticed. (Implies a contrast with the previous thought.)

With a little reworking, however, even a series of strung-together clauses can be fixed up. Conjunctions can be useful but not if they are overused.

Clauses strung together
Francine is always on time, and she frequently comes in before regular office hours, and she never leaves before quitting time.

Reworked into a complex sentence
Francine is always on time, frequently coming in before regular office hours and never leaving before quitting time.

Clauses strung together
He ran down the street, and then he stopped at the main entrance, and he took a deep breath, and then he went inside.

Reworked into a compound predicate
He ran down the street, stopped at the main entrance, took a deep breath, and went inside.

Working with Paragraphs

As the sentence represents a single thought, so the paragraph represents a series of related thoughts. There is no set number of sentences in a paragraph; however, paragraph lengths tend to be shorter today than in the past. Short paragraphs invite readership while long paragraphs "put off" the reader. The key is coherence, which means that ideas must be unified. You can give unity to your paragraphs in several ways: by making each sentence contribute to the central thought, by arranging sentences in a logical order, and by making logical transitions between sentences.

Making Each Sentence Contribute

The first sentence should generally express the theme of the paragraph. Although the thematic statement may actually appear anywhere in the paragraph, the strongest positions are at the beginning or the end; and the end is usually reserved for a transitional lead into the following paragraph.

> Our annual operating budget is somewhat higher than expected due to the increase in state allocations to higher education this fiscal year. The result will probably be an increase in departmental allowances, with the bulk of the increase showing up in the applied sciences. Although Arts and Sciences have been "holding up" well, we don't expect that they will be able to maintain this independence for long. As a result, their departmental budgets will also reflect this positive financial shift. Next year's outlook is a different story.

The lead sentence sets the theme for the entire paragraph, which is this year's budget. The final sentence indicates that the next paragraph will probably deal with next year's budget. What you want to avoid are unrelated sentences. If they are truly unrelated, then they deserve a paragraph of their own. If they are slightly related, then the relationship needs to be pointed out.

Logical Sentence Order

Arrange sentences in a logical order, and provide smooth transitions between them indicating their relationship. There are several ways to group sentences to show ranking: time order, spatial order, and order of climax.

Time order and *chronological order* are sometimes synonymous, although chronological order often implies a direct mention of time or dates, as in the following example:

> The growth of communication in the northernmost regions of America was rapid and coincided roughly with the development of the land itself. In 1867, shortly following the Civil War, the first telegraph line was strung between Dawson Creek and Whitehorse. By the turn of the century, the lines had been extended through to Seattle, on the southeastern coast, and to Anchorage, along Prince William Sound. The

first World War saw a flurry of development as military involvement increased in the region. With this involvement came a windfall of communication development that lasted until 1959.

Time order is appropriate when explaining the steps involved in an action:

Changing a toner cartridge is a relatively easy task, even for an office executive on a Saturday afternoon. First, open the printer and remove the old cartridge. Throw it away. Remove the new cartridge from its box, shake it thoroughly, insert it in the space provided for it, and snap it down. Close the cartridge housing. You are now ready to print.

Spatial order implies movement from one location to another: right to left, up to down, east to west, high to low, and so on:

It rained all day yesterday. The weatherman had shown in glaring detail how the jet stream would carry the warm, moist, low front from the snow-filled Cascades of the Northwest, over the Rockies, onto the plains, and finally into my backyard on the Atlantic coast. Apparently, it hadn't lost anything in the transition.

Order of climax means that arrangement follows from the least important element to the most important element in the paragraph, in ascending order of importance. Most of the time, the climax is the concluding sentence:

If the clerical staff members are uncomfortable with the workload, their immediate supervisors are the first to know. Middle managers are often reluctant to act on "workload" problems, but if pressured, they will pass on complaints to executive officers. If the problem isn't handled to the satisfaction of all the parties involved by the time it reaches the executive level, a vice president may have to intervene; but pity the poor vice president who can't handle the problem. The president's office is a bastion of corporate sanctuary. Woe to the person who would invade it.

When arranging sentences in order of climax, consider moving from the general to the specific or vice versa. Sometimes, moving from the familiar to the unfamiliar will soften the blow of dealing with a new idea:

When we view each member of our office staff as an individual, we sometimes develop tunnel vision. We have to understand the larger picture in order to alleviate this problem. Staff members are all part of a much larger organism. Together they form departments; departments form divisions. A large company is composed of these divisions, and that company is part of a much larger conglomerate. To take the analogy further, the conglomerate is only one of the hundreds of such groupings that help make our system of economics one of the most successful in the world.

Logical Transitions

Related ideas are given further unity by the use of logical transitions between sentences. A good transition usually refers to the sentences preceding it. Remember that a transitional word or phrase also has a meaning. Make sure the meaning adds to the understanding of the sentences or phrases preceding the transition:

> The floor plan was completely haphazard; *furthermore,* it appeared to crowd an already crowded office area. (*Furthermore* indicates an addition to the thought begun in the first clause.)

> Don Johnson was the first to try the new water fountain. *On the other hand,* he was the last to try the potato salad at the last company picnic. (The phrase *on the other hand* indicates contrast.)

> Fourteen employees were found to be in violation of company policies forbidding alcohol on the premises. *Consequently,* inspection of employee lockers will probably become commonplace. (*Consequently* indicates that the second sentence is a result of actions in the first.)

> The rate of consumption has tripled over the past 18 months. *In short,* we have a severe problem. (*In short* indicates a summary or explanation.)

> Jeremy covered the news desk. *Meanwhile,* Judy was busy copying the report before Wally returned and discovered it was missing. (*Meanwhile* is an indication of time placement.)

One of the major problems with the use of transitional words and phrases is overreliance on a very few common groupings. Many people tend to use words such as *however* to bridge every transitional creek. After a while, its use becomes monotonous. The answer? Vary transitional phrases. There's always another word you can use. Think about it.

The same applies to transitions between paragraphs. Use words and meanings that tie the thoughts together and form a smooth bridge between subjects. After all, even dissimilar ideas need to be linked. If they were so dissimilar that you couldn't link them logically, they wouldn't belong in the same document.

Paragraph Development

There are a number of ways to develop your paragraphs to show unity and coherence. Notice that all of the examples below supply relevant details in support of a main idea.

You will often find that developing a definition will add unity to a paragraph:

There are a number of ways of viewing the office water cooler. To a social scientist, it is a communal gathering place at which ideas and information are freely disseminated. It is an informal location, usually outside the territorial boundaries of any one employee and therefore accessible to all on an equal footing. It is the traditional "oasis," shared by any who are in need of water and at which all are free to share. To imply that this communal ground is the "property" of any one individual or department is to negate its real value. At the water cooler, we quench not only our thirst for liquid, but also for information outside the formal boundaries of protocol.

Frequently, classification will serve to relate like ideas in a paragraph:

There are three categories of clerical aid within the company. At the lowest rung of the pay scale is the clerk. A clerk's job includes light typing, no shorthand, much filing, and a tremendous amount of running around. Next up on the scale is the secretary. More typing is involved (at a much faster speed and with more accuracy), much filing, some shorthand, and a great deal of running around. At the top is the executive secretary. Typing is a must (at great speed and accuracy), along with good shorthand, much filing, and more running around than a university track team.

The main idea can be made more coherent by comparing or contrasting it with a like idea:

Comparison
A committee meeting is like a football game. The chair is the quarterback, and as such he is the directing force; however, the members are the players without whom no goal can be obtained. The key to the game plan, then, is to coordinate the players into a single unit with a single goal. The players must be made aware that a unified, or team, effort is integral to the accomplishment of that goal and that the quarterback is the director—he is not the coach. The director recommends; he does not command.

Contrast
The typical office environment is orderly. Without order, little can be accomplished. Remember the recess periods of your schooldays? You were able to act freely, without consideration to the restrictive environment of the classroom. You were free to explore your voice, your agility, and your mastery of fast-paced games not suited to the indoors. Once inside, how-

ever, you were required to conform to the needs of the classroom—quiet and order. Within these confines, work can be accomplished with a minimum of disturbance; and the accomplishment of that work is as important in an office environment as in a classroom.

One of the best ways to develop a paragraph and its central idea is to show cause and effect. Most things in life are a result of something else. For most of us, though, it takes some thought to trace that development:

> The so-called "open office" environment popular in newer buildings today has its roots in several trends. Since the mid-1970s, energy conservation has been a major concern in the United States. The open office requires less heat in the winter and less cooling in the summer, due mainly to the lack of walls. In place of these walls, we now have "dividers" which, although they serve to mask sound, allow for the free circulation of air throughout an entire floor. In addition to conservation, open offices serve to homogenize workers by removing the traditional boundaries of high walls and closed doors. Employees now have access to each other through a network of openings yet maintain the margin of privacy needed for individual productivity.

Obviously, a paragraph need not be restricted to any single method of development but can benefit from a combination approach. The key is to be clear, and any method that promotes clarity is a good one.

Planning and Writing ——————

A sentence usually contains a single idea. A paragraph contains a number of sentences related by a single theme. So too, a complete piece of writing—whether it's a press release, a backgrounder, or an article for the company newsletter—contains a series of paragraphs unified by a single theme and related by logical transitions.

For many of us, the writing is the easy part. Planning is the snag. And the toughest part of planning is deciding exactly what to say and what to leave out. Most of us tend to overwrite. In the words of one observer, "Writing is like summer clothing—it should be long enough to cover the subject, but brief enough to be interesting."

The first task in writing, then, is to choose your subject and limit yourself to the information needed to cover it. There are several ways to accomplish this. One of the easiest ways is to work from a very general topic to a specific topic:

banking → withdrawing and making deposits → avoiding waiting in lines → automatic teller machines (ATMs) → using ATMs in the lobby

This exercise may seem simple, but it does help clear your thoughts and crystallize your ideas through the act of putting them on paper. Naturally, the theme of any piece is intimately tied to its purpose. If, for instance, your purpose is to encourage patrons to use the ATMs in the bank lobby, it may be necessary to come directly to the point in your pitch. However, in doing so, you will probably use one of the traditional writing approaches.

Most of us remember our high school English classes in which we were taught to write various papers for different purposes. Among the most common approaches were:

Exposition—used to inform or explain

Argumentation—used to convince or persuade

Narration—used mostly for entertainment value

Description—used to explain through verbal "pictures"

In public relations writing, narration is the least frequently used except in feature-type stories. The other methods are often used and combined to present information to readers. A lot depends on whether you are trying to be persuasive or are simply presenting information, the two most common goals of public relations writing.

The Central Idea

Once you have decided on the purpose of a particular piece, you should write down a central idea in a single sentence or **thesis statement.** Suppose, for instance, that your goal is to convince employees to come to work on time each day. This will be a persuasive piece. The method you have chosen to use might be argumentation, which will convince your employees. What is your thesis statement? It might be something like this:

> Coming to work on time puts you in step with the other employees who
> work with you, gives you time to adjust to your daily environment,
> allows you the leisure of some prework interaction with others, and
> impresses your employer.

So, in a single sentence, you have set down several controlling ideas that can now be elaborated upon. The next step is to develop a working plan or rough outline.

The Outline

Before you begin an outline, it helps to put down some ideas. These can be in the form of a simple list. For instance, to continue the previous example, perhaps you have decided to stress promptness by comparing the benefits of being on time with the disadvantages of coming in late:

Advantages of coming to work on time:

- Allows time to adjust to daily routine
- Allows time for interaction with fellow workers
- Impresses employer
- Allows time to have coffee
- Allows time to read through the paper

Disadvantages of coming in late

- You are rushed into daily routine without adjustment period
- You have no time to interact informally with fellow workers
- You do not impress employer
- You have no time for coffee
- You have no time to read the paper

Now you have a starting point. It might be that you want to address the points one by one, covering the advantages first, and then the disadvantages. Or perhaps you want to compare the advantages with the disadvantages one at a time.

Outlines are extremely useful as a checklist of key points. You may use the outline simply to check your final written piece against to make sure you have covered all points regardless of final order, or you may have each point represent a complete paragraph or section of your finished document in the order presented in the outline.

In either case, make sure that ideas within each paragraph are related and that each paragraph follows logically from the previous one. The same methods you used to arrange your sentences within the paragraph—time order, spatial order, or order of climax—can be used to arrange your paragraphs within a larger composition.

Unity and Logical Thinking ━━━━

Clarity

We've already learned something of unity by studying the placement of ideas in a logical order within sentences, paragraphs, and whole compositions. Now, let's turn to logic itself. In writing, we should try to present our ideas as logically as possible to enhance understanding.

A major problem hindering understanding is semantics. **Semantics** involves the meanings of words individually and as they appear in a context. We should be extremely careful to select words that hold the same meaning for the reader as for us. One way to do this is to define terms that are likely to be either misunderstood or not understood at all.

> The major cause of antenna malfunction is the lack of foundation stability. The antenna cannot be properly anchored due to permafrost, a permanently frozen layer of ice and soil some three feet below the surface.
>
> All copy to be printed by the in-house print facility should be camera ready (properly sized, clean, and pasted in place).

Often a word can be defined by inserting a synonym.

> The altercation, or fight, lasted only three minutes.
>
> Sled dogs are not only used to running over muskeg—boggy terrain—they often relish the softness of the ground.

Some words or concepts, however, require more careful treatment. Abstracts such as freedom, liberty, and democracy have meanings far beyond those found in the dictionary. We must be careful when we write to give some thought to a word's connotative meaning as well as its denotative, or dictionary, meaning.

> Productivity is the major responsibility of the individual employee. Although management is usually associated with and responsible for rises or drops in productivity, individual employees remain the sole determiners of these fluctuations. Do they arrive at work on time and refreshed, ready to work? Do they spend too much time on breaks or at lunch? Do they perform only the required duties, or do they work beyond those requirements? So, then, productivity is more than producing a greater number of "widgets." Productivity is a state of mind carried over into the workplace. Productivity means caring; and caring means taking responsibility.

The determining factor in deciding to go with a simple or expanded definition is knowledge of your target audience, and that is a concern of planning, not style.

Generalizations

A **generalization** is an assumption based on incomplete evidence. It is a belief that what is true of a few members of a group (regardless of how you categorize that group or what it comprises) is true of the entire group:

> Teenagers are irresponsible.
>
> The British are very formal.
>
> All football players are dumb.
>
> Tall people are good basketball players.

Generalizations can be harmless or they can be dangerous. In writing, generalizations such as the examples above should be avoided. If you do make a generalization, you must support it. This means that you must present adequate evidence that what you are saying is true for most individuals of a particular group:

> Nearly half of all women in the U.S. believe they are overweight. A recent survey conducted by the National Center for Vital Statistics shows that 39 percent of all males and 49 percent of all females surveyed said they considered themselves overweight. The survey, part of the data collected in the most recent Health and Weight Loss Survey, was conducted on a random sample of men and women between the ages of 18 and 55. According to this survey, at any given time, at least 20 percent of the population are on some kind of weight-loss diet.

In this paragraph, the writer has made a generalization and given information enough to be considered adequate support.

Cause and Effect Relationships

Illogical statements often result when the writer fails to set up adequately a cause-and-effect relationship. We can construct such a relationship based on either inductive or deductive reasoning. **Inductive reasoning** proceeds from the particular to the general. A generalization is based on specific evidence that is deemed sufficient to support it. The results of scientific experimentation, for instance, are based on induction:

> A recent study by the Association for Scholastic Testing shows that schoolchildren between the ages of 7 and 14 learn more quickly and absorb more knowledge when the lesson is interactive. Additional studies by National Employment Associates indicate that high-school students with computer skills attain higher-paying jobs upon graduation. It is clear that computer training is fast becoming a necessary component in the education process.

Deductive reasoning involves working from the general to the specific. Specifics are usually determined from generalizations. If you know, for instance, that a high fever usually accompanies influenza, and you have a high fever during the flu season, then you might seek a doctor's care. You have deduced a specific need from a generalization. You may not, in fact, have influenza, but you have made a valid decision based on deduction. The basic assumption, however, must be sound for the deduction to be valid:

> It is clear that computer training is fast becoming a necessary component in the education process. Through this training, students will

become better equipped to deal with a burgeoning technology. Teachers will be eased of the responsibility to be all things to all students because of the interactive nature of computer learning. And students will ultimately benefit through higher-paying jobs.

As you can see, the deductive process in the preceding example was based on a previous inductive process. Most deductions are, in fact, based on previously collected information from which generalizations have been made.

The inductive and deductive processes are prone to problems in construction. The following guidelines will help you avoid the most common problems:

1. Because one item follows another chronologically, don't assume that the latter is a result of the former:

   Helen came in late this morning, and everything has been going downhill since then.

   Fred wouldn't be seeing Marge "on the side" if everything was all right at home.

2. Because one thing is true doesn't mean that you can infer another truth from it. This is commonly called a *non sequitur:*

   The recent, sharp upturn in the economy will certainly result in lower unemployment.

   Liz is something of an "airhead." She'll never make it in the business world.

3. Don't beg the question. In other words, don't draw out an expected response by the way you ask a question. This happens when you assume the truth of a statement you are trying to verify. Sports interviewers frequently do this.

   Champ, was that the greatest match you ever fought or what? (Implies that the match *was* the greatest, thus biasing the response.)

   Janice sneaked in at half past eight this morning. What do you suppose she's up to? (Maybe she slept late and isn't up to anything.)

4. Don't set up an either/or situation unless it really is one.

   Either you're going with me to the meeting or you're not. (Obviously a reasonable statement.)

   Either you're on my side or you're not. (Why can't I see the value in two different arguments without being on anyone's side?)

This is often called the all-or-nothing fallacy because it sets up a false dilemma, ignoring the fact that other variables or possibilities exist:

Employees either come to work on time or they're simply not dedicated.

School systems are either innovators because they acquire and use computers, or they're traditionalists who choose to ignore the future.

Finally, never argue a point that you can't back up with facts simply because you believe it to be true. Although much of what we believe is based on personal predispositions formed throughout our lifetimes, it is never too late to learn something new or to add facts to our existing knowledge.

If you are to be a good, persuasive writer, you must learn to be objective. For most writers, subjectivity indicates that you have a stake in what is being argued or, at least, a personal opinion. Opinions are best left for newspaper columnists or editors, who are paid to express their opinions. Objective writing is the hallmark of the logical writer. If you present the facts objectively, and they support your argument or point of view (whether or not that point of view is one that you personally hold), your argument will be logically sound.

Some Final Thoughts on Writing ———————

Now that you have come to the end of this book, you should have mastered the basics of writing and produced most of the documents common to public relations. This will not, however, make you a good writer—it will simply make you a good technician. Good writing takes skill and imagination. Skill can be gained by practice. Imagination can be gained only by your willingness to experiment. Don't settle for the dry phrase or the lackluster sentence—bring creativity to every aspect of your writing.

Naturally, not every piece of public relations writing lends itself to greatness; however, as writers, we should always strive to present our ideas in the best possible light. In this way, even the most mundane may shine. It is not an easy task. As Alexander Pope said, "True ease of writing comes from art, not chance." Never look at writing as simply a job—it is an art and should be practiced with the care of an artist.

And read. Collect the writing of other professionals whose styles strike you. Read everything that you can in your field. Understand what you are writing about and never be afraid to experiment with your style. Of course you will be edited, and sometimes by those with less skill than you. Don't give up. In the end, good writing pays off—not only monetarily, but in the knowledge that you have the tools to write anything with the clarity and style of a professional, and an artist.

All the rest is mere fine writing.
—Paul Verlaine

KEY TERMS

denotative meaning

connotative meaning

thesis statement

semantics

inductive reasoning

deductive reasoning

The first chapter in which a term is used is indicated in parentheses at the end of the definition.

Accompanying script. The version of a television script sent with the taped spot to the stations that will run it. The accompanying script is stripped of all but its most essential directions. It is intended to provide the reader with a general idea of what the taped spot is about, and is to be used only as a reference for broadcasters who accept the spot for use. (10)

Actuality. An audio- or videotape that features newspeople describing an event, interviews with those involved in the event, or ambiance or background of the event itself for a voice-over. (10)

Advertising. The controlled use of print or broadcast media ensuring that your message reaches your public in exactly the form you intended and at the time you want. (1)

Alignment. The way copy is arranged in relation to column margins. The two most typical alignments are flush left (sometimes called ragged right) and justified. Other options are flush right and centered. (12)

Annual report. One of the most-produced organizational publications, annual reports not only provide information on the organization's financial situation, they also act as a vehicle for enhancing a corporation's image among its various internal publics. (1)

Argument strategies. Persuasive strategies designed to oppose another point of view and to persuade. There are two types: reasoned argument and emotional appeal. Both attempt to persuade by arguing one point of view against another. (3)

Articles and editorials. Usually for newsletters, house publications, trade publications, or consumer publications. In the case of non-house publications, PR articles are submitted in the same way as any other journalistic material. Editorials can be either paid for or submitted uncontrolled to vie for placement with other comments from other parties. (1)

As-recorded spot. A radio spot produced by the originating agency and ready to be played by the stations receiving it. They are usually sent in the format used by the particular station or on reel-to-reel tape, which will probably be transferred to the proper station format. (10)

Backgrounder. Basic information pieces providing background as an aid to reporters, editors, executives, employees, and spokespersons. This is the information used by other writers and reporters to 'flesh out' their stories. (1, 6)

Balance. As it relates to design, balance means that what is put on one side of a page should "weigh" as much as what is on the other side. All the elements placed on the page have weight, even the white space left by not placing elements. Size, color, degree of darkness—all play a part in balance. (12)

Body type. Type set smaller than 14 points and used for body copy. Distinguished from display type, which is 14 points and larger. (12)

Caption. The informational description that appears below or next to a photograph or other illustration. Also known as a **cutline.** (8)

Coercion. Techniques of persuasion not based on reasoned argument (although it may appear to be) but rather on some other method of enticement. (3)

Collateral publications. These include brochures, pamphlets, flyers, and other direct-marketing pieces. They are usually autonomous publications that should be able to stand on their own merits but which can be used as supporting information for other components in a package. (1)

Commercial speech. As defined by the Supreme Court, the concept of commercial speech allows a corporation to state publicly its position on controversial issues. The Court's interpretation of this concept also allows for political activity through lobbying and political action committees. (4)

Compliance strategies. Persuasive strategies designed to gain agreement through coercion. (3)

Consequence. One of the characteristics of newsworthiness of information. Relates to whether the information has any importance to the prospective reading, listening, or viewing public. Is it something that the audience would pay to know? (5)

Controlled information. Information over which you have total control as to editorial content, style, placement, and timing. Examples of controlled information are institutional (image) and advocacy advertising, house publications, brochures, and paid broadcast material (if it is paid placement). Public service announcements (PSAs) are controlled as far as message content is concerned but uncontrolled as to placement and timing. (1)

Corporate advertising. Advertising paid for by corporations but not related directly to products or services. Corporate or institutional advertising takes three basic forms depending on the purpose of the message: (9)

- **Public interest advertising** provides information in the public interest such as health care, safety, and environmental interests. In order to have these ads placed free, they must meet stringent guidelines.

- **Public image advertising** tries to sell the organization as caring about its employees, the environment, the community, and its customers. Unlike the public interest ad, the public image ad always focuses on the company and how it relates to the subject.
- **Advocacy advertising** presents a point of view. This may range from political to social and, by inference, positions the company as an involved citizen of the community or the nation.

Crossheads. Small, transitional heads within an article. (8)

Cutline. The informational description that appears below or next to a photograph or other illustration. Also known as a **caption.** (8)

Dateline. A brief notation at the beginning of a press release used to indicate the point of origin. (6)

Defamation. Any communication that holds a person up to contempt, hatred, ridicule, or scorn. (4)

Design. The act of bringing order to whatever surrounds us. It is planning and organizing physical materials and shaping and reshaping our environment to accommodate specific needs. (12)

Display type. Type larger than 14 points, used for headlines and other emphasized elements. (12)

Dissonance theory. A theory formulated in the 1950s which says that people tend to seek only messages that are "consonant" with their attitudes; they do not seek out "dissonant" messages. In other words, people don't go looking for messages they don't agree with already. This theory also says that about the only way you are going to get anybody to listen to something they don't agree with is to juxtapose their attitude with a "dissonant" attitude—an attitude that is logically inconsistent with the first. (3)

Downward communication. Communication within an organization that imparts management's message to employees. Ideally, even downward communication channels such as newsletters permit upward communication through letters to the editor, articles written by employees, surveys, and so forth. (8)

Emotional strategies. Persuasive strategies designed to gain support through the use of emotional appeal, which involves symbols, emotive language, and entertainment strategies. (3)

Emphasis. Focusing readers' attention on a single element on a page. This is what you want them to see first, and is usually where you want them to start interpreting your page. We emphasize elements by assigning them more optical weight than other items on the page. These emphasized elements are larger, darker, more colorful, or oddly shaped. They draw the readers' attention first among all the other items on the page. (12)

Exclusive. A press release or other information intended for only one media outlet. The same information may not be released to other outlets in any form. (6)

Exposition. An information strategy that involves the dissemination of pure information. Two of the most-used forms of exposition are narration and description. (3)

Fact sheet. An information piece that contains just that—facts—and nothing more. It should elaborate on already presented information, such as a news release, and not merely repeat what has already been said. (6)

Feature style. A less objective style of writing that provides less hard information than straight news style. Features generally take a point of view or discuss issues, people, or places. The style is more relaxed, more descriptive, and often more creative than straight news style. (8)

Font. The classification within a given typeface, such as bold, or italic. (12)

Format (1). The type of music a radio station plays or the information it provides. For example, some stations play only Top-40 hits. These stations usually cater to a teenage audience. Other stations play only Classic Rock or jazz, or provide news. Their listeners vary according to their format. (5)

Format (2). The way you arrange your brochure—its organizational characteristics. (9)

Four-color printing. Used for reproducing full-color artwork or photography. The illusion of full color is accomplished by optically mixing the three primary colors—yellow, red (actually magenta) and blue (called cyan)—along with black. Four-color plates are shot using a screen to reduce solid areas to printable, graduated dot patterns. Because each color is shot through a slightly different angle screen, the colors in the overlaid dot patterns blend to form the full-color image. Also known as **process printing.** (12)

Ghostwriting. Writing something for someone else that will be represented as that person's actual point of view. Public relations writers ghostwrite speeches, letters to the editor, annual report letters from the president, and even quotes. (4)

Grid. Another term for the columns used in a layout. (12)

Hard news. Information that has immediate impact on the people receiving it. By journalists' definition, it is very often news people need rather than news they want. (5)

Information kit. An information piece developed to provide generic background that reporters can then place on file. (5)

Interest. One of the characteristics of newsworthiness of information. Relates to whether the information is unusual or entertaining. Does it have any human interest? (5)

Inverted pyramid style. A straight news story: It begins with a lead, expands on the lead, and proceeds to present information in decreasing order of importance. Also known as straight news style. (6)

Issue statement. A precise definition of the situation, including answers to the following four questions: (2)

1. What is the problem or opportunity to be addressed?
2. Who are the affected parties?
3. What is the timing of this issue?
4. What are your (or your organization's) strengths and weaknesses as regards this issue?

Language fallacies. Typically unethical persuasive strategies that involve the actual use of language, including: equivocation, amphibole, and emotive language. (4)

Lead. The opening sentences of a straight news story or feature article. In a straight news story, the lead should include the *who, what, when, where, why,* and *how* of the story. Feature leads generally begin by setting the scene of the story to follow. (6)

Logic fallacies. Persuasive techniques codified by the Roman orators over a thousand years ago. Commonly referred to as logic fallacies because they are both illogical and deceptive by nature, they include, among others: cause and effect, personal attack, bandwagon, and inference by association strategies. (4)

Media directory. A good directory is an indispensable tool for the media relations specialist. Publishers of directories offer formats ranging from global checkers that include a variety of sources in every medium to specialized directories dealing with a single medium. (5)

Media list. A personalized list that contains details about local contacts and all the information you need to conduct business in your community. Media lists may include regional and even nationwide contacts, depending on the scope of your operation. A media list, once compiled, should be updated by hand at least once a month. (5)

Message strategy. Developing a message, or messages, that will reach and have the desired effect on your target audiences. Message strategies should logically follow your objectives and contribute either directly or indirectly to them. (3)

Newsletter. A brief (usually four pages) printed publication distributed either vertically or horizontally. A newsletter usually contains information of interest to a narrowly defined target audience. The various types of newsletters include the following: (8)

- *Association newsletters* help a scattered membership with a common interest keep in touch.
- *Community group newsletters* are often used by civic organizations to keep in touch with members, announce meetings, and stimulate attendance at events.
- *Institutional newsletters,* perhaps the most common type of newsletter, are usually distributed among employees.
- *Publicity newsletters* often create their own readers. They can be developed for fan clubs, resorts, and politicians.
- *Special-interest newsletters,* developed by special-interest groups, tend to grow with their following.
- *Self-interest or "digest" newsletters* are designed to make a profit. The individuals or groups who develop them typically offer advice or present solutions to problems held in common by their target readers. These often come in the form of a sort of "digest" of topics of interest to a certain profession.

News release. The most widely used of all public relations formats. News releases are used most often to disseminate information for publicity purposes and generally are of three types: (1, 6)

- **Publicity releases** cover any information occurring within an organization that might have some news value to local, regional, or even national media.
- **Product releases** deal with specific products or product lines and are usually targeted to trade publications within individual industries.

- **Financial releases** are used primarily in shareholder relations but are also of interest to financial media.

Objective. The concrete steps you need to take to reach your goal. A project's objectives must relate to the purpose of your message and should be realistic and measurable. For public relations writing, there are three types of objectives: informational, attitudinal, and behavioral. (2)

Offset lithography. A printing process in which the nonprinting area of the printing plate accepts water but not ink, while the image, or printing, area accepts ink but not water. During the printing process, both water and ink are applied to the plate as it revolves. The plate transfers its positive image to an offset cylinder made of rubber that then transfers the reversed image to the paper. (12)

Persuasion. An information strategy that involves moving someone to believe something or act in a certain way. (3)

Pitch letter. Generally sent to reporters and editors you are most familiar with and with whom you have already established a working relationship, a pitch letter alerts them of a story opportunity. Also known as a media advisory. (5)

Placement agency. An organization that will take information, such as a press release, and send it out to media outlets using its own regularly updated media lists and computerized mailing services. (5)

Point. A unit of vertical measurement of type. There are 12 points to a pica and 72 points to an inch. (12)

Positioning. Placing your piece in context as either part of some larger whole or as a standout from other pieces. (9)

Press kit. One of the most common methods of distributing brochures and other collateral information pieces. Press kits are produced and used for a wide variety of public relations purposes, including product promotion presentations, press conferences, and as promotional packages by regional or local distributors or agencies. (5)

Primary research. Data collected for the first time and specifically for the project at hand. (2)

Process printing. Used for reproducing full-color artwork or photography. The illusion of full color is accomplished by optically mixing the three primary colors—yellow, red (actually magenta) and blue (called cyan)—along with black. Four-color plates are shot using a screen to reduce solid areas to printable, graduated dot patterns. Because each color is shot through a slightly different angle screen, the colors in the overlaid dot patterns blend to form the full-color image. Also known as **four-color printing.** (12)

Profile. A feature story written specifically about a person, product or service, or an organization or some part of it. It profiles the subject by listing facts, highlighting points of interest, and tying the subject to the organization being promoted. (8)

Prominence. One of the characteristics of newsworthiness of information. Relates to whether the information concerns or involves events and people of prominence. (5)

Proportion. A measure of relationship in size. It helps to show one object's relationship to other objects in a layout. (12)

Proximity. One of the characteristics of newsworthiness of information. Relates to whether the information is local. (5)

Publicity kit. An information piece designed to be something of a "how-to" aid for those in your organization who are unfamiliar with publicity techniques. It is provides basic training and support in garnering publicity. (5)

Public service announcement (PSA). A radio or television spot aimed at providing an important message to its target audience. The PSA is reserved strictly for organizations that qualify as nonprofit under federal tax laws. (1, 10)

Pull quote. A magazine or newsletter device of "pulling" out quotations from the text, enlarging the point size, and setting them off from the text to draw a reader's attention to a point within an article. (8)

Quick copy. While it used to mean exclusively xerography, many of the newer quick-copy setups, such as Xerox's Docu-Tech, don't use this now-familiar process at all. Instead, these machines (literally computers) use laser technology to print. The result is a rapid-print method that is not limited to black-and-white, like xerography, but can present a wide range of grays. (12)

Quick print. A printing process involving a small cylinder press using paper printing plates. The plates are created using a photoelectrostatic process that results in a raised toner image that takes the ink and is imprinted directly onto the paper. (12)

Rule of ground thirds. A method of creating prorportion which requires that you divide a page into thirds and that you balance the page using a two-thirds to one-third ratio. This two-thirds to one-third ratio is commonly used in newsletter layout, but it is most often apparent in print advertisements in which a large graphic image takes up two-thirds of the page, while the copy takes up the other third. (12)

Sans serif typefaces. A category of typeface without *serifs*—the lines that cross the end strokes of the letters (*sans,* from the French, meaning "without"). They are usually, but not always, distinguished by uniformity of strokes. They usually impart a more modern look to a publication, especially if used as display type. (12)

Script treatment. An informal narrative account of a television spot. It is not written in a script format but may include ideas for shots and transitions. (10)

Secondary research. Data previously collected, often by third parties, for other purposes and adapted to the current needs. This can include demographic information already gathered by another department in your organization, or information gained from research done by other parties entirely outside your company. (2)

Sequence. The order of the elements on a layout, it will literally lead readers through a page. (12)

Serif typefaces. A category of typeface distinguished by a variation in thick and thin strokes, and by *serifs*—the lines that cross the end strokes of the letters. Serif type can be further broken down into *romans* and *slab* or *square serif* faces. Serif faces usually are considered easier to read, especially in body type sizes. (12)

Shooting script. Includes all of the information necessary for a complete understanding of a TV spot idea. It fleshes out camera shots, transitions, audio (including music and sound effects), narrative, acting directions, and approximate times. (10)

Signature. Groupings of pages printed on both sides, usually sixteen to a signature, but sometimes fewer, and always in multiples of four. (12)

Slice-of-life spot. A television commercial that sets up a dramatic situation complete with a beginning, middle, and end. In the slice-of-life spot, the focus is on the story, not the characters. The message is imparted through an interesting sequence of events incorporating, but not relying on, interesting characters. Slice-of-life spots usually use a wide variety of camera movements and postproduction techniques, such as dissolves and special effects. (10)

Soft news. News people want rather than news they necessarily need. (5)

Special. A press release or other information written in a style intended for a specific publication, but being released elsewhere as well. (6)

Speeches and presentations. The interpersonal method of imparting a position or an image. Good speeches can inform or persuade, and good presentations can win support where other, written, methods may fail. (1)

Spot announcement. The simplest type of radio spot, a spot announcement involves no sound effects or music bed and is meant to be read by radio station personnel. (10)

Spot color printing. The placement of a second color (black—or whatever the primary inking color—being the first) in a publication. Also known as **two-color printing.** (12)

Spot. A broadcast message, either paid-for advertising or a public service announcement. (5)

Style sheet. A listing of all of the type specifications you use in a newsletter or other publication. (8)

Subhead. May be (1) a display line enlarging on the main headline, usually in smaller size, or (2) a short heading within the copy used to break up a long block of text. (8)

Swipe file. A collection of publications and designs done by other people or companies used to help with design, layout ideas, and writing style, as well as to communicate ideas to typesetters and printers. (12)

Talking heads spot. A television spot in which the primary image appearing on the television screen is the human head—talking. (10)

Target audience. The end users of your information—the people you most want to be affected by your writing. (2)

Timeliness. One of the characteristics of newsworthiness of information. Relates to whether the material is current. If it isn't, is it a whole new angle on an old story? Remember, the word news means "new." (5)

Two-color printing. The placement of a second color (black—or whatever the primary inking color—being the first) in a publication. Also known as **spot color printing.** (12)

Type. The generic term for the lettering used in printing. (12)

Typeface. The nearly limitless alphabets and ornaments available as type. (12)

Uncontrolled information. Information that, once it leaves your hands, is at the mercy of the media. The outlet in which you want it placed has total editorial control over the content, style, placement, and timing. Such items as press releases are totally uncontrolled. Others, such as magazine articles, may receive limited editing but are still controlled as to placement and timing. (1)

Unity. One way of providing readers with a whole by drawing relationships among its various parts. Perhaps the best way to gain unity of design has more to do with an overall look, a unifying design. (12)

Upward communication. Communication within an organization that provides employees a means of communicating their opinions to management. (8)

Video news release (VNR). Originally prepackaged publicity features meant to be aired on local, regional, or national television, VNRs now are news releases designed as feature stories, usually for local television news programs. (10)

Adjective. Adjectives modify nouns or words acting as nouns. There are two basic types of adjectives: descriptive and limiting.

- **Descriptive adjectives** name some quality of an object.
  white house; small car; worn carpet
- **Limiting adjectives** restrict the meaning of a noun to a particular object or indicate quantity. There are five kinds of limiting adjectives:

    Possessive: my suit; their office

    Demonstrative: this suit; that office

    Interrogative: whose suit? which office?

    Articles: a suit, an office; the office

    Numerical: one suit, second office

Adverb. A modifier of other adverbs, adjectives, verbs, and most other words. The most common way to recognize an adverb is by its *-ly* ending. Although not all adverbs end in *-ly*, most do.

Antecedent. A word or group of words referred to by a subsequent pronoun.

Apostrophe. A punctuation mark used to denote several different things. For example, use an apostrophe to indicate the omission of letters or numbers; to form the plurals of letters, numbers, and words used as words; or to indicate possession.

Bracket. Punctuation mark used to set off editorial corrections or explanations within quoted matter. They are sometimes necessary (but only rarely) to set off another item from an item already set off by parentheses.

Case. Indicates the function of nouns and pronouns in a sentence. Personal pronouns (*I, you, he, she, it*) have different forms for the nominative, possessive, and objective cases. See Chapter 15 for the proper uses of case, especially the troublesome use of *whom* versus *who*.

Clause. A group of words expressing complete thoughts, which may or may not be a complete sentence. The two types of clauses are independent and subordinate.

- **Independent clauses,** sometimes called **main clauses,** always have a subject and a verb and make a statement independent of the rest of the sentence. A sentence always has at least one independent clause; however, it may have more than one.

- **Subordinate clauses,** sometimes called **dependent clauses,** contain an idea less important than that of the independent clause. A subordinate clause relies on an independent clause for meaning and is frequently introduced by a subordinate conjunction.

Colon. Internal punctuation mark used most appropriately to separate two main clauses, the second of which amplifies the first.

Comma. Internal punctuation mark used to indicate a pause. Most commonly used to separate independent clauses joined by a coordinating conjunction.

Complex sentence. A sentence that has a main clause and one or more subordinate clauses.

Compound sentence. A sentence that has two or more main clauses.

Compound-complex sentence. A sentence that contains two or more main clauses and one or more subordinate clauses.

Conjunction. A word used to join words, phrases, or clauses together.

- **Coordinating conjunctions** serve to separate independent clauses. The most common coordinating conjunctions are *and, but, or, nor, for, yet,* and *thus.*
- **Subordinate conjunctions** such as *because, if, since,* and *when* join subordinate clauses with independent clauses.

Conjunctive adverb. Conjunctive adverbs, like coordinating conjunctions, join complete clauses that are linked by a common idea.

Dangling construction. A construction in which the second clause in a sentence does not logically modify anything in the first, although it seems to at first glance.

Dash. Internal punctuation mark used in place of a comma to add emphasis to parenthetical expressions that abruptly interrupt the structure of the sentence. Some writers use **parentheses** to set off less emphatic statements.

Degree. Adjectives and adverbs show degree or quantity by means of their positive, comparative, and superlative forms.

- The **positive** form expresses no comparison at all: *slow, quickly.*
- The **comparative** form permits a comparison between two (and only two) things by adding *-er* or the adverb *more* to the positive form of the word: *pretty, prettier; rapid, more rapid.*

- The **superlative** form, which involves a comparison between three or more things, is achieved by adding *-est* or the adverb *most* to the positive form: *pretty, prettiest; rapid, most rapid.*

Gerund. The form of a verb that ends in *-ing.* The gerund is always used as a noun.

Hyphen. a punctuation mark used in compound words that are not yet accepted as single words; to join two or more words that act as a single adjective before a noun; to spell out compound numbers from 21 through 99 and to separate fractions; to avoid ambiguous or awkward combinations of letters; and with the prefixes *self, all, ex,* and the suffix *elect.*

Indefinite pronoun. A pronoun that does not refer to a particular person or thing and has no antecedent (*everybody, anybody, someone*).

Internal punctuation marks. Indicate the relationship of elements within a sentence. In English, five punctuation marks are used for this purpose: commas, semicolons, colons, dashes, and parentheses.

Linking verb. A verb that connects the subject of a sentence with the subject complement (the word that modifies the subject).

Mixed construction. The most common error results from shifting from one verb tense to another or from one "person" or "voice" to another in pronoun references.

Noun. Words that name a person, place, or thing. Subjects of sentences are usually nouns, as are objects of verbs and prepositions.

Parallel structure. Involves putting similar ideas into the same kinds of grammatical constructions.

Parentheses. Internal punctuation mark used in place of a comma to set off less emphatic parenthetical expressions that abruptly interrupt the structure of the sentence.

Participle. A participle is the form of a verb that ends in *-ing* in the present tense and in *-ed* or *-en* in the past tense. A participle acts as an adjective.

Parts of speech. The categories in which words belong. Most words are classified in three ways:

- By their **grammatical function** (such as *subject, object,* etc.).
- By their **grammatical form** (such as the *-s* form added to the end of plural nouns).
- By their **meaning** (such as the names of things as in the case of *nouns,* or statements of action as in the case of *verbs*).

Preposition. A word used to connect parts of a sentence. A preposition usually relates a noun, pronoun, or phrase to some other part of the sentence.

Pronoun. A word that substitutes for a noun. Common pronouns are *he, she, you, they,* and *it*. Pronouns usually take an **antecedent**—a noun usually preceding the pronoun to which the pronoun refers.

Semicolon. Internal punctuation mark normally used as a substitute for a comma when a relationship exists between two clauses whose ideas are strong enough for each clause to function almost as a separate sentence. Can be used in place of a comma when separating main clauses joined by a coordinating conjunction, especially when the clauses already contain commas.

Simple sentence. A sentence that has a single independent clause.

Verb. An action word that makes a statement about the subject of the sentence.

INDEX